EGYPT

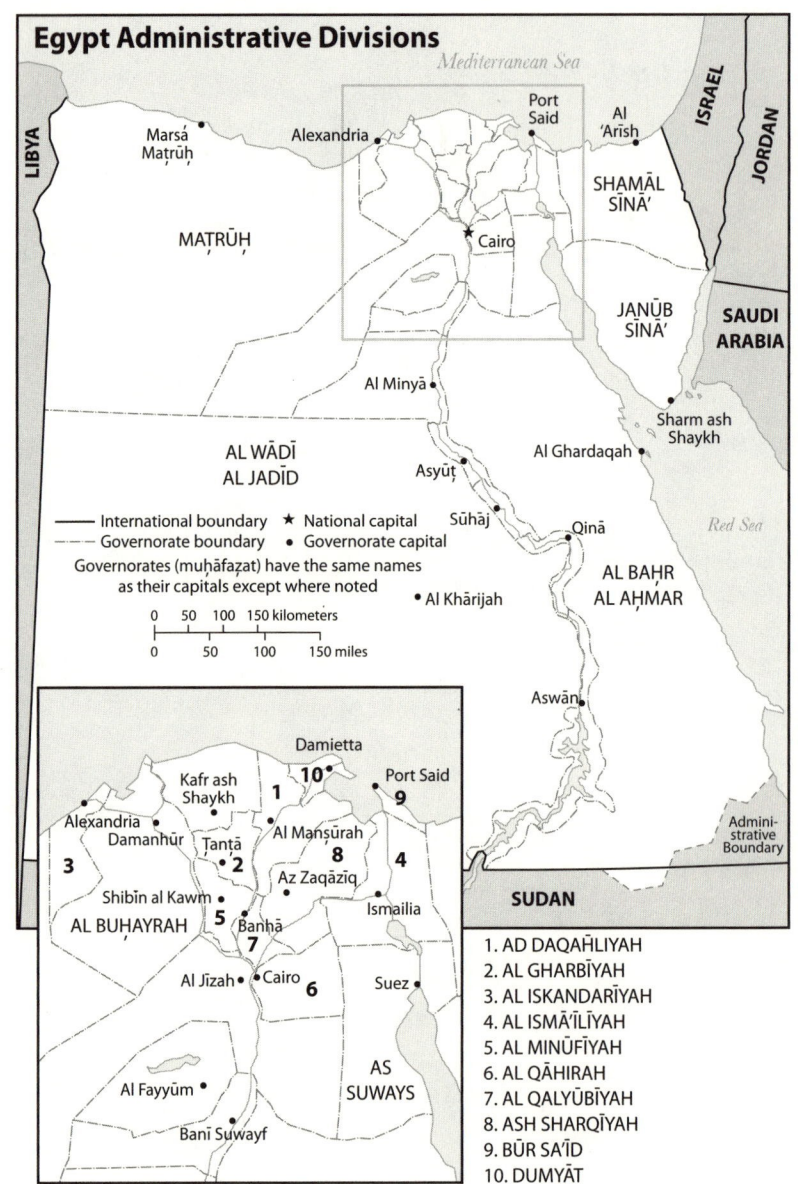

Map 1. Map of Egypt

E G Y P T

A SHORT HISTORY

ROBERT L. TIGNOR

PRINCETON UNIVERSITY PRESS PRINCETON & OXFORD

Copyright 2010 © by Princeton University Press

Published by Princeton University Press,
41 William Street, Princeton, New Jersey 08540

In the United Kingdom: Princeton University Press,
6 Oxford Street, Woodstock, Oxfordshire OX20 1TW

press.princeton.edu

All Rights Reserved

Library of Congress Cataloging-in-Publication Data

Tignor, Robert L.
   Egypt : a short history / Robert L. Tignor.
      p. cm.
   Includes bibliographical references and index.
   ISBN 978-0-691-14763-5 (alk. paper)
   1. Egypt—History. I. Title.
   DT77.T54 010
   962—dc22

                              2010017939

British Library Cataloging-in-Publication Data is available

This book has been composed in ITC Mendoza & Penumbra HalfSerif

Printed on acid-free paper. ∞

Printed in the United States of America

10 9 8 7 6 5 4 3 2 1

CONTENTS

ILLUSTRATIONS

COLOR PLATES

Following page 174

ILLUSTRATIONS

MAPS

FIGURES

CREDITS

I would like to thank the following individuals and institutions for permission to reproduce photographic materials in their possession: Laura Cobb (plate 23); Mary Cross (plates 18 and 20 from Cross, *Egypt*); Joel Gordon (figure 5); Simon Hayter (figure 2 and plate 11); The Princeton Art Museum (plate 24); Richard Seaman (plates 4, 5, 7, 12, 13, 14, and 15); Sandra and Trevor Selby (plates 6, 8, 9, 19, and 25); Darius Sitek (figure 1); The Victoria and Albert Museum (plate 1); and John Waterbury (plates 17 and 22 and figure 3). Map 1, Egypt, administrative divisions. Scale: ca. [1:8,100,00]. Lambert conformal conic projection. [Washington, D.C. : Central Intelligence Agency]. 1997. Publisher's no.: "Base 802526 (R00622) 5-97."

PREFACE

I have been involved with Egypt and Egyptians for half a century, though I hardly imagined when I first began to travel to Egypt that late in my scholarly life I would try to write a brief and synthetic essay on the history of a country as rich as any territory in historical experiences. I first arrived in the country in 1960 in pursuit of a Ph.D. in history. I was investigating the British occupation of Egypt during the Cromer years, with a particular view of understanding the nature of the British impact on Egyptians, whether for good or for ill. Over the years my interest in the modern history of Egypt and my affection for the Egyptian people grew with each new Egypt-centered research project and each new sojourn in the country, many of which were for extended periods. Although I am a modern historian, occasionally I was pressed into writing overview histories of Egypt, but only from the Arab-Muslim conquest of the country in the seventh century to the present. Repeated queries from friends eager to visit Egypt who pressed me to recommend books that would prepare them for their sightseeing, especially books that offered brief and reliable histories of Egypt from the earliest days to the present, left me in a quandary. The tourist literature is abundant. There are superb travel guidebooks, works that contain magnificent illustrations of the antiquities, the architecture of Cairo, and the favored tourist spas, but I had nothing to recommend that covered in a brief and accessible form the history of the country from the pharaohs to the present. I decided to try my hand at such a study.

For me the most daunting aspect of the assignment was surveying the history of Egypt before the arrival of Arab Muslims. I knew that the literature on the pharaohs, the Greeks, and the Romans in

Egypt was voluminous, sophisticated, and highly technical. What I did not appreciate at first was how captivating the very best historical works on pre-Islamic Egypt were and what a pleasure consulting them would bring. Hence, my first debt of gratitude is to the many generations of historians who have inspired, humored, and spurred others to match their high standard. It would be unfair to single out those that I most enjoyed, since my list would slight numerous worthy authorities. But what I discovered—a truth that I have observed in all fields of historical endeavor—is the immense pleasure and satisfaction that comes from starting first with the classics even though so many of these works have been superseded and most no longer even appear in standard bibliographies. Their importance to newcomers is that they created new fields and spurred their successors to deepen and improve upon their work. They set the parameters of the fields and prepared the way for further work.

Start with the classics, but move on to the best and most authoritative recent work—that would be my advice on how to read history. I hope that I have accomplished this goal in preparing to write this book, and where I have missed important new works, I apologize to those scholars whose findings should be here but are not. Now I need to thank many friends and fellow scholars who brought some recent work to my attention and who have thrown up cautionary flags where my eagerness to espouse a particular interpretation needed to be rethought. Special and warm thanks to Beth Baron, Peter Brown, Michael Cook, Jon Durbin, Khalid Fahmy, Molly Greene, Heath Lowry, Holly Pittman, Pamela Long, Joseph Manning, Roger Owen, and Edward Watts. They read all or parts of the manuscript at various stages of its development. Under no circumstances can they be held accountable for any mistakes in fact or interpretation that this work contains. I appreciated the advice that Grant Parker offered when I sought ideas and bibliography on how the ancients, particularly the Greeks and the Romans, viewed Egypt. Finally, but hardly last of all, I am grateful to Brigitta van Rheinberg, editor in chief at Princeton University Press, for her enthusiasm for this project and to Clara Platter, history editor at the press, who answered a bevy of questions, technical and otherwise, on how to get this manuscript ready for publication. If this book has a pleasing appearance and is a pleasure to read, much credit goes to Heath Renfroe and Richard Isomaki, experts in art and English style at Princeton University Press.

EGYPT

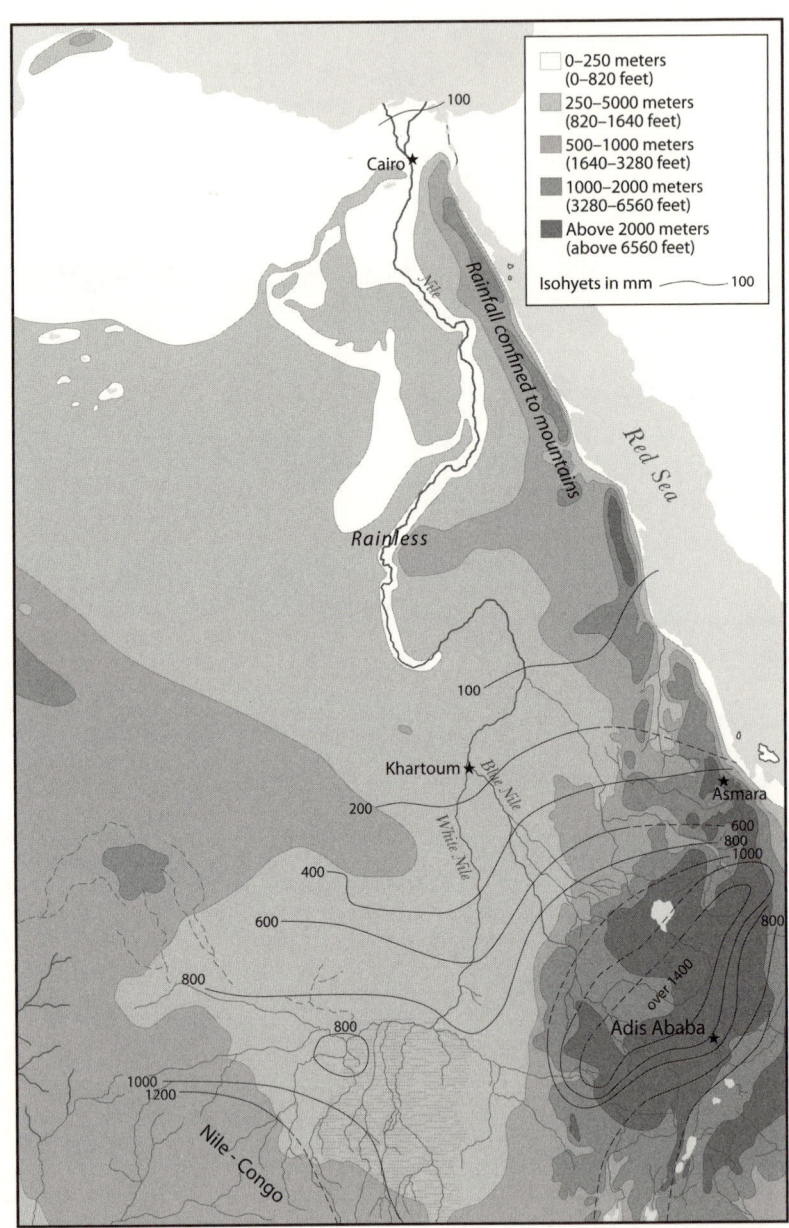

Map 2. Map of the Nile River basin

CHAPTER ONE
The Land and People

As the jumbo jet descends from cloud cover, the attendant announces that the plane is on its final descent into Cairo International Airport. As usual, the cabin is full, not a seat to spare. The occupants include Egyptians returning from work and play overseas, businesspersons, and a large number of tourists. Whether the passengers are longtime residents or first-time visitors, those with window seats scan the ground to see what they can of the fabled city and its marvelous antiquities. At first only sand dunes are visible. The flight is in luck. Wind currents require the plane to pass over the great pyramids of Giza. When these monuments appear, cheers, gasps of delight, and murmurs break out all over the cabin. Those among the passengers who have been to Egypt know that this view does not compare with seeing the structures for the first time from ground level. Yet, even at 3,000 feet, their monumentality is awe-inspiring. Even to the inveterate Cairene passengers the puzzle of how individuals more than 5,000 years ago constructed such magnificent burial sites arises. Thoughts of ancient Egypt are in everyone's mind.

In the drive in to the center of the city from the airport, motorists pass along the boulevard where the Egyptian military holds its ceremonial parades. At one location they observe the impressive grave site of President Anwar al-Sadat. Even the untutored visitors cannot help but be reminded of the Giza pyramids. They served as burial chambers for three of Egypt's early and mighty pharaohs. If the travelers know their history of Egypt, they are aware that the city of Cairo is dotted with many such memorials to the greats. Almost from the beginnings of human habitation in the Nile River basin

Egyptians have memorialized their most powerful and respected rulers, using grandiose monuments to extol their services to the people and to the land. The bigger and more impressive the sites, or so the theory goes, the more splendid the reigns were.

The Sadat tomb has even deeper connections with Egypt's past. Across from the burial grounds are military grandstands in the middle of which is a single seat, painted in black. It is the chair that Anwar al-Sadat occupied when he was gunned down during the October 1981 military parade, held to celebrate the triumphs of the October 1973 war with Israel. If one also remembers the words that the assassin, Khaled al-Islambouli, announced at his trial, "I have killed pharaoh," the Egyptian past seems ever present. Egypt's last three rulers (Gamal Abdel Nasser, Anwar al-Sadat, and Husni Mubarak) have frequently been compared with pharaohs or other of Egypt's earlier rulers. Sadat in particular tried to associate himself and his actions with Egypt's pharaonic past, carrying his baton upright in his hand like a pharaoh carrying the key of life and dressing in regal splendor on high ceremonial occasions. One contemporary observer calls the new rulers Egypt's neo-Mamluks.

Many observers stress the continuity, even the unchanging nature, of Egypt over the millennia. They argue that climate, geography, and the unvarying routines of the Nile River, cresting in summer into floods, impose a unity that human ingenuity cannot alter. Geographically Egypt is cut off from the east and west by deserts, in the north by the Mediterranean, and in the south by fierce Nile rapids, called cataracts. Its inhabitants therefore are crammed into a small band of arable land that the Nile makes available to them, a dependence that the most brilliant scientists have been able to change only a little.

Yet change has also been a prominent feature of Egypt's long history. The period breaks are palpable. Ancient Egyptian culture, lasting nearly three millennia, ultimately gave way to Greek and Roman conquests. The ancient language of the Egyptians fell out of use, and many of the great monuments of antiquity were either covered by sand or torn down so that their materials could be used elsewhere. Then the polytheistic culture of the Greeks and Romans gave way to Christianity, followed by Islam, which brought a new world religion and a new language. Nor was Islam a single entity, for one set of Muslim conquerors succeeded another. The Fatimids, a shimmering Shiite dynasty, gave way to Ayyubids, then to Mamluks, and finally to Ottomans. Next came a new set of foreign conquerors: first the French, followed, after a stunning interlude of Turko-Circassian rulers, by the British. Although contemporaries compare Egypt's present-day regime with the pharaohs and the Mamluks, the men who have ruled Egypt since the 1950s boast of their Egyptianness and assert that they are the first native-born sons to rule the country since the pharaohs.

Change and continuity are, thus, hallmarks of Egypt's long history. These themes are critical to the history of Egypt. Few countries have had as much written about their pasts as has Egypt; yet only a few books offer overviews. The demand is ever pressing. Tourists clamor for a general guide to the rich history of the country—one that will allow them to set the country's omnipresent historical monuments in an understandable narrative. Scholars and experts are eager for a work that will encapsulate the history of periods that are not their specialties. Alas, little exists. Guidebooks abound, but they specialize in certain periods and particular regions. Most are short on history. The reasons for this gap are not hard to discern. In many ways Egypt has too rich a history, too many distinctive historical periods. Each has its linguistic, ethnographic, and documentary requirements, and each has a voluminous, highly specialized, and sophisticated historical literature. Egyptologists find it difficult to converse with modernists. Graeco-Roman scholars have much in common with Islamists since both sets of scholars write about the same geographical entity and the same ethno-linguistic community; yet their linguistic and historical training often keeps them apart.

How much has Egypt changed over the centuries and how much has it remained the same? For millennia the rhythms of everyday existence revolved around the Nile. And they continue to do so even today though the country has not experienced annual Nile floods for more than half a century. Does the presence of the Nile and the relatively narrow band of arable land surrounding the Nile give a unity to the history of Egypt that transcends its many historical periods?

Because of Egypt's unquestioned geographical and strategic importance, lying at the corner of three continents (Europe, Asia, and Africa), the land has attracted numerous outsiders, often as invaders. Hyksos, Greeks, Romans, Arabs, Mamluks, Ottomans, French, and British (some would now even add Americans) have ruled over the country, importing their languages, their populations, and their ways of life. But how effectively have they imposed their cultures on the men and women who lived alongside the banks of the Nile? Certainly much has changed over the course of a long and diverse history. Hieroglyphs passed out of existence, not to be deciphered until the nineteenth century through the work of modern linguistic scholars. Much of the pharaonic culture that so intrigues Egypt's contemporary visitors was buried under centuries of sand deposits. It too only came into prominence through the efforts of a hardy band of scholars known as Egyptologists. Egypt was once the most Christian territory in all of Christendom. But following the Arab-Muslim invasion of the seventh century Christianity gave way to Islam, though not totally. The Coptic population today constitutes nearly 10 percent of Egypt's total, and the Coptic language, with connections to ancient Egyptian, continues in use today, though confined to a clerical class.

Change is obvious. But so is continuity. Monumental architecture, prevalent in pharaonic times, can still be seen in the monuments dedicated to Egypt's modern leaders. So, too, some would argue, does the cult of an all-powerful ruler, whose task it was in ancient times to ensure order and prosperity and whose responsibilities, under Nasser, Sadat, and Mubarak, remain much the same. Religion was at the core of the culture of the ancients. Much in early Egyptian religious belief and practice passed, though in a radically modified form, into Christianity and Islam. In a world that seemed ready to sideline religion Islam has refused to give way. Egypt has played a central role in the emergence of a resurgent Islam. Change and continuity, these are the themes of Egypt's historical narrative. They are writ large.

Peoples and countries often owe their names to foreigners. Spaniards, the first Europeans to arrive in the Americas, believed that they had landed somewhere in East Asia. They called the Native Americans Indians. So it was with Egypt and Egyptians. The ancient Egyptians referred to their territory as *kemet*, the black or arable land, thus distinguishing the cultivable portion of their area from the desert, which they called *deshret*, or the red soil. It was the Greeks who coined the word *aigyptos* (Egyptian) to represent the name of the inhabitants of the Nile River basin as well as the territory in which they lived. This Greek word had an ancient Egyptian derivation. It was a Greek corruption of the ancient Egyptian name for the pharaonic capital city, Memphis: *Hi-kiptah* (the castle of the god Ptah), thus establishing a tradition of using the name of the capital city to stand for the entire territory and the people. Later, the Arab conquerors of Egypt called their new capital, located near the old pharaonic capital of Memphis, *Misr*, which they also employed as the term for the entire territory and whose inhabitants were called *Misriyyin*, the inhabitants of *Misr*.

THE NILE RIVER AND ITS IMPORTANCE TO EGYPT

The Greeks were fascinated with Egypt, a fascination that impelled Alexander's conquest of the country and must account for his many, largely successful efforts to embrace Egyptian ways. To the Greeks, especially to that most accomplished of Greek historians and travelers, Herodotus, Egypt was paired in their imagination with Scythia. The Egyptians represented the most ancient and sophisticated of peoples in contrast to the nomadic, less sophisticated Scythians. To Herodotus we owe many truisms about ancient Egypt, not the least of which was that the land was the gift of the Nile. The Egyptian descriptions that he offered in his book *The Persian Wars* owed much to conversations he held with Egyptian priests in Memphis, Heliopolis, and Thebes during his fifth-century BCE travels in the country. The clerics assured him that their land was "the most ancient of mankind." Certainly, Herodotus's admiration for the people and the land was unbounded. He described Egypt as a territory that "possesses so many wonders; nor has any [other country] such a number of works which defy description. Not only is the climate different from that of the rest of the world, and the river unlike any other rivers, but the people also, in most of their manners and customs, exactly reverse the practice of mankind." He noted that women went to markets while men stayed at home to weave cloth. Only men were priests; yet instead of growing hair, which was the practice in Herodotus's homeland, they shaved off their hair. Even more perplexing to him was the fact that Egyptians ate out of doors and urinated indoors.

Herodotus's precise words about the Nile are worth repeating: "The Egypt to which the Greeks go in their ships is an acquired country, the gift of the Nile." Yet his acute perception of the Nile's centrality to the people of Egypt was only partially right. Certainly, without the Nile's life-giving waters, the vast territory of Egypt (37,540 square kilometers today) would have been little more than desert, interrupted here and there by life-supporting oases. Its 7,500,000 acres of arable land, which today support three growing seasons a year and constitute one of the world's richest and most productive agricultural land areas, would have lain barren.

Herodotus took the Nile and its generous annual floods for granted. In reality, the Nile had not always been so beneficent. Although a great river existed for many millions of years, it was only 12,500 years ago that today's Nile took shape. Earlier Niles, of which there were many, either brought too much water or too little. They could not have produced the way of life that Egyptians take for granted. They would never have created the splendid cultures that marked Egypt's long and resplendent history.

The Nile is the longest river in the world, slightly outdistancing the Amazon. It is fed by innumerable streams and rivers, but its most remote source rises in the hills of Rwanda, some 4,238 miles south of its ultimate destination, the Mediterranean Sea. Its tributaries and main branches flow through eight countries—Rwanda, Burundi, Tanzania, Kenya, Ethiopia, Uganda, Sudan, and Egypt—encompassing more than one million square miles, no less than one-tenth of the whole of the African continent. Yet, for a river that traverses such an immense area, it delivers only a tiny quantity of water. Compared with the mighty Amazon River in South America it transports a mere trickle of water, carrying only 2 percent of the totals that the Amazon supplies. Its volume is no more than that of Germany's Rhine, rarely thought of as one of the large rivers of the world.

Although the Nile has innumerable tributaries, especially in its distant locations in central and equatorial Africa, three branches do most of its work. First, the Atbara River, descending out of the highlands of Ethiopia, carries one-seventh of the river's total annual volume. A raging torrent during the flood season, when monsoon rains and melting snows in the Ethiopian highlands fill its channel, it becomes a dry bed during the nonflood season. The Blue Nile, also rising in the highlands of Ethiopia, was the critical source of Egypt's agricultural prosperity until the twentieth century, bringing vast quantities of silt-laden waters from the Ethiopian highlands during the flood season and depositing this rich soil in the Nile valley basin. It carries four-sevenths of the river's total capacity, much of it during the flood season. Finally comes the White Nile, crashing down out of Lake Victoria and meandering its way northward through the marshlands of the southern Sudan, known as the *sudd*, to merge with the Blue Nile at Khartoum. It carries the remaining two-sevenths of the Nile waters. It, too, is critical to Egypt's annual flood, for it provides a steady source of water year round, thereby moderating the main Nile River and keeping the floodwaters from being violent and unpredictable, as they so often are in the other major rivers of the world. From Khartoum to the Mediterranean Sea the Nile flows on a further 1,600 miles, with the aid of only a single tributary, the Atbara, and without significant rainfall. Yet it leaves enough water and rich soil to create "an elongated oasis" stretching all the way from Aswan to the Mediterranean Sea. It was in this elongated oasis that the Egyptians created their pioneering ancient culture.

The surface of the earth undergoes radical, tectonic changes from time to time. These changes produce new land masses, create mountains and valleys, alter climates and habitats, and change the course of rivers. One such change occurred in central Africa approximately six million years ago. The earth's crust rose to form the Rift Valley, causing dramatic changes in climate, geography, human habitation, and river direction. Previously the waters of central and equatorial Africa had drained toward the Red Sea and the Congo basin. An uplifted Rift not only created the highlands of present-day East Africa where the first hominids appeared and the great lakes of equatorial Africa—Tanganyika, Albert, Edward, and eventually the largest of them all, Victoria—it also redirected river systems and drainage patterns northward toward Egypt and the Mediterranean Sea. Still, the present-day Nile had yet to appear. Several pre-Niles scoured out channels for themselves within Egypt as they progressed to the Mediterranean, though they were hardly the usable river of the modern era. Sometimes these early Niles were fed by waters from equatorial Africa; other times, during periods of great aridity, the central African connection was broken. Occasionally the Nile dried up altogether, leaving Egypt a desert, devoid of all life. Around 800,000 to 700,000 years ago, during an African wet phase, the waters from Ethiopia again broke through to Egypt and turned the Nile into a mighty, though highly unpredictable river. Then 12,500 years ago, during another wet phase, the waters of Lake Victoria, fed by the other lakes of equatorial Africa, spilled out of its basin and plunged northward to form the White Nile, which joined the Blue Nile at Khartoum to become the main Nile River on which Egypt's livelihood soon depended.

Mighty rivers are dangerous forces of nature. Their floods are often unpredictable. People who reside within their floodplains put themselves at risk. Large-scale floods can ruin crops and destroy villages. Insufficient floods produce inadequate harvests and lead to starvation. Yet, what we often refer to today as civilization had its birth in these river basins—the locations of the earliest, complex societies. Naturally, these areas are the subject of intense archaeological inquiry since they offer insights to historians, archaeologists, anthropologists, and other experts on how human beings became prolific, prosperous, and the dominant species on the planet. The peoples residing in three of these floodplains—the Tigris-Euphrates, the Indus, and the Nile—led the way in creating the world's first urban-based, hierarchical, and complex societies. The breakthroughs to complex, large-scale cultures occurred roughly between 7,000 and 5,000 years ago. We know little about the Harappan culture of the Indus River basin; its early remains were regularly covered up by annual floods and new settlements. Mesopotamia and Egypt are better known, and though the similarities in the histories of these two centers of advanced culture, often referred to as the cradles of civilizations, are notable, their contrasts are even more striking. Many of the differences, not surprisingly, sprang from the rivers that the local populations learned to master.

The modern Nile is a remarkably kind and productive river, especially when compared with the Tigris and Euphrates. Its floods are highly predictable. They arrive at the most opportune time for the growing season and require little hydraulic engineering. The Nile's annual flood crested toward the end of the summer months and left its silted waters on the soil at the very moment that Egyptian farmers were ready to plant their crops. All that was required, once the waters had drained back into the main Nile channel, was for the peasants to broadcast their seeds and livestock to trample the seed under foot.

Compare this with the challenges that faced Mesopotamian cultivators. They were confronted with altogether more formidable problems that required elaborate arrangements for controlling raging floodwaters. Because the Tigris-Euphrates annual floods came at the apex of the growing season, agriculturalists had to create an irrigation system that would protect the crops under cultivation and also provide water when the floodwaters had receded. First, the riverbanks needed to be heightened to ensure that water did not spill onto the fields and destroy crops. In addition, Mesopotamian agriculturalists fashioned a sophisticated set of irrigation canals to siphon off the waters of the Euphrates when they were at their low point but were most needed on the land. Moreover, the waters did not flow back easily into the main river channel, as the Nile did, with the result that the low-lying lands in the Mesopotamian delta were at risk of salting up and becoming unusable.

Herodotus himself noted how benign the Nile waters were. No doubt he exaggerated when he observed that "at present, it must be confessed, they [the inhabitants of the Egyptian delta] obtain the fruits of the field with less trouble than any people in the world, the rest of Egypt included, since they have no need to break up the ground with the plough, nor to use the hoe, nor to do any of the work which the rest of mankind find necessary if they are to get a crop. But the husbandman waits till the river has of its own accord spread itself over the fields and withdrawn again to its bed, and then sows his plot of ground, and after sowing, turns his swine into it after which he has only to await the harvest."

The Egyptians, too, were fulsome in their praise of their mighty and life-giving river. In words carved on a pyramid some forty-five centuries ago, an Egyptian poet exclaimed:

> They tremble that behold the Nile in full flood.
> The fields laugh and the river banks are overflowed.
> The visage of men is bright, and the hearts of the gods rejoiceth.

And some centuries later another poet also sang the river's praises:

> Praise to thee O Nile, that issuest forth from the earth and comes
>   to nourish the dwellers in Egypt.
> That givest drink to the desert places which were far from water;
>   his dew it is that falleth from heaven.

The Nile produced another immeasurable benefit, leading ultimately to the unity of the land from the Mediterranean Sea to the first cataract or rapids at present-day Aswan. Not only did its currents flow northward, but its winds blew in the opposite direction. Sailors could set their sails to capture the Mediterranean breezes as they traveled south; they could coast under the currents of the river as they traveled north. Yet unity did not come easily or quickly. It came about through hard-won struggles, still only dimly understood.

The Nile divides Egypt into two parts. The southern half of Egypt, called Upper Egypt because it contains the upper waters of the Nile inside Egypt, has a narrow floodplain, surrounded on both sides by hills and mountains. Its cultivable lands stretch out over a long north-south dimension, but never exceed ten miles east and west of the river's banks. At a location where Cairo now sits and where the political center of Egypt was often found, the Nile branches out. Today there are two branches, one debouching at Damietta, the other at Rosetta. In pharaonic times, there were many more branches leading to the Mediterranean. Northward of Cairo in what is termed Lower Egypt exists a large delta area, stretching at its widest nearly two hundred miles from east to west. For millennia, Lower Egypt has been the country's breadbasket. Often it supplied much of the eastern Mediterranean with vital foodstuffs.

Today's Nile, tamed by vast hydraulic works, is a languorous and calm river. To the naked eye it hardly seems to have a current. The only cataract within Egypt itself, at Aswan, no longer produces the vast churning, hissing, and spitting of waters that occurred during the high Nile state when floodwaters crashed against massive rock formations in the main channel. In the days before the high dam south of Aswan had cut the supply of water to the first cataract, visitors flocked to Aswan during the flood season to witness this force of nature. Foreign businesspersons eventually built the Old Cataract Hotel on the very site of the cataract to ensure that vacationers and tourists could see this marvel of nature. Even today, when river turbulence no longer exists, the hotel, with its turn-of-the-twentieth-century charm and amenities, remains one of the favorite spas for those seeking repose from a troubled and turbulent world.

Speaking of repose, if one wants to find serenity in the hustle and bustle of Cairo, take a felucca ride on the Nile. Even at Cairo the Nile waters are far from impressive. The distance from one bank to the other is not great, a far cry from, say, the Mississippi River. Nor do the muddy waters beckon one to go for a swim. Feluccas look worn and in need of repair. Nearly all of them have patches on their sails. But expert boatmen navigate them, and as one meanders from the east to the west banks of the Nile, one feels the pull of history. Here are reeds like those where the baby Moses was said to have been hidden from the wrath of the pharaohs. Overhead is the bridge to Cairo University, where protesters often gathered to shout their defiance against the British or officials of the Egyptian government. And as twilight descends on the city (and it does so with alarming speed), Cairo's lights shimmer off the river, projecting an image of graceful splendor.

The Beginnings of Human Habitation in the Nile Valley

The earliest records of human habitation in the Nile valley date from 400,000 years ago. They consist of flaked stone tools that suggest that *Homo erectus* dwelled in this area as these early hominids, predecessors of modern men and women, moved through the African continent before populating other parts of the Afro-Eurasian landmass. Unfortunately, no bones have been found, so our evidence rests entirely on the discovery of tools. Just when modern men and women—*Homo sapiens*—entered the Nile basin has yet to be determined. The earliest settlements known so far date from 7,000 years ago. They were found at Merimde, on the edge of the Western delta, and in the Fayyum region southwest of present-day Cairo. Where these early humans came from is still an open question. Some scholars suggest that they arrived from the Libyan Desert during a drying-out phase when humans flocked into river basins for sustenance. Others argue for a northeast origin, believing that these people entered Egypt from Southwest Asia, migrating across the Sinai Peninsula.

In their new setting *Homo sapiens* adapted to the rhythms of the Nile without great difficulty. They divided the arable lands into irrigation basins of quite varying sizes, ranging from 1,000 acres to 40,000 acres, in preparation for the annual flood. Cultivators divided basins by means of simple earthen walls and then allowed the waters when they flooded into the basins to soak into the soil for a period lasting between forty and sixty days, depositing new layers of silt. Only then did farmers cut the barriers and permit the waters to flow on to basins further downriver or drain back into the main Nile channel. The view of the flooded plain at the height of the flood season was magnificent to behold. Harold Hurst, a British hydraulic engineer and part of a last generation to see the Egyptian countryside when it was still fully flooded, commented: "In the bright sunlight and the temperate weather of the autumn in Egypt this was a wonderful sight with the desert hills and the pyramids in the background." All of Egypt's arable land lay under water save for the mounds on which the villages nestled. People moved from village to village by means of boats. (See plate 1 for an artist's rendition of the Nile in flood.)

The irrigation technology required to trap the annual Nile floods was simple. Each village, usually under the control of local notables, took responsibility for its own irrigation. This did lead to village rivalries and disputes, some of which became violent and produced bitter histories. What the central government was needed for, when it finally came into being sometime 5,000 years ago, was to store seed grain for the next year and provide emergency supplies of foodstuffs if the floods were inadequate. The state also maintained Nilometers, which were placed strategically along the upper reaches of the river to provide advanced indications of when the floods would come and how large they would be. A true canal system did not come into being until the nineteenth century, when Egypt's rulers, Muhammad Ali first of all during the first half of that century and the British after their occupation of the country in 1882, constructed a series of barrages and dams across the Nile that replaced the basin system of irrigation, largely unchanged since pharaonic times, with a system of perennial irrigation. Whereas in ancient times basin irrigation had permitted only a single growing season, perennial irrigation, which made Nile waters available the year round, enabled Egyptian cultivators to take full advantage of the fertility of the soil and the climate to grow two, sometimes three crops per year. What the modern cultivators sacrificed, however, was the regular deposit of new soil carried in the floodwaters from the Ethiopian highlands. As a result cultivators turned to larger and larger quantities of fertilizers as the only way to maintain the fertility and high productivity of the land.

The ancient Egyptians were among those first groups of peoples who moved from being hunters and gatherers to engage in settled agriculture and husbandry. They were not the first, however. They learned many of the techniques for planting seeds and harvesting crops either from the peoples of Southwest Asia, usually regarded as the first settled agriculturalists in the world, or from the peoples living to their west in present-day Libya, who were driven into the Nile River basin by the growing aridity of the world. Cultivators, dependent as they were on the Nile floods, grew only a single, winter crop. The main cultigens were wheat, beans, berseem (Egyptian clover), lentils, barley, and chickpeas. Farmers maintained orchards and vineyards, which were the only lands that enjoyed year-round irrigation. These estates had to be walled off from the flood, which would destroy the trees and vines, and were watered regularly from wells and reservoirs. The Egyptians also possessed domesticated animals, notably cattle, sheep, goats, and pigs.

Although the Nile floods did most of the work in irrigating and renewing the soil, Egyptian cultivators employed a simple technology to lift river basin and canal waters on to the land when and as needed. Following the Amarna period of the New Kingdom, around 1200 BCE, Egyptians invented a simple device known as the *shaduf*, which, using a fulcrum, lifted a water bag that enabled cultivators to irrigate the lands from the spring and summer low-water Nile. *Shadufs* made it possible to grow winter crops, such as cotton and additional cereals. Later, during the Ptolemaic period the buffalo-driven water wheel, known as the *saqia*, and the Archimedean screw allowed farmers to make more than a very modest use of the low Nile waters that the *shaduf* alone had permitted. Egypt's vaunted agriculture, based on two and occasionally three crops per year, became reality only after the pharaonic period had come to an end and after Alexander the Great's conquest of the country in 332 BCE. (See plates 2 and 3 for illustrations of *shadufs* and *saqias* in use today.)

WHO WERE THE ANCIENT EGYPTIANS?

But who were these early inhabitants of the Nile River basin? The question of their identity has roiled scholars and commentators.

Much of the debate revolves around the issue of whether the ancient Egyptians were African peoples, that is to say, people with black skins and the physical features that are prominent among African peoples today. Or were these ancient men and women living along the banks of the Nile similar to present-day Egyptians, who have olive-colored skins? In several books, particularly *The African Origins of Civilization: Myth or Reality*, the Senegalese writer Cheikh Anta Diop marshaled linguistic, literary, and artistic evidence in support of the theory that the ancient Egyptians were black Africans. Citing the writings of Herodotus on Egypt and asserting that the images on the friezes and paintings of the ancient Egyptians display unquestionably black African features, Diop asserted that "ancient Egypt was a Negro civilization," adding that "instead of presenting itself as an insolvent debtor, the Black world is the very initiator of the 'Western Civilization' flaunted before our eyes today."

The entry of Diop into the sacred domain of the Egyptologists has spurred a vigorous and informative set of replies. Here the consensus is that Diop was wrong in claiming that Herodotus described the ancient Egyptians as being black Africans. Quite the contrary, Herodotus and other classical authorities made a careful distinction between Egyptians and the black-skinned peoples who lived to the south, whom they referred to as Ethiopians. So, too, did Egyptian craftsmen of the time distinguish between themselves and peoples to the south. They depicted the latter in paintings, sculptures, and mosaics as black, while portraying Egyptians as mildly dark and Asians as having paler skins. Scenes from the tombs of Seti I and Ramses III in the Valley of the Kings in Upper Egypt offer a full array of the peoples with whom the Egyptians had contact. In them the Egyptians are shown as having reddish-brown skins.

More recently, a scholar of Chinese political thought, Martin Bernal, has thrust himself into this very same debate. Employing a provocative title, *Black Athena: The Afroasiatic Roots of Classical Civilization*, Bernal argues that the influence of Egypt on Greece and through Greece on Western civilization was profound but that generations of Western scholars, eager to show that the West owed its greatness to Indo-European achievements and not to African or

Semitic influences, denied the Egyptian contribution to the Western experience. Alas, Bernal's main point—the indebtedness of the West to Egypt—got lost in part because of the weakness of his scholarship, the heated responses from aggrieved classical scholars, who stepped forward to defend their field, and the always present controversy over whether the Egyptians were a black African people.

Of course, as modern scholarship has come to understand just how intermixed the peoples of the world truly are and how little genetic difference there is among the so-called races of the world, some scholars refuse to employ racial categorizations altogether. Instead, they identify peoples not by physical appearances but by languages. If, in fact, one uses language as the basis of determining who the ancient Egyptians were, the answer is clear and unequivocal. The early Egyptians were a people who spoke and wrote what linguistic scholars call an Afro-Asiatic or Hamitic-Semitic language, one of a body of languages based in North Eastern Africa and Southwest Asia that numbers among its branches Berber, Chadic, Hebrew, Ethiopic, Cushitic, and Arabic as well as ancient Egyptian.

Still, this retreat into identities, based on language, seems deeply unsatisfying. One should not allow racial prejudices to blind one from trying to offer physical descriptions of the ancient Egyptians since they exist in abundance in paintings, carvings, and even for that matter in mummified remains. Such an attempt can reasonably be made at the present time.

Roughly ten thousand years ago the growing aridity of Africa caused peoples living south, east, and west of the Nile River basin to flock into a region where they could grow crops, herd livestock, and sustain their traditional way of life. Thus, the earliest inhabitants of the Nile valley were of mixed African, North African, and Southwest Asian origins. Moreover, there were noticeable physical differences between the peoples living in Upper Egypt and those living in the delta in Lower Egypt. The Upper Egyptians were small, had long narrow skulls, dark wavy hair, and brown skins, while those of the delta and those who congregated around the region where present-day Cairo is located were taller and had broader skulls.

PREDYNASTIC HISTORY

Already by 5000 BCE the Egyptian portion of the Nile River basin, which had originally been only thinly occupied by fishing and herding peoples, had given way to a series of largely autonomous villages. At this time the inhabitants of this portion of the Nile River basin gave few hints that they would be among the first communities in world history to establish a central polity and a distinctive and unified culture. Most of the Nile River basin dwellers lived in tiny villages, subsisting on the grains that they cultivated, mainly wheat and barley, hunting, foraging, and fishing, and the produce of their domesticated animals—sheep, goats, and pigs. As yet, they had no written language. They probably spoke different dialects and had no massive irrigation works. Little status or wealth differences set one group of inhabitants off from another. The villagers, having only limited contact with their neighbors, lived in small mud hovels.

With the passage of time, these tiny villages were able to grow into important towns and eventually become cult centers for the worship of local gods, who were propitiated in order to ensure the fecundity of the land and provide stability to the lives of the peoples. The move to larger village communities was at this early stage more pronounced in Upper Egypt than in Lower Egypt, especially in the bigger Upper Egyptian settlements known as Naqada and Hierakonpolis. The south or Upper Egypt sustained its early advance over the north, and ultimately the communities living in the south found themselves strong enough to unify the whole of the Nile valley from the first cataract, just south of present-day Aswan, to the Mediterranean. Upper Egyptians, in addition to having spawned larger village settlements, also had the advantage of access to the mineral deposits in the hills of the eastern desert and Nubia, south of the first cataract.

Egypt's predynastic era divides into several distinct historical periods. The first of these, known as the Badrian period, named after the village of el-Badri, located in Upper Egypt, lasted roughly from 5500 to 4000 BCE. Little is known about these centuries except that the Badrians were farmers who cultivated crops and managed herds. Some believe that they domesticated animals on their own. If, as seems more likely, they did not, their contact with cultures of Southwestern Asia, where domesticated animals were in use, enabled them to assimilate these skills. Many lived in tents made from animal skins. Next came the Naqada period, from 4000 to 3100 BCE, taking its name from the site of Naqada in Upper Egypt where the British Egyptologist Flinders Petrie discovered a cemetery in 1895 that contained more than 3,000 graves. The burials here were of a quite rudimentary nature, consisting of simple mats thrown over the bodies of the deceased, which in turn were deposited in pits. Yet the fact that men and women were burying their progenitors, rather than exposing them to the wild animals, suggests that these early humans regarded themselves as different, more exalted, than the rest of the animal world, perhaps even able to survive into an afterlife. Even at this early date, Egyptians buried the dead on the west bank of the Nile, where the sun set, presumably in hopes that like the sun, the dead, too, would arise and ascend into a new life after death.

By the Naqada II phase, life in Upper Egypt had become more complex. Social and occupational hierarchies existed. A privileged and wealthy class emerged. Its members engaged in hunting activities not in order to support themselves but as a symbol of their rank and their prestige. Some members of this group promoted long-distance trade, as the well-to-do sought to obtain luxury commodities from afar. Specialized artisans produced wares for the rest of society, fashioning more elaborate commodities for the well-to-do. The wealthy and powerful were now buried in larger, more elaborate tombs. Their bodies were surrounded by many of the very same objects of beauty and pleasure that they had enjoyed during their lives. Upper Egypt at the time had at least three relatively large urban conglomerations: Naqada, known as the gold town; Hierakonpolis, further south, and Abydos, where the necropolis of the first kings was located. Hierakonpolis was the most impressive of the three, possessing a wall that was 9.5 meters thick in places and inside which was an enclosed temple where scholars later found the Narmer palette. Although Egypt lacked the magnificence that the cities of Sumer had at this time, the city of Hierakonpolis was a virtual twin of the great Mesopotamian city of Uruk. Indeed, artifacts found at Hierakonpolis suggest some actual connection and borrowing between the inhabitants of these two locations. Perhaps as many as 5,000 residents lived within the city walls of Hierakonpolis.

At the end of the Naqada III period, some time around 3100 BCE, Upper and Lower Egypt were united. The unification was not entirely peaceful. One major artifact of this era—the famed Narmer palette, discovered in 1898 and now prominently displayed in a Cairo museum—features a powerful ruling figure, who having caught one of his enemies by the hair—unquestionably a northerner—holds a mace over his head as he prepares to slay him. This smiting image became one of the standard motifs in Egyptian representation and was intended to demonstrate the power of the ruler. Certainly by 3000 BCE most of the Nile valley from the delta to Aswan was united.

The early kings of the first Egyptian dynasty were buried at Abydos, while Hierakonpolis had become a vital cult center for the god Horus. Although Egypt's cities were not as large as those in Mesopotamia, the territory had numerous urban centers, the remains of which have been covered up by Nile floods and later settlements. By the time that the famed third dynasty arrived on the scene, Egypt was a unified polity. It had developed a monumental style of royal architecture and buried its royalty in elaborate tombs.

EGYPT'S HISTORY MATTERS

Historians of Egypt of all ilks—Egyptologists, Coptologists, papyrologists, Islamists, and modernists—rarely wonder whether what they do has relevance. They know instinctively that it does. But the question deserves an answer. Perhaps Egypt's place in the world historical drama can be compared to the legendary appearances of movie character Forrest Gump, in the Oscar-winning movie of that same name. Forrest Gump, rather like Egypt and the Egyptians, seems to appear at all of the great historical moments. In the case of Egypt,

Figure 1. Narmer palette

however, its inhabitants often assumed a starring role. As the narrative of this volume will demonstrate, they did so by being one of the first communities to create centralized polities and complex social hierarchies. They also were innovators in one of humankind's most magnificent achievements—the invention of the alphabet. Although many of the symbols of hieroglyphs are pictograms and ideograms, standing for individual words, and others represent consonants, the Egyptians went a step further, pioneering the introduction of symbols that stood purely for the single letter in an alphabet.

Equally important to world history was the role that Egyptian cultivators played in supporting some of history's great empires. After the ancient culture of the pharaohs had given way, Greek and Roman conquerors looked to Egypt to feed their large imperial populations. So did later Fatimid, Mamluk, and Ottoman empire builders. In all of these imperial states, Egypt was the empire's most populous and prosperous state. Early Christianity owed much to Egyptian religious fervor, and Islamic conquerors, naturally, sought to implant their religion in this vital territory. Mamluk Muslims saved Egypt, North Africa, and possibly even Western Europe from the Mongol ambitions of world conquest, defeating a powerful Mongol army in Syria in 1260. The world's modern empire builders—the French, the British, and the Americans—have understood the strategic importance of Egypt, lying astride Europe, Africa, and Asia, and have wanted to incorporate it within their imperial structures.

There is also a great paradox in Egypt's fabled history. Once Egypt had been unified, 5,000 years ago, the territory and its inhabitants were to enjoy an extraordinary period of isolation from the outside world that permitted the dwellers along the banks of the Nile to promote a distinctive way of life and an internal unity that lasted uninterruptedly for 1,500 years, right down to the Hyksos invasion around 1500 BCE. For a millennium and a half, the deserts, the Nile cataracts, and the Mediterranean proved insuperable barriers from the outside. They allowed the Egyptians to perfect the institutions of the pharaonic era (described in chapters 2 and 3) and to create a sense of Egyptianness that has weathered a long line of conquerors and foreign empire builders. In many ways, the long sweep of Egyptian history is a tale of how a people that had originally established a proud sense of their unique religious, political, economic, and cultural identity over a nearly three-thousand-year history then struggled to retain their Egyptianness in the face of a long line of conquerors.

In his oft-quoted *Egypt's Liberation: The Philosophy of the Revolution*, Egypt's longtime president and revolutionary leader Gamal Abdel Nasser argued that, historically, Egypt functioned within the orbits of three circles and that Egypt's role in world affairs was dictated by its central location in these settings. The first of these was an Arab circle, but equally important were the African and Islamic contexts. "It is not without significance that our country is situated west of Asia, in contiguity with the Arab states with whose existence our own is interwoven. It is not without significance, too, that our country lies in northeast Africa, overlooking the Dark Continent, wherein rages a most tumultuous struggle between white colonizers and black inhabitants for control of its limited resources. . . . All these are fundamental realities with deep roots in our lives which we cannot—even if we try—escape or forget."

Nasser was a formidable leader, deeply schooled in his country's history. In the preceding passage Nasser speaks of the primacy of geography in Egyptian history, its vital location at the corner of Africa and Asia. Here, too, he stresses Egypt's ties with what we today call the third world and that he identified as the world emerging from European colonialism. Yet his account is historically impoverished, as this study will demonstrate, for Egypt was also completely tied to the world of the Mediterranean Sea. Its influences on Europe and Europe's influences on it, so apparent at virtually all stages of the country's history, get short shrift in Nasser's reading of Egyptian history. But the pharaohs influenced the Greeks, who, along with the Romans, occupied Egypt and sank deep roots into the Egyptian mentality. Egypt was the most Christian of countries until the Arab-Muslim conquest of the seventh century, after which its primacy within Islam knew few limits. Yet in the nineteenth century the

Egyptian khedive Ismail could proclaim that Egypt had finally joined the European concert of nations, and during the British occupation, Egypt's centrality within the British Empire was never gainsaid. Identity and place in world historical events are issues writ large in the history of this magnificent territory.

LEARNING ABOUT EGYPT IN MUSEUMS

Egypt has an abundance of world-class museums that make experiencing the history and seeing the artifacts of the country a joy. Perhaps, however, first-time visitors should prepare themselves by going to one of their own national museums, almost all of which abound with artifacts from the pharaonic period. For Americans the Metropolitan Museum of Art is an obvious choice. Its superb ancient Egyptian collection includes an entire wing of the museum devoted to the splendid temple of Dendur, originally built 80 miles south of Aswan in Nubia by the Roman governor of Egypt around 15 BCE and now gloriously reassembled through the good offices of the Egyptian government. The Egyptians offered it to the Metropolitan Museum of Art as a token of gratitude to American taxpayers whose generosity enabled the government to save many monuments that would otherwise have been submerged by the Aswan high dam constructed in the 1960s. For Britons the British Museum has an even more extensive collection of Egyptian antiquities, topped off by the Rosetta Stone, which literally greets visitors as they proceed into the rooms that house the Egyptian materials.

Yet these extraordinary collections pale next to the objects on display at the Egyptian Museum, located right off the main square in the center of Cairo, inside an inspiring pink stucco building, first open to the public in 1902. It has on display some 120,000 objects with another 150,000 stored in the basement. Here, too, visitors upon entering encounter one of Egypt's most important artifacts—the Narmer palette, already described and pictured in this chapter, the iconic symbol of territorial unity. Yet few pause before the Narmer palette, so eager are they to reach the second floor, where a plethora of rooms house what must be the world's most opulent collection—that of the Pharaoh Tutankhamen. Can one not help imagine what the tombs of other, longer-lived and more powerful pharaohs must have contained if this relatively minor pharaoh's tomb contained such treasures?

Cairo offers more. The Coptic Museum, built in 1947 and newly refurbished, located in Old Cairo in a residential area where many Copts live, has a stunning collection of Coptic art, probably the best in the world, as well as fine examples of textiles for which Coptic weavers were justly famous. The Museum of Islamic Art was the brainchild of the Egyptian khedive Tawfiq and displays pieces of medieval Islamic art that were gathered from the homes, mosques, and palaces of Cairo over the years. A magnificent replica of a wealthy Ottoman's house can be seen in the Gayer Anderson Museum, easily visited after viewing the Ahmad ibn Tulun mosque, one of Cairo's most magnificent.

There are impressive museums outside Cairo. Alexandria has the Graeco-Roman Museum, opened in 1892 by khedive Abbas, which displays beautiful tomb paintings and several busts of Alexander the Great. A small museum honoring the Greek poet Constantine Cavafy (1863–1933) exists in the flat where he lived during the last twenty-five years of his life, while not far away is the Cecil Hotel, now restored to some measure of its interwar greatness, when it served as a meeting place for literary and cosmopolitan Alexandrians, including the British novelist Lawrence Durrell, best known for his *Alexandria Quartet*. Finally, not to be missed is the new library of Alexandria, opened in 2002 and standing prominently on the corniche. The wall surrounding the building, made of Aswan granite, is etched with letters from most of the languages of the world. At present, the library's holdings are not large, but the administration aspires to assemble a collection of some 8 million books.

The most recent museum is the Nubian Museum at Aswan. Opened in 1997 and displaying many objects from Nubia that would otherwise have been submerged by Lake Nasser behind the high dam of Aswan, it is a gem. Its architecture, the gardens surrounding the structure, the layout of the collection, and the beauty and uniqueness of the Nubian artifacts reflect the skill of its Egyptian architect, Mahmud al-Hakim, and the love and devotion of the men and women who combed the region to assemble the pieces on view there.

Egypt during the Old Kingdom

A short bus, car, or taxi ride from the center of Cairo brings travelers to the three great pyramids at the edge of the desert just west of the Cairo suburb of Giza. They are the only one of the Seven Wonders of the World still standing today. Yet although first-time visitors will have seen these structures countless times in photographs, pictures fail to capture their majesty and immensity. They tower above the skyline of the city of Cairo and continue to defy explanations of how people five thousand years ago raised the huge stone pieces to such heights and with such perfect symmetry.

Arriving at the foot of the great pyramid, inveterate visitors or first-timers can think of little else than getting to the top and seeing the world from there. Well into the nineteenth century, the great pyramid was the tallest structure in the world. Climbing the pyramids is no longer permitted. Too many injuries and even some fatalities persuaded the authorities to prohibit what is every person's fond wish—to spread out a prepared lunch on a twelve-foot-square area at the very pinnacle, once a favorite gathering place where a party of climbers could eat, drink, and survey the countless pyramids to the south and Cairo's urban sprawl to the east. The prohibition did not come into being until the 1940s, so it was customary for even the least athletic of tourists to attempt to ascend the great pyramid in earlier decades. Baedeker's popular guidebook *Egypt* encouraged visitors to try, stating that the ascent "though fatiguing was perfectly safe" as long as one adhered to well-established practices. The climber should select three young and athletic Bedouin guides. Two of these men would go ahead and help the tourist up the three-foot-wide stone steps, one man pulling on each arm. The third man would push from behind. The guides were naturally in a hurry since the more tourists they helped to reach the top, the more money they made. Baedeker's guidebook claimed that climbers could reach the top in ten or fifteen minutes, an assertion hard to believe. The handbook recommended taking half an hour to reach the top in the summer so as to avoid the discomfort of arriving breathless and heated. The descent was quicker but not much easier. "Persons liable to giddiness may find it a little trying, but the help of the Bedouin removes all danger."

Entering pyramids is not for the faint of heart. Many of the passageways are narrow and winding, and the heat and darkness are discomforting. Anyone afraid of closed in and dimly lit locations should avoid this activity. The great pyramid naturally attracts the most visitors. Who can return from a visit to Egypt without having entered this most famous of constructions? These days, entering the great pyramid is not so hazardous or unpleasant as it once was. The interior corridors have been cleaned and lighted. This was not the case throughout much of the nineteenth century, as one visitor's remarks made clear. "We emerged dusty, dirty; faces covered with perspiration from the heat, and blacked by the smoke of torches, we looked as I have seen men look in battle."

Today's visitors enter the great pyramid through an entrance made by a Muslim Caliph in the ninth century, just below the original one. The opening is reached after clambering over thirteen tiers of large stone rungs. Even though the stones have had steps chiseled in them in order to make the climb manageable, ascending even that relatively short distance is no easy task.

The designers of the pyramids endeavored to hide the entrances and also carved out a number of false openings in order to baffle tomb robbers; they were never successful. Once inside the great pyramid, heat and dankness have to be dealt with. Next comes a long and ascending gallery, thirty feet high and forty-one feet long that leads into the king's chamber, empty except for a lidless sarcophagus. Here Egyptian priests laid Khufu to rest nearly 5,000 years ago.

The small pyramid at Giza brings a different set of challenges. There is no ascent to the burial chamber. Something more eerie awaits. Guides routinely turn off their flashlights when visitors are inside the tomb room. The chamber's darkness is so total that one cannot even see one's hand in front of the face, and frightening enough to induce panic. What if, perchance, the batteries on the flashlights failed? But, of course, this is part of a well-rehearsed plan. The light appears, and fears dissipate.

The three great pyramids of Giza represent the most impressive and visible symbols of a complex and sophisticated high culture that arose in Egypt virtually without warning. Almost overnight cities appeared where only tiny villages had existed. A civil service took the place of rule by village notables. A semidivine king ascended the throne of Egypt supplanting tribal chiefs. Something new, far more complex culturally and politically, crystallized in the valley of the Nile around 3000 BCE. The foundations of this culture remained durable for two and a half millennia, straight down to the time of Alexander the Great, who conquered Egypt in 332 BCE and produced the first major rupture in the Egyptian historical narrative. Although Alexander's conquest set in motion forces that allowed Greek and Roman culture to replace many of ancient Egypt's institutions, the country's new foreign rulers did not erase all of the deeply rooted institutions and cultural beliefs of the pharaonic period. The Greeks and the Romans came admiring the Egyptians and endeavored to learn from them.

In our present era of rapid cultural, economic, and political change, the mind boggles at a cultural system surviving and prospering over two and a half millennia. Modern empires rise and fall in a few centuries. Spain's empire in the Americas lasted an impressive three centuries. The British ruled over India for that same length of time. Usually, great powers enjoy their moment of prominence for no more than a century. Yet the ancient Egyptians, while experiencing significant changes in their ways of life, including periods of economic and political chaos intermingled with moments of unexcelled political and artistic achievement, witnessed no "breaches, profound changes, and dark ages."

The narrative of ancient Egyptian history is much like a great classical symphony. Fast and slow movements interchange; sadness and joy make their appearances; many variations are explored; but the primary themes return with a reassuring and pleasing familiarity. The reasons for the extraordinary persistence of institutions and ethos in ancient Egypt are not difficult to discern. First among them was a determination among Egypt's ruling elites to return to ways that had served them well. Ancient Egyptians remembered, with justifiable pride, the magnificent architectural and artistic triumphs and the unparalleled political stability and economic prosperity of the six centuries that stretched from 2700 to 2100—the period that historians later labeled the Old Kingdom. These centuries represented an ideal world that the ruling group wished to preserve or re-create.

Literate Egyptian elites looking back on 2,500 years of a single, dominating cultural system were, of course, eager to pick out turning points and highlight the decisive moments and events that they believed had shaped the course of their history. The first historical chronology of the ancients came from an Egyptian scribe, writing in Greek in the third century BCE. Manetho's writings were lost and have come down to us only through the works of later commentators; yet his identification of thirty-one Egyptian dynasties from the first unification of Egypt around 3100 BCE to the conquest by Alexander in 332 has stood the test of time. Manetho's chronology remained the most widely used method for periodizing pharaonic history until the nineteenth century, when scholars introduced new, and what for them were more helpful, ways to periodize the history of the ancients. These scholars suggested that the culture of the pharaohs could be divided into three periods of high cultural and political success (the Old Kingdom, the Middle Kingdom, and the New Kingdom), which were interrupted by periods of political and cultural instability. These were designated as the first, second, and third intermediate periods. The following table gives *The Dictionary of Ancient Egypt*'s dates and dynasties for ancient Egyptian society.

3100–2686 BCE Predynastic period (first and second dynasties)
2686–2181 BCE Old Kingdom (third through sixth dynasties)
2181–2055 BCE First intermediate period
                (seventh through tenth dynasties)

2055–1650 BCE Middle Kingdom
          (eleventh through thirteenth dynasties)
1650–1550 BCE Second intermediate period
          (fourteenth through seventeenth dynasties)
1550–1069 BCE New Kingdom
          (eighteenth through twentieth dynasties)
1069–747 BCE Third intermediate period
          (twenty-first through twenth-fifth dynasties)
747–332 BCE Late period
          (twenty-sixth through thirty-first dynasties)

THE CULTURE OF ANCIENT EGYPT

Ancient Egyptian culture had a unique, one might even say easily identified and distinctive set of characteristics that were numerous, varied, and inextricably related to one another. The major traits are easily listed. They consist of a centralized state, ruled over by a godly king; an efficient bureaucracy; a priestly class, concerned with ordering the worship of numerous zoomorphic and anthropomorphic gods, who were believed to have influence on human events; a monumental architecture, based on an impressive knowledge of certain exact sciences, notably mathematics; and a distinctive and unmistakable artistic style that varied little over the entire period of pharaonic rule. Just as the people of Western Europe looked back to the Roman Empire after its fall, so the peoples of Egypt remembered the glories of the pharaonic centuries even after the last of the pharaohs had gone and even after the ancient language had been lost. For many centuries they tried to re-create this way of life. Egypt's early conquerors, the Greeks and Romans, brought new ideas and new institutions, but they, too, admired the elegance and stability of ancient Egyptian civilization and wanted to retain much from these centuries. It was only the Christians and the Muslims, with their hatred of polytheism and zoomorphic deities, who sought to eradicate Egypt's classical traditions. Yet here, too, much that was important religiously to the ancient Egyptians made its way into Christian and Muslim belief and practice.

The Art of the Ancient Egyptians

The art forms of the ancient Egyptians are a good place to begin a description of ancient Egyptian culture. Exquisitely beautiful art became in many ways the most revealing feature of this enduring ancient world. It is to be found in abundance on friezes and walls of temples and funerary constructions and reveals the realism with which Egyptians viewed, and pleasure that they took in, their own lives and the natural world that surrounded them. And it influenced all subsequent art that had contact with the world of the Mediterranean. The Greeks and the Romans learned from it and improved on it, and its influence can even be seen, though remotely, in later Western art from the medieval period into the Renaissance. Artists in other ancient cultures rarely matched the techniques and aesthetic sensibilities of Egyptian artists. Yet in spite of the fact that the art of the ancient Egyptians achieved a "natural and unconscious realism, exercised with a technical ability of the highest order," it lacked the kind of individuality that characterized the painting and sculpting of later artists, notably that of the ancient Greeks and Romans.

In the first place, while Egyptian creators of artworks and patrons of what we today call the arts undoubtedly had strong aesthetic sensibilities, art was not undertaken for its own sake. It had well-understood functions. Specifically, wall paintings, sculptures, and stelae were intended to represent objects that were vital to the cult of the gods and to the afterlife of humans. When artisans created religious figures, they did so in order to give form and provide a location where the deities could manifest themselves and where ritual actions could take place. Likewise, when they depicted kings, queens, and other notables, they did so in order to ensure good lives in this world and in the next.

With some notable exceptions, especially during the reign of Akhenaten in the New Kingdom (see the next chapter for a fuller discussion), Egyptian artists adhered to rigid rules for depicting human and animal forms if, as they often did, they drew them two-dimensionally on walls rather than as statues in three dimensions.

Their primary goal was not to portray animate and inanimate objects as they would be seen from a particular vantage point, but rather as nature presented them to the viewers, stressing the most telling features of the objects. This meant drawing trees from the sides and ponds from above, even when both objects were incorporated in the same drawing. This technique can be seen most clearly in the two-dimensional representations of human beings. Typically, the artists presented the face in a profile, with only one eye showing, while drawing the trunk of the body as if seen straight on. The legs were presented in profile. What is so astonishing is how little Egyptian artists deviated from this style even as one century replaced another and one set of dynasts and one generation of artists gave way to others. (See figure 2 for an example of how Egyptian artists represented the human form in two dimensions.)

CENTRALIZED GOVERNANCE AND A SENSE OF THE DUALITY OF THE UNIVERSE

One should not be surprised that the Egyptians formed a centralized polity and a unified state. Some commentators believe that Egypt was the first nation-state in world history. The territory running along the Nile River from the first cataract at Aswan to the Mediterranean Sea possessed many advantages for creating a unified and centralized polity. Its land mass constituted a geographical, if not an ethnic, unity that few other peoples possessed. Its population was nestled inside the Nile valley, largely protected in its early stages of development from southern invaders by the Nile River cataracts that began at Aswan. These made the Nile unnavigable south of Aswan. Egyptians enjoyed protection from populations living to the east and west because of deserts that armed units did not penetrate until the Hyksos entered Egypt in the seventeenth century BCE. Similar protection extended to the north, where the Mediterranean Sea offered security from the outside world until seafaring peoples like the Phoenicians, first, and the Greeks and Romans, later, mastered oceanic currents, winds, and sailing technology.

Figure 2. Wall painting of Nebamun, who died around 1350

In spite of the inherent unity of the Nile valley, Egyptians had an intense sense of dualism in their lives. Basic to this sense of two-ness was Egypt's division into its upper and lower parts, the south and the north. Even after the territory's conquest and unification, the pharaohs wore two crowns, one that symbolized the north and the other the south. Often, when the country disintegrated into periods of political instability, the north and the south drifted apart. Equally important, however, was a sharp dualism between the arable land and the desert, a separation expressed in colors. The red part of the country represented the sand, and the black the arable land. The fact that the inhabitants of the Nile valley could physically straddle the desert and the arable land, placing one foot in sand and the other on cultivated soil, made this duality a harsh reality of Egyptian agriculture. Not surprisingly, Egyptians carried a sense of counterposing forces into politics and culture. They saw the world as oscillating between order and disorder, the universe divided between night and day and between the heavens and the earth. In the same fashion, they believed in a mortal life and an afterlife. Critical to sustaining order in the face of constant pressures for disorder was the ruler, the pharaoh, whose task it was to understand the rhythms of this world and to ensure that through his wise and just rule order prevailed over disorder.

The Pharaohs

At the heart of ancient Egyptian society and culture was the king, the pharaoh, a word taken from the Greek form of *pero* or *per-a'a*, which was the Egyptian designation for the royal residence. The king was thought to be divine, a god-man, the offspring of a human mother and a deity. He was expected to ascend into the eternal world of the gods after his death and to live there forever. In the central cosmology of the ancient Egyptians, the pharaoh was associated with the hawk god, Horus, in this life, and with the god of regeneration and the afterlife, Osiris, in the next. Horus's consort, Hathor, the goddess of sensuality, like Horus himself, and the other gods of a polytheistic spiritual world were thought to be under the dominion of the solar god, Ra, whom the ancient Egyptians increasingly came to regard as the most powerful and important of all of their deities.

The Egyptians developed elaborate paraphernalia, featuring insignias, regalia, and titles, to underscore the power of the king and his central government and to extol the virtues of central power that included an administrative bureaucracy, a priestly class, and landed notables. State officials, while subordinate to the king, were vital instruments in promoting the well-being of the people. Hence, they, too, received homage and enjoyed great prestige. Illustrative of the influence of the most powerful of all the agents of the state—the pharaoh—is the fact that the Egyptian kings were among the first rulers to wear crowns. Their capital city during the Old Kingdom period was located at Memphis, not far from present-day Cairo, the joining point between Lower and Upper Egypt. This area housed the pharaoh's administration, though not the priestly classes, who were often associated with different locations in Egypt. The god Ptah, believed by many to have been the creator of the universe, had his main religious site at Memphis. This creation story provided religious authority for the political and cultural centrality of Memphis. But other gods had their own locations. Their advocates vied with one another for the preeminence of their deities and the paramountcy of their cities. The powerful sun god, Ra, had his cult center at Heliopolis, not far from Memphis. Over time, this area became an autonomous and rival source of legitimacy as the powers of the Heliopolis priestly element waxed and as belief in the sun god became more widespread.

Pyramids

No monuments better represent the spirit of the Old Kingdom and the esteem attached to the ruling family than the pyramids that feature so prominently in the architecture of this period and that have so influenced the way that later generations have viewed the ancient Egyptians. The breakthrough in pyramidal building occurred during the rule of King Djoser (r. 2667–2648). Its design was the product of the fertile imagination of the king's chief minister, Imhotep. As we have observed, predynastic Egyptians had been accustomed to burying the dead in pit graves. By Djoser's time, grave sites of the kings had taken on a greatly enhanced significance. Not only were the kings now expected to ascend, after death, to the heavens, where they would join their fellow gods, but the grave sites themselves were designed to serve as temples for the worship of gods and kings. The place chosen for the burial of King Djoser was Saqqara, not far from present-day Cairo, located on high and firm ground capable of supporting a large and heavy mass of stones. Previously, Egyptians had buried important personages in structures called *mastabas*, which were low-lying yet massive stone buildings, resembling benches that rose above the earth's surface. These burial structures had many rooms, including a chapel, and featured scenes from the deceased's life as a reminder of the world that he had inhabited. Underneath the *mastaba* was the actual burial chamber itself, usually hewn from the rock bed.

Imhotep wished Djoser's burial site to project the pharaoh's awesome power and wealth. No doubt the viewer can divine elements of bravado in the builder's ambitions. Imhotep surely was aware that when finished the construction would exhibit his own architectural genius. Not satisfied with a single bench, he kept adding new layers, or steps, from whence the pyramid has derived its historical name as the step pyramid. Eventually the building had six benches or steps, rose to a height of 204 feet, and contained 10,000 stone blocks, weighing 850,000 tons. Each of the stones was cut into perfectly rectangular small blocks so that it could be erected alongside the others and fastened onto the table below. (See plate 4 for an illustration of the step pyramid of Saqqara.)

The step pyramid set a standard for later builders. The king lay at the very center of the burial pyramid, which was set within a large funerary complex and was enclosed by walls that were covered with a shimmering limestone finish. The full construction site featured many rooms, including a temple and a palace court. Scattered about the location were numerous statues and relief sculptures, the most impressive of which was a statue of Djoser himself, fashioned in Egypt's unmistakable realistic artistic style. The statue was an early life-sized representation of the human form in ancient Egypt. The complex of buildings, walkways, halls, temples, palaces, and the like was nothing less than a small city itself, which priests and cult figures maintained for decades after the death of Djoser as a tribute to his greatness in life and his eternal existence.

Djoser was a third-dynasty ruler. Some scholars would group him and the other third-dynasty rulers with Egypt's archaic dynasties. But the fourth dynasty, building on the achievements of Djoser, undoubtedly moved to a higher stage of architectural achievement. The reigns of Khufu (r. 2589–2566), his son Khafra (r. 2558–2532), and his grandson Menkaura (r. 2532–2503) represent the ruling elites' embrace of monumental construction, centered on pyramidal mortuary buildings. It was at this time that pyramids attained their highest artistic and technical levels. So skilled were Egyptian architects and craftsmen that they were able to make the heaviest stone pieces seem as light as feathers. In their hands stones became plastic forms, capable of taking on many shapes.

Egypt's achievement in stone building is all the more impressive because prior to the third dynasty, when the Saqqara step pyramid was erected, Egyptian builders had worked primarily in mud-brick, reed, and wood. Yet just as the wonder of ancient Egypt seemed to appear almost overnight, so the magnificence of pyramidal and other works in stone appeared almost out of nowhere. Just how the Egyptian learned to build in stone with such incredible precision and unmatched beauty is yet another of the mysteries of this ancient culture.

The precursor of the three great pyramid builders at Giza was Sneferu (r. 2613–2589), the first ruler of the fourth dynasty and Khufu's father. He built the Meidum pyramid as well as two stone pyramids at Dahshur, all of which attained a new level of massiveness, consisting of more than 3.5 million cubic meters of stone. But here work on structures jutting skyward was still experimental. The most obvious example of an experiment gone wrong is the bent pyramid, about ten miles south of Giza, where, quite obviously, the architect and builders became aware that the angles at which the complex was thrusting itself into the air would not support all of the weight yet to come. Hence, the builders had no alternative but to break off the angles of the pyramid and close the structure off sharply at the top, ruining its triangular shape. (See plate 5 for an illustration of the bent pyramid.) A nearby pyramid reflected another important experiment. The builders encased the final structure in magnificent limestone so that it could reflect the sun's rays and project a shimmering image of austere beauty.

The stage was thus set for the splendors of Giza, the apex of the artistic and architectural achievements of Old Kingdom culture. Although there are no fewer than seventy pyramids in Egypt and Sudan, none equals the majesty, size, and architectural virtuosity of the three structures of Giza. The largest pyramid, constructed by Khufu, was known until recent times by the ruler's Greek name, Cheops. The second largest pyramid and the only one to have any of its original limestone casing intact was built by Khufu's son, Khafra, while the third and smallest of the three belonged to Khufu's grandson, Menkaura. Like the pyramids at Saqqara and Dahshur, these structures were much more than funerary sites. Each had three distinct parts, representing different aspects of this life and the afterworld. They had a chapel, devoted to the worship of the prominent god or gods of the ruler, a causeway with scenes from this life and anticipations of the next life drawn along the walls, and the pyramid itself, inside which, not beneath, the body of the great king was laid to rest and from which he was expected to ascend into the heavens. In order to aid him in his ascent, the pyramid builders usually left a solar boat near by, some of which were of immense size. One can be seen today just outside the great pyramid. (See plate 6 for an illustration of the Sphinx and the pyramid of Khafra.)

Later generations have marveled at how these ancient builders and workers, without the aid of wheeled carriages, pulleys, and cranes, were able to erect such immense monuments and to do so with little margin of error. The great pyramid of Khufu rises 481 feet above ground. How did the workmen hoist such massive blocks of stone, some weighing more than two tons, to such great heights? The answer is that builders employed sturdy brick ramps that enabled workmen to lift heavy stones and dug canals from the Nile to the base of the Giza plateau, where a harbor was constructed for handling the huge stones. Another undoubted advantage was a group of skilled and semiskilled workers, who were housed and fed in villages near the work site and were put to work the year round.

Herodotus visited the great pyramid and left one of the first written accounts. He asserted that the great pyramid had taken twenty years to construct and had involved more than 100,000 workmen who toiled for four to six months at a time before being replaced by another group of 100,000. Herodotus's account eventually became the scholarly consensus, accepted by virtually all later commentators. But Herodotus was wrong, or so claims John Romer, author of a 2008 publication, *The Great Pyramid*. Herodotus's information was badly out of date, based, as it was, on myths that circulated among Egypt's priestly classes. To begin with, extracting 100,000 workers every year from a society with a population 1.6 million would have produced an economic catastrophe for the rest of Egypt. A more likely scenario is that the pharaoh created a permanent workforce, probably numbering 21,000 at the beginning, when the largest quantity of stones had to be put in place at the base of the pyramid, and falling off to 4,000 for the last stage of the construction. Even so, this workforce would have had to labor at "savage work rates," something on the order of ten-hour days and 300 days in the year, in order to "reduce the economic consequences on Egypt's population of erecting such great pyramids." At that rate, they would have finished the task in fourteen years, not the twenty that Herodotus claimed.

The workmanship in the three pyramids of Giza was of the highest quality, especially that of the great pyramid of Khufu, which stands as the most impressive monument from the Old Kingdom period. By the time that the builders were prepared to erect Khufu's pyramid, many experiments, some of which had gone badly wrong, had taught the builders how to erect a perfect triangle. The fundamental requirement was that the upper half of the pyramid must have precisely half as much area as the bottom half: quite an achievement at any time, but especially for so early in the human saga. Equally stunning was the exactitude achieved in the directions of the four corners of the building. The corners were designed to face precisely due north, south, east, and west. The north and south sides were off by a mere 0.09 percent from the mark, while the east-west axis missed its true course by 0.03 percent. The great pyramid had 2,200 blocks, each weighing on average two and a half tons. The stones were quarried from the east side of the valley. In all, the great pyramid contained 5.5 million tons of limestone, 8,000 tons of granite, and half a million tons of mortar. (See plate 7 for an illustration of the great pyramid of Giza.)

Pyramids proclaimed the king's divinity and the Egyptian belief that kings, and perhaps even others, would enjoy rich and pleasurable afterlives. The builders were masters in the use of stone. They could fit one stone into another with almost no grating, and they could position stones flawlessly in the directions they wanted. Each pharaoh began the construction of his pyramid at the time of his ascension to the throne, but since construction could take up to twenty-five years, some did not see them through to completion. The most magnificent had outside casings of smoothed white limestone, only a few of which, however, have survived years of wear and tear and the ravages of looters. The fourth dynasty was Egypt's pyramidal era *par excellence*; the twelve-mile stretch of territory from Dahshur in the south to Giza is even to this day littered with the burial sites of kings, queens, royal family members, and even some of the dignitaries of the era.

COSMOLOGIES AND RELIGIONS

The religion of the ancient Egyptians has not enjoyed the favor of the outside world. The Greeks, while adopting some of the Egyptian deities and even forming a cult around the Egyptian goddess Isis, derided the Egyptian people and their priests for believing in gods that had animal heads and human bodies. The Israelites fashioned a whole new religious system in opposition to the polytheism of ancient Egypt, of which they had an intimate knowledge. The most powerful Jewish prophets condemned the Egyptians as pagans and idolaters, worshippers of false gods, and ignorant of the one true god, Yahweh, who bestowed his special blessings on the Hebrew peoples.

Yes, the ancient Egyptians did believe in a plethora of gods and worshipped strange animal-human deities, such as the falcon-headed god, Horus, identified with the pharaoh; the ibis-headed god of wisdom, Thoth; and Anubis, the jackal-headed god associated with embalming. Rather than seeing these beliefs through the prism of later monotheisms, one should note how well they represented the most positive aspects of Egyptian life. The gods and goddesses of the ancient Egyptians reveal the people's love of their world, the animals who surrounded them and in whom they took such delight, the sun, which never failed to regenerate the soil, the Nile River, with its bountiful and predictable supply of water and new soil, and the kings, who maintained the social order. Nor was the religion of these ancient people so diametrically opposed to the monotheisms that supplanted them and that held them in such low regard. While it is true that the Israelites and their Christian successors used ancient Egyptian beliefs as foils for their own religious tenets, in many ways Egyptian thought penetrated deeply and formatively into Judeo-Christian traditions. The most obvious influence was the belief in human resurrection, but equally important was a belief that godlike figures descended to live among humans and were the offspring of god-fathers and human mothers.

Of the ancient beliefs that have had a profound influence on later thought, the Egyptian belief in resurrection is the most obvious. The Egyptians spared no expense or thought in preparing their most powerful figures for a full and pleasurable afterlife. The body was to be preserved for eternity through elaborate procedures, which involved drawing out the internal organs, with the exception of the heart, and preserving these organs in special jars. What was left of the body then was swabbed with embalming fluids and wrapped in linen garments before being placed in elaborate coffins for final burying. At first, these mummification techniques were reserved for the pharaohs and members of the royal family. With the passage of time, powerful and wealthy men and women believed that they, too, could move on to a happy afterlife; it was even the case by the time of the New Kingdom that common folk, if they could afford the expenses, prepared themselves in a similar way so that they, too, could participate in the eternal life.

The Egyptian cosmological and religious beliefs were complex and diverse. Thus far, they have defied scholarly efforts to see them as one set of unified tenets or as a group of beliefs evolving over time in an orderly fashion. Perhaps one of the reasons that these belief systems seem so disorderly and fragmented stems from the fact that the ancient Egyptians were not at first a unified people. They lived well separated from one another in distinctive and localized communities, each of which had its own set of ideas about the universe and its gods. Each of the rising urban conglomerations of the ancient Egyptians had its own gods, usually dominated by a founding god, who was believed to protect the local community and ensure its well-being. Not surprisingly, therefore, certain gods loomed large in the Egyptian religious beliefs and were associated with specific locations where they were believed to be most powerful and where their cults were most highly developed.

All the same, several religious tenets tended to gain prominence over others. Over time, they achieved widespread acceptance. Egyptian religious ideas did evolve in specific ways, starting with a belief in the magical power of objects, moving then to a belief in the supernatural powers of animals, and finally settling on a faith in human forms themselves as the ideal representations of the divine. In this way the admixture of the human and the animal as portrayals of Egyptian divinities actually represented the historical development of Egyptian thinking about the divine. Certainly, by the time of the Old Kingdom, it was common to associate certain gods with specific functions and activities. The god Ptah was seen as the divinity that created something from the nothingness that had once existed. Yet if Ptah was the universe's creator, he lacked a powerful intervening presence. That kind of puissance inhered mainly in the great sun god, Ra, who some believed had succeeded Ptah on the throne and who had become for many the most supreme of this plethora of deities. Not to be overlooked, however, was Osiris, the god of regeneration, at first associated with the rebirth of the soil following the annual flood season, but soon connected to rebirth and resurrection in general. Osiris was the god who presided over the underworld and the afterlife and who took the deceased pharaohs into their eternal dwelling place.

Of all the cosmological stories of the ancient Egyptians that descended down through the ages, the most frequently cited was the saga involving the family of Seth, Osiris, and Isis. The story owes much of its historical significance to the Greek writer and historian Plutarch, who was the first to write down the saga, but there is no doubt that he was rendering in written form a narrative that had a long oral history. No doubt the story retained its historical power because of its overlap with Judeo-Christian themes.

Here is how Plutarch presented the tale. Early in time, perhaps even at the moment of creation, two gods, Osiris and Seth, fought for preeminence. Seth prevailed over his brother, Osiris, and after killing him, scattered the broken parts of his body over the length and breadth of the valley of the Nile. Fortunately, Osiris's wife, Isis, reassembled her husband's body and then charged her son, Horus, with the task of taking revenge against Seth. This Horus did, and in the process he came to represent the living king, while Osiris came to represent the resurrected king, who presided over the kingdom of the afterlife. Seth in turn symbolized the evil forces in life. The themes of resurrection and the competition between the forces of good and evil were of course motifs that reasserted themselves in all of the most important Near Eastern religions and also found their way into Greek and Roman thought.

The Egyptians built many temples for their gods; but these places of worship functioned quite differently from those with which modern men and women are familiar. Structures that housed the gods were not available to ordinary people except on special festival and ceremonial occasions, when the deity, usually a wooden image, from one and a half to six feet tall, was brought out and shown to an admiring public. Temple affairs revolved around ensuring that the god was kept happy—a task that was accomplished by providing food, drink, and various forms of entertainment for the god. A priestly class looked after the well-being of the gods and alone had access to the temple itself. Priests were endowed with agricultural estates, the profits of which were employed to provide the food and drink for their gods. In this fashion, the priests, especially those who looked after gods who were known to be powerful, like Ra at Heliopolis, and Isis, Osiris, Hathor, and Horus, became major political and economic forces, even to the extent of challenging the pharaoh and his court for ultimate supremacy.

The materials that provide the fullest and most revealing insight into the ethos and the spiritual tenets of the Old Kingdom are the texts carved into the walls inside and surrounding the pyramids. These texts first began to appear during the fifth dynasty and cover a period of three centuries, spanning the late Old Kingdom period and the first intermediate era, beginning around 2375 and lasting until 2055. They represent sayings that were thought to have magical powers and that ensured the safe passage of the deceased pharaohs to the afterlife. They also constitute the oldest religious writings and literature of the ancient Egyptians and provide an invaluable window into the spiritual lives and the beliefs of the ancient Egyptians. Constituting much more than beliefs connected with the all-powerful kings, they articulate the ethos of the people and are "the oldest chapter of human thinking which has survived to mankind." They also reveal just how deeply indebted the great monotheistic religions of the Near East (Judaism, Christianity, and Islam) were to the ethical tenets of their Egyptian predecessors.

The pyramid texts, as they are known today, stressed filial piety and extolled righteous and orderly behavior. The virtue that they most frequently underscored was encapsulated in the Egyptian word *maat*, which many have translated as righteousness, justice, and truth. To the ancients *maat* meant living according to a correct moral order, in which human beings conducted their lives in accordance with the tenets of the great Ra, and rendered obedience to their superiors on earth, the most important of whom was the gods' representative on earth, the pharaoh.

WRITING

Writing is one of humankind's most glorious achievements. It overcomes the problems of misunderstanding and forgetfulness that arise when information must be transmitted orally from individual to individual and generation to generation. It allows for the preservation of data that would be too complex to be memorized, and it enables cultures to create and retain vital records attesting to where they have come from and how they have evolved. A written language facilitates a shared understanding of events, actions, and decisions. Not surprisingly, then, the earliest written records were commercial and economic documents, since this information needed to be precise and was difficult to commit to memory. Only in time did written records set forth religious sentiments and human sensibilities.

Inventing systems of writing is one of humankind's most diffi-cult breakthroughs. This innovation occurred independently in only a few places in the world—probably only in Mesopotamia, Mexico, and China, though there is some dispute over whether Egypt was an independent source of writing. Once a system of writing had been invented, it spread quickly to other peoples and was modified and improved upon as it moved into new territories and was absorbed by new cultural groups.

Egypt may not have been one of the areas of the world where writing was invented, for the consensus seems to be that the Egyp-tians borrowed the idea from the Mesopotamians, adapting it to their purposes and making it a flexible vehicle for keeping records and expressing a wide range of ideas. At least 5,000 years ago, the Egyptians were making use of their own system of writing, called hieroglyphs. The first hieroglyphs date to the early dynastic period (2920–2575), though they were probably in use before this era. The last hieroglyphic inscription dates from the temple complex at Phi-lae in 394 CE, at which time hieroglyphs passed out of existence and out of people's memories. They were not recaptured until the nine-teenth century CE through the work of Egyptologists, most notably Jean-François Champollion, who, working with the Rosetta Stone, on which a single document, inscribed in three languages (Greek, hieroglyphs, and demotic Egyptian), made possible the deciphering of the language and gave modern people access to the culture of the ancient Egyptians.

Hieroglyphs employ three different ways to represent language in a written form. The first—the pictogram—shows the object itself. In other words, a picture of a duck refers to the word for duck. The second form is an ideogram, in which a picture stands for an ab-stract idea, such as love. The third form—the phonogram—stands for a sound. Here, one finds the beginning of the alphabet, and as recent work in the western desert has demonstrated, the ancient Egyptians were probably the first peoples to make that all-important leap from using a sign not to represent a word or an idea or even a sound, which requires a consonant as well as a vowel, but a single letter. This decisive breakthrough in human achievement occurred sometime early in the Middle Kingdom, probably around 1800 BCE, though the inspiration may well have come from Asian mercenaries living in Egypt, probably serving in the pharaoh's army.

To illustrate the progression from simply picturing objects as a way to represent them to using signs to stand for letters alone, let us take the example of the duck once again. The pictogram of the duck standing by itself represents the animal. But if the image of a duck is drawn with a figure of a man above it, it represents a sound, in this case the sound "sa." Standing alone, unconnected to other images representing other sounds, sa means a son. Finally, the image of a duck stood for the letter s itself, with the accompanying vowel implied within the meaning of the sentence. Over time, the alphabetic or phonetic part of Egyptian hieroglyphs came to contain a twenty-six-letter alphabet. In all, ancient Egyptian had about 500 common signs or hieroglyphs.

Hieroglyphs were mainly inscribed on stones and walls. They conveyed religious and moral messages. In time, a cursive form of hieroglyphs evolved, used primarily for legal documents, administrative records, and literary compositions. The Greeks called this form of writing hieratic since they believed that the priestly classes monopolized it. Finally, an even simpler version of the hieratic appeared around the seventh century before the Common Era. It was called demotic. These three interrelated scripts became increasingly alphabetic, particularly as Egyptians increased their contact with the Greeks, who had adopted an alphabet from the Phoenicians and had demonstrated its utility and ease of use. Later, as hieroglyphs gave way to Greek and Latin, the Coptic Christian community became the instrument for preserving parts of the ancient Egyptian language. Their educated classes developed a language that employed the Greek alphabet, but to which they added seven letters so as to be able to express sounds that did not exist in Greek but had been part of the sounds used in ancient Egyptian.

The mastery of writing created a privileged and powerful class that was reserved for those few who learned the complexities of hieroglyphs. This knowledge brought with it great prestige. According to one poem in praise of scribal life, the author noted: "Be a scribe that thy limbs may be sleek and thy hands soft, that thou mayest go forth in white attire, honor done thee, and the courtiers may salute thee." Or another sentiment: "Set thy heart on books. Would that I might make thee to love books more than thy mother, that I might put their beauty before thine eyes. It is greater than any profession. . . . Behold there is no calling whereon a man hath no master save that of the scribe, and he is himself the master." The life of the scribe was deemed infinitely better than that of the ordinary peasant since the scribe was "freed from coerced labor and protected from all work." Even the soldier was at a disadvantage since he "knoweth not whether he be alive or dead." Nor could the priest count on such protections since he might be called upon to work in the canals, where he was likely to be "drenched in the river."

SCIENCE

The best-known and in many ways the greatest of the Egyptian achievements in science was the invention of the calendar of 365¼ days. Although the length of the year was well known to ancient men and women, the Egyptians made an advance on other calendars by separating their year from the widely used lunar calendar of twelve months of thirty days each. The lunar calendar left 5¼ days unaccounted for and meant that this calendar was always falling out of relation with the seasons. The Egyptians rectified this problem by creating a twelve-month solar calendar that consisted of thirty days each, with five days added at the end of each year. They divided their calendar into weeks of ten days each, and the day in turn into twenty-four hours. The year began, not surprisingly, at the advent of the flood and was divided into three seasons of four months each, coinciding with the growing, harvesting, and fallow parts of the year. These innovations, which have constituted the calendar that most humans still live by, was already in place sometime between 2937 and 2821 BCE. In reality, the Egyptians operated with two calendars, one solar and one lunar. The solar was used for administrative purposes and ran side by side with the lunar calendar, which regulated temple affairs.

The pyramids revealed just how proficient the ancient Egyptians were in yet another scientific endeavor—mathematics. This skill can also be seen in several manuscripts that, while written down during the Middle Kingdom, reflected the mathematical knowledge that Egyptians possessed probably at the time of the Old Kingdom and that architects and builders employed in constructing the temples and pyramids. The Egyptians had a decimal numerical system that featured separate signs for 1, 10, 100, and beyond. They also used body parts as the main way to measure the length of objects. The primary unit of measurement was the length of the arm from the elbow to the tip of the thumb. This was known as the forearm. In turn, the forearm consisted of six palms. Artists employed these measurements in their drawings of the human body. The best-known of Egypt's mathematical treatises, the Rhind papyrus, dates from the middle of the second intermediate period (1650–1550) and reveals a sophisticated grasp of fractions and calculus.

Finally, many Greek observers were impressed with the Egyptian knowledge of the body and medicine. Herodotus observed that "each physician applies himself to one disease only and not more; someone for the eyes; others for the head; others for the teeth; others for the intestines; and others for internal disorders." A seventeenth-century BCE *Book of Surgery* has been considered the work of "the first scientific observer known to us, and in this papyrus we have the earliest known scientific document."

FIRST INTERMEDIATE PERIOD

The Old Kingdom came crashing down almost as rapidly as it arose. Already in the fifth dynasty indications existed that the energies of the ruling groups were not as formidable as they had once been. The pyramidal constructions after the fourth dynasty were much less impressive than those at Giza. Workmanship was not precise. Many structures were never completed, and none had the full complex of temples, mortuary rooms, causeways, and statues that the earlier monuments possessed. In addition, power seemed to slip away from the pharaohs and their central bureaucracies as landed notables paid less attention to the dictates of Memphis and exercised closer surveillance over their local populations. Nonetheless, the Old Kingdom fell into disarray largely because of climatic conditions that afflicted all of North Africa and Southwest Asia. Sometime between 2200 and 2150 this part of the world suffered acutely from aridity and droughts. The Mesopotamians and the Harappans of the Indus valley were as hard hit as the Egyptians. For the Egyptians drought took the form of low and inadequate Nile River floods, the result of lesser amounts of monsoon rains feeding the upper regions of the Nile, particularly the Blue Nile arising in the mountains of Ethiopia.

Egyptian sources leave no doubt that the Nile failures were catastrophic between 2180 and 2150 and then again for several decades around 2000. The documents from these years are replete with references to the suffering and despair of the people and their utter disbelief that a community of people that had enjoyed such widespread prosperity and peace had now sunk to such depths of unhappiness and disorder. Many of these comments, chiseled on the walls of buildings and funerary complexes, speak of a world turned upside down, where the wicked prospered and the good suffered. Source after source speaks of famine spreading from one village to another. The heroic figures cited in these records are no longer the pharaohs and their subordinates but rather local notables, who, in contrast to others, protected their followers and mitigated the effects of famine and local warfare.

Listen to the following tomb inscription: "All of Egypt was dying of hunger to such a degree that everyone had come to eating his children." Or another: "The tribes of the desert have become Egyptians everywhere. . . . The plunderer is everywhere, and the servant takes what he finds." And yet another: "Barbarians from outside have come to Egypt. There are really no Egyptians anywhere." One Egyptologist calls this Egypt's "first dark age."

The impact of this disorder on a culture that had known prosperity and political stability was long-lasting, traumatic, and transforming. The optimism that had suffused the Old Kingdom period was dashed. Egyptians now understood that order and well-being were not guaranteed, that disorder could descend as fast as prosperity had been achieved, and that a land that had been spared conquests from the outside now had enemies settled on its peripheries eager to exploit its weaknesses. The first intermediate period lasted a mere century, but left an indelible imprint on the mentality of the ancient Egyptians.

CHAPTER THREE
The Middle and New Kingdoms

In the New Kingdom Egypt became a world power. Its influence stretched from the southernmost part of Nubia all the way to Mesopotamia. Subject peoples and admirers sang the praises of the pharaohs. Even when Egypt did not control Mesopotamia, its bureaucrats engaged in sophisticated diplomatic negotiations with the chief ministers of the Tigris-Euphrates region. To cement good relations with the powerful Egyptians, Mesopotamian rulers sent their most eligible and regal daughters to live in Egypt and marry into Egyptian royal families.

Deserts and cataracts had served Egypt well in the Old Kingdom era. They had isolated the inhabitants from the rest of the world and allowed the diverse peoples living in the Nile River basin to create a unique culture and to form a deep sense of their Egyptian identity. But new technologies eventually allowed people and weapons to cross deserts and bypass cataracts. Horses and chariots carried Egyptian warriors across the Sinai desert into Southwestern Asia and around the cataracts into Nubia. The Egyptian rulers of the New Kingdom took full advantage of these technological breakthroughs, creating a majestic Egyptian empire.

Old Kingdom Egypt was a self-contained culture, cut off from the other communities of North Africa, Sudan, and Southwest Asia. While its rulers sporadically mounted military expeditions beyond its borders and its traders traveled into distant areas to exchange luxury goods, the isolation of the country that had been so important in building an ethnic, cultural, and political unity was still intact at the end of the Old Kingdom period. It was to remain free from major external influences until the invasion of the Hyksos peoples at the end of the Middle Kingdom and the rise of the New Kingdom. Egypt's pharaohs during the era of the New Kingdom projected power well beyond the country's natural boundaries. They created one of the world's first territorial empires. As imperialist figures the pharaohs' names were familiar across North Africa and Southwest Asia and into Nubia. They are still familiar today: Akhenaten, Egypt's most radical pharaoh, a tyrannical monotheist, whom one admirer called "the first individual in human history"; Ramses II, who planted the Egyptian flag and built monuments to himself in Nubia and sent his armies into Southwestern Asia; and Queen Hatshepsut, one of the few women to place her name and achievements squarely within the history of this ancient civilization, who sent naval expeditions into the Red Sea and accumulated vital information on Egypt's less frequently visited neighbors.

To understand the difference between the Old Kingdom and its successor regimes in the Middle and New Kingdoms, visit Egypt's ancient imperial headquarters at Luxor. Most visitors arrive by airplane, but the overnight train from Cairo is a pleasant way to make the four-hundred-mile journey. The luxury train leaves the main Cairo station in the evening, and passengers, after taking a tasteful meal in their rooms, retire to beds for the overnight journey, arriving refreshed at the Luxor station early the next morning.

Imperial cities are much the same wherever they are. They glory in the magnificence of their monuments; their pomp projects far-flung imperial successes. They celebrate the military and political exploits of their most successful rulers and revel in wealth and power. Thebes (present-day Luxor) was no exception. Here, at the pylon that forms an entrance to the wondrous temple of Luxor, Ramses had his artists depict his heroic battlefield exploits in the famous battle of Kadesh in which, according to Ramses' account, the Egyptian army defeated the Hittites. Few promenades in the world can rival that at Luxor, with its long avenue of sphinxes leading to the Luxor temple. The avenue of sphinxes once stretched all the way from Luxor to Karnak, more than a full mile, but even in its present-day reduced scale it is breathtaking. Military, religious, and political parades must surely have taken place here and inspired onlookers with the might of Egypt's ruling classes. (See plate 8 for an illustration of the avenue of the sphinxes at Luxor.) Across the river, where the pharaohs had their tombs chiseled into the sides of hills, more tributes to pharaonic power abounded. The Ramesseum is the first object that the visitors see once they have crossed the Nile, a magnificent mortuary temple built by Ramses II, a funerary cult center, meant to celebrate the power and achievements of this mighty pharaoh. Its pylons contain more scenes from the battle of Kadesh. The valley of the kings and queens itself has unparalleled mausoleums to Egypt's fabled rulers, far more impressive than, say, the tombs to the greats of the British Empire at Westminster Abbey. Of course, they were not meant to be viewed by outsiders but were hidden away from the eyes of tomb robbers. Today, many of the most spectacular of these constructions are closed because of their recent rapid deterioration. The most stunning of all, in the opinion of many, is the tomb of Seti I, not so important a pharaoh as many others, but whose tomb will cause him to live on vividly and forever in the imaginations of visitors. The colors, especially the dark blues, are as brilliant today as they were thousands of years ago. Alas, because Seti's site has attracted so many visitors in the past and has suffered much deterioration, it is rarely opened these days.

THE FIRST INTERMEDIATE PERIOD AND THE MIDDLE KINGDOM

Historians often gloss over Egypt's intermediate periods, which certainly get short shrift from visitors to Egypt and museum collections. Powerful pharaohs command attention, and Egypt on the move, establishing its authority outside the Nile River basin, excites people's imaginations. But the intermediate periods created opportunities to be free of the established institutions and to experiment with new political and cultural forms. During Egypt's first intermediate period, when centralized state power waned, local figures enjoyed a political and intellectual freedom denied to them when the pharaohs and the civil and religious bureaucracy were powerful. Local notables filled the breach caused by a failure at the center; those that were adept became the protectors of local stability. Writers and intellectuals were released from priestly oversight; Egyptian cultural brokers prepared the groundwork for a literary renaissance that flourished during the Middle Kingdom.

During the first intermediate period Egypt was politically fragmented and had many local monarchs, some of whom aspired to reunify the country. One of the most successful of these rulers was a family based in Thebes. Concerning themselves with the welfare of their subjects, these men laid the foundations for Egypt's eleventh dynasty and the onset of the Middle Kingdom era. The pharaoh who is credited with solidifying the power of this dynasty has come down through the historical annals by the name of Mentuhotep II. He ruled for fifty-one years, roughly from 2055 to 2004 BCE, during which period he not only reunified Upper and Lower Egypt but carried out military campaigns in Syria and Nubia. In some reliefs depicting his exploits, he is shown smiting his enemies, but in these representations his enemies are not foreigners, as they are in so many of the later ancient Egyptian representations of pharaonic power, but Egyptians.

Mentuhotep II enabled Egypt to enter upon two centuries of renewed centralized authority, economic prosperity, and intellectual achievement. This period, known as the Middle Kingdom, was dominated by the twelfth dynasty and witnessed the emergence of the city of Thebes, where present-day Luxor is located, as a new political capital as well as a religious center dedicated to the god Amun.

The Middle Kingdom is the classical period in ancient Egyptian history. It was a time when literature, the monumental style of architecture, polytheistic religion, and the governmental institutions that were introduced in the Old Kingdom were brought to a high state of perfection, ready to be passed on to the even more puissant pharaohs of the New Kingdom. Unfortunately, much less is known of the Middle Kingdom than the Old and New Kingdoms, except for its literature. Fewer monuments from this era have survived, ironically, because of the artistic excellence of the period. Architects and builders used high-quality stone, mostly limestone, which successors were eager to cannibalize for their own building materials.

The Middle Kingdom's decision to locate its major city at Thebes was an unlikely choice. In the Old Kingdom, the center of authority had been the city of Memphis, strategically located between Upper Egypt and the delta. Prior to its emergence as a center of wealth and power, Thebes was little more than a rustic village, and its triumph over the city of Herakleopolis due west of modern-day Beni Suef was unanticipated. Herakleopolis was closer to the old capital city at Memphis and closer to the population centers of the delta. But the rulers of the eleventh and twelfth dynasties had ties to the Theban area and chose to situate themselves in one of the few locations in Upper Egypt that was not tightly bounded on both sides by hills. In contrast to most of Upper Egypt, Thebes had a wide floodplain.

The pharaohs of the eleventh and twelfth dynasties elevated the local god, known as Amun, into a countrywide deity and ultimately into an imperial cult. Egyptian priests and believers merged their belief in Amun, which means "hidden" and refers to the immanent nature of the universe, with the great sun god, Ra. The new deity acquired the name Amun-Ra and claimed prominence over the pantheon of other Egyptian gods. Some devotees believed that Amun-Ra was the source of all divine power. The worship of Amun-Ra came to be closely associated with the economic prosperity and political power of the country, and the pharaohs were thought to represent this deity on earth. Many Egyptians held the view that pharaohs were the offspring of the great sun god and an earthly mother and thus had both a divine and a human nature.

Although the rulers and the ruling elite associated with the Middle Kingdom consciously sought to revive the traditions and institutions associated with the Old Kingdom, new elements appeared. In the first place, Southwest Asian and Nubian-African influences made their presence felt, and though the Middle Kingdom did not aspire to the expansionist impulses that became dominant during the New Kingdom, Egyptian culture and society were no longer insulated from the rest of the world. Moreover, the breakdown of the Old Kingdom and the rise of local, territorial notables compelled the pharaohs and the ruling elite to be far more accommodating to the interests of their subjects than the rulers in Old Kingdom Egypt had been.

In the Middle Kingdom period, rulers portrayed themselves as good shepherds whose duty it was to secure the well-being of the population. Old Kingdom pharaohs had depicted themselves as holding untrammeled power and living outside the realm of human emotions. Not so the pharaohs of the Middle period. In their statues and frieze portraits, artists show their faces lined with creases of worry and their mouths turned downwards with sadness for their subjects. Amenemhat I (r. 1985–1955), founder of Egypt's twelfth dynasty and a powerful ruler, expressed well what the people expected of their pharaohs:

> I was one who cultivated grain and loved the harvest-god;
> The Nile greeted me in every valley;
> None was hungry in my years, none thirsted then;
> Men dwelt in peace, through that which I wrought, conversing of me.

Still the overwhelming power of the ruler persisted. The mighty temples and monuments dedicated to the pharaohs that have attracted so many visitors to Luxor in Upper Egypt had their beginnings in this period. Although the most impressive of these structures were the handiwork of the rulers of the New Kingdom, most notably Ramses II, the twelfth dynasty laid the foundations for these edifices.

Although the ravages of time destroyed much of the splendor of Middle Kingdom art and architecture, they did not do away with the Middle Kingdom's most important gift to posterity, its literature. The literature of the Middle Kingdom period is of an exceptionally high quality, some of which has overcome barriers of distance in time and culture to resonate among modern readers. The best known of these works is *The Tale of Sinuhe*, a twelfth-dynasty account of banishment from the homeland and eventual reconciliation. Recast as a novel in Finnish in 1945 and translated into English four years later under the title *The Egyptian*, it became an overnight best seller and was subsequently made into a hit movie in 1954. Written by an unknown author, sometimes labeled the Egyptian Shakespeare, the poem recounts the flight of a fearful royal courtier, Sinuhe, from his beloved homeland, following the assassination of the pharaoh, Amenemhat, and his rehabilitation in a foreign kingdom in Syria. Here, Sinuhe grows wealthy and powerful and enjoys an esteem that he had not achieved in Egypt. But he longs for reconciliation with the rulers of his beloved homeland. Some of the passages in the poem, like the following one, project Egypt as an ideal society and may have been intended by the author as political propaganda:

> [The new ruler in Egypt] is a hero, active with a strong army,
>   a champion without compare. . . .
> He is unique, God-given. How joyful this land since he has ruled.

In spite of his prosperity in the new land, Sinuhe aches for Egypt and has no stronger desire than to live out his life and be buried there. His joy is unbounded when he receives a decree from the pharaoh inviting him to return. When he finally arrives in Egypt, prostrating himself before the king, he is overcome with emotion and rendered mute.

> I was like a man seized in the dusk.
> My soul had perished, my limbs failed,
> My heart was not in my body
> I did not know life from death.

THE SECOND INTERMEDIATE PERIOD AND THE HYKSOS CONQUEST

Like its predecessor, the Middle Kingdom began to disintegrate through internal tensions and conflict. This time, pressure came from incoming populations, who had settled in the Nile valley, attracted by its prosperity. The most dynamic of these incomers was a group known as the Hyksos. Although they have left virtually no written records and hence historians have had little opportunity to study them, the Hyksos were a Semitic-speaking people who came into Egypt from Southwest Asia. At first they arrived in small numbers and sought to assimilate the local culture; eventually Hyksos military forces, assembled outside the country, overthrew Egypt's local rulers and established their own monarchy.

The most impressive contribution that the Hyksos made to Egyptian history was the introduction of a new military technology that was sweeping through all of Europe, Asia, and North Africa at this time. The key to their military successes was the horse-drawn chariot that their warriors used to rout Egyptian infantry-based militias. The new military technology revolutionized warfare all across the Afro-Eurasian landmass, sending waves of shock and awe through those armies that had not encountered armed charioteers before. Probably perfected by Indo-European peoples from the steppes of central Eurasia, chariot warfare succeeded because it combined four new and essential features. First and foremost were the chariots themselves, made from metal, at first bronze and, later on, the more plentiful iron. They were so light that a warrior could pick them up with one hand and so swift and nimble that they could move rapidly through slow-moving infantry units. The other three ingredients were well-trained horses, expert drivers, and skillful archers, who could spray deadly arrows against defenseless adversaries. Egyptian army units were no match for the Hyksos war charioteers, who also possessed other superior weapons, such as javelins and spears that charioteers also hurled from their speeding chariots. In addition, Hyksos infantry soldiers wielded bows and arrows and protected themselves by wearing bronze and leather armor. Even more frightening was the heavy, crushing falchion, a single-edged sword.

THE NEW KINGDOM

What is known as the second intermediate period lasted a mere century (1650–1550), about one-quarter of the length of time of the Middle Kingdom era. Yet the nomadic Hyksos left an indelible mark on the Egyptian culture, compelling their Egyptian successors to master the new military technology, which they did, and which they used with incomparable efficiency to create a powerful expansionist state and a full-fledged territorial empire of their own. At its height the landmass of the New Kingdom stretched from the fourth Nile cataract in what is today Sudan all the way to the Euphrates River in present-day Iraq. At the height of its powers the Egyptian army was a formidable force, possessing its own well-trained legions of warriors who were led by veteran soldiers and were motivated as armies have been ever since by awards and decorations.

Ahmose I (r. 1550–1525 BCE) ushered the New Kingdom into being and became the founder of Egypt's eighteenth dynasty. He accomplished what other aspiring Egyptian rulers had failed to do: he crushed the military machine of the Hyksos and drove its people and their supporters out of the country.

The expulsion of the Hyksos is yet another significant event in the annals of Egyptian history and a major marker of the Egyptian narrative. As we have already observed, many groups entered Egypt, attracted by its wealth and the comfort of life in the Nile River basin. Following the breakdown of the New Kingdom, many of these groups came as conquerors. Yet, with some notable exceptions, the conquerors sought to assimilate to Egyptian ways and at the least to display their admiration of the country and its talented people. Many stayed on as welcomed members of the larger Egyptian society even after their tenure of power had ceased and they had been replaced by a new set of rulers, usually foreign. Not so the Hyksos. As the campaigns carried out by Ahmose and a successor, Thutmose I, make clear, the Asian Hyksos peoples did not win the favor of the local people or embrace Egyptian mores. The Egyptians regarded them as foreign oppressors and exulted in their defeat. Thus, by the time that the New Kingdom emerged, the Egyptians had reestablished their identity distinct from that of their conquerors and enunciated a set of practices and beliefs decidedly different from the nomadic and invading Hyksos, whom the new dynasts slew or drove from the country.

A series of powerful rulers followed in Ahmose I's footsteps, culminating in Egypt's two most successful warrior-pharaohs, Thutmose III and Ramses II. Yet, in spite of the powers attributed to the pharaohs and the widespread belief in their divinity, a greater degree of individualism, pluralism, and professionalism set the New Kingdom off from its predecessors. Priests, professional military men, and scribal bureaucrats were more autonomous than ever before. No longer were the kings and members of the royal entourage the only ones to be provided with state burials and destined to rise into the heavens after their deaths. Important notables and wealthy commoners copied the practice of the royals, though not in such an elaborate fashion as to suggest that their lives were somehow on a par with their rulers'. Nonetheless, they, too, had themselves buried in tombs, surrounded by amulets, and had prayers inscribed on the tomb walls as insurance for their well-being in the afterlife. They, too, believed that they would be resurrected and would live as comfortably as the pharaohs.

The eighteenth dynasty's most successful expansionists and empire builders were Thutmose I (r. 1504–1492), Thutmose III (r. 1479–1425), and Amenhotep II (r. 1427–1400). During the reigns of the Thutmoses, though more so under Ramses II's rule, Thebes became a formidable imperial city, replete with monumental constructions that were dedicated to the gods, mostly Amun-Ra, and to the empire's most powerful monarchs.

Not surprisingly, an empire built on military valor attached great importance to physical strength and glorified sports. Artists depicted their rulers as men with perfect physiques, capable of vigorous athletic pursuits, possessing the necessary talents to inspire men in battle even when their actual appearances were far from the ideal. The most aggressive expander of them all—Thutmose I—was a man scarcely five feet tall. Yet Thutmose I marched further and brought more territory under the rule of the homeland than any other monarch. The priestly prayer for one of his successors, also a great expansionist (Thutmose III), captures the military and aggressive impulses of the age:

Oh my son, my avenger, Menkheperre, living forever
I have given to thee might and victory against all countries

I have set thy fame, even the fear of thee, in all lands
Thy terror is as far as the four pillars of heaven. . . .
I have made powerless the invaders who came before thee
Their hearts burned, their limbs trembled.

The Egyptologist James Henry Breasted, in his characteristic dramatic and occasionally exaggerated rhetoric, called Thutmose III "the first character possessed of universal aspects, the first world hero." Thutmose III's army, well supplied with horses and chariots as well as skilled charioteers, numbered somewhere between 25,000 and 30,000. At the battle of Megiddo, during which he conquered the neighboring territory of Palestine, his forces won an unprecedented bounty. They seized 924 chariots, 2,238 horses, and 200 suits of armor. They also captured vast herds of cattle and took as part of the victor's prize immense quantities of gold and silver. They transported the precious metals to Egypt and laid them at the feet of the priests of Amun-Ra, thereby creating the great wealth and power of this priestly class and ensuring priestly support for expansionist policies.

MIGHTY PHARAOHS

During the Middle Kingdom and especially the New Kingdom periods, Egypt entered a new era. The substantial documentation that exists for this period has permitted historians to explore the lives and activities of rulers, leaders, and even to some extent the common people in greater depth than any of the other eras of the pharaonic period. The abundant historical records consist of papyrus manuscripts, stelae, and hieroglyphs carved on the walls of temples and palaces. The documentary base of Egyptian records from the New Kingdom is no less full than the materials available to medieval European historians. More documents allow for a deeper understanding of the inner workings of Egyptian society. The personalities of pharaohs come to life. Queen mothers enter the historical record as manipulators of power and proponents of their offspring in competition with other aspirants to power. The Egyptian narrative becomes more than a mere recitation of rulers' names, but is replete with intrigue, struggles for power, outsized egos, and cowardice.

Thutmose III

The institution that benefited the most from the abundance of source materials is the monarchy. Let us start with one of Egypt's mightiest rulers, Thutmose III, who ruled during the fifteenth century BCE. Although he had to share power with the queen regent, Hatshepsut, one of the wives of his father, on her death Thutmose III ruled with great vigor and for many years. He and his armies were constantly at war, extending the territory of Egypt into Southwest Asia. His forces won one of the most stirring battles of the ancient period—the battle of Megiddo—where at a fortress known as Armageddon, Thutmose III defeated the king of Kadesh and brought the rebellious province of Palestine under Egyptian control. He also sent his troops into Nubia and conquered territories in Sudan all the way to the fifth cataract. As the founder of Egypt's first major territorial empire, he maintained a large standing army, and to ensure the compliance of conquered territories he retained the sons and daughters of their ruling and noble families in his capital city. One of Egypt's most energetic warrior-kings, he led no fewer than seventeen military campaigns during a feverish twenty years of expansionist activity.

Queen Hatshepsut

Equally influential and virtually unique in the annals of Egyptian pharaohs was Queen Hatshepsut (r. 1473–1458), the daughter of Thutmose I and wife of Thutmose II. She acted as regent at first for Thutmose III, but later had herself declared a pharaoh. Although there had been a few female pharaohs before her, none exercised the power that Hatshepsut did; nor did any of these women remain on the throne as long. Although Egypt's rulers were expected to be males, Hatshepsut held power for nearly two decades before

Thutmose III replaced her. During her reign, she was customarily portrayed wearing male attire, and more often than not, though not always, scribes used the male pronoun when referring to her. Unlike her husband and her successor (Thutmose II and Thutmose III respectively), Hatshepsut was not an expansionist. Instead, she gathered information on the neighboring peoples who were not well known to the Egyptians; the purpose was to establish commercial contacts and promote the exchange of products. Her most notable expedition was a voyage of discovery that she commissioned to bring back information and products from the Red Sea regions. This voyage, often referred to as the expedition to Punt, was made up of five ships and included among its crew artists as well as sailors and traders. The royal ships made their way along the west coast of the Red Sea, coming into contact with the African peoples there. They also crossed the Red Sea and landed on the shores of the Arabian Peninsula. So significant was the voyage to Hatshepsut that she had pictures of the boats and the areas explored inscribed on the walls of her temple at Deir el-Bahri.

One cannot leave the life of this remarkable woman without mentioning the magnificent temple that she had constructed for herself at Deir el-Bahri. The work, which today attracts vast crowds of tourists, was only part of the architectural outburst associated with her rule. She also had ceremonial roads constructed throughout Thebes. The temple, her masterpiece, was built on the edge of the desert, just below the foothills, on the western side of the Nile. Here workmen lived in the nearby workmen's village so as to be able to devote all of their energies to the building of a place of worship that heralded Hatshepsut as a divinely born daughter of the god Amun and as a legitimate ruler of the country. (See plate 9 for an illustration of Queen Hatshepsut's temple.)

To experience Hatshepsut in all her glory, visit the room dedicated to her at the Metropolitan Museum of Art in New York City. This astonishing gallery has more than twenty statues of the queen-pharaoh, none of which is exactly the same. Most of them are standard pharaonic images, however, depicting her as an athletic, masculine figure, with broad shoulders, a strong physique, and the mandatory fake pharaonic beard. But spend a moment viewing two full-length statues of her along the far wall of the gallery. The statue in highly polished limestone, known today to its admirers as the white Hatshepsut, is magnificent, truly one of the most elegant and pleasing artistic pieces from the entire ancient Egyptian era. Equally arresting is a statue nearby, which depicts Hatshepsut as a woman, with breasts and a soft and lovely feminine face and figure, the very opposite of the stylized masculine portraiture demanded of virtually all pharaonic images.

Akhenaten

In 1887 an Egyptian peasant woman digging in the area around the village of Amarna on the east bank of the Nile River in Upper Egypt came upon 300 cuneiform tablets. Her discovery set off a buzz of excitement among antiquities scholars and led to careful explorations of a region around which little previous archaeological work had taken place. The team, headed up by the British Egyptologist Flinders Petrie, brought to light an aspect of ancient Egyptian history previously lost to the scholarly world. There, at Amarna, lay the remains of a whole ancient political and religious capital city, the work of one of the New Kingdom's most powerful leaders, yet little known to later generations—Akhenaten (r. 1352–1336). This pharaoh had introduced a whole new set of religious tenets into his society and moved the center of his polity to a new city where he worshipped what he considered to be the one and only true god, Aten. His successors, including his son, the famous Tutankhamen, repudiated the innovations of this man and attempted to efface all memories of his reign. This they accomplished almost miraculously. Yet their efforts at destruction did not win out over the persistence and ingenuity of modern Egyptology. Although the pharaoh Akhenaten's rule was in many ways a radical aberration of what had gone before and what was to come later, the twentieth-century discoveries of what has now come to be labeled the Amarna period add yet another magnificent chapter to the history of pharaonic Egypt.

Akhenaten was one of the later rulers of the eighteenth dynasty. He was also the most controversial monarch of ancient Egypt. A man of vaulting ambitions and deep-seated contradictions, he was undeniably a religious heretic, a political and religious tyrant, and possibly a mentally and physically deformed individual. He nearly destroyed the cultural foundations that had made ancient Egypt one of the world's most successful, stable, and long-lived civilizations. He was also a pioneering monotheist, a man whose religious concepts were so progressive that they may have influenced the tenets of Judaism and Christianity. An innovator in a culture that spurned new ways, he patronized a new, more realistic and naturalist art form. "The first individual in human history," Akhenaten distanced himself from the canons of his culture and imagined the universe in different forms from previous pharaohs and the powerful priestly classes. A sympathizer has called his reign "the most exciting epoch in Egyptian history, adding that "Akhenaten himself cannot be omitted from any intellectual history of humankind."

Akhenaten came to the throne in 1352 BCE, the son and successor to Amenhotep III. He ruled until 1336. He took as his wife and queen Nefertiti, whose name, meaning "the beautiful one," has come to symbolize the elegance, beauty, and sophistication of New Kingdom Egypt. The portrait bust of her housed in the Berlin Museum is one of the most revered works of art from this era, though recently its authenticity has been called into question. It made its way to Berlin in spite of vigorous protests of the Egyptian antiquity authorities at the high-handed actions of a German excavations team that had carried out work in the Amarna area. A last effort by the Egyptian authorities to have the piece returned to Egypt made it all the way to the German dictator, Adolph Hitler, but failed. Hitler refused to part with an object that in his opinion had flawless Aryan looks. (See plate 10 for an illustration of the statue of Queen Nefertiti.)

If we are to believe the artistic representations of Akhenaten, he was effeminate-looking, with slanting eyes, big lips, narrow shoulders, a distended belly, large hips and thighs, and tiny legs that appeared quite incapable of supporting his large torso. Later scholarly critics have even used these portraits as well as some of his actions to suggest that the Egyptian pharaoh was mentally unbalanced as well as physically awkward. In a recent study, Nicholas Reeves has argued that Akhenaten suffered from Marfan syndrome and that this ailment may explain his radical departure from Egypt's traditional beliefs. Yet it is likely that the sculptors and others who were given the privilege of portraying the king were encouraged to do so in a naturalistic style that had not been employed in Egypt up until then. They took the new winds of creative change blowing through Egypt as an invitation to exaggerate some of the king's abnormal features, much as cartoonists in modern times exaggerate the faces of leading figures. (See plate 11 for an illustration of a statue of Akhenaten.)

Whatever the case, early in his reign, the king embraced a new religion, centered on the sun, portrayed purely as a solar disk. Akhenaten called the supreme deity Aten. Unlike Egypt's other deities, Aten had no anthropomorphic or animal features, except for hands that appeared in the images of the sun god as the farthermost extension of the sun's rays. (See plate 12 for an illustration of the solar disk and supreme deity, Aten.) Having broken with Egypt's traditional religious tenets, Akhenaten underscored the novelty of his reign by changing his royal name from Amenhotep to Akhenaten, which meant the spirit of Aten. Soon after that, he moved the capital of Egypt from Thebes to a site midway between Memphis and Thebes. In this new location, on the east side of the Nile River, approximately 200 miles north of Thebes, he erected a new city dedicated to the god Aten. He called the new city Akhetaten, meaning "horizon of Aten." Akhenaten's rule is often referred to as the Amarna period in Egyptian history because the location where Egyptologists uncovered the first evidence of this era, its graves sites, was around the present-day village of el-Amarna. Here, in fact, the royal city existed some 3,500 years ago. During the pharaoh's reign the city occupied seventy-seven square miles, housed temples to Aten, a great palace, and a magnificent royal road, and served as a residence for 20,000 to 50,000 dwellers.

Akhenaten set about to efface the memories of the earlier gods, which he believed ignorant rulers and a misguided and power-hungry priestly class had imposed on Egypt. He had temples and monuments that glorified early rulers and their religious beliefs torn down. What he did not eliminate he set about to disfigure so that references to earlier rulers and other gods would not be seen. Unfortunately for Akhenaten, his religious and philosophical innovations did not endure. One of his immediate successors, his son Tutankhamen, began the counterrevolution. Repudiating his father's beliefs, he returned Egypt's capital to Thebes, restored the power of the old priestly class, whom Akhenaten had sought to eliminate, and set about to do what his father had done to his own predecessors: he carried out a ruthless campaign of erasure of his father's rule. This meant allowing the city of Akhetaten to fall into ruins. It also meant destroying all signs of the Amarna period throughout the entire Nile valley. So effective was his work that Akhenaten's name and influence passed out of Egyptian history until scholars, exploring the area around the village of el-Amarna in the 1820s and 1830s, came upon the grave sites that had not been seen for three millennia. Although the first bits and pieces of information on the Amarna period date from these early decades of the nineteenth century, it was not until Flinders Petrie began full-scale excavations in 1892 that this extraordinary moment in ancient Egyptian history revealed its secret to an astonished public.

The heart of Akhenaten's intellectual revolution was a strict monotheism that stood in striking contrast to the rich polytheistic tradition of his predecessors. Similarities between the Hymn to Aten and the Hebrew Scriptures Psalm 104 suggest that the Israelites may have been inspired by Akhenaten's religion and transported his insights from their captivity in Egypt to Palestine.

From the Hymn to Aten:

When thou settest in the western horizon,
The land is darkness like death. . . .
All creeping things, they sting.

> At daybreak, when thou arisest in the horizon . . .
> Thou drivest away the darkness. . . .
> Men awake and stand upon their feet. . . .
> All the world, they do labor.
> How manifold are thy works!
> They are hidden from man's sight.
> O sole god, like whom there is no other,
> Thou hast made the earth according to thy desire.

And from Psalm 104 from the Old Testament:

> Thou makest darkness and it is night,
> Wherein all the beasts of the forest creep forth.
> The young lions roar after their prey.
> The sun arisest, they get them away. . . .
> Man goeth forth unto his work.
> And to his labor until evening.
> O Jahweh, how manifold are thy works!
> The earth is full of thy riches.

Other religious features were part of the new Egyptian religion. Akhenaten's god was a more accessible deity. The temples to the other Egyptian gods were closed structures, and the image of the god was hidden away in the farthest and darkest part of the temple, available only to the most revered priests. In contrast, the temples to Aten were open to the outside. Nor was the priesthood permitted to monopolize worship activities. The new religion was a more compassionate and feeling faith. Its practitioners encouraged men and women to view the sole god as a personal and forgiving being, whose outstretched rays, with human hands, reached down to humans and guided them in their daily actions.

Yet Akhenaten's god, Aten, had only a single intermediary, the pharaoh himself. Despite the apparent openness of the god Aten, in reality Egyptians were forbidden to have contact with their new god. Only the pharaoh had the right to interpret Aten's dictates to the larger society. Akhenaten's new faith was deeply autocratic, perhaps even tyrannical. Put in a simple, but accurate way, "The god of Akhenaten's religion was Akhenaten himself."

Akhenaten's emphasis on monotheism had an underlying political and social context. Not only did it draw on previous attempts to elevate a single god to great prominence, it also reflected the larger, Mediterranean and Africa-wide expansion of the Egyptian state. A far-flung empire like Egypt made it easier to envision an overarching deity, one less tied to specific locales, as was the case in Egypt's traditional cosmology. In addition, Akhenaten's emphasis on a new god was nothing less than a monarchical power play against the influence and authority of the priests of Amun-Ra. The priestly class, centered at Thebes, had enjoyed the bounty of the state's expansion, becoming a virtual state within a state, even able to challenge the king and his royal followers. As the warrior-kings who had preceded Akhenaten brought back more treasure from Southwest Asia and Nubia, so the wealth and power of the priesthood increased. Akhenaten's decision to make Aten the single deity in the Egyptian religion and to move his capital city to Akhetaten was a riposte to the status of Amun-Ra's priestly class. As such it aroused bitter resentment. When subsequent pharaohs restored the old religious order and returned the center of the empire to Thebes, the clerics exacted their revenge. They, too, endeavored to remove all traces of Akhenaten and the elements that had supported his radical religious and political stances.

A final area in which Akhenaten's innovating spirit was felt was in the world of artistic expression, although here, too, there were antecedents. Artistically, the Akhenaten years were marked with an emphasis on realism, even surrealism, rather than formulaic prescriptions about how artists should render all forms of life, human, animal, and vegetable. Akhenaten encouraged artists to depict even the mighty pharaoh as he really was, rather than in a stereotypical form. Modern critics call the art of this period expressionistic and see it as a rebellion against the classical period and its stylized representations. In some scenes, wall engravers presented horse and chariot in "an ecstasy of speed" and portrayed the royal family in scenes of loving intimacy. The ruler permitted portraitists to depict him and his wife holding hands and kissing their children; in one poignant scene the artists even exposed deep emotion, showing the king and queen grieving over the death of one of their daughters. In contrast to the past, artists in this era spurned animal and human representations of the gods. Instead, they depicted Aten purely as a disk, whose hands stretched downward from the heavens to humankind on earth.

The artists in the Amarna period broke with a two-millennia-long tradition. They employed forms that "can even be called frightful; movement, expression, emotion, and disregard for reality are now the rule. The essence of this art, which was at first designated disparagingly as merely 'ugly' or even 'sick' can be understood by comparing it with schools of modern art that deal freely with the human form." The innovations of the Akhenaten period were highly naturalistic, ranging all the way from "the grotesque to the mildly unconventional." Yet artists also had an eye for repose and beauty. The famous portrait of Nefertiti, Akhenaten's wife, struck just these new chords in Egyptian representation. Her elongated neck and dreamy expression and the sloping lines throughout the head and shoulders not only projected sophistication, but demonstrated the ability of the artists of the Amarna years to depict elegance and refinement.

Ramses II

The last of the mighty pharaohs to be considered here is by far the best known: Ramses II (r. 1279–1213 BCE), son of Seti I and grandson of Ramses I. The latter was a military usurper and founder of the nineteenth dynasty. Ramses II had one of the longest reigns in the history of ancient Egypt. He died in 1213 at the age of ninety, having ruled alone for sixty-six years after a nine-year period of regency rule.

Like his father and grandfather and the rulers of the previous dynasty, the eighteenth, Ramses II had imperialist ambitions. At the end of Ramses' regency period, the territories of Palestine and Syria had begun to slip away from Egypt and come under the authority of the Hittites. Ramses II led a large Egyptian army against Muwatallis, king of the Hittites, who claimed authority over the contested lands.

The battle of Kadesh took place near the Orontes River in present-day Syria in 1274. Military historians consider it to be one of the most notable military conflicts of the ancient period. The Hittite forces numbered between 18,000 and 19,000 and included 2,500 horse-drawn chariots. Ramses' forces were even larger, numbering 20,000. They also boasted a large contingent of charioteers. Yet the different divisions of the Egyptian army became separated from one another, allowing the Hittite forces to ambush the central regiments under the command of the pharaoh. Just as the Egyptian force was on the verge of being routed, Ramses II rallied his soldiers single-handedly, plunging headlong with his chariot into the midst of his adversaries at enormous risk to himself. His bold actions snatched military victory from what appeared certain defeat. Or so at least the Egyptian account goes. Ramses made sure that the population in the Nile valley believed in their ruler's military exploits. He ordered the account of the battle of Kadesh to be represented in numerous written sources and on the walls of temples and other constructions from this period as a superb military victory, achieved largely through royal valor. In reality, Egypt failed to reassert its control over this region, though the battle established Ramses' reputation as a powerful warrior-king.

The major Egyptian accounts of this event may be found on the temple at Abydos, the hypostyle hall in Karnak, and the mortuary temple, known as the Ramesseum, on the west bank of the Nile opposite Thebes, as well as in an official written account of the battle.

During Ramses' period of rule, Memphis reemerged as the capital of the Egyptian empire. Because of the impressive economic activity achieved in these years, the capital became a bustling port city, receiving goods from all over the Mediterranean trading zone. It also had a substantial residential area and a royal citadel, which shone with white walls. Yet Thebes also prospered, though its appearance was noticeably different from that of Memphis. No longer a rustic agricultural village, yet not so grandiose as Memphis, it enjoyed a burst of energy as Egypt's religious and cultural center. On the east bank of the Nile, Thebes was already an impressive imperial city, composed of palaces, villas, residential areas, and an ever-growing complex of halls, temples, and monuments dedicated to the gods and to the great kings. Ramses, of course, left his mark on the city. Across the banks of the Nile, on the western side, in the plain surrounded by desert cliffs, other monuments of the ancient rulers existed. Here Ramses set about creating his mortuary temple, the Ramesseum, which was intended to, and in fact did, overshadow the constructions of all previous rulers of Egypt. Ramses also left his imprint in the valley of the kings and queens, for not only did he construct a large and magnificent chamber for his own burial site, but he also built a vast set of chambers for the more than 100 sons and daughters whom he sired, many of whom he outlived. These chambers have only recently been uncovered and constitute, according to their excavator, Kent Weeks, the most exciting and revealing discovery since Howard Carter found the burial chamber of Tutankhamen in 1922.

By the time of the next dynasty, the nineteenth dynasty, nearly all traces of Akhenaten's flirtation with a single god had disappeared. Ramses was avidly polytheistic, patronizing all of the main gods of Egypt. At Thebes he paid tribute to Amun, whose priesthood once again thrived under his rule. This did not mean, however, that the worship of the sun lost its prominence. Quite the contrary: Ra continued to have his followers, and his main religious center at Heliopolis enjoyed much attention. Once again gods were hidden away in the most secret chambers of temples and attended to in loving concern by a priestly class, whose sole purpose in life was to be in service to their special deities.

Everything about Ramses II, except his stature (he was five feet, five inches), was outsized. He secured his historical reputation by having enormous monuments represent his life and present his image. He erected at least eleven larger-than-life statues to himself, the most recent one being discovered just outside of Cairo in 1962. This statue was twenty-four feet tall, and made of Aswan granite, which was towed all the way down the Nile and erected inside the city of Memphis. Today, it can be seen enclosed in a vast hall, lying on its side near the place where it was found. Modern Egyptians have shared a few of these statues with the outside world, so today monuments to the great pharaoh can be found in cities as widely dispersed as Paris and Denver. For many years, a statue to Ramses II was located just outside the main Cairo railway station, but it had to be moved to the outskirts of city because pollution was eating away at the stone.

The most notable of Ramses II's monuments is Abu Simbel, the history of which is worth recounting. The monument consists of four sixty-five-foot-high statues of the ruler, with his wives and children assembled at his feet. Originally carved out of the cliffs in one of the farthermost areas of Upper Egypt and intended to demonstrate that the power of the monarch stretched into the southernmost parts of his kingdom, this stunning construction, which some have called grotesque in its celebration of royal authority, was eventually covered over by sand and lost to the world. It was rediscovered only in the middle of the nineteenth century. Imagine the astonishment of the excavators as they uncovered a historical treasure that had intrigued Greek historians and travelers and had been commented on extensively in ancient times and then seemed to have been lost forever. The European traveler who was first to bring it to the attention of the world, J. L. Burckhardt, wrote that he was about to leave the area "when having luckily turned more to the southward, I fell in with what is yet visible of four immense colossal statues cut out of rock; . . . they stand in a deep recess, excavated in the mountain, but it is greatly to be regretted that they are now almost entirely buried beneath the sands, which are blown down here in torrents. The entire head, and part of the breast and arms of one of the statues are yet above the surface; of the one next to it scarcely any part is visible, the head being broken off, and the body covered with sand to above the shoulders; of the other two the bonnets only appear."

More than 100 years later, this magnificent work was again in peril. This time it was Nasser's dream of a high dam at Aswan that put Abu Simbel at risk. Not only would the Aswan dam electrify Egypt but it would also create a vast lake behind its huge walls, drowning many of Egypt's most prominent antiquities. No one was willing to lose Abu Simbel. At a cost of $36 million, the Egyptian government had the monument cut into 1,000 numbered pieces so that it could be moved to higher ground. This undertaking, begun in 1960, has rescued one of the world's most impressive historical monuments. (See plate 13 for an illustration of Abu Simbel in its present location.)

Ramses II's mummification was, not surprisingly, even more elaborate than that of Egypt's other ruling families. It offers a further opportunity to observe this most private and yet most fascinating aspect of the culture of ancient Egypt. The Egyptians, as we have observed, believed in an afterlife, certainly for the ruling family and later in the development of their culture for many segments of society. Yet even while notables and then commoners enjoyed the privileges of being mummified and prepared for an eternal afterlife, the most ornate ceremonies and burial techniques were reserved for the most powerful of Egypt's rulers. Hence Ramses II's preparations for burial and afterlife were lengthy and highly ritualized, encompassing all of the essential features for the preparation of the body for its final journey. The entire procedure for his mummification took seventy days. It began with the extraction of the organs. The brain was pulled out through the nose, and the organs were placed in canopic jars that were set alongside the mummified body in the burial chamber. Egyptians regarded the heart, not the brain, as the essence of being. In Ramses' case burial surgeons removed the heart and then stitched it back into its original location, using golden threads. More commonly, the mummification team left the heart in place. Next came the embalming of the body, washing, and wrapping in linen cloth. The mummy having been prepared for insertion in the burial chamber, the priests carried it into a highly decorated room, chanting hymns of praise and poems for a happy afterlife. The wrapped and embalmed body was placed inside a wooden sarcophagus, which in the case of powerful men and women was painted with bright colors and resplendent etchings.

The most striking part of the sarcophagus was the image or mask of the ruler himself. The interior burial chamber, located at the far end of a tunnel, was adorned with portraits of the life that the pharaoh had lived and enjoyed and that were designed to bring pleasure to him as he embarked upon his journey to the next world.

The reason Egyptian rulers chose to have themselves entombed in the western desert in Upper Egypt rather than have enormous pyramids to celebrate their power and represent their belief in the continuation of life after death was to prevent the looting and despoiling of the tombs that had become commonplace in ancient Egypt. Pharaohs and others buried like them had no greater luck than their predecessors of the Old Kingdom. Their tombs were also robbed. Even that of Ramses II did not escape looters. Seeking to preserve the heritage of their predecessors, later pharaohs and priests had the bodies of Ramses II and others removed from their sites and hidden away in an enlarged tomb of one of the queens. This tomb was sealed and, inexplicably and miraculously, remained untouched and unknown for 2,800 years. Only then did Egyptologists discover the site and find the large quantity of the mummies that today are on display in the Egyptian Antiquities Museum and other locations around the world. They offer delight to later generations of scholars and lovers of the ancient Egyptians.

One of the few tombs to escape devastation from looters was that of Tutankhamen, who was the son of Akhenaten, the twelfth king of the eighteenth dynasty. He ruled over Egypt for only a brief time, from 1336 to 1327 BCE. His largely undefiled tomb was discovered by the Egyptologist and archaeologist Howard Carter, who was convinced that there were still undiscovered tombs, especially of an unknown and apparently short-lived and relatively obscure pharaoh of the eighteenth dynasty. Carter spent fifteen years in search of the tomb, driven on by his belief that the discovery would show the world the magnificence of the treasures that had been stored in other tombs but could only be guessed at because looters had despoiled so many of the burial chambers. Carter finally came upon the burial site in November 1922, but, awaiting the arrival of his patron, Lord Carnarvon, he did not enter the tomb until three months later, in February 1923. The tomb of Tutankhamen proved to be all and more than Carter had promised or anticipated. It was crammed full, in no particular order, with many items that had been part of the pharaoh's life. Its gold-encrusted beds, its beautiful canopic jars, its black-lacquered Anubis dog, and most spectacular of all, its sarcophagus, with the striking burial mask of the pharaoh, astonished the world at the time and have continued to enthrall millions of visitors in awe of the splendor that existed in ancient Egypt. Most of the collection can be seen today in a large and special section of the Egyptian Museum in Cairo devoted to the king, but from time to time some of the best pieces have been sent on traveling expeditions to foreign destinations. (See plates 14 and 15 for illustrations of the funeral mask and the royal chair taken from the burial chamber of King Tutankhamen.)

PEASANTS AND WOMEN IN EGYPT

We know a great deal about the lives of the kings, queens, priests, bureaucrats, traders, and military men of ancient Egypt. Their lives are portrayed in wall engravings and celebrated in written work. Other groups, with one notable exception, women, are understudied because little has been written about them. We can easily imagine the lives of peasants, who are depicted on the walls of Egypt's monuments, whose lives, as they had for millennia before, conformed to the agricultural routines of the Nile River. They worked intensely during the growing season and had less to do during the fallow periods unless the state imposed building or irrigation projects on them. Few of the literati wrote about them, and few of the artists and etchers offered more than stylized portraits of their lives. The exception, however, is women, who have been the subject of much attention in recent years as scholars have tried to provide outlines of women's lives in all societies. Yet even here, most of what we know is drawn from the world of the upper-class, wealthy, and powerful women, rather than that of the peasantry, and this world was entirely depicted by male artists and writers.

Women were clearly subordinate to men in ancient Egypt. The only important female pharaoh was Queen Hatshepsut, who was often portrayed in male attire and shown wearing the pharaonic "fake beard." In the visual and textual images about men and women, men predominated. Funerary scenes give prominence to male figures; women seem to be included as backdrops and in roles serving men.

Yet it is important to realize that Egyptian women, in contrast to their counterparts in Mesopotamia, also well studied, had many more rights and were less beholden to fathers and husbands. They had legal rights equivalent to those of men from the same social class and had the same afterlife expectations as their male counterparts. These rights were unusual in the ancient world of Southwest Asia and North Africa. The representations of Egyptian women typically depict them as smaller than men, possessing cream-colored skin in contrast to the rougher hues of the men. Lower-order men and women were represented as doing the same categories of work. They wove, made bread, and tilled the soil. Whereas peasant women and men wore simple clothing, as befitted individuals who spent their days in the outdoors in heavy labor, men and women of the upper classes were shown wearing formal attire. The artists had clear ideas of what constituted feminine beauty. Markers of beauty consisted of being thin, graceful, having small waists, firm breasts, long necks, pale skins, and bluish-black hair. Such was the image of Akhenaten's wife, Nefertiti, one of Egypt's classic beautiful women. Unlike the women of Mesopotamia, Egyptian women were not veiled. Nor were they confined to special areas of the house.

Egyptian poets, almost all of whom seem to have been males, celebrated the romantic and sensual love of a woman, as the following lines of a love poem illustrate:

My heart beats rapidly
When I think of my love for you
It does not allow me to act sensibly
But jumps from its place.

Most marriages were arranged. Men married at the age of fifteen and women at twelve. The principal domain of women was the home, whether it was the simple hut of the peasant or the magnificent palace of the pharaoh. The influence of queens and queen mothers was enormous, although it had to be exercised from behind the scenes and became visible to the outside world only occasionally. Egypt had only a few queen regents, even though many pharaohs came to the throne before they had reached maturity and relied on a combination of regency figures and the guidance of their mothers. Nor should one lose sight of the fact when measuring the influence of women that some of Egypt's gods, even those of great power, like Isis, were women. Moreover, the queen was increasingly thought of as partaking in the divine, like her husband. Even though what we know about women is exceedingly limited, we do know that the great pharaoh Ahmose I, who was primarily responsible for driving the Hyksos out of Egypt, relied on the advice of his mother, Akhotep, and his principal wife, Nefertari, who outlived her husband and his son, and was deified as their patron by the workmen at Deir el-Medina.

No formal ceremonies were associated with marriage, and customarily women moved into the household of their mates. Divorce was allowed to both husband and wife, and most families were monogamous. The purpose of marriage was to produce children and strengthen the family. From the New Kingdom these lines of instruction underscore the goals of marriage and the importance of family:

> Take a wife while you are young
> That she make a son for you
> She should bear for you while you are youthful
> It is proper to make people
> Happy is the man whose people are many
> He is saluted on account of his progeny.

We do not know whether women learned to read or write in a society where literacy was reserved to perhaps no more than 1 percent of the population. An indication that men began to monopolize positions of power, leaving the management of household affairs to women, can be seen in the fact that while in the Old Kingdom female priestesses existed, they had disappeared by the time of the New Kingdom.

CHAPTER FOUR
Nubians, Greeks, and Romans, circa 1200 BCE–632 CE

History shows us that empire builders and world hegemons were driven to possess Egypt. At first, the most powerful rulers in the world—the world's first empire builders—were Egyptian themselves. Karnak and Luxor broadcast the puissance of New Kingdom pharaohs, one of whom—Ramses II—erected colossal statues to himself everywhere his warriors went. In modern time insatiable empire builders like Cecil Rhodes included Egypt in their ambitions of world hegemony. Rhodes dreamed of British possessions stretching from the tip of South Africa to the Mediterranean Sea, the much publicized Cape to Cairo project, while Napoleon hoped that conquering and occupying Egypt would drive a stake in the heart of Britain's imperial ambitions and foretell the triumph of French power on the world stage. The Fatimids sought to extend their Shiite vision throughout the entire Muslim world and even beyond, and the Mamluks stymied the Mongol project of world dominion at the Egyptian border. Yet none of these power mongers attached as much importance to Egypt as Afro-Eurasia's most driven world conqueror, Alexander the Great.

To the Greeks and to their most energetic military leader, Alexander the Great, Egypt had special importance. They considered it the oldest and originally the most sophisticated of territories, a people from whom the Greeks gratefully acknowledged a cultural debt. Of course, Alexander the Great recognized Egypt's strategic location. But its cultural centrality and oracular wisdom captivated the conqueror as well. Having just asserted Greek control over the country, Alexander risked everything when he took a small party of his most trusted aides into the western desert, eager to visit the oracle at Siwa and take advantage of the oracle's vaunted ability to know the future. Enduring 300 miles of searing desert heat, risking death, and using up six full weeks at a time when his conquering ambitions were at their most intense, Alexander's desire to have answers from this most famous and respected of oracles knew no bounds. Two questions burned in his mind: Would he conquer the world? And was he a god? Since no one accompanied him when he met with the chief priest of the oracle and he gave no full account of the meeting, precisely what the chief priest told the Macedonian warrior is not known. Alexander did admit, however, when his party sought an account of the meeting that "he had been told what his heart desired."

PHARAONIC EGYPT IN DECLINE

Throughout the pharaonic centuries, Egypt's enemies had come from Southwest Asia, Libya, and Nubia. Many of its foes arrived from the western desert (the Libyans) or Sinai (the Hyksos and the Persians). Yet it was from across the seas that the pharaonic era came to its abrupt and stunning end. That moment can be dated with precision. It was 332 BCE when Alexander the Great conquered the country. Even before the Greek conquest, at a time when decline was obvious, local notables and foreign usurpers were still endeavoring to revive the glory days of the pharaohs. But Alexander's conquest put an end to these efforts. It also had another devastating consequence. Native-born Egyptians were not to govern their country for more than two millennia.

The catalogue of foreign names and foreign potentates who ruled Egypt after the pharaohs is luminous. First came the Greeks, followed by Romans, Byzantines, Arab Muslim conquerors, North African Fatimids, Ayyubids, Mamluks overwhelmingly from the Caspian and Circassian regions, Ottoman Turks, Bonapartist French, an alien dynasty established by an Albanian warlord, Muhammad Ali, and the British, at last supplanted by Egyptians in the military coup d'état of 1952. But this is not the whole story. While Nubians, Persians, Greeks, and Romans—the subject of this chapter—ruled

Egypt in the postpharaonic years, Egyptians were not relegated to the sidelines. They inserted themselves into all arenas of action. Particularly in the Christian era and especially thereafter under foreign Muslim rulers, Egyptians dominated the country's intellectual life. They were the clerics and intellectuals who debated the merits of Christian theology and held the high offices of Egyptian Christendom. In the Islamic period, they were the *ulama* and *qadis*, who decided what valid belief was and what was not. In addition, Greeks and Romans absorbed much from ancient Egyptian culture and created a creolized Hellenistic-Egyptian culture. Even Egyptian Christianity preserved many aspects of ancient Egyptian religion though its clerics would never admit their indebtedness.

Following the successes of Egypt's nineteenth dynasty, which had culminated in the military triumphs of Ramses II, the country again sank into decline. There was to be no revival. A series of foreign rulers and foreign military men came to the fore. For the next 3,000 years Egypt's rulers were persons many of whom did not speak the indigenous language or even in some cases subscribe to the prevailing religious beliefs. Often, they lived as isolated and exploiting elites, scorning the local inhabitants, especially the Egyptian peasantry. They regarded the country purely as a source of wealth, a way to aggrandize power for themselves and their superiors, whose seats of power lay outside the country.

In pharaonic times Egypt's rulers were expected to be good shepherds, entrusted with the welfare of the country and its population. All too often, in the centuries that followed, Egypt's rulers treated the people with scant regard.

LIBYANS AND NUBIANS

Egypt continued to be ruled by native-born Egyptian pharaohs for two centuries after the glorious nineteenth dynasty, but its rulers were weak and ineffective men who lacked the resources and the will to assert their mastery over the country. Their epithets attest to their incapacities: The Rescued, The Humble Endures, The Blind, and, most telling of all, No Use. The age was one of deep pessimism and despondency; the men and women of power and wealth counseled the less fortunate to imitate the old ways and adhere to tradition. A rigid traditionalism took the place of the individualism that had characterized earlier eras. The country's elites were now tormented by a sense of failure and sin. They viewed their gods as all powerful and themselves as mere pawns in life's events. Their watchwords were silence, humility, and obedience. The later books of wisdom expanded upon the inadequacy of mankind, as the following aphorism affirms: "God is always in his success, whereas man is in his failure. One thing is that which men say, another is that which god does. For man is but clay and straw, and the god is his builder, and he is tearing down or building up every day. He makes a thousand poor men as he wishes, or he makes a thousand men as overseers."

Egypt suffered from the fate that has afflicted many successful empires. It was overextended. No longer could its rulers and its military forces control subject peoples on its fringes in Southwest Asia, North Africa, and Nubia. Restless populations at the edges of the empire now sought their independence, if not their revenge. In addition, Egypt's priestly classes had recaptured great power at the expense of the political classes. They hampered the efforts of the pharaohs to provide leadership and dynamism. Even Egypt's conquered and colonized peoples lamented the country's decline and longed for the days when the pharaohs had ensured political stability and economic prosperity.

In earlier centuries Egyptian rulers had exercised a constant surveillance over borders, fearful that outsiders would seek to overthrow the central state and establish their dominion, as the Hyksos had done in an earlier age. Thus, it was telling when around 950 BCE a Libyan family began to play the role of the pharaohs. No invasion took place. Rather, Libyans who had entered Egypt as prisoners or had migrated into the country in search of wealth took over the seats of power. Their rule proved short-lived, and for another brief period local Egyptians were again in charge of the affairs of the state. They were no more successful than their predecessors in re-establishing a vibrant culture and a powerful state.

Shortly after the Libyans, peoples from the south came. Nubia was ancient Egypt's backyard, its point of entry to Africa south of the Sahara. Its influences on Egypt have been grossly underestimated, in part because of an earlier scholarly prejudice against Africa and the many contributions that Africans have made to the cultures north of the Sahara. It is also true, however, that the ancient Egyptians themselves contributed to these biases, looking down on the cultures arising in this region, which they regularly called "miserable Kush." They often ruthlessly exploited Nubia's resources, notably its raw materials and its peoples, taken as captives and enslaved. The conventional Egyptian view of the Nubians was in striking contrast to that of Homer, who regarded the region and its people favorably, commenting that the people "are the remotest nation, the most just of men, the favorites of the gods. The lofty inhabitants of Olympus journey to them and take part in their feasts. Their sacrifices are the most agreeable of all that mortals can offer to them." Nubia, too, finally took its revenge on their patronizing overlords from the north, occupying and placing one of their own on the Egyptian throne. Egypt's twenty-fifth dynasty came from Nubia; scholars have called its rulers the black pharaohs of Egypt.

Upper and lower Nubia encompasses the area from the first cataract in Egypt all the way up the Nile to Khartoum, the present-day capital of Sudan. In ancient times, however, the land lying between the first and fourth cataracts, which had heavy population concentrations, attracted the Egyptians. Here a distinctive culture arose at about the same time as did the ancient Egyptian culture, that is to say, approximately 6,000 years ago. Although the peoples of Nubia were in touch with the ancient Egyptians and absorbed many Egyptian institutions and values, their own traditions did not give way. The first powerful state to appear in this region was at Kerma. Its origins have been traced to 2400 BCE, when its merchants were observed trading with the Egyptians and controlling the flow of luxury goods into the northern territories. Kerma's location was about fifty miles north of the third cataract. The Egyptians sent military expeditions into the area, though they did not establish a permanent political or military presence there.

It was not until the New Kingdom that Egyptian rule took on the features of a colonial administration over Nubia. In contrast to the techniques that the Egyptians used in Southwest Asia, where they worked in alliance with local satraps, in Nubia the New Kingdom conquerors sent their own administrators southward and established a civil and military administration that lasted for more than 500 years. Egyptian rule in Nubia involved the imposition of the full panoply of pharaonic culture upon local populations, including Egyptian religious beliefs. The Egyptian presence, begun as a series of military forays by the mighty warrior-king Ahmose, did not end until 1100 BCE, when Egyptians and Sudanese alike seem to have largely abandoned the land, which reverted to a no-man's-territory for several centuries. The region did not return to life until a new set of local kings established themselves at Napata around 850 BCE. Eventually, Piankhy, one of the kings of Napata, even had the temerity to invade Egypt and to place himself on the throne there as the founder of Egypt's twenty-fifth dynasty, the first and the only one to be ruled by peoples south of Aswan. Piankhy turned the tables on Nubia's former rulers and had his own name proclaimed in hymns of praise:

> Oh mighty ruler, oh mighty ruler,
> Piankhy, mighty ruler!
> You return having taken Lower Egypt,
> You are eternal,
> Your might abides,
> Oh ruler loved of Thebes!

Nubians of the twenty-fifth dynasty ruled over Egypt for nearly a hundred years, from 747 to 656 BCE, only to be driven out by military forces dispatched to bring Egypt into the Assyrian Empire. Even after leaving Egypt, the Napatan kings continued to govern the northern part of modern-day Sudan for several hundred more years. Napata had been drawn into the Egyptian orbit from early times and had absorbed a considerable amount of Egyptian influence. Nubian kings called themselves pharaohs, worshipped the Egyptian sun god, Amun, had themselves buried in pyramids, and used hieroglyphs. Yet because of its distance from Egypt and because of the fact that the region was never fully occupied by Egypt but was used mainly as an Egyptian trading outpost, the Egyptian influences were muted. Later, in order to maintain their independence from the heartland of the Nile valley, Nubian rulers moved even further south, establishing the kingdom of Meroe around 300 BCE. This state, renowned for its burial pyramids and its large urbanized population concentrated in the capital city of Meroe, lasted more than 500 years, until it fell in the fifth century CE.

In the sixth century BCE, Achaeminids from Persia extended their authority westward and seized Egypt as a prized possession. The most renowned of the Achaeminid conquerors was Cyrus II, who ruled from 559 to 530 BCE and who entrusted the conquest of Egypt to his son Cambyses. The latter potentate overran the country and established Egypt's twenty-seventh dynasty (525–404). At his death, the Achaeminid throne passed to Darius I (r. 522–486), one of history's most formidable monarchs, an architect of the closer unification of Persia with its western territories.

The Persian interlude was not a happy one for most Egyptians. Although Egypt's next conquerors, the Greeks, exaggerated Persian brutality and oppression, the Persians reminded the Egyptians of the Hyksos: alien conquerors unwilling to assimilate to Egyptians ways. Their response to the Persians was no different from their reactions to the Hyksos. They rebelled, thus proclaiming yet again their distinctive cultural identity and their unwillingness to subordinate themselves to peoples who scorned their ways. The disrespect for Egyptian customs came to a head under the administration of the Persian governor Aryandes, who ruled from 522 to 517. The delta cities launched a revolt against Persian overrule in 496, toward the end of Darius's long reign, at a time when the Persians were preoccupied with Greek territorial and military aspirations in the area. A later rebellion in 465 found an inspiring leader, Inaros, who drew on the cultural identity of the Egyptian people in a movement that can be likened to anticolonial nationalism, displaying many similarities to twentieth-century Egyptian nationalist fervor against the British overlords. Inaros defeated Egypt's Persian rulers, but the country's independence was short-lived, and the Persians reestablished their control and executed the rebel leader.

Alas, this was the Egypt that the Greeks catalogued. Herodotus, whose account of Egypt influenced many later generations, went to Egypt in the fifth century. He arrived at a time of political turmoil and internal rebellions. Innovation had given way to submission. A slavish imitation of the old ways had replaced a thirst for boldness and personal fame. Segments of his account reveal an Egypt in retreat, in thrall to omens and empty rituals.

GREEKS AND ROMANS IN EGYPT

Few rulers were better suited to extinguish Egyptian dreams of restoring pharaonic glories than Alexander the Great. A man of towering abilities and ambitions to match, Alexander entered Egypt with his mighty Macedonian army in 332, routing an already declining Persian force. Egypt was but one of the early stops on Alexander's road to bringing the known habitable world under his sway. In short order, his 50,000-man army, with its crack cavalry corps and its phalanxes of infantry men who wielded eighteen-foot-long pikes, destroyed a much larger Persian army, reputed to be a half-million strong, at the battle of Gaugamela in Iraq in 331. The Persian defeat opened Central Asia and northern India to Alexander's conquering troops. By the time of the ruler's death in 323, at the age of thirty-two, brought on by heavy drinking, his state stretched all the way from Libya to present-day Afghanistan.

Alexander's youthful talents were breathtaking. He had athletic prowess, military skills, personal courage, ambition, charm, and charisma. His knowledge of Greek ways was unparalleled, since his father, King Philip II of Macedonia, had brought Aristotle to the court to steep his son in the arts and sciences that were flourishing on the Greek mainland. Philip was assassinated in 337 at the age of forty-six, and Alexander wasted little time suppressing uprisings against Macedonian authority at home and on the Greek mainland. It was at this time, though it may even have been earlier, that Alexander's determination to rule and dominate came to the fore. Some have speculated that having lost favor with his father, he had a hand in the assassination. Whatever the case may have been, Alexander ruthlessly and systematically killed off other aspirants to power, leaning heavily on the support of his chief and most loyal general, Antipater, and loyal Macedonian troops while minimizing the influence of soldiers from the Greek heartland in his army. Indeed, mainland Greeks consisted of a small regiment; their proportion to the total army rarely exceeded 10 percent.

Although Egypt was territorially only a small part of Alexander's empire, it was a vital element. Alexander found much to attract him in the old pharaonic polity. He admired its hierarchical and centralized government and its close association of religion with political authority. He hoped to learn the pharaoh's secrets of power and to use them as an aid in ruling over his far-flung territories. After the original conquest, Alexander visited Heliopolis, as pharaohs had done when they ascended the throne. He, too, wished to associate the worship of Amun with his power. He traveled to Memphis, the political capital of the ancient state. He went even further afield, as we have seen, visiting the famed oracle of Amun in the oasis of Siwa.

Alexander's early and unanticipated death set in motion a fragmentation of his vast territorial empire, though it did not cause total disintegration. His loyal general Perdicas tried to preserve the empire. Perdicas's efforts to have the other military leaders recognize Alexander's eldest son failed. So did his attempt to create a regency for Alexander's yet-to-be-born son from a marriage with a Bactrian woman. Since the Greek generals objected to subordinating themselves to a half-Macedonian, half-Bactrian child-ruler, an orderly succession had little chance to succeed. Like Alexander himself, the generals were ambitious men. They had marched halfway around the world, or so it seemed to them, and had borne all manner of physical and mental hardships, not the least of which was Alexander's demand that they take Persian wives in order to enhance the legitimacy of the empire in the east. Within a few years of Alexander's demise, the empire fragmented into four sometimes antagonistic units. One of them, in many ways the most populous and prosperous—Egypt—became the preserve of a Greek general, Ptolemy, who in 305 took the title of Ptolemy I. He founded a dynasty destined to endure for three centuries, until in 30 BCE the Roman emperor Caesar Augustus overthrew the Ptolemaic ruler, Queen Cleopatra, and absorbed Egypt into an expanding Roman Empire.

Alexander and his successors had no intention of devolving power on local elites; they encouraged the migration of Greeks into Egypt. Yet their impact was not nearly as disruptive of the old pharaonic order as it might seem at first glance. In the first place, Alexander and most of his army were not from the Greek heartland. They possessed and championed the pastoral and martial values of the Macedonian periphery. Second, and even more importantly, because Greek culture had a considerable Egyptian and Southwest Asia overlay, it was not so unsettling to the Egyptians. A substantial intermixing of Southwest Asian, North African, and African influences had already occurred in Greece by the time that Alexander marched into Africa and Asia—one that reflected the indebtedness of the Greeks to Phoenicians, Mesopotamians, Egyptians, and Persians. Alexander showed the regard in which he held Africa and the Orient when he embraced many Egyptian institutions and practices, and later on when he compelled his top military leaders to take Persian brides. Impressed with the hierarchical, centralized, divineright monarchies of the East, he orientalized his empire.

The East had come to Greece mainly via Cyprus, Crete, and Rhodes. Its agents were craftsmen, priests, doctors, seers, magicians, and merchants who moved freely between North Africa and Southwest Asia and the Greek mainland. Their most critical contribution to the Greeks was the Phoenician alphabet, which had a singular advantage over earlier systems of writing such as those that had developed in Sumer and spread into Egypt and other parts of the world. The Phoenicians had symbols for vowels as well as for consonants. The Greeks took over this alphabet and improved it, making

Greek, in the view of one observer, "the most perfect writing system" in the world at this time.

THE PTOLEMAIC AGE

The Ptolemaic and Roman ages were periods of unprecedented prosperity in Egypt. Employing an administrative system that reached down into the countryside even more effectively than the pharaohs had, though adapting many of the institutions that the pharaohs had first put in place, the Ptolemies and, after them, the Romans expanded the irrigation system and turned Egypt into a veritable breadbasket for the home territories. The cultivated area increased to 16,000 square kilometers for the delta, 10,000 square kilometers for Upper Egypt, and 1,300 square kilometers for Fayyum. Fayyum experienced spectacular growth. What had been for many millennia not much more than a marshy region and a favorite habitat for fish and fowl enjoyed a spectacular flourishing under Ptolemaic engineering talent and settlement to become a favored location for large Greek landowners. Many of the new landed class were retired military men, to whom the rulers had doled out land grants.

Egypt's population had been approximately three million at its high point in the pharaonic years. It soared to perhaps as many as seven million in Roman times, the greatest figure until the nineteenth century, representing nearly 10 percent of the total population of imperial Rome. The most prosperous and populous state in the Greek and Roman empires, Egypt owed its increase in population and the expansion of the cultivated area to technical advances in irrigation. Although simple in comparison with those introduced by hydraulic engineers in the nineteenth and twentieth centuries, they were remarkably effective. The most notable were new water-lifting devices, particularly the Archimedes screw, and the more widespread use of the *shaduf* and the *saqia*, both of which had been employed in earlier times, but were now widely distributed around the countryside. These devices not only enabled cultivators to make more intensive use of the Nile waters during the flood season, but they also made possible the irrigation of lands lying close to the Nile after the flood season was over.

Wherever Alexander advanced, he founded new cities, many of which he named after himself. Of the many cities that boasted the name Alexandria, the one that gave him the greatest pleasure and was the largest and most dynamic was in Egypt. Its foundation demonstrated the many talents of its creator. Seeking to establish a trading port for the eastern Mediterranean, Alexander visited the Greek city of Naukratis, a location that did not satisfy him. It was too far inland and isolated. But a slip of land between Lake Mareotis and the sea filled the bill. The site would support a deepwater harbor, was easily defensible, and caught the cooling sea winds. The great conqueror walked over the land, marking with pieces of meal where the main market and the major temples were to be located. Thus was created in 331 the city of Alexandria, near the Egyptian village of Rhakotis on the Mediterranean, opposite one of the branches of the Nile. Overnight it became a bustling port city, pointing Egypt toward Greece and the northeastern cities of the Mediterranean. Its beauty and comfort attracted a large Greek immigrant population. Alexander adored his Mediterranean metropolis, and his body was interred there upon his death.

Under the Ptolemies, Alexandria continued to flourish. It served as Egypt's capital. Its ever-increasing Greek population had deep roots in Greek culture; before the end of the Ptolemaic era it numbered no less than 300,000—a figure not again attained until the end of the nineteenth century.

Ptolemaic Alexandria projected its veneer of Hellenistic learning far and wide. Reveling in the intellectual achievements of Greek culture and believing that "the art, science, and literature of early Greek civilization were of an unequaled standard, and, thus, of supreme cultural importance for the future," Ptolemy I, from the outset of his reign, brought many of the leading mainland Greek scholars to his territory. He first approached Aristotle's successor, Theophrastus, but when the latter declined to emigrate to Alexandria, he settled for Theophrastus's recommendation—Demetrius of

Phaleron. Demetrius helped to establish a museum and created a library, which became justly famous throughout the entire Hellenistic world. Visitors boasted of its massive collection of volumes, its seminars, and its storehouse of knowledge.

Ptolemy I's goal was to make Alexandria the Athens of Hellenistic thought and culture and to use its intellectual and cultural resources to train the royal family, much as Philip of Macedonia had done for his son, Alexander. Ptolemy II, the next ruler, followed in his father's footsteps, adding to the prestige of the library and attracting numerous Greek intellectuals to the city.

Ptolemy II's pride and joy was the library at Alexandria, which the monarch charged with the task of holding every book written in Greek as well as the sacred and famous works of people outside the Hellenistic world. The actual number of works that the library contained is unknown. It is said that Ptolemy set his sights on acquiring half a million works. Whether the library had 40,000 volumes or 700,000, as some have contended, it housed the largest collection of works in the world. It also had a catalogue. Alas, like the books themselves, the catalogue did not survive the library's destruction.

Myth has it that the Arab Muslim warriors who overran Egypt in 641–42 despoiled the library. The story goes that the Arab general, Amr ibn al-As, who conquered Egypt, wrote back to the caliph Umar in Mecca seeking his advice on what his forces should do with the city's great library. The caliph is said to have responded that "if the books agree with the Quran, they are unnecessary, and if they do not contain what the Quran says, they ought to be destroyed." This picturesque story has no validity in historical fact, however. The first destruction of the library occurred when Julius Caesar was seeking to avoid military defeat at Alexandria and accidentally caused some of the books to be burned through a military explosion. The real decline of the library occurred in the third century and stemmed mainly from neglect and the dispersion of the core of the books into private and semiofficial libraries located around the city.

Under the first two Ptolemies the museum at Alexandria acquired the reputation that think tanks in the contemporary world have. It ran symposia and invited seminar papers from distinguished scholars from the far corners of the Hellenistic world. To be invited to the museum was tantamount to achieving worldwide recognition for one's learning, though in reality, like many contemporary ivory-tower bodies, the museum also had a reputation for producing trivial and esoteric papers that few could understand and fewer still wanted to read. The scholars in residence seemed to have enjoyed the leisure that the state allowed them. They also developed a reputation for consuming large quantities of alcohol.

Despite the efforts of Egypt's Greek rulers, Athens retained its primacy for the study of philosophy, but Alexandria took the lead in mathematics and science. Although the mathematician Euclid was educated in Athens, his work undertaken while he resided in Alexandria under the Ptolemies was the best in its field. Here he wrote his *Elements*, which surveyed the entire area of Greek mathematics and geometry since Pythagoras and remained for centuries the standard textbook in the field. Equally influential and noteworthy was the natural philosopher Archimedes, who was born in Egypt and was able to make significant technical contributions to Egyptian life before he migrated to Syracuse, where he died in 212 BCE. Eratosthenes, born in Libya, moved to Alexandria, where he was appointed as the chief librarian of the great library. He was also an accomplished poet, a mathematician, and a geographer, who made remarkably precise calculations of the earth's circumference and the tilt of its axis. The city leaders were famed for their support of Greek lyric poetry, of which the most notable example was that of Callimachus, who served as librarian at the museum.

Yet Hellenism did not mark a complete rupture with Egypt's pharaonic past. It is virtually impossible for conquerors to obliterate the culture of the local population. And the Greeks were also shrewd colonizers. They knew that ruling over Egypt and other non-Greek-speaking peoples would be simpler if they as conquerors embraced aspects of the local culture. Moreover, they had much admiration for the contributions of the ancients in governance and culture.

In no area of life was the blending of Egyptian and Greek motifs more pronounced than in religion. The incoming Greek conquerors, travelers, settlers, and scholars brought with them a rudimentary knowledge of the Egyptian gods and thus had little difficulty finding parallels between their own polytheistic and nature-oriented beliefs and those of the ancient Egyptians. In the new syncretistic belief system that emerged in Hellenistic Egypt, Amun took the place of Zeus as the high, creator God, while Horus filled the role of Apollo; Thoth of Hermes; Hathor of Aphrodite; and Ptah of Hephaestus. The most impressive temples of this period, particularly the ones at Dendera and Philae, had many Greek features but also were modeled along the lines of the temples of ancient Egypt. Even so, the Ptolemaic dynasty did not make the mistake that its pharaonic predecessors had. Its rulers saw to it that the priests were kept in check. Priestly landholdings were limited, as was the ability of clerics to accumulate the vast amounts of wealth that had been a common feature of the Middle and New Kingdoms, particularly during periods of decline in royal authority.

In Alexandria the most important religious cult to arise during Greek and Roman times was that of Serapis. It represented a blending of Greek and pharaonic religious motifs. While the Greeks were impressed with the similarities between their own gods and those that the Egyptians worshipped, they had little respect for the animal-headed gods and goddesses that so delighted the Egyptians. Their new Hellenistic-Egyptian god Serapis was a combination of Apis, the Egyptian bull god, and Osiris, the god of resurrection, but took on a fully human form. Ptolemy II erected Alexandria's largest temple to Serapis and began the construction of a vast set of buildings for the worship of the god. This area, known as the Serapeum and centered around the temple, contained a library, lecture halls, and subsidiary cult shrines to Anubis and Isis as well as a large figure of Serapis. Serapis soon came to be seen as the protector of Alexandria and the most important Graeco-Egyptian god in the city.

Of all of the religious beliefs that prevailed in Egypt during the Hellenistic era none was more widespread than the cult surrounding the goddess Isis. In ancient mythology Isis had played a powerful role as a symbol of rebirth and regeneration (see the previous chapter for this account). In the story that dealt with struggles for power, murder, and revenge, which many Egyptians accepted as a fundamental religious narrative, Isis represented creation and resided in heaven, while Osiris was the god of the underworld and resurrection and Horus was the divinity that looked over and guided Egypt and its people.

The island of Philae, located where the present-day city of Aswan exists, was often seen as the earthly residence of Isis and assumed prominence as a location for the worship of the goddess. Even before the Greek conquest, toward the end of the New Kingdom era, particularly during the twenty-fifth and twenty-sixth dynasties, a cult had already emerged around Isis, and Philae had become an important site for her worship. Under the Greeks, following their occupation of Egypt and the expansion of their empire through Asia, the cult of Isis spread throughout Egypt and reached into territories in the eastern Mediterranean.

To honor the goddess, her devotees erected a small but exquisitely beautiful temple at Philae where her worship was carried out for at least five centuries. The temple, though submerged during the British occupation of the country following the construction of the first Aswan dam at the turn of the twentieth century, was restored when the high dam at Aswan replaced the old Aswan dam. It is one of Egypt's most attractive tourist sites. Its beauty is unmatched and its size and near-perfect restoration provide visitors with an opportunity to witness the ideal merging of ancient Egyptian and Hellenistic religious influences.

Although the temple of Philae contains only twelve rooms, small by the grandiose standards of the ancient Egyptians and the Greeks, it includes all of the rooms and functions that were critical to religious belief and worship. Its rooms include the hall where the king's coronation took place, a coronation room, an induction hall, and, most important of all, an interior holy of holies where the goddess was said to take up her earthly residence. Isis's worshippers have written some of Egypt's most appealing poetry, inscribing many lines on the walls of Philae as hymns to Isis. They can still be read today. The composer of one of the hymns recognized Isis "as the supreme and universal deity . . . who in her earthly royal residence was surrounded by ancient gods and goddesses, and in the constant company of her brother-husband, Osiris, and their son, Horus." (See plate 16 for an illustration of the temple of Isis at Philae.)

EGYPT AND PALESTINE

Egypt and Palestine have had a long and intimate relationship. The aridity of Sinai notwithstanding, this territory served as a bridge between these two areas of dense populations. Moses led his followers out of their captivity in Egypt through Sinai to a promised land in Palestine, and Mary, the mother of Jesus, is said to have taken Jesus away to Egypt in order to save him from Herod. Nor was the sea route overlooked. Strong east-west currents in the eastern Mediterranean also connected Egypt with Cyprus and the coast of what is now southern Turkey. The Hellenistic period was yet another era when the connections between Palestine and Egypt were most pronounced. Ptolemy I and a number of his successors offered refuge to Jews in their country and succeeded in attracting a large Jewish population, most of whom settled in Alexandria. It is virtually impossible to estimate the size of that community, although the larger estimates that have placed the Jewish community in Egypt as close to one million strong are undoubtedly exaggerated. Although the Jews of Egypt rarely intermarried with non-Jews, they were quick to become fluent in Greek and to occupy many important governmental and mercantile positions in the Greek state. It was during the second century BCE that Jewish scholars translated the Torah into Greek, thus creating the Septuagint.

THE ROMANS

The Romans replaced the Greeks during the first century BCE, though they portrayed themselves as the inheritors and proponents of Greek culture. They, too, looked upon Egypt as a vital possession and had already brought Egypt within the hegemony of the Roman Empire before the crucial battle of Actium in 31 BCE. During the time when the career of Julius Caesar was in the ascendant, a time when Rome was gradually transforming itself from a republic of city-states to an empire of large possessions, Egypt held considerable attraction. Egypt's ruler then was Cleopatra VII (r. 51–30 BCE), a direct descendant of Ptolemy I and the one Ptolemaic ruler who made a conscious effort to familiarize herself with Egyptian ways. Among other things, she took the time to learn the local language.

Cleopatra has come down to the present as a noteworthy historical figure. Countless works of art, literature, and music have portrayed her as a woman of beauty and high intellect. Shakespeare featured her in a play, *Antony and Cleopatra,* and Handel in an opera, and several modern films have presented her as a beautiful woman and an artful ruler. The best known of the modern-day films starred Elizabeth Taylor and Richard Burton and was produced in 1963. What we actually know about Cleopatra is that she was a woman of high intelligence and charm, though whether she was as beautiful as modern-day critics believe remains open to question. Plutarch, the Roman historian of Greek origins, offers a description, writing in *Life of Antony*, the longest of *Plutarch's Lives:* "her beauty was in itself not altogether incomparable, nor such as to strike those who saw her; but converse with her had an irresistible charm. . . . There was also sweetness in the tones of her voice; and her tongue, like an instrument of many strings, she could readily turn to whatever language she pleased." She drew powerful men into her orbit and used her charm and intellect to stave off Rome's imperializing ambitions for some time after she came to the throne in 51 BCE at the age of eighteen. First she formed an alliance with Julius Caesar, whose child she bore, and then she aligned with one of his successors, Marc Antony, to whom she bore twins. Her choice of Marc Antony as lover and political savior proved unwise. In his battle for control over Egypt with his chief adversary, Octavian, Marc Antony failed. At the battle of Actium Octavian defeated Marc Antony's forces, invaded Egypt, and incorporated the country into an expanding Roman state. After the battle both Marc Antony and Cleopatra committed suicide, Cleopatra allowing herself to be bitten by a poisonous snake. With her death, the Ptolemaic period came to an end, and Rome's imperial rule began. It was to last for more than six centuries, until it was sharply brought down by seventh-century Arab Muslim invaders of Egypt.

The Roman period in Egypt, even more so than the pharaonic era, has yielded to later generations superb source materials. The country's dry climate enabled a plethora of papyrus documents to survive the ravages of time and has provided historians with unrivaled opportunities to delve deeply into this era, even to describe the lives of commoners as well as elites. Yet because so many of these manuscripts come from Upper Egypt, where the climate and deserts preserved them, they likely give a distorted view of the people and the country at this time. Many were found in Upper Egyptian villages that lay far above the Nile floodwater plain. No fewer than one-third come from Fayyum, which under the Greeks and Romans was a privileged and prosperous area. Much less fully documented and thus much less well known, though no less important historically, was the delta, where so many of the early records, mainly documents written on papyrus, were submerged under the Nile floodwaters and lost to posterity.

Two large Upper Egypt estates in particular provide the clearest portrait of the Egyptian countryside and the operations of large landholders. The first set of documents provides information on the farmlands of Aurelius Appianus, who resided as an absentee landowner in the third century in Alexandria. Eager to participate in the lively Greek cultural life of Egypt's capital city, Appianus left the management of his landholdings in the Fayyum district of Arsinoite to a local agent by the name of Heroninos. Most of the letters that have passed down to the present were addressed to Heroninos, and most of the account books were his handiwork.

A second important site of documentation was the district (*nome*) of Oxyrhynchus, which lay about one hundred miles south of present-day Cairo. One of the large estates in the district prospered in the Ptolemaic period and even more so during the early centuries of Roman rule, only to fall into decay in the later Roman period. Its abandoned sites at the edge of the desert allowed the records to remain for centuries in a prime condition of preservation.

We can learn a great deal about Roman Egypt from these records. Take, for instance, the well-documented provincial city of Oxyrhynchus, the main urban location in a district that bore the same name and stretched twenty-five miles to the north of the provincial capital and fifteen miles to the south. The Oxyrhynchus nome contained roughly one hundred villages and a rural population totaling 100,000. Another 20,000 to 25,000 persons lived in the capital city, and on the basis of these population figures and others for the additional twenty-nine nomes of Egypt and the provincial capitals and even larger cities, historical demographers have estimated the population of Roman Egypt at its high point in the third century CE at seven million. Although this population was one of the largest and densest in ancient times, the Egyptian countryside did not teem with people, as it does today. Village dwellers, who went out during the day to work on their fields, toiled alone. If an accident befell them, they could lie untreated and unattended for days.

Rome continued apace the Greek trend of undermining and breaking Egypt's connection with its pharaonic past. Hieroglyphs were less used. The last known use of hieroglyphs was in the temple of Philae in 394, although the ancient Egyptian language continued to be spoken and written in cursive or demotic form for a considerably longer time. Nor did local gods retain the same creditability that they had in earlier eras; they were forcefully trampled into the earth during the Christian era in Egypt (described in the next chapter). Moreover, the Roman Empire was a magnificent structure to behold, reaching from the Scottish Highlands in the west to Mesopotamia in the East and encompassing the present-day African countries of Algeria, Tunisia, Libya, Egypt, and Sudan. Although its overall population of roughly 60 million paled in comparison to that of the contemporaneous Han Empire in China, which boasted more than 100 million subjects, such a vast territorial expanse and population density diminished Egypt's importance, however prosperous and populous it proved to be. It was far from what it had been in the days of the pharaohs, when Egyptians thought of themselves as the center of the universe and the source of all sophisticated and cultured life. Moreover, the rise of the Sasanian Empire in Persia as Rome's chief adversary in the third century of the Common Era further lessened the luster of Egypt, which, in fact, became a prized possession fought over by these two warring imperial powers, each of which had world-conquering ambitions.

Even so, as with the Greek presence in Egypt, the Romans did not effect a complete break with the pharaonic past. The Roman authorities retained the old administrative districts that the Greeks had inherited from their predecessors. Egypt continued to be divided into thirty administrative districts. Each nome had an administrative capital where a provincial ruler, known as a *nomarch*, held forth. The supreme ruler of Egypt, or the governor, was sent out from Rome and served a term of one to three years, though occasionally his tenure was extended to five years. Egypt's administrative capital was Alexandria, as it had been during the Ptolemaic era. Here, too, the Romans followed the Greek practice of having Egypt's center of political gravity be the Mediterranean rather than Memphis—the location that divided Upper and Lower Egypt, as had been the case in pharaonic times.

Alexandria prospered even more under the Romans than under the Greeks. Its population expanded, its commercial life bustled, and its intellectual vitality was second to none in the empire, except perhaps for Rome itself. Recent discoveries of a vast complex of lecture halls, theater rooms, gardens, and public baths by a team of Polish archaeologists at the very center of the old city attest to the importance that the Roman rulers and, later on, the Christianized population attached to higher learning. The excavations brought to light more than twenty lecture rooms where advanced students gathered to imbibe the learning of experts brought in from the far corners of the empire. Several larger theater rooms accommodated even bigger audiences, and other features, like the public baths and gardens, were intended to make the attractions of higher learning appealing to its advocates. (See plate 17 for an illustration of a Roman lecture amphitheater in Alexandria.)

Valuing martial abilities, the Romans richly rewarded those who fought bravely and risked their physical well-being in the service of the empire. At its high point in the third century CE, the Roman army totaled 400,000 soldiers, of whom 20,000 were based in Egypt. The Egyptian force consisted of two legions of Roman soldiers, each of whom was a full-fledged Roman citizen. In electing to serve in the armed forces, recruits signed up for twenty-five years. The Roman legions were supported by a large auxiliary force from the outer parts of the empire, whose members were engaged for twenty-six years of military service, after which they attained Roman citizenship and enjoyed all of the benefits that came with citizenship. These benefits included being tried according to Roman law in Roman courts and paying lesser taxes than non-Roman subjects of the empire. Most of the Egyptian auxiliaries were drawn from Egypt's cities and were of Greek descent.

A development that had long-term meaningful consequences for Egyptian culture was the move of the center of the Roman Empire from Rome to Constantinople, founded in 330 by the emperor Constantine and taking its name from him. An eastward shift of the Roman Empire had been under way for some time and signaled the rise of the Byzantine state, although the Roman and Byzantine empires did not become permanently separated until the end of Theodosius's reign (379–95). Constantinople became a booming metropolis at a time when Rome was shrinking in size in its descent into an urban backwater. While the population of Rome declined in the fourth century, that of Constantinople increased dramatically. It reached the half million mark by 500.

The significance to Egypt of the eastward shift of Roman power cannot be overestimated. Constantine asserted control over Egypt after he defeated his rival, Licinius, in a battle in 324 and followed this military victory by demanding that Egypt's imperial taxes be sent to the new capital instead of to Rome. For the next three centuries, until the Arab Muslim conquest in 640, Egypt looked to Byzantium for its political leadership and much of its religious inspiration. Although Latin survived as the language of the top military officers and the top bureaucrats, Greek eventually became the dominant language of the eastern part of the old Roman Empire, Latin being confined to the West.

The Romans and their Byzantine successors imposed another layer of social hierarchy on the local population. The result was a highly stratified territory in which power and wealth were unevenly distributed and movement across social and class lines was difficult. Until the third century CE, when Roman citizenship was made available to all free-born persons living within the empire, at the top of Egypt's sociopolitical ladder was a small number of Roman citizens, who monopolized power and who served as administrative officers, military men, and in a few cases large landowners and merchants. Beneath them came a larger, mainly urban-based Greek community, whose numbers had grown over the centuries of Ptolemaic rule. Next came the large Jewish community, who were well educated and mainly urban based. They had prospered under the Greeks and continued to enjoy imperial protection under the Romans until they fell out of favor and suffered heavy persecution. Last of all were the Egyptians, most of whom were peasants. They bore the brunt of government taxation. They were also the country's essential economic resource, for they cultivated the foodstuffs that fed the large population living in Egypt and that were exported to feed the far-flung subjects of the Roman Empire.

Although the vast majority of Egyptians were on the lowest rung of the social ladder, limited opportunities existed for enterprising Egyptians to better their circumstances. They could become merchants, large landowners, soldiers, even civil bureaucrats, but doing so meant putting aside their Egyptian identities and assimilating themselves to Greek and Roman ways. Such persons, though often of peasant stock, were no longer thought of as part of the Egyptian peasantry.

Greeks, Romans, and Jews were primarily city dwellers. They congregated in Egypt's four major cities—Alexandria, Ptolemais, Naukratis, and Antinopolis. To a Roman, if one was not a citizen, or a resident of one of the large metropolises, or a Jew, then one was an Egyptian, which was tantamount to being a member of a despised group whom most Romans regarded as mere beasts of burden. Even the Greek population that resided in the countryside was lumped together in Roman thought as part of the Egyptian peasantry.

Despite the fact that the Roman rulers regarded only the four large cities of Egypt as worthy places to reside, the residents of the smaller urban areas, many of which were capitals of nomes, imitated their better-off urban residents. They went to public baths, attended plays in amphitheaters, dressed in the Greek and Roman style, and took part in Greek and Roman sporting activities and festivals, engaging in these enterprises on an ostentatious scale, even to the extent of bankrupting themselves and their local governments.

Greek culture pervaded even Egypt's smaller urban areas, and individuals whom the wealthy and powerful regarded as lowly Egyptians thought of themselves as Greek. The strikingly beautiful burial portraits of town dwellers that are known as the Fayyum portraits are stunning testimonials to their Hellenism. The wealthy and powerful urbanites lumped all smaller-town residents as part of an undifferentiated Egyptian population. They were Egyptians, pure and simple. But to themselves, as one can see, in their "mummy pictures," which they had drawn as part of their burial rites, they were entirely Greek. In fact, they spoke Greek, lived a simplified Greek way of life, and saw themselves as distinctive from the vast mass of the country's people. Their portraits display men and women as if they were of pure Greek descent.

The great mass of the Egyptian population—the Egyptian peasantry—lived in ways that were a striking contrast to those of the city dwellers. Egypt had between 2,000 and 2,500 villages, each one encompassing on average 2,000 acres of land and a population of just under 1,300. Since the villages were relatively close to each other, local travel was easy, mostly by means of small boats traversing the network of canals that dotted the countryside. Most farms were small. Yet cultivators often had to walk long distances from their villages to reach their farmlands. Most villages also had a few large estates, some of which were owned by absentee landlords, living mainly in the nearest city or in one of the large metropolises if the landowners were wealthy. Small farmers owned their own parcels of land; yet upward mobility was limited since peasants had few opportunities to pursue forms of work outside of agriculture. In a real sense, then, peasants found themselves tied to the land. The largest burden of taxation fell on them since the country had no income tax or city taxes, though taxes were levied on traders and owners of businesses.

With the exception of Fayyum, where an elaborate system of irrigation had been erected in the Greek period and was maintained under the Romans, the hydraulic technology of Egyptian agriculture looked little different than it had appeared in pharaonic times. Cultivators awaited the Nile floods, praying for moderate inundations. Wheat was the main cultigen, followed by barley, which was used for animal fodder and also mixed with wheat in the making of bread. Lentils and beans produced most of the protein in the local diet; peasant families filled out their diets with cheese from sheep and goats. Peasants ate very little meat, particularly compared with the soldiers, who were given a daily ration of pork. Meat appeared in the local diet only on festive occasions, although the abundant supplies of fish made it a part of the diet of all but the poorest of country folk.

Christian Egypt

Deserts are fearful places. They have few landmarks, support little life, and are avoided by all but the most skilled and knowledgeable of nomadic peoples. To be lost in the desert is to be without hope. Yet their very dangers and their austere beauty give them an irresistible allure for many. Although the importance of the Nile to Egypt is undeniable, the territory is also a land of three vast deserts. In fact, deserts occupy over 95 percent of the Egyptian landmass. Like the Nile, they have shaped the country's historical narrative. The western desert, leading to the border of Libya, is the largest of the three. It has vast rolling sand dunes, a true classical desert, interrupted here and there by life-giving oases. The eastern desert links Egypt with the Red Sea; it is as beautiful as the western desert, though less classical. Its colorful and oddly shaped mountainous outcroppings have attracted hermits to its remote and romantic caves. Finally, the Sinai Desert is the major land link between Africa and Asia. Over it conquering armies traveled; as one would expect, the Egyptians have demanded to control its strategic passes.

Although the deserts of Egypt are sparsely inhabited, they are not empty of humans. Bedouins make their livelihoods wherever they can, and they have inserted themselves into Egypt's historical narrative. Sometimes, they have lived at peace and in a symbiotic relationship with the settled populations of the river basin, supplying the produce of a pastoral life and the desert in exchange for agricultural commodities. But Bedouin peoples are fiercely independent, all the more so when the central government of Egypt has failed and left its inhabitants at the mercy of marauding nomads.

Each of these deserts had important moments in Egyptian history. In leading the Israelites out of Egypt, Moses had to cross Sinai. Although he never reached Palestine, he did ascend Mount Sinai, where it is believed that God gave him the Ten Commandments. A bush, claimed to have been transplanted from the original burning bush at the foot of the mountain where God commanded Moses to lead his people to the Holy Land, can be seen within the confines of the famous monastery of Saint Catherine. Today, tourists can visit this Greek Orthodox monastery, founded in 527 CE, from which trips to the top of Mount Sinai are arranged. (See plate 18 for an illustration of Saint Catherine's monastery in Sinai.)

For many years after World War II Sinai was off-limits to civilians. It was a strategic military territory fought over by the Egyptian and Israeli armies. Since the signing of the peace treaty between Egypt and Israel in 1979, it has enjoyed a spectacular revival as a tourist site. Sharm el-Sheikh, at the foot of the peninsula, has become a fabled location. Tourists fly in for a week of snorkeling and swimming in one of the most appealing locations in the world.

The western desert covers two-thirds of all of Egypt, a vast sprawling and largely uninhabited area of 1.2 million square miles. Its historical fame rests largely on its oases, the best known of which is at Siwa. Today, Siwa attracts many visitors. Its hotels and many amenities enable Cairenes and others to escape the hurly-burly of their lives for a weekend of pristine solitude. Its importance in ancient times was far greater, however. Here in an area where 300 freshwater springs and streams feed olive and date palm trees resided the oracle of Siwa, well known and highly esteemed in the Greek world. Potentates rushed to the oracle to learn of their fates. As we have noted, the oracle's most important visitor was Alexander the Great.

Finally, the eastern desert has a different but no less historical importance, as this chapter will demonstrate in abundant ways. Along with the western desert, it attracted some of the early converts to Christianity. Wishing to renounce the materialism of Roman imperial culture, they sought a deep spirituality, which they believed they could attain only through renunciation and simple prayerful living. Antony was the exemplary monastic figure of the late third and fourth centuries. The caves and austere dwelling places of the deserts were tempting retreats for him and other ascetics. Antony and others fled from settled society in the Nile River basin to a simple existence in both the western and eastern deserts. There they became the founding figures of monastic movements, which eventually spread out of Egypt into Europe.

THE BEGINNINGS OF CHRISTIANITY IN EGYPT

Christianity threatened the ancient Egyptian culture more fundamentally than Greek and Roman beliefs and practices. Yet even here, the religious traditions of the peoples of the pharaoh did not disappear without a fight. In addition, many ancient ideas were assimilated into the new religion.

Nowhere in the early years of the late antique Roman Empire were Egyptians more influential than in the evolution of the early Christian church. Egypt's clerics and scholars were instrumental in debating the major tenets of early Christianity and framing some of its fundamental beliefs. Egyptian Christianity also owed a powerful debt to neo-Platonic thought, much of which was incorporated into the new religion. Nonetheless once Christianity had become an imperial faith the authorities used all of the tools of empire to suppress pagan practices, declaring it illegal to worship any god but the Christian God. Gods and goddesses that had survived, in modified forms, through Greek and early Roman times, were able to withstand the withering Christian attack on polytheism only by infiltrating Christian thought and practice in subtle ways. Yet because Christianity affirmed a belief in a bodily resurrection and held to the view that God had three persons (Father, Son, and Holy Ghost) its underlying messages were familiar to the Egyptians, who in the pharaonic period had their own triune of gods (Osiris-Isis-Horus) and an unquenchable belief that they would be revived in a glorious afterlife.

Yet, in the final analysis, the Christian faith and the creation of a new Greek-Coptic alphabet drove a wedge between the Egyptians and their pharaonic heritage. Judaism, out of which Christianity evolved, and Christianity itself detested the religious ideology of the ancient Egyptians. Devotees of these two faiths regarded the ancient Egyptians as irrational and superstitious polytheists, worshippers of false gods, who, in addition, had oppressed the Israelites during their captivity in Egypt. Egyptian Christians sought to expunge memories of this past.

The earliest followers of Jesus did not intend to create a new religion. The advocates of the "Jesus movement," as some label the early stages of Christianity, were Jews. Jesus himself never spurned his Jewishness and broadcast his message among members of the Jewish faith. His disciples, in spite of Jesus' injunction to go out into all the world and preach the gospel, at first worked avidly within Judaism. Even Paul, Christianity's earliest and most energetic evangelist among non-Jews, spoke in Jewish places of worship throughout the Near East and Asia Minor. In Egypt, the Jesus movement found an interested and receptive audience especially among the large, wealthy, and well educated Jewish population of Alexandria, many of whom made annual journeys to Jerusalem to participate in holy celebrations. In the minds of many Jews in the first century CE, the Jesus movement was little more than a radical, some might even have said lunatic, fringe of Judaism, which at the time was experimenting with many new creedal affirmations. It was only as the Jesus movement failed to gain wide acceptance among the Jews of Southwest Asia and Egypt that its adherents began to carry their message to non-Jews. Only then did it take on the appearance of a new religion, with its own distinctive beliefs and its own separate clergy.

Tradition has it that one of Christianity's most learned disciples, Mark, the author of one of the early works of the life of Jesus, introduced the Jesus movement into Egypt. He is said to have gone there a little more than a decade after Jesus' death and to have suffered a brutal death at the hands of enraged Egyptians who did not care for his preachings. Whatever the case may be, it seems reasonable, despite the dearth of evidence, that knowledge of Jesus and his ideas circulated early and freely in Egypt in the first century of the Common Era. The connections between Egypt and Palestine were close; ideas, texts, and travelers moved freely back and forth between these two worlds.

By the second century of the Common Era Christianity had begun to put down deep roots in Egypt, particularly in Alexandria, which continued to be a flourishing center of intellectual and religious discourse. Where a Greek library and museum had existed during the height of the Greek era a new school, known as the Catechetical School, arose to take its place. It, too, attracted scholars from all over the eastern Mediterranean, but now these men debated religious topics rather than abstract philosophy and sought to give a rigorous form to their new religion. In particular, they hammered out the fundamentals regarding the life and teachings of Jesus and the meaning of his preaching.

Christianity was only one of many different new religious movements that competed for attention as the Roman Empire reached its apex. In the face of stiff competition and intense persecution from the imperial authorities, it owed its ultimate success to the universalistic aspects of its message, the charisma of its holy men, the sacred aura surrounding its scriptural canon, and certainly in the case of Egypt the fit that existed between Christian doctrine and aspects of popular, pre-existing religious beliefs and practices. The new religion made few distinctions, appealing equally to rich and poor, city dwellers and peasants, slave and free, and men and women. It also profited from the zeal and talents of its early converts, many of whom lived in Egypt. Indeed, even though Egypt eventually slipped out of the central orbit of the world-wide Christian faith, losing its preeminence to Rome and Constantinople, its early contributions to the triumph of Christianity and to the shape of Christian action and belief cannot be overestimated.

The success of Christianity was spectacular and in many ways unexpected. The first century of the Common Era offers little evidence of the growth of this new religion, except for the occasional writings of Christian converts themselves. The Jewish chroniclers barely noticed it, and the imperial state felt no threat from its followers. Little had changed, at least on the surface, a century later. Only in the third century did Christians become a force to be reckoned with, and it was at this stage that the Roman emperors, led by Diocletian (284-305), were moved to carry out savage campaigns of persecution. Diocletian's persecutions were formidable indeed. He required all of his soldiers, on penalty of expulsion from the army, to engage in Roman rites. He tore down churches and sent converts to be mauled by lions in sporting amphitheaters. He destroyed all of the Christian writings that he could lay his hand on. Yet it was his immediate successor, Constantine (305–337), who, claiming to having seen a vision from the Christian God that he would succeed in his attack on Rome in 312, granted toleration to the Christians in the following year.

During these early centuries of Christianity's existence, Egypt was a vibrant center of activity, if not the very heart of the new faith. If in the third century most Egyptians were polytheists, believing in the myriad of gods that had been worshipped from ancient times through the Graeco-Roman period, by the sixth century most Egyptians were Christians. Polytheism had been rendered a minority and much persecuted faith.

It is difficult to provide a precise tracking of this monumental change in the religious beliefs of the Egyptians, who eventually turned away from the gods and goddesses of the Egyptian-Greek world and embraced the Christian God. It is clear that the process was gradual but had become virtually complete by the time of the Arab-Muslim conquest of the country in the seventh century. In the 350s, a visitor to the city of Alexandria, destined to be one of the strongholds of the Christian faith, observed a plethora of shrines to Graeco-Egyptian gods and goddesses. He noted that the "lavishly adorned temples, sacristans, priests, haruspices, worshipers, and the best diviners all abound; and everything is performed according to the proper rites. Thus, you will find altars constantly ablaze with the fires of sacrifice and heaped with incense."

By the second half of the fourth century, however, Christian communities were mobilized against the old religious beliefs and practices. Tension came to a head in 391 at the Serapeum of Alexandria where the most important Graeco-Egyptian god of Alexandria, Serapis, was worshipped. The emperor issued a decree that the temple should be closed, but a Christian soldier, believing that the decree did not go far enough, entered the temple and struck the jaw of the image of Serapis. Others then followed, hammering the god and separating its limbs from its torso. The limbs and other broken off parts of the image were taken to various parts of the city and burned, while the torso was publicly burned inside the theater of the Serapeum. If any event marked a turning point in the triumph of Christianity over the Graeco-Roman gods, it was this showdown in the city of Alexandria.

Egyptian leadership in the spread of Christianity was altogether critical. The Catechetical School of Alexandria gave Christianity its first major theologians. The School's founder, a world-class scholar, was the Sicilian-born Pantaemus, whose works have been lost. He passed the torch of learning to Clement (d. 215), originally an Athenian, with a deep appreciation for Greek philosophy. Clement, of whom it was said that he considered "ignorance worse than sin," believed in the compatibility between Christian belief and rational inquiry. He in turn prepared the way for Origen, one of early Christianity's most venerated savants. A native-born Egyptian, who died in 254, Origen may have studied with Plotinus, a master of classical literature and philosophy; his mastery of Graeco-Roman philosophy is in no doubt. Origen traveled widely throughout the Roman world, maintaining ties with many of the leading intellectuals of his age. An individual of massive learning, he wrote commentaries on nearly all of the books of the Old and New Testaments. His major work, *De Principiis*, appeared in four volumes: on God and the Celestial World; on Man and Matter; on Free Will and its Impact; and on the Scriptures. Unfortunately, the originals have not survived, coming down to us only through the Latin translations of later scholars, Rufinus and Jerome.

Monasticism in Egypt

Egypt's centrality in early Christianity was nowhere more prominent than in the country's monastic movement, for the birthplace of Christian monasticism was the western and eastern deserts of Egypt. It was notably in Wadi Natrun in the Western desert about fifty miles north of Cairo and in Upper Egypt that monastic ideals spread throughout the Christian world. Egyptian ascetics were not content merely to live godly lives. They exulted in their spiritual exploits in the deserts and broadcast them throughout the entire Christian universe. Hence, it is no exaggeration to say that Egyptians not only pioneered but also popularized through their writings the two forms of monastic life that came to predominate in Europe centuries later: eremetic and cenobitic monasticism. The fourth century was the culminating age of Egyptian monasticism, and its most notable figures were Antony (251–356) and Pachomius (290–347). While it is wrong to designate Antony as the founder of eremetic monasticism and Pachomius the originator of cenobitic monasticism, since both men had predecessors, their influence was so pervasive and their fame so widespread that their names have forever been associated with the beginnings of these two monastic ways of life.

The two men were entirely different. Antony had no formal education, was intensely shy, deeply religious, and entirely otherworldly. At the age of eighteen he sold all of his belongings and began to live the life of a hermit, moving farther and farther into the eastern desert of Egypt and farther and farther away from all forms of life. He was so given to a simple and ascetic way of life that it was said of him that he "blushed when he had to eat." By the time he died in 356 at the age of 105 he had virtually dropped out of civilization, living a long distance from the nearest villages in an area of utter wilderness. Had it not been for Athanasius, the combative bishop of Alexandria, Antony would not have achieved the notoriety that he enjoyed, for it was Athanasius who was so impressed with Antony's religiosity that he wrote an encomium of him, *The Life of Antony*, which popularized his ascetic ways far beyond the boundaries of Egypt.

Athanasius's *Life of Antony* had even deeper and more significant effects. It extolled an ascetic form of Christianity, holding it up as a model for attaining a virtuous religious life. It also served as a caution against using traditional Greek and Roman forms of learning to achieve an understanding of Christian truths and stressed the primacy of the written, scriptural word. The treatise was an integral part of Athanasius's attack on the doctrines of Arius, a presbyter in the bishopric of Alexandria (see below in this chapter), which the bishops of Alexandria, and especially Athanasius, regarded as insufficiently detached from pagan philosophical approaches to religious truth and insufficiently steeped in knowledge of the Holy Word.

Much different was Pachomius, who eschewed the isolated monastic way of life. He did not believe as Antony did that a true Christian had to mortify the body. Yet he, too, had a preference for asceticism, although he wanted to accomplish his renunciation of worldly pleasure within a communal setting. Press-ganged into Constantine's army, then converted to Christianity, Pachomius brought much of the empire's military regimen into his religious order. Monks lived in cells and adhered to strict routines; all devotees rose at an appointed time, wore the same clothing, ate together, and worshipped at regular times during the day. His monastery in Upper Egypt was constructed like a Roman fortress, surrounded by high walls and entered only by those with a deep commitment to the Christian faith. Pachomius's movement led to the formation of numerous large-scale cells in Upper Egypt, so that by the end of the seventh century the monastery he founded at Tabennesis had 7,000 monks, while that at Arsinoe had another 10,000 followers.

Both of these monastic movements arose within Egypt in locations that had existed on the fringes of the Graeco-Roman world. The eremetic form of Egyptian monasticism took shape at the edge of the Nile delta. One of the most significant locations for eremetic monasticism was at the sites of Nitria, Scetis, and Kellis, nearly suburbs of the bustling city of Alexandria. The hermits living there supported themselves by selling produce on the open market or receiving gifts from believers. In contrast, the cenobitic form of Egyptian monasticism arose in poor rural areas in Middle Egypt, where survival depended on being well-organized and where monks supported one another in impoverished settings.

In both situations, the monastic movements had the effect of transporting Christian belief and practice into the villages of Egypt. It provided inspiring images for peasant families as they began to put aside their traditional religious beliefs in favor of the new religion. It was not uncommon for church leaders, especially those associated with monastic movements, to transform temples, the location of so much popular religious belief and so centrally associated with the ancient gods, to places of worship for the Christian God. Thus, Egyptian monasticism made Christianity a mass movement just as the Catechetical School of Alexandria made it a force to be reckoned with among the scholarly elite of the Graeco-Roman world.

Women played a vital role in Egyptian monasticism. One of the most influential of the Egyptian monastic movements, the White Monastery, based in Upper Egypt, included female monks from its very foundation. Shenoute, who was head of the White Monastery from 385 until his death in 465, exercised authority over no fewer than 4,000 monks, of whom 1,800 were women. Believing that the most favorable setting for living a truly Christian life and attaining salvation was within a well-organized corporate body, he imposed strict discipline on his followers. Monks were expected to live ascetic lives filled with hard work and prayers; their dress, food, shelter, and sexuality were designed to set them apart from the other members of the larger society and to facilitate their entry into paradise. The members of Shenoute's monastic order attempted to live "with their companions in peace without sin and deceit, like God and his angels who live in heaven."

Shenoute was a fierce advocate of Christianity and used his influence to stamp out pagan practices in the vicinity of his monastery. Few used the bully pulpit more ruthlessly. Situated across the Nile River from the important city of Panopolis, the White Monastery broadcast a message of condemnation against those in the area who had not embraced the Christian faith. A particularly rich and oppressive, but unnamed landlord living in Panopolis found himself the target of Shenoute's fire and brimstone, identified repeatedly and shamelessly as a faithless and godless man, a fool, a wretch, a child of pestilence, and a sinner.

Egyptian Gnostic Christianity

The vitality of early Egyptian Christianity has become all the more clear to later scholars when in 1945 Egyptian villagers discovered a group of Gnostic scrolls in the town of Nag Hammadi in Upper

Egypt. Although publication of the texts was delayed for thirty-two years and although the writings vary in authorship and in time and place of composition, they provide unique insights into the evolution of early Christian orthodoxy and heresy. The Nag Hammadi collection consists of twelve codices, or books, plus eight leaves removed from a thirteenth book and placed inside the cover of the sixth book. Each of the books, except the tenth one, consists of collections of brief texts; in all, there are thirty more or less complete texts and ten fragmentary ones.

Previously what we knew about the Egyptian Gnostics came only from their most severe critics, men like Irenaeus, Ignatius, and Tertullian, who succeeded in characterizing as heresy the doctrines circulated among Gnostic scholars and the religious texts that the Gnostics preferred. In contrast, the Nag Hammadi texts provide original Gnostic writings that scholars can check against the complaints of their critics. They include the Gospel of Thomas, the Gospel of Philip, and the Gospel of Truth, which circulated widely in Egypt and the Near East in the second century and were read as avidly as the other writings that eventually came to make up the accepted version of the New Testament. Although one cannot tell who the precise authors of the individual texts were, we do know the names and the major ideas, however distorted, of the leading Gnostic scholars from the attacks of their critics. The best known and most reviled by the critics were Valentinus and Basilides, who must surely have found voice in these books.

Doctrinally, the Gnostics sought to achieve closeness with Jesus, not through reading the scriptures but rather through knowing oneself. The Gnostics saw Jesus as a guide rather than a savior. Many considered him to be an exemplary human being, possessing a spark of the divine, like the rest of humanity.

The texts themselves were originally written in Greek and drew inspiration from a Platonic Christian tradition. They were translated into Coptic, not very skillfully, and, then, a group of them was hidden away around 400 CE. What gives the Nag Hammadi collection its considerable intellectual unity is a utopian and highly individualistic view of human society, and an asceticism that manifested itself in the renunciation of earthly goods. The Gnostics saw the resurrection of Jesus as a spiritual rebirth, not a physical one. They believed in the power of individual reason and intuition and did not accept the power of the rising Christian clergy to arbitrate religious doctrine.

Not surprisingly the heaviest criticism of the Gnostic approach came from Egypt's clerical class, who believed that only specially trained and ordained ranks of the clergy, from bishops down to individual priests, had the final and definitive say on what was correct belief and which writings were truly Christian and which were not.

THE CREATION OF A SEPARATE CHRISTIAN CHURCH IN EGYPT

Egypt, an arena of spirited and heated religious disputation in the heartland of Christendom, witnessed a radical new departure in the fourth century. It saw the creation of a national Egyptian Christian church that hived off from the other Christian churches and polities. This rupture within the Christian world owed much to the energy of several bishops of Alexandria, most notably Athanasius, whose long tenure, interrupted by five periods of exile, lasted from 328 to 373. In its early days the Christian church in Alexandria had many leaders, and it was only gradually that a single bishop assumed such preeminence that he was often referred to as a papa or pope. One of the reasons for Athanasius's success in elevating himself and his office, the bishopric of Alexandria, to a high level is that he brought the various monastic movements within the confines of the church, championing the teachings and actions of men like Antony and Pachomius, who were the most influential monks in this century of creative Christian thought and action in Egypt.

The theological dispute that most roiled the Egyptian scholarly and clerical class and proved an even more decisive challenge to the authority of the bishopric of Alexandria was the controversy over the ideas of Arius. The issues that the Alexandrian presbyter raised provoked the most severe intellectual crisis in the fourth-century Roman world. Here, too, the position and actions of Bishop

Athanasius were altogether decisive. Today it is difficult to understand how clerics could argue so passionately over such seemingly arcane matters as the relationship between God the Father and God the Son, Jesus Christ. But behind these seemingly obscure theological arguments lay crucial questions that have been at the heart of Christian doctrine ever since. Decisive questions were being debated at this time: Who was Jesus, was he a son of God or the only begotten son of God? Was he purely divine or both divine and human? What revelations did he bring? What were the authentic sources of knowledge about his life and teachings? And what powers should the clergy have over the laity, especially in matters relating to approaching God and Jesus? These issues drove wedges through the church and set friends and fellow scholars against one another.

Arius was the source of much of this controversy. Born into a wealthy Libyan family around 280, he emerged into prominence at the very time that Christianity was asserting itself as a dynamic force throughout the Roman Empire. Schooled in Platonic thought and serving as the leader of a small circle of parish churches at the outskirts of Alexandria, he became a popular preacher, beloved by his followers. Using his oratorical skills to great effect, he set forth a compelling view of Christianity, extolling the humanity of Christ and contending that God could communicate with humans only through a divinity lower than himself. He also believed that Christians should be judged by the religiosity of their lives rather than by any strict adherence to a set of clerically determined dogmas. Stressing the virtues of ascetic living, Arius called on his followers to reject this world's material pleasures.

In many of his views, but especially his notion that Jesus Christ was not the equal of God the Father, he came into conflict with Egypt's clerical elements. His early chief antagonist was Alexander, the bishop of Alexandria, who while asserting the primacy of the See of Alexandria throughout the entire Christian world was determined to bring all of the parishes in Egypt, including those in which Arius functioned, under his authority. On the issue of Christ the Son and God the Father, Alexander believed that these two essences were one and the same. They were equal, and as such they were of the same substance. In Bishop Alexander's view, God the Father and God the Son were, to use the language of the period, consubstantial—a doctrine that Arius rejected. In Arius's view, God the Father had always preceded God the Son and thus Jesus, the Son, was not of the same or equal substance as God the Father.

Arius's oratory and his general humanity had great appeal to many segments of Alexandrian society. Lay preachers appeared on the streets of Alexander to broadcast his ideas, which the bishops of Alexandria, originally Alexander and then his successor, Athanasius, saw as a challenge to their authority and an impulse for a highly individualistic view of the Christian faith.

Such disputation irked Emperor Constantine, a pragmatic man, who had embraced Christianity, expecting it to be a bulwark of the imperial system. Determined to end the controversy, Constantine called a conference of leading clerics, perhaps as many as 250, at the city of Nicaea in 325. He attended the council himself, where he played a role in persuading the attendees to endorse the final creedal statement. The main message of the Nicene Creed represented a triumph for the anti-Arian bishops: Its words rang out clearly for consubstantialism: "We believe in one God, the father almighty, maker of all things visible and invisible—and in one Lord, Jesus Christ, the Son of God, the only begotten of the Father, that is of the substance of the Father; God of God, Light of Light, true God of true God, begotten, not made, consubstantial with the Father, by whom all things were made, both which are in heaven and on earth." All but two Libyan bishops subscribed to the creed; the Libyans, along with Arius, were excommunicated. Yet Arius continued to promote his religious views, only to meet an even more formidable adversary in Athanasius.

While the Council of Nicaea repudiated one influential Egyptian, Arius, it endorsed the position of Egypt's most powerful clerical officeholders, Alexander and Athanasius. Egypt's place in the firmament of the church stood at such a high level following Nicaea that its rivals, especially the bishoprics of Rome and Constantinople, which sought to elevate their own positions, showed their concern by claiming that the bishop of Alexandria had become "a veritable pharaoh of the church." Egypt's supremacy proved short-lived, however, for the question of the divinity and humanity of Christ was far from resolved. The Council of Chalcedon, called in 451 and attended by no fewer than 600 bishops, proved a disaster for the Egyptian delegation. At earlier councils, Egypt had been represented by intellectual and scholastic heavyweights, notably Athanasius and Cyril. Now a person of much lesser diplomatic and debating skills, Dioscorus, led the Egyptian delegation. He held rigidly to what his critics called a monophysitic position. By this, they meant that Jesus Christ had a single nature that was both fully human and fully divine, which was at variance with the Chalcedonian creed, affirming that Christ had two natures, one of which was fully human and the other fully divine. For the Egyptian clerics, Jesus was, in a sense, a human being turned into God. "God with us" was their slogan. The council condemned the Egyptian position, whose delegates, no longer prepared to remain within the fold of the Roman or Byzantine Christian faiths, bolted and asserted the independence of the Egyptian Coptic Church.

Although, once again, the theology of the dispute is difficult to unravel or even to understand fully, what is undoubtedly true is that the Egyptian bishops and major clerics used the dispute to assert the independence of their national church. Coptic Christianity was an expression of Egyptian separatist identity and Egypt's distinctive culture. It represented opposition to the rising prominence of Rome and Constantinople and created in Egypt a national church that, unfortunately for Egypt's relations with the rest of the Christian world, left Egypt as a separatist dominion of the world church. Not only did the Council of Chalcedon recognize Rome as the primary seat of ecclesiastical authority, followed by Constantinople, but it also undermined the authority of Alexandria by condemning its bishop and then exiling him.

The one exception to the isolation of Coptic Christianity was its relationship with the fledgling Ethiopian Christian church. In the earliest days, however, this relationship was like that of a parent to a child. Nearly all of the guidance and inspiration flowed from Egypt to Ethiopia. The close tie between these two outposts of the Christian faith began in the fourth century when the Egyptian archbishop, Athanasius, appointed Frumentius as the first bishop of Ethiopia. From that moment forward, the head of the Coptic Church in Egypt assumed responsibility for naming the leader of the Ethiopian church. Moreover, Egyptian Coptic literature served as the main religious and theological inspiration for the sister church in Axum in these early centuries. Egyptian clerics were instrumental in transmitting a large number of Christian texts written in Greek, including the Bible, the monastic rules of Pachomius, *The Life of Antony*, and other documents, to the Ethiopians, who then translated these books into their language, Ge'ez.

A powerful ingredient supporting an independent and national Coptic Christianity was the Coptic language, which was, in the words of a leading scholar of the Coptic religion, "the last phase in the evolution of the language of the ancient Egyptians" and thus one of the few long-term connections Egyptians had with their pharaonic past.

As we have observed, hieroglyphs were modified and simplified as hieratic and then made even less formal as demotic. When Alexander the Great and his successors introduced the Greek language into the country, following Alexander's conquest, an early form of Coptic emerged as a way to transliterate Egyptian demotic into Greek. But the Egyptian clergy found the language inadequate for representing all of the native Egyptian sounds of demotic and, later on, for reproducing the Christian scriptures. Accordingly, scholars and scribes added seven letters to the Greek alphabet to represent sounds that did not exist in Greek. This became the Coptic script and language, which during the Christian era in Egypt gained wider and wider acceptance at the expense of Greek. The first known Egyptian document to be transliterated into Greek characters was written down a century and a half before the Common Era. Demotic Egyptian, written in Greek letters, was still being used in the early fifth century CE by priests associated with the worship of Isis. In time Arabic eventually supplanted Coptic, but the retreat of Coptic to the point that it became purely a religious and liturgical language, used by the

Coptic clergy in their religious services, took place only after several centuries of Arab Muslim rule. In fact, during the first two centuries of Arab Muslim rule in Egypt, Coptic experienced a literary flourishing, and it was not until the tenth century that numerous Egyptian Christian authors began to compose their works in Arabic.

Egypt within Islamic Empires, 639–969

Cairo is a city of mosques. The first large-scale building that one sees upon arriving in the city is the Muhammad Ali mosque built on an outcropping of the Muqattam hills. It towers over the city's other buildings and, as intended, projected the power of Egypt's new dynast. Although it was built in the nineteenth century and therefore is not one of Egypt's early mosques, its dominance reminds all that Egypt, in spite of its magnificent pharaonic past and its Graeco-Roman-Christian heritage, is at heart a Muslim country. Its majestic minarets greet Cairenes every day of the year, proclaiming the centrality of Islam in the life and culture of the country. (See plate 19 for an illustration of the Muhammad Ali mosque.)

Early each morning, often as early as 5:00 AM, in every nook and cranny of the city, from small, recently built constructions to the oldest and most revered mosques of the Islamic period, the morning call to prayer echoes forth from minarets. In recent times recorded messages have produced the well-rehearsed words: Allah Akbar—God is Great. Muezzins are no longer needed. Fridays are truly devoted to religious activities. Mosques are crowded with believers who come to pray and to seek insight from the learned words of imams. Cairo is one of Islam's most notable and dynamic cities. It houses Islam's oldest and most highly respected school of religious learning—al-Azhar—and religious buildings grace the newest quarters as well as those locations that formed the original Muslim city. Yet Egypt was not always the heartland of the Muslim religion. In the first three centuries of the Islamic empires it ceded a long-held and much-cherished primacy in the North African–Southwest Asian world to other regions. In a narrative of Egypt's history it is necessary to make a detour into the Arabian Peninsula, Southwest Asia, the Iranian plateau, and Central Asia in order to gain a proper understanding of the Muslim belief and practice that swept over the land of the pharaohs and superimposed themselves on the culture that Greeks, Romans, and Christians had established in the Nile River basin.

In the seventh century Egypt left center stage. One of the cradles of civilization, then a world power in its own right, the breadbasket of the Greek and Roman empires, a favored colony of Alexander the Great, and a vital center in the triumph of Christianity as a new world faith, Egypt lost it preeminence to areas that Egypt's leading figures had once scorned. The new dynamism of the Near East originated from a small hillock in the southwestern portion of the Arabian Peninsula in 610 CE. Here, a simple merchant claimed to have had a divine revelation. In this dramatic moment Muhammad believed that God had come to him and commanded him with the following message:

> Recite in the name of thy Lord who created
> created man of a blood clot
> Recite and thy Lord is the most bountiful
> who taught by the pen
> taught man what he knew not
> No, indeed, surely man waxes insolent,
> for he thinks himself self-sufficient
> Surely unto thy Lord is the returning.

Other revelations followed until his death, many of which came to him while he was wrapped in blankets and shivering, as if in a trance. Soon, a new religion was born, whose adherents swept out of the Arabian Peninsula defeating the Byzantine and Persian armies that had controlled Southwest Asia, Egypt, and North Africa and installing the new religion of Islam wherever their forces prevailed. While Egypt was quickly and decisively drawn into the Islamic fold, the Arabian Peninsula, Syria, and Iraq eclipsed it in religious and political centrality during the next three centuries.

By the seventh century Egypt had become one of the most thoroughly Christianized countries in the realm of Christendom, although even here significant pockets of traditional religious practice persisted. Yet the country would soon participate in another world-changing event: the arrival of Arab Muslim conquerors and the gradual conversion of the country's population to Islam. To understand the collapse of the Roman-Byzantine empire in Egypt in the seventh century and the spread of Islam, we must turn to a relatively isolated part of the Afro-Eurasian continent: the Arabian Peninsula, where momentous events were under way at the end of the sixth century.

The Arabian Peninsula had gradually been drawn into the outside world from the third century onward. Especially affected was the western part, known as the Hijaz, through which trading caravans and travelers passed, making their way to Persia, Syria, Yemen, and even across the Red Sea to Ethiopia. Not only did long-distance merchants who led the caravans bring commodities from Persia and Syria, they also introduced new religious beliefs. Yemen was a center where Jews and Christians worshipped, and even in parts of the Hijaz, especially the city of Yathrib, later known as Medina, Jewish communities were active. Religions purporting to promote universal truths for all peoples of the world, like Christianity, or beliefs in a single God, like Judaism, thus were increasingly familiar to the Arab tribesmen who inhabited the peninsula.

One of the commercial and religious centers of the Hijaz was Mecca. The location was not an imposing place, rather a town made up of simple dwellings. In the words of a contemporary poet Mecca was a desolate place where "no waters flow . . . not a blade of grass on which to rest the eye; no hunting. Only merchants, the most despicable of professions." Although the poet calls attention to Mecca's mercantile importance, though in a derogatory manner, the village also enjoyed high standing as a holy city, a sanctuary, as well as a location for active long-distance commerce. Peoples from all over the area came to worship at the Kaaba, an unimpressive set of unmortared stones, piled on top of each other, but nonetheless believed to be the site of the chief god of the Meccans, Allah, who could resolve disputes and who promoted peace among warring clans, factions, and tribes, though not the only god worshipped by the Meccans. Into this world a man destined to change the shape of history was born around 570 CE.

MUHAMMAD, THE PROPHET AND FOUNDER OF ISLAM

Muhammad was a member of the powerful Quraysh clan, but unfortunately for him his subclan was not one of the most influential. Muhammad's father died before his birth, and his mother passed away when he was only six. The task of raising the youngster fell first to his paternal grandfather, Abd al-Muttalib, and then to his uncle, Abu Talib. For approximately forty years, Muhammad lived an undistinguished life, serving as an agent of a successful merchant woman, Khadijah, whom Muhammad later married despite the fact that she was considerably older then he. No doubt Muhammad's merchant journeys, perhaps as far as Syria, played a role in his later religious beliefs.

In 610, while on a spiritual retreat on a nearby hillside at Hira, where Muhammad often went to meditate, he experienced a religious awakening. He believed that God (Allah in Arabic) had come to him and had called him to introduce his community to important religious tenets. Muhammad continued to have divine revelations, and although he was illiterate, his early followers copied these messages down on "scraps of parchment and leather, ribs of palm branches, camels' shoulder blades and ribs, pieces of board, and the breasts of men." These fragments were eventually brought together in a single book, which became the Quran. The early messages emphasized the need to live an upright life in anticipation of an impending day of judgment. They were short and hortatory. Because the Quran would be arranged with the longest revelations coming first and the shortest last, most of the early messages are located among the later suras, or chapters.

Muhammad carried his message of a day of judgment and the need to live righteously to the men and women of Mecca, winning a few converts, including his wife, Khadijah. Most Meccans, especially the wealthy and influential members of the Quraysh clan, paid him little heed. Only when he became more assertive and began to win additional converts did the Quraysh leadership turn against him. Spurned at home, the Prophet directed his attention to the strife-torn city of Medina. Here, in Medina, clans fought with one another, and here, too, resided an important Jewish community. Some of Medina's leaders approached Muhammad, asking him to become their leader and a source of unity. Muhammad accepted their invitation, and with a few devoted Meccan followers, he left his home and migrated to Medina in 622. The year of the move to Medina, known as the *hijra*, is the first year of the Muslim calendar. It was in Medina that Muhammad was able to build a strong community of believers, which came to be called the *umma*, and which accepted Muhammad and his tenets as having a higher authority than even their own families and clans.

In Medina, Muhammad began to articulate the social, cultural, economic, and political tenets of his new religion. Inevitably, as he promulgated these requirements, which came to him as revelations from God, his messages became longer and more complicated. Muhammad believed that the revelations coming to him were the same as those that had been given to Jews and Christians. Later, he called Christians and Jews "peoples of the book," asserting that they, too, had holy scriptures, and hence deserved tolerance within the new order. Yet Muhammad's difficulties with the Jewish community living in Medina became a source of friction and disappointment to him, causing him to promote practices that would distinguish his faith from Judaism and Christianity. Although, at first he had instructed his followers to face Jerusalem when praying, later, after the Jews in Medina had refused to accept his preachings and had allegedly conspired with his enemies, he told his followers to turn toward Mecca as they prayed. He also set aside a full month, the month of Ramadan, for fasting, rather than single days, and he required Muslims to pray five times daily rather than three times. It was also in the face of Jewish antipathy toward his preaching that Muhammad enunciated his belief that his doctrines were the last word that God offered to mankind and that consequently he was "the seal of the prophets," correcting the errors that earlier Jewish and Christian communities had made in their understanding of God's message.

Islam permits Jews and Christians to worship their God and to live at peace within their own communities, but they are expected to be politically subservient to Muslim rulers and to pay a special tax, called the *jizya*. Yet Muhammad's failure to persuade the Jews of Medina to accept him as a prophet in the tradition of Moses and other Hebrew prophets resulted in hostile passages in the Quran against Jews. Eventually, Muhammad's bitterness against the Jews led him to drive them out of Medina or kill them. After he did so, he handed over their lands to his followers.

Muhammad and his new religion were a success at Medina. They brought order and stability to a community that had been beset by internecine warfare. But the Prophet never lost sight of his birthplace, and later he mounted a military campaign to win back Mecca. In this effort, he introduced the idea of *jihad*, a holy war. Although he failed militarily to defeat his Meccan adversaries, eventually the leading Quraysh figures realized that Muhammad's supporters were damaging their long-distance trade and that they would be better off, and perhaps even prosper, if they came to terms with their erstwhile resident. Hence, in 630 the Meccan leadership accepted Muhammad and his religious leadership in their city.

The core religious text of Muslims is the Quran, which was passed along by word of mouth and then written down periodically. It was finally brought together after Muhammad's death during the caliphate of Uthman, who ruled over the Muslim community between 644 and 656. Uthman created a commission to produce an authoritative rendering of God's word. The definitive version was finally available around 650, and Uthman ordered that all other texts be destroyed. The Quran has, in all, 114 suras. The first, called the *Fatiha*, or the Opening, reads, as follows and is often on the lips of the devout:

In the name of God, the Merciful, the Compassionate,
Praise belongs to God, the Lord of All Being, the

> All Merciful, the All Compassionate, the
> Master of the day of Judgment, thee only we
> serve; to thee alone we pray for succor. Guide
> us in the straight path, the path of those whom
> thou hast blessed, not of those against whom
> thou are wrathful, nor of those who are
> astray.

Many non-Muslims find the Quran difficult to read and are unable to appreciate its beauty and power. But it has survived the centuries and continues to inspire. One of its English translators, A. J. Arberry, captured its brilliance, remarking that it was "amongst the greatest literary masterpieces of mankind." While conceding that the English translations were poor, he claimed that the original would "move men to tears and ecstasy."

SUCCESSORS TO MUHAMMAD

Muhammad died in 632, having made no preparations for his succession. His community of believers was plunged into crisis. Some groups sought to secede, believing that they had pledged themselves only to Muhammad and that they were now free to go their own way. Others sought to transfer the mantle of the Prophet to themselves. Three groups vied for power: the *Muhajirun*, early converts to Muhammad's mission who had migrated to Medina; the *Ansar*, those members of the community at Medina who had invited Muhammad to become their political and religious leader; and the Quraysh, which was Muhammad's tribal group, but whose leading figures had opposed the Prophet at the outset. The Quraysh asserted their claim to authority on the basis of their wealth and power.

Finally, the community chose Abu Bakr as their leader, or caliph—a choice that proved to be providential and that played a decisive role in keeping the new faith and the new political community alive. Abu Bakr was an early convert as well as a respected and influential member of the Quraysh community. He was also an old man and thus not likely to rule for long. In fact, he died after serving as the community's caliph for only two years and was succeeded by Umar, another early convert, who ruled from 634 to 644. Umar was succeeded in turn by Uthman, also a member of the Quraysh tribe, who ruled from 644 to 656, and by Ali, a cousin of the Prophet and husband of one of his daughters. Ali ruled from 656 to 661.

These four successors to Muhammad have come down in Muslim history as men of strong religious beliefs and preservers of his legacy. They are known to Sunni Muslims as "the rightly guided caliphs," and deservedly so, because they did, indeed, hold the still inchoate *umma* of Muhammad together. But they did so amidst much turmoil. Their rivalries left powerful and enduring divisions within Islam. The three caliphs who succeeded Abu Bakr met their death at the hands of assassins, so that by the time of Ali's assassination in 661, one of Islam's most bitter divisions had already begun to take shape. While Ali accepted the legitimacy of his predecessors, he chafed under the rule of Uthman, who seemed to him to lean too much toward the secularizing and aggrandizing segment of the Quraysh clan. Moreover, Ali, as cousin of the Prophet and husband of Fatima, one of the Prophet's daughters, believed that succession to the caliphate of Islam should pass through him and his heirs. Hence when he was killed and power passed to Muawiya, the provincial governor of Syria, a member of the Quraysh tribe, and one of the deceased Caliph Uthman's protégés, the followers of Ali were deeply and permanently alienated. In time, some of the early supporters of Ali's claim to the caliphate created a separatist movement within Islam known as Shiism. (See chapter 7 for an extended discussion of Shiism.)

Even before Muhammad's death, the Prophet contemplated expanding the faith beyond the Arabian Peninsula into territories that were then under Sasanian and Byzantine rule in Iraq and Syria. The Arabs of Arabia had many contacts with migrant Arabs living in these locations, so that military forays beyond Arabia seemed a logical extension of the Prophet's mission. Muhammad's immediate successors implemented these plans; by the time of the caliphate of

Uthman, Arab forces, using their skill in camel warfare and their religious and economic passion for conquest, had defeated Byzantine and Sasanian forces.

THE CONQUEST OF EGYPT

The year 636 was an altogether decisive one for these Muslim warriors. During the course of it, they defeated the Sasanians at the battle of Qadisiyya and the Byzantines at the Yarmuk River in Palestine. These two military successes opened up the prospect of pushing further east into Iraq and eventually into the Iranian Plateau and moving westward into Egypt and later into North Africa.

The military commander who cast his eye on Egypt was Amr ibn al-As, who sought the authorization of the caliph before undertaking such a bold and meaningful expansion into a land that was still one of the most valuable territories within the Byzantine Empire. At the time of the Arab conquest of Egypt the population of the country had declined to about three million. Greek and Coptic were the two major languages of the country, which was garrisoned by no fewer than 30,000 Byzantine soldiers as compared with Amr's army, which at the outset was little more than 3,000 strong. During the conquest it grew to 10,000 men. Amr had knowledge of Egypt, having traveled in the country as a merchant. He also was confident that his conquest would succeed. He noted that "no country in the world [was] so wealthy and so defenseless." He realized that the Byzantine forces were not the top regiments of the emperor's forces, and the emperor, in addition, was well aware of the increasing discontent against Byzantine rule in Egypt and the difficulties that the empire was likely to encounter if it threw all of its resources into defending this territory. Accordingly, he withdrew his crack forces to more defensible frontiers in northern Syria, and while he did not concede Egypt to Muslim adversaries, he did not assemble a powerful force to resist their intervention.

Amr's defeat of the Byzantine forces was rapid. He took the old Byzantine administrative capital, Babylon, in 640 and Alexandria in 641. By November 641 the Byzantine commander signed a treaty with the Muslim forces conceding control over Egypt. Bringing the whole of Egypt under his authority took longer. Amr did not establish control over Middle and Upper Egypt for another six years and did not negotiate an agreement with the Nubians on Egypt's southern border until 651.

Amr's stunningly swift conquest was the result of factors that accounted for Muslim military successes elsewhere. Religious zeal and eagerness to acquire booty from conquered territories accounted for much of the success of the Muslim forces against larger but less well disciplined armies. In addition, particularly in Egypt, the Byzantine Empire received little support from the local population, which had chafed under an increasingly heavy burden of taxation and marginalization because of Egypt's monophysite religious beliefs.

Amr had ambitious plans for the conquered territory. First, he endeavored to strengthen the commercial connection of Egypt with the Hijaz, promising to establish a safe and secure caravan route between Egypt and the Arabian Peninsula. In a letter to Caliph Umar he boasted: "I will send to Medina a camel train so long that the first camel will reach you before the last one has left me." By the time he left Egypt in 644 no fewer than 10,000 Arab Muslim soldiers garrisoned the country.

Amr also had to make a crucial political decision: where to site his political capital. Alexandria beckoned. The pearl of the eastern Mediterranean, it was Egypt's most populous and sophisticated city. Its splendors astonished the desert-loving tribesmen. In a letter to the caliph in Mecca Amr wrote that he had "captured a city from the description of which I shall refrain. Suffice it to say that I have seized therein a city of 4,000 villas with 4,000 baths, 40,000 poll tax paying Jews and 400 places of entertainment for royalty." A few of Amr's men took over luxury houses in Alexandria, but Caliph Umar called them back to their primary duties, carrying the banner of Islam further west. He reminded Amr and his men that they were warriors, whose task it was to expand the domain of Islam. They must spurn citified life, and they should locate Egypt's capital so that it looked eastward toward the Arabian Peninsula rather than northward to the Mediterranean. Caliph Umar wrote that he wanted no water between himself and his soldiers in Egypt. He demanded that when "I travel to you from Medina, my horse must take me to the place where I join you." Accordingly, he instructed Amr to build his capital where the old Roman fortress of Babylon had existed.

Fustat, as the new city was called, arose with extraordinary rapidity west of present-day Cairo. Within a century of the original conquest it had attained a population of 200,000. Nor did Amr neglect his religious duties. Almost his first act at Fustat was the construction of a mosque, subsequently named after him. Amr's mosque was originally built along the bank of the Nile, but as the Nile moved westward in later centuries, the mosque moved inland.

Over the years, the mosque has been added to and refurbished so that virtually nothing remains of the original construction except for its placement. Yet we know from chronicler accounts that in its early days, it was a large and open-aired structure. The original mosque was a roofless building, with a large courtyard, to which was later added imposing minarets at each of its four corners. It could accommodate 700 worshippers, not the estimated 12,000 men who made up the army stationed at Fustat. Mainly, it served the political and military elite under Amr and his successors. Later, in 673, it was enlarged to provide a place of worship for more of the Muslim inhabitants of the city. Although it is not as frequently visited as some of the more famous mosques in Cairo, such as the ibn Tulun mosque and al-Azhar mosque, it still retains a striking beauty that projects the innocence and simplicity of Islam in its earliest days.

The Arab forces that settled just outside the old Byzantine city of Babylon occupied an area that came to be known as Fustat and that constituted the beginning phase in the evolution of the city of Cairo. Fustat, also known as Misr, which also represented the Arabic name for Egypt, began its existence in 642. It stood on the east bank of the Nile, just south of the area where the Nile divided and spread out into the delta. By claiming Fustat as their political capital, the Arab conquerors were returning the center of Egyptian life to the interior of the country, to the dividing point between Upper and Lower Egypt, much as it had been in ancient times, and away from

Alexandria and the Mediterranean, where it had been located under the Greeks and the Romans.

Yet it needs to be recalled that Fustat was purely an Arab Muslim garrison city, in the midst of a predominantly Christian population and dependent on this population for political stability. Just outside Fustat, in the old Christian city of Babylon, there were no fewer than ten churches, and many more churches and monasteries nearby. Gezira island had a church, and Giza, just beneath the pyramids, did as well, along with one of the two Jewish synagogues. One of the major transformations in Egyptian history—the Arabization and Islamicization of the population—had not yet taken place. Islamicization was a gradual and incomplete affair that was not accomplished until the Mamluk era in the fourteenth century. Even at this later date, Coptic Christians continued to represent a significant minority of the population, probably just less than 10 percent. Arabization made more rapid progress, no doubt aided by the migration to Egypt of large numbers of Arab-speaking tribesmen and women out of the Arabian Peninsula. Of far greater importance was a 706 edict by the governor of Egypt requiring all government decrees to be written in Arabic. As Arabic documents became widespread, the number appearing in Coptic and Greek diminished. The last Greek papyrus dates from 780.

SYRIA AND IRAQ AS THE CENTERS OF ARAB POWER

The Umayyad Dynasty

Amr, the chosen warrior of the caliphs Umar and Uthman, was a military commander who did the bidding of the Umayyad branch of the Quraysh. Thus, when the fourth caliph, Ali ibn al-Talib, died at the hands of an assassin, power passed to Muawiya, a leading Quraysh notable. The new caliph moved the capital of the Muslim empire from Medina to Damascus, in Syria. This move pleased the Arab conquerors of Egypt, who found themselves closer to the center of political authority. Nor were they displeased when one of the later Umayyad rulers, Caliph Abd al-Malik, began to issue Islamic coinage in place of the old Byzantine currency and when he built the Dome of the Rock in Jerusalem in 692 precisely on the location of the Temple Mount and at a place that towered over the site of the Christian Church of the Holy Sepulcher. This magnificent building, which has inspired observers over the centuries, openly proclaimed the message that Islam ruled supreme in a land once dominated by Jews and Christians. One of its mosaics carried the Arabic message that Muslims, unlike Christians, believed in a single God, not three Gods.

The Umayyad state, which ruled over the world of Islam until 750, was essentially an Arab political and religious entity. Because the Arab conquerors lacked experience in administering large, settled populations, they borrowed freely and openly from the Byzantine and Persian practices of their predecessors. Yet if an individual wished to exercise power and escape the heavy *jizya,* or head tax, on non-Muslims, he was expected to become a Muslim. The avenue to becoming Muslim at first was exceedingly limited and over time created deep resentments against Umayyad power. The only sure pathway to assimilation was to become a client of an Arab, a *mawla.* Only through winning the patron's favor, which naturally entailed learning the language, adopting Arab customs, and accepting Islam as one's faith, could an individual enter the Muslim fold. Naturally, the assimilation process was slow and opened the door only slightly to the vast non-Arab populations that were steadily being brought under Islamic authority and seeking conversion to Islam. As the gradual Arabization and Islamization of much of the Islamic world began to accelerate and produced large numbers of Muslims, many of whom were fluent in Arabic but who were still treated as second-class members of the empire, resentment and opposition increased.

Moreover, the non-Muslim populations also began to feel alienated from their Arab Muslim rulers. At first Jews and Christians had accepted their new rulers, who were more tolerant and less oppressive than their Byzantine and Sasanian predecessors. But as the Umayyad state refined the distinctions between Muslims and non-Muslims, these restrictions became increasingly onerous. Laws subordinating non-Muslims, enforced with more rigor by the later Umayyad caliphs, limited the construction of new churches and synagogues, required non-Muslims to wear special clothing, and imposed a special tax on these communities (whose members were known in the Islamic world as *dhimmis*), rather than the general land tax, or *kharaj*, that all who owned land had to pay.

The Abbasid Dynasty

Opposition finally came to a head in the middle of the eighth century and resulted in the overthrow of the Umayyads and the installation of a new regime. The new rulers, known as the Abbasids, came to power in 750 and moved the capital of the Islamic empire from Damascus to the newly founded and soon resplendent city of Baghdad, established at a location on the Tigris River and close to the old Mesopotamian centers of political authority. The move to Baghdad represented an eastward shift in power, away from the Arabian Peninsula, the Fertile Crescent, Egypt, and North Africa. It came about in part because the center of opposition to Umayyad authority was east, in the distant province of Khurasan, where Iranians dwelled in great numbers and resented their subordinate status. Although the Abbasid regime clearly represented a triumph for the elements within the Islamic empire that were not Arab, including the Berbers of North Africa as well as the Iranians and Turks, the rulers themselves remained Arabic-speakers, and the primary language of politics, culture, and religion continued to be Arabic. Still, Abbasid rule was a boon to Turks and Persians, who had been converting to Islam without renouncing their language and culture and continued to do so in increasing numbers.

The Abbasid era was one of dazzling successes. To Muslims, and indeed, to much of the Afro-Eurasian world, Baghdad became the center of the universe. Some Islamic maps located Baghdad as its center. One of the advocates for choosing Baghdad as the Abbasid capital described the area as "surrounded by palm trees and near water so that if one district suffers from drought or fails to yield its harvest in due season, there will be relief from another." Overnight, the city became a thriving locus for administration and commerce. Products flowed to it from across the Afro-Eurasian landmass. From China came silk, paper, and porcelain. Indian traders arrived with pepper, and East Africans supplied ivory, gold, and slaves. Known to some of its inhabitants as "the navel of the earth," Baghdad attracted peoples "from all countries far and near, and people from every side have preferred Baghdad to their own homelands." To its residents, Iraq was "the most elegant country," from which goods "can be procured so readily and so certainly that it is as if all the good things of the world were sent there, all the treasures of the earth assembled there, and all the blessings of creation reflected there."

It should not be surprising, then, that during the Abbasid period many of the fundamentals of the Muslim faith and the Muslim institutional framework crystallized. Muslims scholars, known as ulama, scoured the Arab Muslim heartland for as much information as they could collect on the life of Muhammad and his early companions. It was in the eighth century that the first biographies of the Prophet appeared, and it was during the eighth and ninth centuries that scholars traveled far and wide in search of additional information on Muhammad's activities. The most revered collector of the sayings attributed to Muhammad, known as *hadith*, was a scholar known as Bukhari, whose compilation was the fount of Muslim religion, law, and politics. One of the reasons that Bukhari and others had sought out additional information about the early days of the faith was that the Quran addressed only a limited number of issues. Yet the empire required a panoply of laws and institutions and sought to provide religious authenticity to these practices. After all, Muhammad had been the seal of the prophets, God's last messenger to mankind, and hence his words and actions, including those that were not contained in the Quran, were deemed essential guidelines for the daily lives of all Muslims.

It was also in the eighth and ninth centuries that various Muslim schools of jurisprudence evolved. The key locations for the elaboration of Islamic law, known as the *sharia*, were central Iraq, especially Baghdad, and the Arabian Peninsula. Eventually, four great schools of Islamic jurisprudence emerged. They are the Shafii, Maliki, Hanbali, and Hanafi schools. Here Egypt had influence. The juridical scholar that many have regarded as the master of Islamic legal reasoning and the most erudite of the Islamic scholars of jurisprudence was Muhammad ibn Idris al-Shafii (767–820). It was he who laid out the methods by which laws were to be considered binding on the community of believers. While al-Shafii was born in Gaza and migrated to Mecca at a young age, where he served in the Abbasid bureaucracy, he lived the latter years of his life in Egypt. He was buried there, and his tomb still exists there. The jurist's cenotaph is well worth a visit. An exemplary piece of Ayyubid woodwork, it was crafted from teak imported from Syria and is one of the largest mausoleums in the Muslim world, soaring to a height of twenty-nine meters in a domed cube. Nearly all of al-Shafii's scholarly works that have survived were written while he lived in Egypt.

Al-Shafii believed that God would not leave humankind without a sure guide to action and belief. That sure guide was to be found in the life, teachings, and actions of the Prophet Muhammad. In essence, al-Shafii argued that the Quran and the hadith provided a full guide to all of the questions that confronted human beings in their daily lives. If, on occasion, individuals, even highly trained Muslim scholars, were unable to find the right guidance in the Quran and the hadith literature and had to employ legal reasoning, this was only because they had failed to understand these two fundaments of Islamic life and law as fully as they might have. No Muslim, of course, doubted the primacy of the Quran. Al-Shafii, with his emphasis on hadiths, elevated this legal source to a higher level than it had achieved prior to his influence. Henceforth, it became important for Muslim scholars to examine the sayings and actions of the Prophet in order to ensure that they were authentic, a requirement that entailed verifying the sayings attributed to him through an accurate and incontrovertible chain of authorities, known as an *isnad*. Al-Shafii and the leaders of the other major schools of Muslim jurisprudence considered such a legal system fully sufficient for individual actions and institutional behavior.

The Abbasid era was one of the most resplendent moments in Islamic history. The era is sometimes best known to modern outsiders through the *One Thousand and One Nights*, in which tales of magic, splendor, wealthy merchants, dangerous seafaring voyages, and beautiful women were narrated to the Muslim caliph to amuse and impress. Many tales were set in Baghdad under the caliph Harun al-Rashid, who ruled from 789 to 809 and whose rule has often been considered the apogee of Islamic sophistication.

Although al-Rashid's rule may well have represented the zenith of Abbasid splendor, one of his immediate predecessors, the caliph al-Mutasim (833–42), made political decisions that had even more profound effects on Islamic history. Not only was it in this period that the Sunni-Shiite differences hardened, but, perhaps in response to the threats represented by Shiism, the caliph expanded his armed forces and increasingly placed the military might of the Abbasid state in the hands of foreign-born military men. At first, these foreign-recruited soldiers numbered only 3,000 to 4,000, though their high level of military training and their unquestioned loyalty to the caliphs made them an elite military corps, a true palace guard. In time, their numbers expanded, but their integration into Baghdadi Arab society and into the cultural and social networks of the empire was never more than minimal. The vast majority of these highly specialized recruits were Turks, drawn from the peripheries of the empire. The result was that militarily, and also increasingly politically, the Islamic state came to be dominated by foreign-born minority elements. In such a fashion and for the first time, a military cadre, recruited from outside the frontiers, arose within Islam, set off from the rest of society. The distinction between civilians and the military, which had not been a feature of the early Islamic state, when the expanding Muslim-Arab forces were virtual citizen armies, now became a marked characteristic of the Muslim polity.

Many empires that expand rapidly decline because of overextension. This was the case in the Roman and Han empires. It eventually became a factor in the fragmentation of the great Abbasid Empire.

Maintaining control over distant parts of the empire, notably communicating rapidly over long distances, limitations of military resources, and problems of assimilating diverse linguistic and ethnic groups affected the Abbasid state as deeply as they did the Roman and the Han. The distance from the western end of the Abbasid state in Spain to its eastern outposts in central Asia and northern India was 6,000 miles, a true impediment to effective control from Baghdad. No matter how hard the Abbasid caliphs tried to control Persians, Turks, Berbers, and other groups and no matter how loyal and large their military forces became, they could not keep regional elements from asserting their autonomy.

The Tulunid Regime in Egypt

Autonomous challenges to Abbasid authority began from the very beginnings of Abbasid rule. One of the defeated Umayyads made his way to Spain in 750 and established an independent regime there, which by the tenth century had become a beacon of prosperity and stability. Not long after the Umayyad state of Spain appeared, Egypt and North Africa began to pull away from Baghdad. In the early ninth century, the Aghlabid dynasty asserted its autonomy from the Abbasids in parts of North Africa. Egypt's first autonomous regime did not come into being until the ninth century, however, when Ahmad ibn Tulun arrived in the country. He inaugurated what became known as the Tulunid dynasty (868–905). Ahmad ibn Tulun was sent to be governor of Egypt as agent of the Abbasid caliph, bringing with him the political and military qualities that he and other members of his family had witnessed in the political court of Samarra in Iraq where he had served. Soon he and his successors were asserting their independence from Baghdad, refusing to send the requisite tax payments to the caliph and issuing decrees in their own name. Tulunid rule lasted only until 905, when the Abbasids reasserted control over Egypt—a control that was to prove short-lived, however. A half century later Egypt fell victim to the power of another outsider regime, this one featuring the Shiite Fatimid rulers who were based in North Africa. They conquered the country in 969.

Although Tulunid rule lasted a mere thirty-seven years, the regime left a magnificent gift to future generations. The mosque of ibn Tulun is one of Cairo's most elegant, yet simple mosques, manifesting, as Amr ibn al-As's mosque did, the ardor and religious certainty of these Samarran rulers. The mosque itself, with its graceful open courtyard surrounded by four arcaded halls, was made of brick except for its single stone minaret. The work, begun in 876 and completed in three years, was built in response to citizens' complaints that the old mosque of Amr ibn al-As was too small to accommodate all of those who wanted to worship. The new structure quickly came to constitute the center of the Tulunid capital, a location that was north of Amr's capital at Fustat, called Qatai. Although Qatai was soon to be superseded by the splendid capital at al-Qahira that began to take shape soon after the Fatimid conquest of Egypt in 969, this urban area was a site of beauty and spaciousness. The city came into being because Ahmad ibn Tulun found the old city of Fustat too small for his purposes. Qatai had a number of impressive constructions, including a palace, a hospital, and an aqueduct, which remains. Still, its most important building was the mosque itself, as ibn Tulun intended. Today it is the oldest remaining mosque in Cairo, the vast interior of which covers six and a half acres and brings an immense feeling of repose to visitors and worshippers. At the time of its building, it was claimed to be able to accommodate all of the inhabitants of the city of Qatai for the Friday prayers. (See plate 20 for an illustration of the mosque of Ahmad ibn Tulun.)

THE PLACE OF EGYPT WITHIN THE GREAT ISLAMIC EMPIRES

As we have observed, Christian Egyptians had distanced themselves from their pharaonic ancestors. To Jews and Christians, ancient Egypt was a desolate site of idolatry, nature worship, and priestly and regal oppression. Arab Muslim conquerors held much the same view of the ancient Egyptians, whom they, too, saw as infidels whose monuments they believed had been erected to false gods. Yet because the Christians had swept aside so many of the religious beliefs of the ancients, Muslim scholars were less inhibited from studying and even valuing some of the achievements of the ancient Egyptians. Egypt had a special interest to erudite Muslims, who, like the Greeks and Romans before them, regarded the territory as one of the cradles of civilization and hence worthy of close attention.

The Christian era had marked a rupture with Egypt's glorious ancient past, even more severe than had occurred during the Greek and Roman periods. This rupture was especially pronounced in the field of religion. During Greek and Roman times, many of the old Egyptians gods continued to have devotees and even a priesthood. The cult surrounding the goddess Isis lasted for centuries. But Christianity regarded such beliefs as blasphemous, and though in subtle ways ancient religious beliefs and practices were assimilated to Christianity, the Christian clergy would not tolerate practices and priestly classes that were openly associated with these ancient deities. In truth, the Christians were so successful either in stamping out or assimilating what they regarded as pagan practices that their Muslim successors were left with a religious landscape relatively free of early pre-Christian and pre-Muslim practices.

It was in the eleventh century, long after the Umayyads and Abbasids had ceased to rule over the country, that the Egyptian fascination with the ancient civilization became a passionate undertaking among some members of the scholarly classes. Only then did geographers and chroniclers, who wrote so prolifically and so perceptibly about the world that they inhabited, begin to devote much attention to the pyramids, temples, and other monuments that would have been common sights to all of the people living in the Nile valley. First they had to overcome the strongly negative images in the Quran of the pharaohs and the scholars' own belief that Egypt was a godless and defiantly pagan culture. During the early centuries of Muslim rule, Egypt's antiquities were seen as cautionary tales of the ruination that God brought to peoples who ignored his message and refused to heed the message of his prophets. The Arab poet al-Mutannabi (915–65) thought that the ruined pyramids showed the folly of human efforts unguided by God's teachings. He wrote: "Where is he among whose structures the pyramids belong? . . .

These monuments have survived their inhabitants, though only for a while. For when annihilation seizes them, they too will surely follow." Even as late as the thirteenth century, Jamal al-Din al-Idrisi (d. 1251) held to this view, claiming that the monuments of Egypt, in an obvious state of disrepair, "called on believers to consider the fate of those who did not accept God's message."

Yet by the twelfth century, the Iraqi scholar and traveler Abd al-Latif al-Baghdadi (d. 1231) visited Egypt and left one of the fullest and most flattering accounts from the medieval period about the monuments that the ancients had left behind. Nowhere in his accounts is there any disparagement of the ancients, but rather great respect for their numerous achievements. In particular, al-Baghdadi marveled at the engineering genius that lay behind the construction of the great pyramids at Giza. About them he wrote: "If you reflected upon them, you find the most noble intellects were put into them and the highest minds were behind them. . . . The pyramids are almost capable of talking of their peoples and telling their status and speak of their science and intellects and expose their biographies and chronicles."

The eleventh- and twelfth-century Arabic Egyptian texts that revel in Egypt's marvelous ancient culture have caused many later scholars to claim that Egyptians must surely have had a sense of the land's singular identity within the Islamic world. But, in fact, this interest in the ancient Egyptians did not gain momentum until the twelfth and thirteenth centuries and appears largely to have been confined to the literati, so there is little reason to believe that Egypt was accorded any significant degree of primacy within the Umayyad and Abbasid empires because of its ancient splendors. More importantly, it was in Iraq and the Arabian Peninsula that much of the intellectual vitality of early Islam showed itself. Here most of Islam's great jurists laid out the fundamentals of the sharia, an important exception being imam al-Shafii, and, as we have seen, it was in the Iranian plateau that Persian and, later, Turkish elements began to make their mark on Islam.

The notable exception to the subordinate place of Egypt within the large Islamic empires of the first three centuries was the land's preeminence in craftsmanship and industrial production. Egyptian artisans had enjoyed fame and popularity during the pharaonic, Greek, and Roman eras for the elegant textiles that they wove. Many of these textiles had messages written on them or interwoven into the fabric. Some merely contained the name of the ruler, written in black ink. Other incorporated longer messages that spoke of religious beliefs or funerary injunctions. Still others were of a quite mundane nature, containing laundry or shopping lists. Drawing upon pharaonic, Greek, Roman, and Coptic practices, the artisans of Egypt in the first several decades of Islamic rule continued to spin and weave the finest textiles known to the world. Although silk was supposed to be forbidden to devout Muslims, few of the wealthy could resist purchasing and displaying the gorgeous silk brocades that Egyptian craftsmen interwove with gold lace. Drawing on these earlier techniques, Muslim artisans produced woolen, linen, and cotton fabrics that were prized throughout the Islamic lands. The second caliph, Umar, ordered the embroidered silk covering of the Kaaba from Egypt. Most of the finest fabrics from Egypt were produced in small highly specialized workshops, in which spinning, weaving, dying, and embroidering were undertaken in separate work units. Patrons ordered individual pieces from the best of these specialist artisans.

Yet it was not until the Fatimids overran Egypt in 969 and created a new capital city, al-Qahira, with magnificent mosques and learning centers, that Egypt's role in the Muslim world began to rival that which it had enjoyed within North Africa and Southwest Asia in earlier times.

WOMEN AND ISLAM

One of the most important changes to occur in Egypt with the arrival of Islam involved the status and place of women in society. In pharaonic times women were considered subordinate to men. Few of them became literate and even fewer rose into positions of power, although a few queens did exercise the power of pharaohs. The place of women in Egyptian society changed little under the

Greeks, Romans, and the Christians, but the Arabization and Islamization of the country wrought decisive transformations. These changes had their beginnings in the Arabian Peninsula at the time of Muhammad and represented the Prophet's efforts to determine the place of women in the new Islamic *umma*. In pre-Islamic Arabia women had exercised many rights and powers. Men married into women's families and moved into their wives' locations. Women could ask for a man's hand in marriage. In addition, as the career of Muhammad's first wife, Khadijah, made clear, women could engage in business activities. Khadijah was a merchant and a person of considerable standing in her community. Women could also divorce their husbands.

Muhammad altered many of these arrangements as he began to define relations between men and women. Here the main influences came not from Egypt, Greece, and the Roman-Byzantine world, but rather from ancient practices that had held sway in Mesopotamia for centuries. Particularly during the Babylonian period, the women of the well-off and powerful classes were veiled and did not interact with men outside the household. In large part, this requirement was designed to separate respectable women from less respectable ones, especially from prostitutes, who were forbidden to wear the veil and who were whipped and dealt with in other harsh ways if they were caught wearing the clothes and acting the part of a noble woman. In addition, the women of the well-to-do had special quarters in the home set aside for them; these were out of bounds to all men except for husbands and sons.

As Muhammad elaborated the new social and religious principles of Islam, he brought his Muslim world into greater conformity with that of Southwest Asia. Before Khadijah's death, he took no other wife, but after her death he married a number of women. They wore the veil and remained in the home unless they had obligations outside. He permitted men to take up to four wives, though he enjoined men who took more than a single wife to treat each of these wives equally. If a man thought that he could not do so, he was not to marry a second wife. The Prophet also made divorcing a woman easy, stipulating that a man had only to say three times that he was divorcing a woman for that desire to become a reality. Women, however, were not permitted to divorce their husbands. Men could take as many concubines as they wanted. Muhammad's favorite wife after Khadijah's death was a young woman, Aisha, whom he married when she was only nine or ten years old and on whom he enforced strict veiling obligations. Now, it is true that Muhammad's injunctions on marriage and the social status marked in certain crucial areas an improvement on what had been common in pre-Islamic Arabia. Before the communities accepted the new religion of the Prophet, wealthy and powerful men had taken many wives. He also had dowries paid directly to the bride rather than the bride's guardians, and women now could inherit property, though of a lesser proportion than men. Still, the application of Islam's gender principles to countries like Egypt brought the Mesopotamian system of patriarchy and the diminishment of women's autonomy to many territories where other systems had prevailed and where women had enjoyed more freedom than they now did under Islam.

Fatimids, Ayyubids, and Mamluks, 969–1517

Muizz Street is a narrow lane that connects the walls and gate of Bab al-Zuwayla in present-day Cairo to the walls and gate of Bab al-Futuh to the north. It is also a stirring reminder of medieval Cairo. Not only is the street named after the first Fatimid caliph to rule over Egypt, but a sojourner walking this short distance traverses the length of the royal city that the Fatimids built as their new political and religious capital after their conquest of Egypt in 969. Walkers should pause for a moment at the recently restored and magnificent gate at Bab al-Zuwayla, a massive portal that closed the royal city off at night and offered residents protection from raiders. Also take a moment and climb up on the walls, even ascend one of the minarets of the mosque of sultan al-Muayyad, a Mamluk ruler. The view of Cairo from this vantage point is breathtaking. Minarets, domes, and burial constructions, all from different Islamic periods, serve as testimonials to the depth of religion in the life of the country.

Few structures from the Fatimid era remain. The royal palaces no longer exist, and the great mosque of al-Azhar is much different from the less ornate and smaller one that the Fatimids built. Many of the most striking buildings along the street date from Mamluk and Ottoman times, but the narrow lane with its two- and three-story domiciles, whose balconies jut precariously out over the street below, blocking the sun's rays, are unmistakably medieval. Today, the crowds of businesspersons, hawkers, and shopkeepers who ply the lane are dressed differently from their medieval counterparts, although those wearing galabiyas provide reminders of the dress of a millennium ago. The noises, animals, and carts that intermingle with a teeming human population are additional echoes of an earlier period.

In 969, the brilliant Fatimid general Jawhar engineered the conquest of Egypt from his center of power in North Africa. Almost at once, he set about the task of constructing a royal city, northeast of the old center of power at Fustat. His royal city took the name of al-Qahira, the Victorious. It would be known in the English-speaking world as Cairo. Jawhar required only four years before he felt that the new city was ready to receive the supreme Fatimid religious and political leader, the ambitious and imperializing imam-caliph al-Muizz (r. 953–75), who arrived regally in Cairo in 973, prepared to make this new location the center of Fatimid power. From here, he intended to bring the entire Muslim world under Shia political authority.

Egypt had not been Islam's vital center during the Umayyad and Abbasid empires, although it was clearly an important and wealthy province. During the Umayyad and Abbasid eras, Egyptians continued to distance themselves from their pharaonic, Greek, and Roman pasts, viewing the ancients with a jaundiced eye. At the same time the population inhabiting the Nile valley had been compelled to cede intellectual, political, and religious preeminence to Syria, Iraq, Iran, and even Central Asia. All this was to change when the Fatimids entered Egypt in 969. Dispatched to Egypt with a 100,000-man army and commanded by the Fatimid caliph al-Muizz to found a city from which he and his successors could rule the world, the military commander, Jawhar, took control of Egypt on behalf of an independent, powerful, and dynamic new dynasty that remained in power until 1171. Jawhar encountered little resistance from the rulers of Egypt, no doubt intimidated by the massive size of the Fatimid army and its advanced weaponry but also calmed when Jawhar promised to allow Sunni Muslims, Christians, and Jews to adhere to their religious beliefs and practices. Although the Egyptian people continued to be ruled by foreign governors under the Fatimids and their many successors (Ayyubids, Mamluks, and Ottomans), Egypt became as vibrant an economic, political, and cultural territory as it had been under the pharaohs. Particularly during the Fatimid era, Egypt's wealth overshadowed that of other Muslim regions, and its high culture was the envy of Muslims and knowledgeable Europeans.

The rise of the Fatimids is a complex and often confusing story, shrouded in arguments and polemics involving Shiite and Sunni claims to supremacy within Islam. Yet it is important to unravel this narrative, given the fact that for two glorious centuries Egypt was ruled by a powerful and shimmering Shiite dynasty. It is also the case that Shiism has come to play an increasingly influential role in Muslim affairs and global politics in the late twentieth- and early twentieth-first centuries.

The narrative of Shiism begins with the birth of Islam itself. The movement began innocently as a political argument over the succession to the Prophet Muhammad but quickly spiraled into disputes over complex theological matters, religious law, hadiths, and the political authority of religious leaders, known as imams in the Shiite sect. These differences persist to the present. The majority of Muslims, who came to be called Sunnis, accepted the order that unfolded historically during these early centuries. They believed that the four first caliphs, or successors to Muhammad, were legitimate rulers, and they also accepted the subsequent regimes, first the Umayyads and after them the Abbasids. A minority, eventually called Shiites, objected. They held that Ali, the Prophet's cousin, husband of the Prophet's daughter, Fatima, and an early convert, should have succeeded Muhammad. Many even affirmed that Muhammad had designated Ali as his successor. One tradition claimed that Muhammad had said to his followers: "He whose master I am has also Ali for his master." Although the earliest supporters of Ali's legitimacy were the *ansar*, that is Muhammad's followers from Medina, who resented the primacy that the old Meccan elite assumed at the beginning of the Islamic state, soon other groups rallied to the cause of Ali. These included peoples who felt themselves distant from the seats of power, notably the peoples of lower Iraq, who resented the domination of Syria under the Umayyads, and of middle Iraq under the Abbasids, and the Berber tribesmen of North Africa, who complained that Arab invaders had deprived them of their independence.

Other opposition elements existed in Islam, but none proved as enduring as the Shiite movement. At first a group known as the Kharijites, who believed that Muhammad's successor should be Islam's most pious individual, gained a large following. Similarly, many groups supported the claims of Ali and his heirs. The first Abbasid caliph, Abu al-Abbas al-Saffah, claimed descent from Ali. But when the Abbasids severed their ties with other opposition groups, particularly with those who held that the proper heirs to the Muslim caliphate were only those individuals who traced their descent through Ali and his wife Fatima, the chief source of opposition to Abbasid authority found its focus among the supporters of a descent line from Ali and Fatima. At first these elements were referred to as the *shiat* Ali or the party of Ali, soon simply as Shia.

The early history of these Shiite movements contains much tragedy and suffering and created powerful symbolism for martyred opposition. Both of Ali's sons by Fatima, al-Hasan and al-Husayn, put forward claims to the caliphate. Al-Hasan abdicated and his claims fell to his brother, who, however, was killed along with a small coterie of followers, numbering a mere seventy-two, at the battle of Karbala in 680. Although surrounded by a 4,000-man Umayyad army, al-Husayn and his followers chose death rather than submission and thereby left a memorial and a symbol for their Shiite followers.

Shiism continued to attract pockets of opposition in regions within the Abbasid Empire, especially locations that were difficult to control and groups that felt themselves outside the hallways of power. Yet it was not until a pious and learned man with claims to the legacy of Ali and Fatima, Jafar ibn al-Sadiq (d. 765), appeared on the scene that Shiism acquired an energizing religious and political ideology. Jafar was a man of scholarly inclinations who lived a quiet life in Medina and was thought by the main Shiite groups to be the sixth imam, or spiritual and political ruler, after Ali. It was only after his death, however, that the Shiite movement split into its two main groups, the Ismailis, sometimes referred to as the seveners, who went on to become the Fatimids of North Africa and Egypt, and the proto-twelvers, who became strong in Iran and eventually founded the Safavid dynasty at the beginning of the sixteenth century. This vital split within Shiism occurred over Jafar's successors. The Ismailis believed that Jafar had designated his son, Ismail ibn Jafar, as his successor and that Ismail, whom most people believed died before his father, had in turn designated his son, Muhammad ibn Ismail, as his successor. This group, taking its name from the imam Ismail, then believed that Muhammad, the seventh imam, had gone into hiding and would return as the Mahdi, the redeemer, at the end of the world. In contrast, the twelvers believed that the line of succession from Jafar was different. They traced descent through a different set of imams to a twelfth imam, who, like Muhammad ibn Ismail, had gone into hiding and would also return at the end of the world as the Mahdi.

Although little is known about the life of Jafar, he was influential in crystallizing many of the tenets that lay at the heart of Shiism. In particular, he stressed the idea of the imamate, for he held that Islam required a specially designated spiritual guide—an imam—to provide both religious and political guidance to the faithful. He also believed that the imams were descendants of Ali and Fatima. This belief was nothing short of treasonous to the Abbasid caliphs and their scholarly supporters, since it denied the legitimacy of the Abbasid caliphate and challenged the role that scholars or learned individuals, known as ulama, played in the Sunni world.

Later, following the death of Jafar, Ismaili scholars put forward two other fundamental Shiite principles that further differentiated them from the Sunni Muslim community. The first was that there were two realms of religious truth: an external realm, known as *zahir*, which contained religious prescriptions and laws, including the sharia, and an internal realm, known as *batin*, which contained the deep and internal truths of all higher religions. Since this interior realm of religious truth was known only to the most learned initiates of the Shiite faith, namely the imams and their closest associates, the rulings of imams on Muslim actions and beliefs in religious as well as secular matters were altogether decisive, far more so than the guidance given by Sunni clerics. This deep religious knowledge contained the essence of all of the major monotheistic religions, Judaism and Christianity as well as Islam, and hence made Shiism at its core an all-embracing religion. Yet because these principles were so contrary to the Sunni branch of the faith, and indeed were a dagger pointed at the heart of Sunni Islam, the Ismailis preached the need to practice their second belief—dissimulation, or what they called *taqiyya*. When in contact with the powerful Sunni world of Islam, they encouraged their followers to conceal their true beliefs. Only after the Shiite form of Islam had triumphed, perhaps not until the return of the Mahdi, were Shiites openly to express all of their interior religious beliefs and fully practice their religious ideals.

The death of Jafar left the Shiite movement in limbo, its different factions arguing over succession questions. In the next century (the ninth), however, Ismailism enjoyed a strong revival, preparing the way for the triumph of the Fatimid state at the beginning of the tenth century. The principal reason for the resurgence was the influence of Ismaili missionaries, fanning out across the whole of the Abbasid Empire and disseminating their religious message and their belief in the eventual triumph of an Ismaili political order. They called on their devotees to acknowledge the imamate of Muhammad ibn Ismail and to affirm that his return as the Mahdi, the expected one, was imminent. One of the centers for the dispersion of Ismaili doctrines was Khuzistan, in the southwestern corner of Iran, where a prosperous merchant by the name of Ubayd Allah, whom Ismailis prefer to call Abd Allah, dispatched his followers to spread the word that the Mahdi, Muhammad ibn Ismail, would soon return. This was not a prophecy that the Abbasid rulers wished to countenance, and for his safety, Ubayd Allah fled Khuzistan, moved first to Basra in southern Iraq, and then on to Salamiya at the western edge of the Syrian desert. Constantly on the move, he succeeded in avoiding the reach of the Abbasid state. The ideas of these missionizing agents fell on fertile soil, for the ninth century was one of intense political and religious turmoil. In the east, a revolt of black African slaves, who had been imported into the salt marshlands of southern Iraq and worked under oppressive conditions, drew its inspiration from the same radical ideals that were circulating at the time. The leader of this revolt, which lasted for fifteen years, from 869 to 883, proclaimed himself to be the Mahdi, sent to restore the world to its rightful order. He, too, claimed to be a descendent of the family of Ali.

Even more threatening to the Abbasid state were revolts in the west, particularly in North Africa, where Berber populations had long been a source of opposition to a Sunni political order dominated by Arabs, Turks, and Persians. Ubayd Allah, finding Salamiya no longer safe, moved his base of operations to North Africa. Here he gained the support of an inspiring religious leader and an Ismaili missionary agent named Abu Abd Allah, who had taken up residence in the remote village of Sijilmasa in present-day southeastern Morocco. There Abd Allah announced that he was the precursor of the Mahdi. Although Abd Allah was charismatic and successful and seized political control over much of North Africa from the ruling Aghlabid dynasty, he nonetheless turned power over to Ubayd Allah, his Mahdi, in 909. At this moment, in 910, when Ubayd Allah al-Mahdi moved into the old Aghlabid capital city of Qayrawan, the Fatimid dynasty came into being. Not satisfied with a ruling city that had once been the center of Sunni power, Ubayd Allah moved his capital first to al-Mahdiyya on the Tunisian coast and soon thereafter to al-Mansuriya. Yet he and his successors had even larger plans, no less than the conquest of the entire Muslim world and its political subjugation, if not its religious acceptance, to their Shiite authority. But before this could happen, Ubayd Allah had to deal with his chief agent, Abd Allah, who soon became his most determined rival. He succeeded in defeating Abd Allah's forces and putting his once most devoted supporter to death.

By the time that Ubayd Allah had installed himself in power in North Africa, the tenets of Ismailism had taken on a more elaborate, yet unmistakably Shiite form. These ideas further emphasized the religious and political authority of imams and widened the gap between Sunni and Shiite views of the clerical classes. The Ismailis believed that God had sent a series of prophets to mankind to provide spiritual guidance and religious laws. In all, there had been six such prophets—Adam, Noah, Abraham, Moses, Jesus, and Muhammad. These were the men who gave the world its religious injunctions. But behind them and associated with them were six individuals, known as guarantors, who understood the inner meanings of the religious laws and the deep spiritual truths that connected all monotheistic religions. Adam's guarantor was his son Abel, while for Noah it was his son Seth. Abraham's spiritual guarantor was his son Isaac. Moses' guarantor was his brother Aaron, and for Jesus his most important disciple, Peter, was the guarantor. According to the Ismailis, Muhammad looked to Ali as his spiritual guarantor. Since Muhammad was the seal of the prophets, the last such messenger whom God sent, and Ali the last of the guarantors, the task of interpreting the inner truths of religions henceforth rested with the divinely inspired imams and their specially trained assistants.

The Fatimids' first three efforts to extend their power to Egypt failed, but by the 960s Egypt was already in decline. Its leaders, seeking political stability and economic prosperity, therefore reached out to Jawhar, the skilled military commander of the Fatimid forces, and negotiated a settlement with him. Jawhar was the handpicked agent of the ambitious Fatimid caliph, al-Muizz, the Fatimid "man of destiny."

The core of the Fatimid army that then made Egypt its base for extending its influence further east was composed of Kutama Berbers from North Africa, who had rallied to the Fatimid cause in the late ninth century. But successors to the first Fatimid caliph, Ubayd Allah, had enlarged their ranks in the tenth century by importing Turkish and sub-Saharan African military slaves, who proved much more effective in dealing with the bow-wielding Muslim and Byzantine soldiers that were their most determined opponents. By the time that al-Muizz's successor, al-Aziz (r. 975–96), was on the throne in Cairo, the Fatimid state, now at its territorial apex, encompassed all of North Africa from Morocco to Sicily, Egypt, Palestine, parts of Syria, and the Hijaz, where the Fatimids had assumed responsibility for the safety of the holy cities of Mecca and Medina and the annual pilgrimages to these cites. Moreover, the Fatimid caliphs used Egypt as a base of operations from which they dispatched a host of missionaries, who promoted Ismaili colonies in Persia, Sind (present-day Pakistan and northern India), and Yemen. The tenth century was indeed the century of Shiism, for not only did the Ismailis exercise widespread influence throughout all of the Islamic lands, but the Abbasid caliphate delegated many of its administrative responsibilities to the Shiite Buyid family.

Although the Fatimids were committed to their Shiite beliefs, they did not make a determined effort to convert the people of Egypt from their Sunni practices. Quite the contrary: except for a few episodes, the Fatimid rulers and their clerics pursued a policy of toleration toward the Sunnis as well as toward Copts and Jews, whose numbers, however, continued to dwindle during the two centuries of Fatimid rule. In their selection of officials, the ruling elite chose on the basis of merit rather than religious affiliation. The result was that many Sunnis, as well as an unusual number of Christians and Jews, manned some of the most important offices in the kingdom. As a consequence, when the Fatimids were ousted by the Sunni Ayyubids in 1171, Egypt returned to a Sunni way of life almost effortlessly.

Toleration of others' beliefs did not mean apathy toward the Shiite cause. On the contrary, the Fatimids were imperializers, committed to bringing the whole of the Islamic world under Shiite influence. They employed the wealth and influence of Egypt to dispatch missionaries to the far corners of Islam. More significantly, the dynasts surrounded themselves with a small circle of Shiite intellectuals who were committed to establishing a Shiite set of religious laws to rival the Sunni sharia. These men also collected sayings and traditions of the Prophet and his companions—the Shiite version of hadith—that would affirm the legitimacy of the Ismaili faith. In this cause, the family of al-Numan played the dominant role. Throughout much of the last half of the tenth and the first half of the eleventh centuries its members served as the chief *qadis* (religious judges) of the Fatimid dynasty in Cairo and elaborated a Shiite set of religious injunctions that Ismaili believers were expected to adhere to.

Egyptian Christian commentators living at the time of Fatimid rule called the reigns of the caliphs al-Muizz and al-Aziz a period of "great peace for the churches." The one exception to this statement occurred during the tumultuous reign of al-Hakim, who was the caliph from 996 to 1021. His erratic and often violent policies have suggested to some observers a good deal of mental instability. Be that as it may, although al-Hakim established a House of Knowledge (*Dar al-Ilm*), where both secular and religious subjects were taught and where scholars were paid salaries so that they could pursue their intellectual interests, he also turned against the Christian and Jewish communities in Egypt and other parts of the Fatimid empire. He had numerous Christian churches and monasteries and Jewish synagogues torn down, including the Church of the Holy Sepulchre in Jerusalem. He compelled non-Muslim subjects to wear special clothing, even at times, badges that separated them from the rest of the population. Copts were put under pressure to renounce their beliefs and to embrace Islam, although it was not until the Mamluk era in the fourteenth century that the Coptic population was reduced in size to less than 10 percent of the total. Al-Hakim's destruction of the Church of the Holy Sepulchre played a major role in awakening the Western Christian world's interest in the holy places and causing the papacy in Rome to think about calling for a crusade to reestablish Christian control over Palestine.

Not only were the Fatimids the founders of the city of Cairo, but their influence on the city is palpable to this day. Although there had been an urban conglomeration at the point where the Nile waters divided and descended into the delta for millennia, the Fatimids were the true founders and certainly the namers of the city known in English as Cairo, in French as Le Caire, and in Arabic as al-Qahira. Originally designed as a royal city, housing mainly the palaces of the caliphs, army barracks, and al-Azhar mosque, where the caliphs and their military and civil bureaucracy worshipped according to Ismaili practices, the extraordinary political and economic successes of the Fatimid regime quickly caused the city to expand far beyond its original plans as a military encampment and royal setting. Al-Azhar grew in size and reputation. It attracted students from all over the

Islamic world, serving as a virtual university where initiates could imbibe the learning of the Ismaili faith. (See figure 3 and plate 21 for illustrations of al-Azhar mosque.) The highly controversial caliph, al-Hakim, turned his considerable energies to beautifying and expanding Cairo. He sought nothing less than to make Cairo the equal of the great cities of Afro-Eurasia. And at this he clearly succeeded, building additional palaces, mosques, pavilions, fountains, gardens, and arsenals so that his city would outshine the other great cities that he had knowledge of. He took as Cairo's rivals the Abbasid capital at Baghdad, the supreme center of Eastern Christianity at Constantinople, and the cities of the Umayyad dynasty in Spain. An essential part of al-Hakim's effort to make Cairo a bastion of beauty and learning was his founding of a library, which was reputed to have 100,000 bound volumes, dealing with all manner of subjects, including 18,000 manuscripts on ancient civilizations. The reading rooms were open to all; visitors were supplied with paper, pen, and ink should they wish to transcribe any of the library's documents.

We know about the extraordinary prosperity that Egypt enjoyed during the Fatimid era because of the discovery of a cache of records, dating mainly from the eleventh through the thirteenth centuries, found in the *geniza*, or storage room, attached to the synagogue in Cairo. This remarkable collection of records that included the wills and the correspondence of merchants came to light in the 1890s and was then sold to foreign collectors. The largest body of these materials is to be found in the Cambridge University Library, where researchers have mined them for information on the economic, religious, and social life of Egypt during the late Fatimid and Ayyubid eras.

It was customary for Jewish religious officials to preserve all documents that bore the name of God. Over time many of these storage areas were destroyed or not maintained, but the geniza of the synagogue in Cairo, rebuilt at the beginning of the eleventh century following its destruction by the caliph al-Hakim, remained intact, though not in use, after the end of the thirteenth century. Hence, its existence was not known until researchers came upon its treasure trove of documents at the end of the nineteenth century.

Figure 3. Al-Azhar mosque

The geniza documents, most thoroughly analyzed in numerous articles and books by S. D. Goitein, reveal a world of brisk long-distance trade linking Egypt, North Africa, Europe, Southwest Asia, and the countries surrounding the Indian Ocean. Although many of the commercial records that loom so large in this archive are from Jewish merchants, who had far-flung mercantile networks throughout this extensive region, they also demonstrate that Jewish merchants worked closely and amicably with Christian and Muslim traders. Many of the original merchants who settled in Cairo and fostered Egypt's long-distance trading ties with the Indian Ocean countries and Europe were relatively recent immigrants from North Africa, especially from Qayrawan and al-Mahdiyya, political capitals of the Fatimid caliphs before the conquest of Cairo. These merchants apparently followed their Fatimid patrons to Egypt and used the political stability and economic protection that the rulers provided them and other merchants to expand their trading networks.

What the documents show is that Cairo was an important importer and exporter as well as an entrepôt in large-scale and long-distance trading networks. From Italy came timber and furniture because Egypt was devoid of wood. Italy also provided cheese, a vital protein supplement to the Egyptian diet. From North Africa came many different metals, especially gold, all of which the Egyptians paid for using the marvelous grain harvests that had fed Greeks and Romans since the beginning of the Common Era and that were still in abundance in Egypt. From the east, as far as the Malakas and India came spices and pepper, the trade in which a group of mainly Egyptian-based Muslim traders, known as the Karimi merchants, dominated in the late Fatimid period and during much of the Mamluk era. The agents of this brisk trade with the Orient as it funneled through Egypt, the Karimi merchants were also the main purveyors of spices sold to merchants from Venice, Genoa, Pisa, Marseilles, and Barcelona.

Yet Fatimid power did not endure. The eleventh century began to witness a decline. A succession crisis in 1094–95 contributed to the weakening of the dynasty. Two brothers, al-Mustali and Nizar, fought to succeed their father, al-Mustansir. Although al-Mustali won out and saw his line retain power in Egypt until 1171, when the Ayyubid political leader, Saladin, ended the Fatimid tenure of power there, Egypt found itself surrounded by many enemies, of whom the Saljuk Turks, the European Crusaders, and the Nizaris, who fled to the Caspian region and eventually established a vengeful state in Iran, were the most formidable.

SALADIN AND THE AYYUBIDS IN EGYPT (1171–1250)

Fatimid rule came to an end in 1171. The coup de grace was administered by Egypt's most famous medieval personage, Salah al-Din ibn Ayyub, known to history through his Europeanized name, Saladin. Though a Kurd, Saladin was a major figure in a Turkish and Sunni reconquest of the Islamic heartland. In particular, Turks had been infiltrating the Islamic heartland from the tenth century onward, moving first into Persia, where they adopted the Persian language and embraced Persian-Islamic culture. In the eleventh century Saljuk Turks entered Baghdad from eastern Persia and brought an end to Shiite influence at the caliph's court, persuading the Abbasid rulers to nominate them as their sultans. The two most powerful of these Saljuk sultans, Alp Arslan (r. 1063–72) and Malik Shah (r. 1072–92), were instrumental in extending Abbasid nominal rule from Iran all the way to Syria. Naturally, one of their goals, and a goal of the Abbasid caliphs as well, was to bring an end to heretical Shiite Fatimid authority in Egypt and reestablish Baghdad's power over this vital area.

By the twelfth century the Islamic heartland was in political turmoil. Various powerful and ambitious groups vied for supremacy, and Egypt was a strategic battleground for these competing groups, particularly since the Fatimids no longer possessed the power that they had displayed in the previous century. So weakened were the Fatimid caliphs that they turned with increasing frequency to powerful, non-Shiite viziers to control the domestic population and to hold at bay the growing power of external enemies.

A new competitor for power in Egypt and Syria raised the stakes even higher. At the Council of Clermont in 1095 Pope Urban II awakened European Christians to the Holy Lands, calling on believers to reconquer Palestine and arguing that Christians there were being oppressed and the holy sites in peril. No doubt the pope remembered the persecutions carried out by the Fatimid caliph, al-Hakim, in the early part of the century and his dismemberment of the Church of the Holy Sepulchre. In reality, Muslim-Christian relations had been repaired, and Christians no longer lived in danger of their lives or their livelihoods. Nonetheless, the pope's message struck a responsive chord. A crusade, led by some of the leading princes of Christian Europe, assembled the next year and entered Palestine in 1099, capturing the city of Jerusalem and establishing four relatively small Christian enclave kingdoms in Palestine and Syria. These were at Edessa, Antioch, Tripoli, and Jerusalem. Inevitably, since the Fatimids had always regarded Syria as a central part of their empire, the caliphs soon engaged their armies against the Crusaders.

At the same time that the Crusaders were making an appearance in the Islamic heartland, the Saljuk Turks were also extending their power into Syria and beyond. An important agent in this expansion was Nur al-Din, dispatched to Syria by the Abbasids as their military agent and political representative to advance Abbasid interests westward. Nur al-Din seized Syria in 1154, receiving a diplomacy of investiture from the Abbasid caliph that proclaimed him as ruler of Egypt along with Syria and urged him to act quickly to bring Egypt under Abbasid authority. Unfortunately, Nur al-Din was preoccupied with the Crusaders who controlled Jerusalem, one of Islam's (and Christendom's) holiest places. Hence Nur al-Din turned responsibility for advancing on Egypt to his trusted lieutenant, Saladin, who in 1168, as a reward for providing military assistance to the Fatimid ruler, was made vizier of the Fatimid state. When the Fatimid caliph al-Adid died in 1171, Saladin allowed no successor to take his place and announced that as the ruling figure in Egypt he would restore the country to the Abbasid Empire. Yet when his own commander, Nur al-Din, died three years later in 1174, Saladin seized the opportunity to proclaim his supremacy over Egypt and to embark on campaigns to bring the whole of Syria and Palestine under his rule. He did this, no doubt, driven forward by personal ambition as well as religious zeal, for Saladin saw himself as a man engaged in holy war or jihad in defense of Islam's heartland. Yet in spite of his ambitions and his many military and political successes, he never formally asserted his independence from the Abbasid caliphate in Baghdad.

Saladin's capabilities as a soldier and statesman have been closely debated and remain a subject of historical controversy. This is largely the result of the source material, which itself is sharply divided between those authorities who portrayed him as a great leader of men and an accomplished warrior for Islam and those on the other side who viewed him as a shrewd manipulator of ideology for sheer personal gain. One of his latter-day biographers (Hamilton A. R. Gibb) concluded his study by describing Saladin as "far from outstanding as a general or strategist. . . . Nor was he a good administrator," but he was a charismatic leader who gathered around him capable men and inspired them "by his unselfishness, his humility and generosity, his moral vindication of Islam against both its enemies and its professed adherents." Gibb adds that he was "utterly simple and transparently honest." Saladin saw the decline of Islam manifested in its loss of Jerusalem and other vital centers in Palestine and Syria to the Christian Crusaders and set about to revive the Islamic spirit and to establish a single united empire, not under his own rule, but under that of the Abbasid caliph.

This flattering image of Saladin found support among many of his Christian adversaries, who praised Saladin for his humanity and his respectful treatment of his foes. An ardent admirer, William of Tyre, the archbishop of Tyre and chronicler of the Crusades and the Middle Ages, saw Saladin as a worthy and thoroughly praiseworthy foe. So positive was the image of Saladin in the European world that Dante included him among the virtuous pagan souls who were allowed to live in limbo, and spared the ravages of hellfire because of their noble lives and noteworthy deeds.

Without doubt Saladin's greatest military triumph was the battle of Hattin in 1187. This battle pitted the armies of the Crusaders against the army of Saladin and proved to be an unqualified victory for Saladin and his forces. The Crusader loss of life was immense, numbering, according to some accounts at the time, anywhere from 30,000 to 40,000 men. So decisive was the battle that Saladin's forces were able to march into Jerusalem and reclaim this city of nearly 100,000 people for Islam. Yet unlike his Christian predecessors, who, when they conquered Jerusalem nearly a century earlier in 1099, slaughtered the Muslim inhabitants, Saladin spared the large Christian population. Those able to pay a rather substantial ransom he allowed to leave the city and take up residence elsewhere. Those who could not pay the ransom, some 15,000 men and women, were incorporated as slaves to the conquering Muslim population. Although by modern standards, this peace treaty hardly seems generous, by the standards of the time it was. It went a long way to burnishing Saladin's reputation in the West as a man of humanity and fair-mindedness.

Saladin did what so many of Egypt's new rulers before him had done. Amr ibn al-As and al-Muizz had built new capital cities following their conquests of the country. Saladin elected to do the same, relocating the seat of government to the east of Fustat and al-Qahira. Although further away from the Nile, the new site, set on high ground, enabled Saladin's forces to command the city below and also protect it from the country's many adversaries. The Citadel was the most striking of the Ayyubids' many contributions to the architecture of Cairo. Saladin located it in that part of the city which had the freshest and purest air. The story was told that the ruler placed meat at various locations around the city and sought the site where the meat stayed fresh the longest. Built on a spur of the Muqattam hills, it continued to be the location where Egypt's rulers resided from Ayyubid times down to the reign of Khedive Ismail (r. 1863–79), who established his residence at Abdin Palace near the center of Cairo. Saladin also established a parade ground just below the Citadel where his troops gathered for their military exercises and parades and where they also engaged in sporting activities, including games of polo. Seeking to make his capital impregnable to Crusaders and other enemies, he surrounded the old Fatimid city of al-Qahira and Fustat with fortified walls, some of which remain in place today. (See plate 22 for an illustration of Saladin's Citadel.)

MAMLUKS IN EGYPT, 1250–1517

Historians of Islam regard the Mamluk system of political and military power, perfected in Egypt in the thirteenth and fourteenth centuries, as Islam's most imposing and influential form of governance. Mamluk rule represented autocratic rule by foreign-born but locally trained military men. It was a way of ruling that had already become widespread in the Muslim world by the time that Egypt's Mamluk rulers seized power. But these men carried its methods and its ethos to a high state of perfection. The techniques of domination, honed by the Mamluks in Egypt, were then widely copied throughout the Muslim world, where they remained long-lived and virtually unique to Islam.

Rule by military slaves (*mamluks*) had deep roots in Muslim history, going all the way back to the ninth century, and forms of Mamluk rule continued to flourish in Egypt and elsewhere even beyond its attempted suppression by Napoleon's French forces during their invasion of Egypt at the end of the eighteenth century and Muhammad Ali's slaughter of the remaining Mamluks a decade later. In many ways, Muhammad Ali's rule in Egypt (1805–48, see chapter 9) resurrected numerous Mamluk features. The Mamluk system of governance provided much of the military energy that fueled Islamic expansionism and contributed to the endurance of Islamic polities over a full millennium.

The first ruler to make extensive use of Mamluks in his court was the Abbasid caliph al-Mutasim, who ruled from 833 to 842. Yet elements of the practice had precedents in the pre-Islamic tribal societies of the sixth century in the Arabian Peninsula. There it was common for successful tribal leaders to take as clients less powerful and dependent individuals, even to accept them as slaves, and then to manumit them after years of service. These ties of clientage and manumission created enduring bonds of loyalty and obedience between master and slaves, and, later on, the manumitted clients of the Abbasid rulers proved to be the military and political agents with the deepest bonds of loyalty and unswerving obedience to their masters. Although this Mamluk system of rule had existed in the Islamic world from Abbasid times until the nineteenth century, it reached its most fully developed form in Egypt after the overthrow of the Ayyubids in 1250 and thrived for nearly three centuries until the Ottoman invasion of Egypt in 1517. It is hardly surprising that this period is known in Egyptian historical annals as the Mamluk era.

The rise of the Mamluks to overwhelming authority owed much to one of the last of the Ayyubid rulers, al-Salih Ayyub (r. 1240–49), who came to the sultanate at a time of political and military unrest. Numerous competitors for power beset Egypt and Syria. At the time of his reign the most determined of these forces belonged to the Crusaders, but Mongols invaders were already making inroads into Muslim lands. They would sack Baghdad in 1258 and would set their sights on Syria and the biggest prize of all, Egypt. Seeking to strengthen his power and to surround himself with men with military skills and loyalty to his rule, al-Salih Ayyub, imported a large number of military slaves, in fact more than any previous Ayyubid ruler. The region from which he brought most of these recruits was the impoverished Kipchak area north of the Caspian Sea. Parents in this locale were willing to sell their sons at a hefty price to Islamic merchants, who transported them to Egypt, where they received military training and rose to positions of power. The sultan made these recruits, some 800 to 1,000 strong, the core of his army. The Kipchak region was a polytheistic border area, contested between Islam and Mongol invaders, noted for the horse-riding and martial skills of its population. Hence, it was immensely attractive to the ruling element in Egypt, desperate for a loyal, obedient, and committed military component in their midst.

Alas for the rulers who succeeded al-Salih upon his death in 1249, the decade of the 1250s was a chaotic one, and eventually one of these Kipchak Mamluks, al-Malik al-Zahir Baybars, seized power for himself and his followers. Baybars inaugurated a Mamluk political regime that lasted until the end of the fourteenth century and has often been referred to as the Bahri period because the location of the chief barracks of the ruling Mamluks was the Bahri barracks on an island of the Nile not far from Cairo. The Bahri Mamluks were, in turn, succeeded by a group often referred to as the Burji Mamluks because their primary barracks was the tower (*burj*) at the citadel in Cairo. They are more frequently referred to as the Circassian Mamluks because the vast majority of these men came from the Circassian region of the Caucasus.

At the outset, the Mamluks won legitimacy for themselves as well as a reputation as great warriors because they cleared Syria and Palestine of the remnants of the Crusaders and, even more importantly, stopped the advance of the vaunted and feared Mongol forces at the battle of Ain Jalut in Palestine in 1260.

Ain Jalut is a momentous event in the annals of Egyptian history. Had the Mongols won, not only would the country have been absorbed into an expanding Mongol Empire, but Mongol warriors would have continued their inexorable march westward. This was the clear message that the Mongol commander, the fearsome Hulaga, dispatched to the Egyptian leaders, warning them that his forces were "the army of God on his earth" and cautioning them to avoid "the fate of others and hand over your power to us before the veil is torn and you are sorry and your errors rebound upon you. . . . You have heard that we have conquered the lands and cleansed the earth of corruption and killed most of the people." The Mamluks were well aware that these words were not idle threats, for Mongol warriors had a mere two years earlier ravaged Baghdad, boasting that they had taken the lives of 200,000 people. There they spared no one, seeking out their adversaries in wells, latrines, and sewers, and pursuing them onto rooftops. One observer of the devastation noted that "blood poured from the gutters into the streets. . . . The same happened in mosques and . . . Baghdad, which had been the most civilized of cities, became a ruin with only a few inhabitants." Though newly arrived in Egypt, the Mamluk warriors were determined to defend Cairo and save it from the depredations that Baghdad had experienced. Their leader left the Mongols in no doubt that his forces would not capitulate. He ordered the Mongol emissaries to be executed and had their heads placed on pikes at the Bab al-Zuwayla gate.

Early military triumphs gave Baybars (r. 1260–1277) and his immediate successors, most notably, al-Mansur Qalawun (r. 1279–1290), the opportunity to install an elaborate military and political recruiting and training system in Egypt. Using Muslim merchants who knew the northern border areas of Islam well, the rulers in Egypt dispatched these men to purchase from their families youngsters who were just attaining the age of puberty. The young men were chosen because of their physical abilities and their good looks and were then transported under the care of the merchants to Egypt.

Once in Egypt, the recruits were incorporated into Mamluk households and sent to schools where they received an intensive training in religion and military skills. Most of the teachers in these schools, of which there were approximately twelve, each of which could accommodate 1,000 trainees, were eunuchs, valued because they were loyal to their masters and were adept at keeping the older Mamluk students from preying on their younger counterparts. In the early years of the captive's training religious principles were stressed, and though the Mamluks as adults often violated Muslim precepts, they nevertheless gained a deep knowledge of Islam. As they advanced in their education, they began to concentrate on military skills, notably horsemanship and archery. The Mamluk forces were well known for their cavalry skills and were experts in riding and shooting arrows while galloping at full speed. Once their training was completed, they graduated as a group in a large passing-out parade, at which time they were manumitted. This intensive form of education produced a strong sense of loyalty to one another and to the Mamluk master who had sponsored and freed them.

A striking feature of the Mamluk system of recruitment and training, at least when it was operating according to its basic principles, is that it produced a one-generation aristocracy of rulers and warriors. In spite of what must have been a strong desire for the freedmen to pass power on to their offspring, in fact, the Mamluk households brought in new recruits to take their places and passed over their own offspring. The noted Islamic scholar Ibn Khaldun, who though born in Tunis spent much of his adult life in Egypt, understood the virtues of this unusual procedure. He wrote: "The rulers choose from amongst these Mamluks, who are imported to them, horsemen and soldiers. These Mamluks are more courageous in war and endure privations better than the sons of Mamluks who had preceded them and who were reared in easy circumstances and in the shadow of rulership." Perhaps it was the political and military instability that afflicted the Islamic world at this time that caused Muslim rulers to abstain from promoting their own offspring and caused them instead to form ties with new recruits who were being brought from distant lands and who, under most circumstances, manifested the most intense bonds of obedience to their new masters.

The Mamluk ruling elite was itself stratified and hierarchical. The most powerful units were those of the sultan himself. Young boys fortunate enough to belong to the sultan's household expected to rise to high positions within the Mamluk hierarchy and to spend most of their days as soldiers and administrators in the capital city of Cairo. They constituted the royal Mamluks. Beneath this group in the military and political hierarchy were the various grades of amirs, of which there were four: amirs of one hundred Mamluks, amirs of forty, of ten, and of five. These units, although trained in much the same fashion as the sultan's Mamluks, were not so privileged. Their training was less elaborate, and they served outside Cairo. Finally, there was a third unit of free cavalry, many of whom were the sons of the Mamluks. They did not enjoy the respect or power that the proper Mamluks commanded. Over time, they became increasingly less important, less disciplined, and less well organized.

The first two strong Mamluk rulers—Baybars and Qalawun—were the men who installed and then perfected the Mamluk political and military system. Forced to create a stronger army than had existed in Ayyubid times in order to hold off the challenges of the Mongols and the Crusaders, they established a unified military structure. All officers and nonofficers knew their places within the military hierarchy and understood that they owed supreme allegiance to the ruling sultan. Baybars and Qalawun took a deep interest in the efficiency of the army. Baybars inspected his royal Mamluk units as often as twice a week and paid particular attention to the military equipment of his soldiers and how well they were able to make use of it. He rewarded his top officers with large land grants, but he refused to play favorites, believing that such arrangements would undermine the solidarity and fighting spirit of his forces. He also enhanced his legitimacy by bringing the Abbasid caliph from Baghdad, after the Mongol conquest of that city, and installed him at Cairo.

Both Baybars and Qalawun used the new military schools to instill obedience, loyalty, discipline, and a sense of hierarchy in the trainees. The schools featured military tournaments where the martial skills of the students were tested and enhanced. The heads of the schools were men who inspired respect and awe in their students and who refused to tolerate any breaches of discipline. It was said of one powerful head of the royal Mamluk school that hardly a student escaped being struck or cursed; yet the men, when they were manumitted and rose to become amirs of the fighting force, looked back upon their tutor with the utmost admiration.

Unfortunately, toward the latter years of the Bahri period and then with increasing frequency in the Circassian era, this strict sense of hierarchy and discipline began to break down. In order to stay in power, sultans played favorites, rewarding those who were loyal to them with larger land grants than those who were of a higher rank. What worked for these rulers in the short run undermined the strict hierarchy and steadfast loyalty that had been a cornerstone of Mamluk governance under Baybars and Qalawun. By the end of the fourteenth and the beginning of the fifteenth century Mamluk rule no longer inspired fear and respect. Sons of Mamluks now found a position for themselves inside the army, and the rank and file of the population discovered that their acts of rebellion resulted in reforms intended to pacify them. The Mamluk forces were to prove no barrier to the conquest of Egypt by the Ottoman army in 1516–17.

One of the noteworthy aspects of Mamluk rule was the gulf that separated the rulers from the rest of the population. The rulers came from distant lands, adopted or already had Turkish names, spoke Turkish rather than Arabic, and lived apart from the rank and file of the population. Often they abused their power over the Egyptian people and looked down upon the masses as inferiors. The one bridge between the Mamluk rulers and the Egyptian people, ironically enough, was the offspring of Mamluks. Though often spurned by their fathers, they learned the Arabic language of their mothers, were given Arabic names, and used what influence they had as sons of Mamluks to occupy intermediate positions within Egyptian society. Many of these sons were merchants. Others became bureaucrats, and still others pursued notable careers as religious scholars and bureaucrats. They had a greater feel for the life of the ordinary Egyptian, and if they had any influence with those in power, they used it to communicate some of the realities of ordinary life in Egypt to the rulers.

Although contemporaries and later historians have often portrayed the Mamluks as loutish individuals, only partially assimilated to Islam, the commitment of the sultans and the elite to honoring their Islamic training was second to none. The old city of Cairo, though built by the Fatimids and added to by the Ayyubids, was very much a manifestation of Mamluk fidelity to Islam. Many of Cairo's medieval buildings, especially the mosques that have survived into modern times, bear the stamp of Mamluk architecture. The mosque and the madrasa (school) of Sultan Hasan that sit at the foot of the Muqattam hills under Saladin's citadel are among the finest examples of Islamic architecture in the city. Both are unmistakably Mamluk and inspire awe in believers as well as visitors. The madrasa was begun during the uninspiring reign of Sultan Hasan (1347–61) but was not completed until after his assassination. It is a massive construction, as were so many of the Mamluk buildings, intended to display the power and wealth of the ruling elite. The building was constructed between 1356 and 1363 at the end of the Bahri Mamluk period. It possesses the tallest minaret in Cairo, at eighty-four meters, and the tallest portal. It also served as a mosque and contained four madrasas, placed in vaulted recesses and dedicated to the four legal traditions of Sunni Islam. The most expensive mosque ever built in medieval Cairo, it was deemed the greatest mosque in the entire Muslim world upon completion. (See plate 23 for an illustration of Sultan Hasan mosque.) Opposite the madrasa is the mosque of al-Rifai, which was built in the middle of the nineteenth century, during the reign of Khedive Ismail; it was constructed in a neo-Mamluk style so as to add to the magnificence of the location and instill in the whole area religious enthusiasm and a sense of past religious glories.

An intellectual achievement of the Mamluk period that owes much to the presence of the Mamluks, though ironically, are the writings of a group of intellectuals led by the noted Islamic scholar Ibn Taymiyya of Syria (1263–1328), whose ideas have experienced a brilliant revival in the twentieth and twenty-first centuries. Ibn Taymiyya and an Egyptian scholar with similar intellectual leanings, Ibn al-Hajj (d. 1336), both espoused a strict and traditionalist interpretation of Islam. To them, the presence of the Crusaders and the Mongols in the heartland of Islam, the power exercised by foreign, and to these men, insufficiently Islamized Mamluk rulers attested to the failure of Muslims to adhere to the original teachings of Muhammad and the first generation of believers. Ibn Taymiyya and Ibn al-Hajj demanded that Muslims set aside the innovations of recent times and cling to the simple and easily understood beliefs of the Prophet himself. Their treatises also challenged the authority of the Mamluk rulers, for these two intellectuals wanted the educated classes—the ulama—to count for more in the world of Islam than military men. While their message hardly threatened the Mamluks, they helped to create a commitment to Islam and intellectual pursuits that the scholarly classes enjoyed.

These two men and other less famous, but nonetheless influential ulama were, as we have observed, part of a long historical tradition in which native-born Egyptians made a place for themselves in a society dominated by foreign rulers. These individuals used their intellectual prowess, especially their achievements in religion and philosophy, to carve out a site of influence for the well-educated element in a society otherwise dominated by military men. Although Ibn Taymiyya was born in Turkey, he found the intellectual climate of Mamluk Syria more to his liking. Similarly, perhaps Islam's most widely respected intellectual, Ibn Khaldun described Cairo as "the garden of the universe, the orchard of the world."

Not only did Ibn Taymiyya and other conservative ulama dispute the power of the Mamluk rulers, they also wrote vehemently against a movement that had come to prominence at the end of the Ayyubid period and had thrived during Mamluk times—Sufism, or mystical Islam. Mystics had always been prominent religious figures in the history of Islam. In the early centuries of Islam they had achieved notoriety through their ascetic and exemplary ways of life. Through constant prayer and denial of personal pleasures to themselves, they sought nothing less than union with God. Perhaps the most noteworthy, and also notorious, of these early mystics was a man born in Persia, who settled in Baghdad and wrote in Arabic, an Iraqi by the name of al-Husayn ibn Mansur al-Hallaj (858–922). Unlike many other mystics, he sought to spread his notions of religiosity among the people, counseling them to seek union with God as he did. He often fell into trances during which he believed that he was in the presence of God. On one such occasion, he announced that he was the truth and through his complete union with the Deity had become God himself.

The political authorities feared al-Hallaj, whose following was substantial, and they received support from the ulama, who argued that al-Hallaj's ideas were heretical. Tried and imprisoned for eleven years, he was put to death in 922 in a most brutal way. Some reports stated that he was beheaded and his hands and feet cut off.

Sufism did not die with al-Hallaj. Individual mystics continued to flourish within Islam, perhaps the most famous being Ibn al-Arabi, the Spanish devout (1165–1240), who persuaded many that his mystical form of Islam brought religious ecstasy and personal happiness. It was during his lifetime in the twelfth and thirteenth centuries, a time when Islam was under great pressure from Crusaders, Mongols, and Turkish military tribes moving westward, that this mystical form of Islam began to find institutional settings across the entire Muslim world. Sufi brotherhoods, extolling a founding figure or saint, came into being and established their own religious centers, often called *Khanaqahs*, where the leading Sufis of the order lived and where initiates were instructed in the Sufi ways. It was, in fact, in the twelfth century that Egypt's most long-lived and influential Sufi brotherhoods came into being. Although the Sufi orders continued to worry members of the scholarly classes, who often accused the Sufis of holding to heretical beliefs, they increasingly became the religion of the common people and a social organization that maintained community welfare.

THE DECLINE OF MAMLUK POWER

The bubonic plague, also known as the Black Death, tore through the Afro-Eurasian land mass in the fourteenth century. Egypt experienced the full measure of its destruction. Its impact weakened the Mamluk polity and economy and eventually opened the way for the Ottoman conquest. The plague reached Cairo and Alexandria in 1347, spreading its lethal bacilli through the urban populations of these two metropolises, but also wreaking havoc on the tightly packed populations of the countryside. The noted Egyptian chronicler al-Maqrizi (1364–1442), who lived through the later stages of the plague, commented: "The country was not far from being ruined. . . . One found in the desert the bodies of savage animals with bubos under their arms. It was the same with horses, camels, asses, and all the beasts in general, including birds, even ostriches." Nor was the epidemic confined to animals. It ravaged the human population. Al-Maqrizi went on to say that "Cairo became an empty desert, and there was no one to be seen in the streets. A man could go from Zuwayla Gate to the Bab al-Nasr without encountering another soul. The dead were so numerous that people thought only of them." Ibn Khaldun, who lost his mother and father and a number of his teachers to the Black Death, believed that it threatened the very foundations of civilization. "Cities and buildings were laid waste, roads and way signs were obliterated, settlements and mansions became empty, dynasties and tribes grew weak. The entire world changed."

Throughout the Afro-Eurasian landmass, the appearance of the Black Death meant destruction. It took a horrifying toll on local populations, carrying off anywhere from one-third to one-half. Although we do not have precise figures on Egypt, there is no reason to believe that its impact there was any less lethal than on the devastated populations of China and Western Europe. The population of Egypt may have been in the neighborhood of six million at the beginning of the fourteenth century. By 1500, after numerous epidemics of the disease, Egypt's numbers were halved. Nor did the population of the country reach pre-1300 levels until sometime in the nineteenth century.

Under the Mamluks, Egypt was much slower to recover from the Black Death than Western European countries and China. The failure to spring back stemmed largely from a centralized landholding system, in which Mamluk landowners refused to release peasant farmers from their rent and taxpaying obligations following the decline of the population as readily as did the landowning elite in Western European countries. Not only were Mamluk fief holders absentee landlords, and therefore ignorant of rural conditions and the plight of the peasantry, but they had the coercive means to enforce their will on the rural dwellers, even when these measures prolonged rural decay and delayed agricultural progress.

Ottoman Egypt, 1517–1798

In 1599 Mustafa Ali, a high Ottoman functionary and one of the empire's leading intellectuals whose world history is justly celebrated among Ottoman historians today, visited Egypt for a second time. His sorrowful account of the state of Egyptian society at the time distressed the authorities at home in Istanbul. They could ill afford to see their most important and lucrative province slip into decline, and they wondered whether Egypt would continue to provide the same level of financial and material support that had swelled the coffers of the imperial state. Mustafa Ali was a gloomy man, convinced that the inability of the Ottomans to expand their territory and fulfill their mission of world empire augured the decline of their civilization. He was also fixated on the approach of Islam's first millennium and thought it offered further proof of Ottoman decline as well as a prelude to the end of the world and the arrival of a Mahdi figure.

Mustafa Ali's notion of a declining Ottoman culture found many believers within the scholarly elite and became a mantra of Ottoman thought for centuries thereafter. Although Europeans were not yet ready to write the Ottoman Empire off, still concerned about Ottoman forces besieging Vienna and other important European cities, Bonaparte's expedition to Egypt in 1798 persuaded many (see chapter 9) that indeed Ottoman Egypt was but a pale imitation of its ancient glories and that Islam, especially as practiced by the Ottomans, was an impediment to progress. By the nineteenth century European statesmen and intellectuals described Turkey as the sick man of Europe and eagerly anticipated the day when the great powers of Europe would carve up Ottoman imperial possessions.

For these and other reasons, the Ottomans have not enjoyed a good historical press. Their decline has been a staple of Ottoman historiography from the seventeenth century right down to the present. British and French statesmen invoked this perspective when justifying their parceling out of the Arab territories of the Ottoman Empire after the Turks' defeat in World War I. But this view is entirely unfair. The empire endured longer than any other in world history (from 1400 to 1919). Its administrators demonstrated talents of governance that today's ruling elites, unable to accommodate religious, ethnic, and linguistic division at home and abroad, must surely admire. Its merchants, rather than despairing when Europeans began to dominate the Muslim world of trade in the Indian Ocean, adjusted with surprising ingenuity. And its scholars and artisans, far from slipping into somnolence, produced works of long-lasting beauty. In all of these arenas, Egypt, the Ottomans' most important and lucrative imperial possession, excelled.

To return to the critical and gloomy Mustafa Ali, his description of Cairo conveys a powerful message of decline and worry. It divides into two unequal parts: "the good sides and welcome points as over against the objectionable aspects." In the first part, by far the shorter, the author makes the customary obeisance to the virtues of the Nile, praising it as "unequal among the rivers" of the world. It afforded Cairenes "an extremely good-tasting water and . . . in its utmost pleasantness more beneficial to digestion, purer, and sweeter." Even those noteworthy items that virtually all commentators on Egypt extolled, like the pyramids, of which he boasted "there are no monuments, no like marvels in any other country," he saw negative aspects, condemning their builders, the pharaohs as "mischievous." He reveled in the multitude of Cairo's coffeehouses, describing them as ideal places for people to assemble, but at the same time he complained that most of the patrons were "dissolute persons and opium eaters." As for the negative features, which far outweighed the positives, he had little complimentary to say about the beauty of Egyptians. In his view few native-born Egyptians were attractive; if one were to encounter a good-looking Egyptian, more than likely that person had inherited his pleasing features from

Turkish ancestors. Mustafa Ali saved his severest remarks for Egyptian women, whom he described as "unseemly in appearance," although "their abilities and skills in graceful behavior and especially in coquetry and sexiness is more than one would expect." They were appallingly bad homemakers, purchasing indigestible food in the local markets and serving it to unsuspecting husbands.

THE OTTOMAN CONQUEST OF EGYPT

The Ottoman conquest was well nigh inevitable. Ottoman warriors had been expanding in two directions—northward into the Balkans and southward toward the Arab territories—ever since the principality first came into existence in the early fourteenth century. The push toward the south had become irresistible once an expansionist Shiite regime had assumed power in Iran and had set its political and religious sights on Iraq. In 1517, Ottoman forces under the personal command of Sultan Selim readied themselves for a southern campaign. Whether the sultan's forces intended to wage war against the Safavid foe in Iran or turn on the Mamluk regime in Egypt, which had made common cause with the Savafids, was uncertain. But when conditions favored a thrust against the Egyptians, Selim did not hesitate. The battles that ensued were fought with intensity and savagery, though the outcome was never in doubt. The Ottomans had more troops, were better armed, and had mastered the technology of infantry warfare based on rifles and gunpowder. In contrast, the Mamluks still extolled cavalry forces and thrilled at the cavalry charge. They scorned infantry units as practicing an inferior kind of warfare. Emotions ran high between the two warrior states. Both prided themselves on military prowess. Beheading enemies was practiced on both sides. The Mamluks did not shrink from placing the heads of fallen Ottoman soldiers on pikes erected at the main entrances to Cairo. In revenge, the Ottoman conquerors plundered, raped, and killed an estimated 10,000 inhabitants of Cairo in their conquest of the city. To demonstrate their utter contempt for their Mamluk adversaries, the Ottomans hanged the last Mamluk ruler, Tumanbay, at the Zuwayla gate, projecting the message to the

PLATE 25. Egyptian school girls, wearing head scarves and standing in front of ruins of the temple of Dendera

PLATE 24. Artist's rendition of Napoleon in Egypt. Jean-Leon Gerome. Oil on canvas. Princeton University Art Museum, Princeton, NJ.

PLATE 22. The Citadel

PLATE 23. Sultan Hasan mosque

PLATE 21. Al-Azhar mosque

PLATE 20. Ahmad ibn Tulun mosque. Image from Cross, *Egypt* (Harcourt, 1991).

PLATE 18. Saint Catherine's monastery in Sinai. Image from Cross, *Egypt* (Harcourt, 1991).

PLATE 19. Muhammad Ali mosque

PLATE 16. Philae temple

PLATE 17. Roman amphitheater in Alexandria

PLATE 14. Mask of King Tutankhamen

PLATE 15. The royal chair of King Tutankhamen

PLATE 12. The solar disk god, Aten

PLATE 13. Abu Simbel

PLATE 11. Statue of Akhenaten

PLATE 10. Bust of Queen Nefertiti. Altes Museum, Berlin.

PLATE 8. Avenues of the sphinxes at Luxor

PLATE 9. Queen Hatshepsut's mortuary temple

PLATE 6. The Sphinx with the pyramid of Khafra behind

PLATE 7. The great pyramid of Giza

PLATE 4. The step pyramid

PLATE 5. The bent pyramid

PLATE 2. *A shaduf*

PLATE 3. A *saqia* or buffalo-driven water wheel

PLATE 1. The pyramids during the Nile flood. V&A Images/Victoria and Albert Museum, London.

city dwellers that their former ruler deserved nothing more than the treatment that would be given to a common criminal. When the decisive battle of Marj Dabiq in Syria was over, "the battlefield was strewn with corpses and headless bodies and faces covered with dust and grown hideous." The destruction carried out in Cairo was such as "to strike terror into the hearts of man and its horrors to unhinge their reasons." Ibn Iyas, a chronicler of this period and a historian of note, said that the Islamic world had not seen such devastation since the notorious Mongol conquest of Baghdad in 1258.

Ottoman rule changed Egypt. Previously an independent state, possessing its own imperial territories in Syria and the Arabian Peninsula, Egypt now became a colonial province. Cairo, which had been an imperial capital in Fatimid, Ayyubid, and Mamluk times, dispatching its administrators to Damascus, the holy cities in the Arabian Peninsula, and Nubia, now descended in status to a provincial center. Incorporated as an outlying province into an expanding Ottoman Empire, its major resources of money, grains, and fighting men were at the disposal of rulers headquartered in Istanbul.

While the inclusion of Egypt into the Ottoman Empire was a diminishing moment in Egyptian history, it had a transforming effect on the Ottoman historical arc. Before the conquest of Egypt, the Ottomans had run a frontier, warrior state. Their northward expansion, across the Dardanelles into the Balkans, had made them rulers of large Christian populations. They ruled the Balkans, but as minority religious conquerors. The Ottoman's most glorious military achievement, Mehmed II's conquest of Constantinople in 1453, underscored this condition, for while it elevated the Ottoman sultan to the throne of the old Byzantine Christian empire, it brought more Christian territory and Christian populations into the empire. In contrast, the drive into Syria and Egypt and subsequent advances in Iraq and North Africa brought numerous coreligionists under Ottoman jurisdiction, counterbalancing the massive Christian communities ruled from Istanbul. The Arab conquests also elevated the Islamic purposes of the Ottomans, shifting the responsibility for the well-being of Islam's holy places in the Arabian Peninsula from Mamluk Egypt to the Ottoman sultan and bringing under imperial authority two heartland Islamic territories, Egypt and Syria. The Arab states of the empire represented more than one-fifth of the empire's total population, and Egypt, the empire's most populous and lucrative province, quickly assumed a decisive importance in imperial affairs. Following his conquest of Egypt, Selim was quick to proclaim his state as heir to the great Islamic empires of the past. And by the turn of the sixteenth century, the Ottoman Empire had indeed become a settled state, possessing a complex and sophisticated bureaucracy. It was henceforth fully committed to strengthening and expanding Sunni Islam against its Christian and Shiite adversaries.

Yet the original conquest of Egypt in 1517 was neither complete nor decisive. As soon as the victory had been achieved, the sultan withdrew large numbers of his soldiers in order to continue his struggles with the Shiite Safavid regime along the Iraq-Iran border. Selim also made a fateful decision. He permitted the Mamluk units stationed in Egypt, though not those based in Syria, to reform. He did so for obvious reasons, though he must surely have understood that allowing military men with political ambitions to remain in existence was extremely risky. In the first place, he needed his best soldiers on the Iran-Iraq border, where the Safavid-Ottoman war was at its hottest. Second, he had to hope that reprieved Mamluk military men would assist the remaining Ottoman troops in controlling and administering Egypt itself, especially its large and potentially rebellious Bedouin tribes. To cement this alliance with the Mamluk forces in Egypt, Selim appointed Khair Bey as the province's first governor. As the governor of Aleppo, Khair Bey had defected to the Ottoman cause at a decisive moment in the battle of Dabiq Marj, earning for himself the sobriquet of the traitor. Selim's critical decision enabled the Mamluks to rebuild their fortunes and put them in a position by the beginning of the seventeenth century to challenge Ottoman predominance in Egypt.

Khair Bey served as governor of Egypt from 1517 until his death in 1522, at which point disaffected units of the Ottoman army in Egypt in league with disgruntled Mamluks sought to break away from Istanbul's authority. On the throne in Istanbul at the time was a formidable new sultan, Sulayman I, subsequently known as "the Magnificent" and "the Lawgiver," whose tenure in power from 1520 to 1566 is often regarded as the apogee of Ottoman influence. Sulayman had no intention of allowing his prize imperial possession to slip away and hurriedly dispatched his chief administrator, Ibrahim Pasha, to suppress the revolt and reestablish Ottoman suzerainty. After defeating the rebels, Ibrahim Pasha promulgated a set of laws in 1525, known as the *kanun name*, that were to establish the guidelines for the administration of Egypt throughout the Ottoman period.

Ibrahim's code of laws had an overarching purpose. The laws were designed to give Egypt an orderly form of government, thus restoring the political stability so badly shaken by the last turbulent years of Mamluk rule and the conquest, and by reestablishing political tranquility, enabling the local population, its farmers and merchants most notably, to be productive, taxpaying assets of the empire. The code also reflected an Ottoman desire to give the Mamluks no further cause to participate in breakaway revolts like that of 1524. By adopting many of the rules that had governed Egypt in the late fifteenth century during an effective period of Mamluk rule, it sought to mollify Mamluk grandees and encourage collaboration with Ottoman overrule.

The *kanun name* was divided into two parts. The first dealt with military matters. It stated that Egypt was to be the home base for six military units, subsequently increased by a seventh in 1554. One of the original six was a Mamluk unit. Each military unit was commanded by an *ogha*, whose chief lieutenant was called a *katkhuda*. Two of the units were infantry, and the remaining five were cavalry. Throughout most of the sixteenth century the force totaled 10,000, of whom nearly 90 percent were native-born Egyptians. The two largest and most prestigious units were both infantry corps—the Janissaries and the Azabs—both of which were stationed in Cairo's vital political center, the Citadel. Unlike the Mamluk army, at least in its early stages, the Ottomans were not committed to a one-generation army and administration. The sons of the military corps were not forbidden from entering the military. In addition, although the *kanun name* prohibited peasants, Bedouins, and Circassians from entering the army, in fact they did. As a consequence, in the Ottoman era, in striking contrast with the Mamluk period, a much closer relationship existed between the ruling elite and the Egyptian population. The irony of this situation should not be lost on historians and must have been felt by the Egyptian people. Although Egypt had been demoted to a colonial status, in fact native-born Egyptians had far more say in the affairs of their country than they had exercised under the Mamluks.

The second part of Ibrahim's *kanun name* dealt with civil administration. It too drew heavily from Mamluk practices. The sultan appointed Egypt's governor, also referred to as the pasha or the *wali*. The appointment was for a single year, but most governors were renewed. Yet long tenures were unheard of. Only one governor served for more than a decade, and during the entire 281 years of Ottoman rule Egypt had 110 governors; hence the average length of service was a little more than two and a half years. The pasha was obligated to govern in conjunction with a council, called a *diwan*, which met four times a week and was composed of the most important Ottoman officers in the country, including the treasurer (*daftardar*), and the *amir al-hajj*, the officer charged with the duty of organizing the annual pilgrimage to the holy cities of the Arabian Peninsula. *Diwans* existed in other provinces of the Ottoman Empire, but no other was so essential to provincial governance and none was required to meet four times a week.

The code of laws also dealt with taxation and expenditures. The country's revenues, garnered largely from land taxes and customs duties, were to be used to pay for the administration of the country, the military units stationed there, the army and navy units in Yemen, Ethiopia, and the Red Sea, the security of Mecca and Medina, and the pilgrimage caravan to the holy cities. What was left over was sent to Istanbul as tribute.

In legal matters, the *kanun name* empowered the sultan to appoint the chief *qadi* of Egypt, who oversaw Egypt's courts. The chief *qadi* was always from the Hanafi school of legal jurisprudence, the legal school that the Ottomans preferred. Although Egypt was predominantly a Shafiite country, having a Hanafite at the head of Egyptian court system did not constitute a radical departure. The Mamluks had allowed all four schools of legal reasoning to function in the country.

Finally, Ibrahim's code of laws divided the administration of Egypt into fourteen provinces, thirteen of which were in lower and middle Egypt. The fourteenth encompassed the oases of Kharja in the western desert. In a concession to the political power of the tribal groups living in Upper Egypt, the Ottomans delegated the administration of all of Egypt from Asyut southward to the shaykhs of the Banu Umar tribe. The *kanun name*'s willingness to concede authority to the Arab tribesmen of Upper Egypt was a reflection of how powerful these groups had become under the Mamluks and would remain during the Ottoman years. Unwilling to subordinate themselves to state officials, the Arab tribesmen of Upper Egypt agreed to collect taxes on the state's behalf. In return the governor allowed them to exercise authority over this large region.

Egypt's settled Arab tribes must be distinguished from the nomad communities, most of whom dwelled in the western desert and from whom the settled Arab tribes offered protection to the rest of the Egyptian people. In the Ottoman era, Egypt had forty-five of these settled tribes, one group of which, the Hawwara tribesmen, came to exercise unchecked control over Upper Egypt in the eighteenth century. Many of the Arab tribesmen of Upper Egypt had entered the country in the fourteenth century, arriving from North Africa, and seizing control of large swathes of territory there during the last century of Mamluk rule. Not to be overlooked, though not so powerful, were Arab tribesmen who dwelled in Lower Egypt, living outside the most heavily populated regions though in close proximity with the peasantry.

WHO WERE THE OTTOMANS?

The Ottomans were part of a wave of nomadic Turkish peoples who had migrated from Central Asia into Iran, Armenia, Anatolia, the Caucasus, Russia, the Balkans, Iraq, and Syria in the tenth century.

Of these communities the Saljuks were at first the most powerful, taking over the seat of authority of the Abbasid Empire at Baghdad in the eleventh century and briefly establishing a successful autonomous state in Anatolia, known as the Saljuk of Rum. The Saljuk military triumph over a Byzantine force at the battle of Manzikert in the Armenian highlands in 1071 was a significant event for westward-migrating Turkish nomadic and warrior groups since it opened up Anatolia to them. Nonetheless, the Saljuk of Rum state was weak and short-lived, its influence on Anatolian affairs proving limited. Its leaders ceased to be important politically after suffering a military defeat at the hands of the Mongols in 1243. Among the many successor states that followed in Anatolia were the Ottomans, who would not, however, have been perceived as the likely winners in the fierce competition for power that ensued in this region. Certainly, they would not have been seen as the creators of a powerful and long-lived Islamic state.

Inspired leadership, favorable location, and several critical decisions made the difference in the Ottomans' rise. The early Ottoman warriors, notably the founder of the dynasty, Osman (r. 1281–1324) and his immediate successor, Orhan (r. 1324–62) took full advantage of the location of their principality in the northwestern corner of Anatolia. A warring and commercial borderland between the Christian Byzantine Empire and Muslim warrior states, this area profited economically from the vital trade routes that passed through it. Like other wild and turbulent frontiers, heroic military leadership and popular forms of religion, which included religious borrowings across Christian and Muslim borders and extolled mystical expressions of religiosity, were powerfully on display in this locale. Here, too, Byzantine, Crusader, and Muslim armies competed with one another to expand their boundaries, and Christian and Muslim religious ideas circulated freely. Religious experimentation occurred, and syncretistic religious beliefs were rife.

Altogether critical for early Ottoman political legitimacy was Osman's seemingly insignificant military victory at Baphaeon in 1301 against a largely disinterested Byzantine military force. The triumph boosted Osman's prestige and enabled his principality to attract other warrior groups and settlers, who looked to Osman to lead them to new military triumphs and whose allegiance to him was strengthened as the booty acquired in warfare abounded. A second critical moment occurred in the fourteenth century when the Ottomans crossed the Dardanelles and planted the banner of Islam in the Balkans. This military foray opened up a vast area for military prizes, not the least of which was the recruitment of fresh supplies of soldiers from conquered populations.

Nomadic warrior states have frequently appeared in history, raiding settled societies and even establishing their authority over these communities. Before the Ottomans, the most successful and long-lived of these nomadic warrior states was the Mongol Empire, but the Mongol states, like their predecessors and most of their successors, disintegrated because of internal rivalries and an inability to create a stable bureaucratic form of government. Altogether critical in enabling the Ottoman chieftains to rise above their nomadic inheritance were the administrative and military innovations made by Orhan's two successors, Murat I (r. 1362–89) and Bayezit I (r. 1389–1402). To prevent the kind of internecine warfare that frequently destroyed nomadic empires before they were able to establish stable bureaucratic regimes, Murat and Bayezit created a slave army and a corps of administrators whose loyalty to the ruler was unquestioned. They did so by bringing into their army and administration the very men whom they had conquered. Bayezit went one step further, establishing elaborate arrangements for recruiting and training the vital military and administrative cadres that the state required. This system, which came to be known as the *devshirme* system, involved selecting young men, on the basis of their physical and mental talents, from conquered Christian communities in the Balkans and enrolling them in state-administered schools where they were instructed in Islam and learned the arts of warfare and administration. The best and brightest moved on to elite schools in the imperial capital and were earmarked for the top military and administration offices in the Ottoman state. Of course, this system was not new in the Muslim world. The Mamluks were already perfecting it in Egypt at this time, and the Ottoman predecessors in Anatolia, the Saljuks, had employed it.

The conquest of Constantinople in 1453 by Mehmed II, known as "the Conqueror," was not only a world-changing event but it demonstrated that the small principality in Anatolia had become a world power, now endowed with a stable and effective bureaucracy. Mehmed II achieved an ambition that had inspired Muslim rulers from the first campaigns conducted outside the Arabian Peninsula: the defeat of the Byzantine Empire and the occupation of Byzantium's primary city, Constantinople. In triumph, Mehmed announced that he was the successor to the Roman emperors, offering his state as heir to Rome's imperial glory. After seizing Constantinople and proclaiming the city as his imperial capital, Mehmed declared that "the world empire must be one, with one faith, and one sovereignty. To establish this unity, there is no place more fitting than Constantinople." He also believed that, through his person as well as the office of the sultanate, he brought together Roman, Islamic, and Turkish political and military traditions.

THE THREE PHASES OF OTTOMAN RULE IN EGYPT

Rule by Ottoman Governors to 1609

Throughout the Ottoman period, Istanbul's sultans had a clear set of demands that they placed on Egypt and its people. First and foremost, they required the population to recognize the Ottoman state as Islam's only legitimate government. To that end, they expected Egypt to make annual tribute payments to Istanbul in the form of gold, obtained from Sudan and other parts of Africa, and grain shipments, with which other parts of the empire would be fed. The Ottomans also required that they be allowed to station significant army units in Egypt, which the Egyptians paid for and which kept order in Egypt but were also available for duties elsewhere in the empire. These units totaled somewhere between 10,000 and 15,000 men.

The first period of Ottoman rule lasted for the better part of the century and came to an end roughly in 1609 when a series of soldiers' rebellions, though eventually suppressed by a strong governor, weakened the legitimacy of Istanbul and prepared the way for the rise of Mamluk households. During this era Egypt was governed as an orderly and relatively peaceful and prosperous province of the empire, controlled by the sultan's appointed governors and able to make its annual tribute payments without undue suffering.

In Egypt, as elsewhere in the Ottoman provinces, the rulers divided the population into two groups: rulers and subjects. The ruling element, called *askeri*, a word that meant "military," included civil administrators and high-level ulama as well as military men. None of these individuals was taxed. The rest were designated *reaya*, the subject peoples, whose taxes paid for the agents of the state and its many important functions. In this first stage of Ottoman rule Egypt's administrators were paid salaries, unlike those who served in the Balkans and other parts of the empire, where a tax-farming system existed and where local administrators paid themselves out of the taxes that they collected, sending only the surplus to Istanbul.

The Beylicate, 1609–1740

Mamluk power could not be held in check for long, and it reasserted itself at the beginning of the seventeenth century. Not only were the Mamluks permitted to form their own military unit, but they continued to import young slaves from the Balkans, mainly from Georgia and Circassia, train them as they had in their heyday, and use them to swell the power and size of their households. The term *beylicate*, which is often employed to describe this era, refers specifically to the rise in the seventeenth century of Mamluk officials, many of whom held the rank of bey, after Ottoman control over the country waned. In Egypt, beys did not govern provinces as they did in other parts of the Ottoman Empire but were recipients of government stipends, paid from the Egyptian treasury. An official holding the rank of sanjak bey in Egypt was not the ruler of an administrative division, as he was elsewhere in the Ottoman Empire, but the holder of a rank in the Ottoman service. Increasingly in the late sixteenth century and then throughout the seventeenth and eighteenth centuries, individuals holding the title of bey and sanjak bey in Egypt were drawn from the Mamluk community.

Households, rather than high military rank or important administrative office, became the real source of power in seventeenth- and eighteenth-century Egypt. By the seventeenth century three kinds of households existed in Egypt. Each was in competition with the other two. First was the household that formed around the Ottoman governor of the country. In the sixteenth century this household was the dominant force in Egypt. The household of the governor took as its model the sultan's household in Istanbul and those of the leading administrators in the capital city. Alongside the governor's household were the households of the leading Ottoman administrators and military men, namely the *daftardar*, or treasurer of the Egyptian government, the *amir al-hajj*, the officer responsible for the annual pilgrimage to the holy places, the heads of the seven military units based in Egypt, and the administrators of Egypt's districts. The third set of households were those of Mamluk grandees, whose power waxed as they imported more and more young slaves from the Caucasus and as Ottoman power waned. By the eighteenth century, households were no longer confined to these three groups but included anyone who had influence and wealth and was able to attract followers. Hence, merchants, landed elites, and ulama began to create their own households and to enter the competition for political influence.

Households usually rallied around a single leader, although there were occasions when several strong men aligned. The leader was often the head of one of the military regiments stationed in Cairo or a powerful district administrator. Households swelled in size when their leaders brought Mamluks into their ranks, attracted retainers and Bedouins, and found the resources to enlist and pay free-born Ottoman mercenaries. The competition to win the lucrative offices of *daftardar* and *amir al-hajj* was intense since having the funds from these offices provided households with the resources to attract even more followers.

Between 1640 and 1730 two Mamluk households (the Faqaris and the Qasimis) polarized all of Egypt in their competition for preeminence, forcing virtually every element in the society to pick a side. Bedouins, merchants, artisans, ulama, and wealthy peasants were drawn into the fray to the extent that Egypt was plunged into a virtual civil war in 1711, an entire year given over to disputes and confrontations between the warring factions. For a time the Qasimi faction prevailed, but the Faqaris reasserted themselves in 1730, annihilating their foes and preparing the way for the third period of Ottoman Egyptian history, the dominance of the Qazdaghli faction.

A new way of taxing the population, called the *iltizam* system, accompanied the rise of households and was a factor in declining Ottoman power. *Iltizams* were tax farms, a practice that was widely used elsewhere in the Ottoman Empire but had not been introduced into Egypt at the time of the conquest. By the seventeenth century, however, tax farming had made a place for itself in Egypt. An administration, eager to lay its hand on funds more quickly and with less effort than having salaried officials collect taxes, now chose to parcel out Egypt's agricultural lands, political offices, and taxable enterprises to the highest bidders at public auctions. Those who won the auctions, called *multazims*, assumed the full burdens of local administration, including maintaining law and order, and they, rather than salaried officials, collected the taxes, delivering those sums that the state required of them and pocketing the surplus. Egypt's new tax farmers exploited the peasantry more harshly than the salaried Ottoman administrators had and were less worried about the long-term productivity of their farms. Their interest was in extracting wealth from their taxable areas as fully, quickly, and fiercely as possible. The economic effect on the peasantry was predictable and devastating. At first, the tax farmers were Ottoman and Mamluk officials, but as the financial needs of the central administration increased and as the desire to raise increasing amounts of money through the auctioning off of lands and offices to highest bidders intensified, the state simply sold *iltizams* to persons of wealth. By the eighteenth century merchants, wealthy artisans, ulama, and even women were bidding at these auctions and becoming *multazims*.

Another predictable and negative consequence of tax farming was the increased proportion of the agricultural lands set aside as charitable or religious endowments, called waqfs, which paid their donors, in this case former *multazims* as well as their heirs, stipends as administrators. Since these lands were only lightly taxed or not taxed at all, the creation of waqfs deprived the state of much-needed revenue. The use of waqfs was especially popular with non-Mamluk and Ottoman *multazims*, fearful that the state would reassert control over their holdings in order to repair budgetary deficits. With less revenue, the state found the tasks of administering the country increasingly harrowing. By the end of the eighteenth century fully one-fifth of Egypt's agricultural land was under waqfs.

The Qazdaghli Period, 1730–1798

The Qazdaghli household dominated the last period of Ottoman Egyptian history prior to the French invasion of 1798. The founder of the household, Mustafa Qazdaghli, had arrived in Egypt from Anatolia in the seventeenth century and joined the prestigious Janissary corps, rising to the rank of *katkhuda* or second in command before his death in 1704. At first the Qazdaghlis worked within the Faqari faction, which destroyed its bitter Qasimi foes in 1730, but by the 1740s, the Qazdaghlis had become the dominant force in Egypt. In addition to gaining control of most of Egypt's important administrative offices, the Qazdaghlis drew wealth from Egypt's flourishing coffee trade.

The most impressive of the Qazdaghli leaders in this period was a ruthless but dynamic man, Ali Bey al-Kabir, who ruled Egypt from 1760 to 1772. He made Egypt virtually autonomous from Istanbul. Not only did Ali Bey depose two governors whom the sultan sent to Egypt, but he also had his name recited in the Friday prayers immediately after that of the sultan and in place of the imperial appointee. He also had coins minted in his name. Although he had sprung from one of the non-Mamluk, Ottoman military units in Egypt—the Janissary corps—in fact his period in power and that of his successor, Muhammad Bey Abu al-Dhahab, who ruled from 1772 until 1775, more closely resembled the old Mamluk era than any other period in Ottoman Egyptian history. These two rulers, often designated as neo-Mamluks, sought to turn Egypt into an independent state and to detach it from Ottoman suzerainty. Ali Bey invaded Syria against the wishes of his superiors in Istanbul and conducted his own diplomatic negotiations with European diplomats. But these two renegade rulers were ultimately not successful. The Ottomans reestablished their control over Egypt in 1775, only to lose it to the French, who invaded the country in 1798, and then to an Albanian military adventurer, Muhammad Ali, who prevailed in a three-cornered struggle with the Ottoman governor, the Mamluks, and his Albanian stalwarts and had himself installed as the ruler of Egypt in the early nineteenth century.

SOCIAL AND CULTURAL LIFE IN OTTOMAN EGYPT

Largely owing to the influence of the Qazdaghlis and the absence of epidemic diseases and food shortages, Egypt enjoyed an extraordinary period of political stability and economic prosperity in the second half of the eighteenth century. It had not known such halcyon days since the apex of Mamluk power. The arts flourished, Cairo gained much beauty, book reading and intellectual salons were in vogue, and Sufi groups functioned with great vigor. According to Egypt's most acute observer, the historian al-Jabarti, Egypt at this time "was peaceful, free from strife and violence. Cairo's beauties were brilliant, its excellence apparent, vanquishing its rivals. The poor lived at ease. Both great and small lived in abundance."

Undergirding the country's cultural florescence and political well-being was an economic surge, based largely on the coffee trade. Well into the sixteenth century, Egypt had continued to be a major entrepôt for Asian spices and other high-value commodities making their way from Asia to Europe. But the entrance of the European powers into the Indian Ocean and the new trade routes circling the

Cape of Good Hope in South Africa threatened Egypt's importance in global commerce. Coffee came to the rescue. Originally cultivated in Ethiopia, then after plant rootings had been transported to Yemen, grown in Yemen, this southern Arabian principality became the major location for the cultivation of coffee and its only source for export in the fifteenth century and continuing well into the sixteenth century. By the seventeenth and eighteenth centuries coffee had achieved a status similar to that of tea in the nineteenth century and tobacco and alcohol in the first half of the twentieth century, in demand in every corner of the globe. Coffeehouses sprang up as sites where the rich and powerful gathered to discuss the latest commercial and financial news and to plot their political fortunes. More religiously inclined persons flocked to them to consume a beverage that gave them a burst of energy and prolonged their religious mediations. They even provided solace for the poor and downtrodden who came together in shops to grumble and imagine a world turned upside down. Cairo was far in advance of even the wealthiest locations in Europe in its addiction to coffee. London's first coffeehouse opened in 1652 at a time when Cairo was already saturated with 643 such establishments. By 1800 the number of coffee establishments in Cairo had doubled, and fully one-sixth of the city's caravanserais stored coffee beans.

As long as Yemen was the only territory where coffee was grown (and the Yemenis held onto their privileged position tenaciously, refusing to allow any cuttings to leave the country), Egypt's commercial preeminence was assured. The entire coffee trade to Europe passed through the country. Not surprisingly, then, the richest and most influential merchants in Egypt even as late as the eighteenth century were coffee traders. The Sharaybi family, whom al-Jabarti described as possessing an enormous fortune, were the dominant merchants in Egypt's seventeenth- and eighteenth-century coffee business. They lived resplendently in the Cairo's most fashionable quarter, Azbakiyya, on an estate built on the edge of the quarter's attractive lake. Their palatial home, featuring twelve massive sitting rooms, served as a popular meeting place for Cairo's well-connected persons. Mamluk beys came to be entertained there but lingered to discuss current political and commercial affairs. The Sharaybis, who had merchant agents based along the Red Sea coast and throughout Egypt, employed their wealth to serve the public good. They organized salons where the scholarly classes exchanged insights, and founded libraries where large collections of books were made available to anyone with an interest. The funeral of the family's founder, Muhammad al-Daba, revealed the wealth and the esteem that the public attached to this public-spirited individual. It was attended by all of Cairo's elite; the funeral procession stretched all the way from the family house to the mosque.

Material prosperity enhanced spiritual devotion. Sufi orders thrived in Ottoman Egypt, no doubt owing to the close relationship that the Ottoman ruling classes had always enjoyed with Anatolian Sufi orders and the ruling family's embrace of mystical and popular forms of Islamic worship. During the transition from Mamluk to Ottoman rule the leading Egyptian Sufi adept was Abd al-Wahhab al-Sharani (1493–1565), whose learning and devout life gained a large following. One of his disciples built a *zawiya*, or religious building, consisting of a school and a small mosque. In time, as al-Sharani's fame spread, his *zawiya* was enlarged, so that at its high point it housed 200 resident Sufi adepts and provided food and shelter for 500, not all of whom were required to be Sufis. Al-Sharani was an admirer and devoted student of the Spanish-born Sufi mystic Ibn al-Arabi (1165–1240) and encouraged his followers to emulate al-Arabi's all-embracing teachings about Islam and his devotional and meditative practices, which al-Sharani believed facilitated mystical union with God.

Equally influential in Egypt was the Khalwati Sufi order. Taking its name from the Arabic word *khalwa*, meaning to withdraw, the Khalwati Sufis sought to avoid the hurly-burly of daily life in order to meditate and engage in mystical experiences. Although the order had originated in the Caucasus, Anatolia, and Azerbaijan in the late fourteenth century, its vitality in Egypt in the fifteenth century caused its influence to spread into North Africa and across the Sahara. The most revered of the Khalwati shaykhs in Egypt was Damirdash al-Muhammadi (d. 1523). Known for his attention to the poor, he founded an orchard of fruit trees, the produce from which he distributed to people in need. His followers, too, built a *zawiya* for him, which was said to have fifty *khalwas*, or private rooms, where Sufis withdrew for meditation.

Perhaps the most enduring of the cultural attainments of the Ottoman era were the buildings that were erected in Cairo during these three centuries. Although the Mamluks are usually thought of as Islamic Cairo's most creative architects and beautifiers, in fact, a substantial proportion of the most important buildings from the medieval and early modern past were erected in the Ottoman centuries.

At the time of the Ottoman conquest, Cairo consisted of three major urban centers. First and foremost was al-Qahira, the old Fatimid royal city, to which was joined the Citadel, both of which were enclosed within city walls. Most of the Ottoman grandees either took over the best houses in al-Qahira after the conquest or had new, even more spacious residences built for them there. The second urban location was Old Cairo, which had a large Coptic population and was southwest of al-Qahira. This was "a rather decayed town," many of whose inhabitants lived in poverty. One kilometer to the west of al-Qahira was the third urban area, Bulaq, which also served as the city's port. By the second half of the seventeenth century, as the population of Cairo continued to expand from the 100,000 inhabitants who had lived there at the end of the Mamluk era and was well on its way to the one-quarter of a million inhabitants that the French encountered in 1800, residents were filling up the empty areas that separated these three urban conglomerations. Among the new locations, Azbakiyya was considered the most desirable. Built around a pond, it boasted a number of Cairo's largest and most elegant residences.

The political figure who did more than anyone else to beautify Cairo was a member of the Qazdaghli ruling elite, Abd al-Rahman Katkhuda, who lived from 1714 to 1776. His life story is unique among powerful members of the Qazdaghli family. Though birth, family wealth, and inherited high office favored his rise to political prominence, he evinced little interest in political combat. As head of the Qazdaghli family and leader of the powerful and prestigious Janissary corps, he would have been expected to surround himself with political subordinates and retainers so that he could rule the country as ruthlessly as his predecessors had. But political ambitions did not drive him. His disinterest in politics, even a naïveté hard to fathom in a member of this family, ultimately proved to be his undoing. Seeking to rule by consensus and eager to promote men of talents, he brought about his own political and personal ruination by facilitating the rise to power of Ali Bey al-Kabir. The latter's political ambitions were ill-concealed and unbounded, and in 1765 Ali Bey ended his patron's career by sending him into exile in the Hijaz. In contrast to his predecessor, Ibrahim Katkhuda, an effective Qazdaghli ruler, and his successor, Ali Bey, what excited Abd al-Rahman Katkhuda was architectural beauty and urban splendor. In his dedication to making Cairo more commodious and more spiritually fulfilling, he spared no expense.

Perhaps one of the reasons that Abd al-Rahman did not fit the mold of a Qazdaghli political chief was that he was more Egyptian than Ottoman or Mamluk. Born of a free-born Egyptian woman and educated in Egyptian ways and institutions, he acquired a fine knowledge of Arabic. Yet for much of his career he functioned in the shadow of Ibrahim Qazdaghli, a natural-born ruler, whose political ambitions dominated Egypt from 1747 to 1754. But Ibrahim Qazdaghli's death in 1754 propelled Abd al-Rahman into his patron's position. His preference for consensus prevented him from destroying his adversaries as his predecessors would have. Although his critics, including al-Jabarti, who had little good to say about the Qazdaghlis, were incredulous when viewing his political behavior, they marveled at his religious devotion, his charitable works, and especially his refurbishment of Cairo. Of his additions to al-Azhar mosque, which al-Jabarti considered his supreme architectural triumph, the Egyptian chronicler commented, "had he no other achievement to his credit than the buildings that he added to al-Azhar mosque, an accomplishment unequalled by kings, this would have been enough." Yet he did much more, and did so in a highly personal architectural style, unlike that of other Ottoman rulers, who tended to imitate their Mamluk predecessors. His buildings stand out as unique contributions to the Ottoman era.

The most attractive buildings of the Ottoman era were *sabil-kuttabs*, constructions that combined religious schools for children, usually on the second floor, with drinking fountains attached on the ground floor where passersby could slake their thirst. The most impressive of these *sabil-kuttabs,* considered by many to be the finest piece of Ottoman architecture in Cairo, was that erected by Abd al-Rahman on the main street of the Fatimid royal city (Muizz Street) and completed in 1744. It can still be seen today and projects the religious enthusiasm of its patron and his unrivalled architectural brilliance. Open on all three sides, its most striking feature is a magnificent, large grated window from which water was distributed to pedestrians. On the second floor is a classroom where young students were taught to read and write.

Yet, in many ways, the most striking of the Ottoman structures in Cairo was not erected in the Ottoman era at all. The mosque that Egypt's Albanian viceroy, Muhammad Ali, constructed at the Citadel atop a spur of the Muqattam hills is a nineteenth-century work. Known as the Muhammad Ali mosque, it dominates the skyline of Cairo and is the first religious structure that greets visitors to the city. It has all of the features associated with Ottoman religious buildings—a dome over the central place of worship, and tall and slender minarets, projecting the power of Islam high into the sky, in this case no fewer than eighty-two meters, entirely reminiscent of the great Suleimaniye mosque and other notable mosques in Istanbul. Yet the Muhammad Ali mosque was not pure Ottoman architecture. It had European influences, including a clock presented to the Egyptian Pasha by the French monarch Louis-Philippe and installed in a clock tower. Its interior, in the opinion of many observers, is quite un-Islamic and is more profane than religious. Its critics, of whom there are many, consider it a "barbarous mosque" in comparison with the other fine religious constructions that surround it, but over which it towers.

No discussion of the social and cultural life of Ottoman Egypt can be complete without dealing, however briefly, with the vast mass of the population—the Egyptian peasantry—without whose contributions Egypt's economic prosperity, cultural vitality, and political stability could not have been achieved. Alas, not nearly enough is known about the lives of the ordinary peasants, save that for most of them the intrusions of the central government were onerous and resented. The officials that did the bidding of the rulers, even those who lived in their midst, were viewed with suspicion and rightly seen as exploiters. In many respects the only solace of village life was family, friends, and the popular form of Islam that suffused the lives of ordinary folk.

During the Ottoman period, as before, the Egyptian village constituted the country's basic administrative and financial unit. A not extensive, but nonetheless efficient group of local administrators, who themselves resided in the villages, served as the agents of the central government, responsible to the authorities above them, mainly the *multazims,* for the collection of taxes and the maintenance of law and order. The *multazims'* primary village agent was the village shaykh, usually one of the wealthiest and certainly one of the most venerated members of the local community. Large villages might have as many as twenty shaykhs. In turn they were assisted by bookkeepers and treasurers, often drawn from the Coptic population, who kept the tax and land records and assisted the shaykhs when collecting the land and other taxes. Other officials included village watchmen, responsible for protecting the villagers from robberies, and local *qadis*, who applied the religious law when disputes arose and legal questions had to be answered. Sadly for the peasantry, these officials worked aggressively on behalf of their political masters in the central government and spared no effort to enhance their own political and financial well-being. Rarely did they seek to defend the peasants from the outside world.

Napoleon Bonaparte, Muhammad Ali, and Ismail
Egypt in the Nineteenth Century

Thomas Carlyle claimed that the history of the world was but the biography of great men. Karl Marx added that great men made history but not always as they pleased. The history of Egypt from the beginning of the nineteenth century—1798, to be exact—until 1882, the year when the British invaded and occupied Egypt, revolves around three great figures: Napoleon Bonaparte, who led a massive French invasion of the country in 1798, bringing Egypt face-to-face with the most radical of Europe's nation-states; Muhammad Ali, who ruled Egypt from 1805 until 1848 and set in motion modernizing programs that transformed nearly all corners of Egyptian society; and Khedive Ismail, ruler of Egypt from 1863 to 1879, whose ambition it was to make Egypt an outpost of Europe. Each man had grandiose visions for Egypt. Each failed in his own way. Napoleon stayed only a year in Egypt and then saw his French troops forced out of the country just three years after his invasion. Muhammad Ali's forces stood on the doorsteps of Istanbul, but were forced to disgorge most of their territorial conquests under European diplomatic pressure and to limit the size of the Egyptian army and the country's economic ambitions. Ismail celebrated the opening of the Suez Canal in 1869 as proof that Egypt had finally joined the concert of European nations. Yet his European adversaries deposed him ten years later. He departed from a country mired in bankruptcy.

FRANCE, BONAPARTE, AND EGYPT, 1798–1801

On July 1, 1798, a massive French fleet of 400 vessels and close to 54,000 men appeared off the coast of Alexandria. On board were

36,000 soldiers and 16,000 sailors. Egyptians had never seen an invading army of this size, certainly not one that had come by sea. The Ottoman land invasion of 1517, Egypt's last major foreign invasion, had involved fewer soldiers and had come overland across the Sinai Peninsula. France's invading forces were under the command of Napoleon Bonaparte, a twenty-eight-year-old general, who was already the rising star in the firmament of French military and political figures thrown up by the Revolution. The people of Alexandria were filled with fear when they beheld the French off their coast. Nicholas the Turk, an eyewitness, claimed that when the residents looked at the sea they could see only sky and ships and "were seized by unimaginable fear." (See plate 24 for an artist's rendering of Napoleon in Egypt.)

When news of the arrival of the French forces reached the capital city, the Cairenes, too, were afraid. Many packed up their belongings and fled to the countryside. Only the proud Mamluk warriors showed little apprehension. They had, in fact, received an earlier warning when a British naval squadron under the command of Horatio Nelson sailed through Egyptian waters and cautioned the Egyptians that French naval and land forces were in the area and might be planning an attack on Egypt. The Mamluks paid little heed to the British warnings. They remained secure in the belief that even if the French invaded the country, their own forces would prevail. "Let the Franks come; we shall crush them beneath our horses' hooves."

The French forces had left Toulon in mid-May and had been at sea for six weeks, except for a short stopover to invade and bring Malta under French control. Most of the men on the ships had not known of their destination when they boarded and learned of it only midway on their voyage to Egypt. It was only then that Bonaparte announced that the fleet was bound for Egypt and that the soldiers would have the glorious mission of bringing the ideals of the European enlightenment and the French Revolution to one of the cradles of world civilization. Bonaparte's announcement thrilled the men, most especially the 151 scholars whom Bonaparte had chosen to accompany his troops and who were enthralled by the prospect of observing a once great center of civilization to which they would bring their own form of culture. Yet after such a long time on board, all were weary of the cramped quarters and the rough Mediterranean Sea. In truth, only the good fortunes of climate had prevented most of the French fleet from finding itself at the bottom of the Mediterranean. On one fog-filled day, the French ships and Nelson's fleet passed one another unobserved.

The French had little difficulty landing their forces or anchoring their fleet in Abukir Bay, near Alexandria. Their first impressions of Egypt were distinctly negative. Expecting to see a city that Alexander the Great had founded and antiquities that reflected its long and storied history, the French instead saw only a small fishing village containing a mere 6,000 inhabitants. They noticed few signs of historic importance. The only monument immediately visible was a column, known for many centuries as Pompey's pillar, but which in reality was part of a temple that had been erected to the sun god, Serapis, around 300 BCE. One of the French savants opined: "We were looking for the city of the Ptolemies, the library, the seat of human knowledge. And we found instead ruins, barbarism, poverty, and degradation."

The decision to invade Egypt was not the brainstorm of Bonaparte alone, though he had great influence on it. He had been put in charge of the army to invade England. Realizing that as long as the British controlled the oceans, an invasion was certain to fail, he chose instead to strike what he and the other French leadership regarded as a blow to Britain's empire. Egypt was one of the strategic lifelines to India, the cornerstone of Britain overseas. The French felt sure that by invading it, they would strike a blow at British prestige and commercial power. In addition, Egypt had been in the minds of many leading French intellectuals and politicians for some decades. Several French travelers had alerted the home population to its importance. The most widely read of these travelers was Constantine-François de Volney, who had published in 1787 an authoritative two-volume travel account of the Middle East, *Travels Through Egypt and Syria in 1783, 1784, and 1785*. Moreover, the French had a growing commercial connection with Egypt, which had moved into second place, though a distant second, in French overseas commerce, still lagging well behind the sugar islands of the Caribbean. Forty or fifty French merchants resided in Egypt, where the French had opened three consulates—at Alexandria, Rosetta, and Cairo. Finally, when Talleyrand became foreign minister of France in 1797, the die was cast. Talleyrand was unequivocally in favor of the Egyptian expedition and hopeful that France would not only establish a colony in Egypt but use this territory as the core of a large French empire in the Middle East. He sought nothing less that an empire that would rival that of the British Empire in India and the Americas.

As the French forces began their march up the western branch of the Nile on their way to Cairo, harassed along the way by Bedouin forces, Bonaparte issued a proclamation to the Egyptian populace. The document, written in Arabic, endeavored to appeal to the rank and file of the Egyptian population and to portray his soldiers as liberators of Egypt from Mamluk misrule. Invoking the themes of the French Revolution that had served the French army so well in Europe, Bonaparte said that he and his soldiers came as friends of the Egyptian people, as believers in the equality of men, and servants of a state in which men of virtue and intelligence would exercise power. Moreover, he asserted that his forces were not the foes of Islam, that they were, in fact, "faithful Muslims."

While the ideals of the French Revolution won many supporters on the European continent, they fell on deaf ears in Egypt. Egypt's astute chronicler al-Jabarti, who wrote no fewer than three separate accounts of the French invasion and whose observations provide that often missing perspective of the conquered community, had nothing but scorn for the French proclamation. After pointing out its numerous errors in the use of Arabic, he attacked its ideology. The French were hardly friends of any religion, he wrote, having sacked the Papal See in Rome. "They do not hold fast to any religion. You see that they are materialists who deny all God's attributes." He went on in the same vein to remind his readers that the French had slain their own monarch and that their doctrine based on the equality of individuals was a falsehood: "God made some superior to others as is testified by the dwellers in the heavens and on earth."

Nonetheless, the French army impressed al-Jabarti as it marched inexorably toward Cairo with a discipline and a zeal that shamed the panicked Mamluks and reminded the author of the early Muslim armies at the time of the Prophet Muhammad. Nor was al-Jabarti's estimation of the difference between the two military forces wrong. At a battle just outside Cairo, not too far from the pyramids (hence bearing the name that Bonaparte gave it, the Battle of the Pyramids), the French routed the Mamluk forces and entered Cairo largely unopposed. The outcome of the battle could hardly have been in doubt. Not only had the Mamluks divided their forces, placing one group on the east bank of the Nile so that the other group, stationed on the west bank, had to withstand the full force of a 28,000-man French force. In addition, the French had better weaponry and better battle tactics. According to al-Jabarti, "the rifles of the French were like a boiling pot on a fierce fire." Of the battle, he added that "the uninterrupted shooting was deafening. To the people it appears as if the earth were shaking and the sky was falling." Still, the French had much admiration for their opponents as dedicated, if doomed, adversaries. One of the French officers described the Mamluks arrayed against them as garbed in "brilliantly colored" costumes and armed "with sabers, lances, maces, spears, rifles, battles axes and daggers, and each has three pistols. This spectacle produced a vivid impression on our soldiers by its novelty and richness. From that moment on, their thoughts were set on booty." Nonetheless, while routed, the Mamluks were hardly conquered. Of their two leading military figures—Ibrahim Bey and Murad Bey—one retreated to Syria and the other to Upper Egypt, prepared to fight on.

Bonaparte's entry into Cairo did not alter his judgment of Egypt's decline. Although the population was a robust 250,000 and the city had many luxurious palaces, which the French generals and the savants quickly took over, Bonaparte wrote back to his superiors in France that "it would be difficult to find a richer land and a more wretched, ignorant, and brutish people." Bonaparte claimed the deserted palace of Muhammad al-Alfi Bey in the Azbakiyya section of Cairo. He charged his savants with locating suitable quarters for themselves at a distance not too far from his residence and headquarters. After considerable searches, they took over a palace and its grounds at a distance of about two kilometers from Bonaparte's house.

Three events in quick succession doomed the French expedition to failure. The first occurred on August 1, 1798, when the British fleet under Nelson returned from searching for the French fleet along the coast of Syria and found it at anchor in Abukir Bay. Not even waiting for the next day, Nelson sent his ships against the French ships in the dead of the night. Frenchmen watching from a balcony at Rosetta saw explosions and firestorms occurring throughout the night and were convinced that they were watching a great French naval victory. They were wrong. By morning many of the most powerful of the French ships had been sunk, not least of which was the command ship, *l'Orient*, in which Bonaparte had installed a magnificent general's room and an elaborate bed for himself. When news of the naval disaster reached Cairo, Bonaparte threatened to have the tongues removed from those individuals who were spreading the bad tidings. But the truth was soon there for all to behold. Nelson had indeed scuttled the French fleet, leaving Bonaparte, his soldiers, and scholars trapped in Egypt, with no way of escaping. In fact, the British had such full control over the seas that the Frenchmen in Egypt were now no longer able to communicate with their comrades at home. Isolation and a sense of gloom descended upon the French, while the Egyptians, the powerful and the powerless alike, gathered hope that the beginning of the end of what for them was proving a test of wills would result in a French defeat.

This possibility became all the more likely in the middle of October 1798, when the second event occurred: a large number of Cairenes rose in revolt against the French presence. Opposition to the French had been building ever since the soldiers entered Cairo. Egyptian notables resented the fact that Bonaparte required them to wear tricolor rosettes on their garments. They were ill at ease in the councils, called *diwans* in Arabic, that the French commanding general asked the most influential to join. They also balked at the takeover of Cairo's most sumptuous dwellings and the rude and, to them, uncivilized bearing of many of the French soldiers. Despite

Bonaparte's demand that the French troops respect the Egyptian population and honor their religion, not all of the soldiers behaved civilly to the conquered people. Al-Jabarti was troubled, as many of the local population must have been, by the interactions of the French soldiers with Egyptian women. Finally, because Bonaparte required financial support to establish and pay for his government in Egypt, he exacted a number of taxes that the local population found oppressive and regarded as illegitimate.

The primary rallying point for opposition to the French proved to be the mosques, where religious leaders, often inspired by rumors of Bonaparte's death or an invasion of Ottoman and British forces, began to call for a holy war (jihad) against their opponents. For two full days, groups of rioters rose up against the French, and the city administration spun out of control. The rebels fought with clubs, truncheons, sticks, and hammers, but they were not well organized and, in al-Jabarti's words, "ran around like wild asses and fanaticism increased." Bonaparte's response was both brutal and chilling. He launched a ruthless counterattack, sparing no one who had anything to do with the rebellion. Wheeling his cannons up to the Citadel, he "opened fire with cannons and bombs on houses and quarters, aiming specially at the mosque of Azhar, firing at it with these bombs." French forces entered al-Azhar, ravaged student quarters, defiled the mosque, and broke up bookcases. Although al-Jabarti had little sympathy with the rebels, he was appalled at the behavior of the French soldiers. "The French trod in the Mosque of al-Azhar with their shoes, carrying swords and rifles. . . . They ravaged the students' quarters and ponds, smashing the lamps and chandeliers and breaking up the bookcases of the students . . . and scribes. . . . They treated the books and the Quranic volumes as trash, throwing them on the ground, stamping on them with their feet and shoes. Furthermore, they soiled the mosque, blowing their spit in it, pissing and defecating in it. They guzzled wine and smashed the bottles in the central court and other parts. And whoever they happened to meet in the mosque they stripped." These reprisals left those elements in Egyptian society previously drawn to the French in no doubt that the actions of the French soldiers were not those of "faithful Muslims." Bonaparte had crushed a rebellion, but in the process he had created a population entirely hostile to French authority.

The third event was a disastrous military campaign in Syria. Cut off from France, Bonaparte's one obvious solution was to establish a viable French colonial possession in Egypt. His pro-Muslim edicts and his efforts to create collaborating Egyptian councils (*diwans*) were part and parcel of this attempt to turn Egypt into a French colony. So also was his military foray into Syria, which, in the minds of all of Egypt's rulers from pharaonic times to the present, was strategically linked to the valley of the Nile. Bonaparte assembled a formidable army of 13,000 battle-tested soldiers and moved into Syria. Here everything went wrong. The British and Ottoman fleets harassed the advancing French soldiers as did Bedouin tribesmen, who preyed on stragglers. The military coup de grâce came at the battle of Acre, where a strong Ottoman army repulsed the French, who suffered great loss of life. The battle losses were, however, small in comparison with the losses to disease. Plague swept through the French army, leaving a trail of dying and dead. The French had always known the Middle East to be an unhealthy place. To counteract the threat of disease, they had brought a large contingent of physicians, who, however, were powerless in the face of this epidemic disease. They were equally powerless to deal with the ophthalmic disorders, which, while they did not kill, spared hardly a single French soldier. By the time Bonaparte took the distasteful decision to withdraw his army from Syria, he had lost no fewer than 2,000 men of the 13,000 with whom he had set out.

Bonaparte lasted little more than a year in Egypt. With affairs going poorly in France as well as in Egypt, the ambitious general stole away from Cairo with a few of his trusted advisers. He departed on August 18, 1799, twelve and a half months after he had landed in Egypt. He left Alexandria on August 22 and arrived back in France, having avoided British Mediterranean naval squadrons, to be named the first consul in a government with three consuls. A mere five years later, in 1804, after he had turned the military fortunes of France around, he became Emperor Napoleon I. Although he claimed that he had not deserted his troops in Egypt, but had left to answer a higher calling in France, many of his men did not agree. Most displeased was the man whom Bonaparte left in charge, Jean-Baptiste Kléber. Bonaparte had not even told Kléber of his plans to leave or of his intention to leave him in charge of the French Egyptian army.

Kléber was livid. He already thought the Egyptian adventure a failure. Now he regarded Bonaparte as a coward for having left his loyal army to fend for itself. Kléber's only thought was to get the troops out of Egypt, but at this he failed. Before he could arrange terms for an evacuation or a surrender, he was assassinated by a Muslim opponent. The terms of surrender and return to France were negotiated between his successor, Jacques Abdallah Menou, and Sydney Smith of the British Mediterranean fleet. Finally, on July 31, 1801, almost exactly three years and one month after they had set foot on Egyptian soil, French soldiers began to leave Egypt. By September the entire French army, now only 20,000 strong, had been evacuated.

What made the French invasion stunning among modern wars was the fact that Bonaparte had taken with him no fewer than 151 scholars, drawn from among the leading young French intellectuals, who were imbued with the ideals of the French Revolution. Much to the chagrin of his military comrades, Bonaparte doted on these men of science. Regularly every evening, he would meet with his loyal scholars in his command center on the lead ship, l'Orient, where he engaged in lively philosophical and scientific discussions on all manner of scholarly activity. Once the army arrived in Egypt, he gave them great leeway to poke around Egypt, make drawings of the antiquities that they happened on, and write papers about their favorite intellectual pursuits. Most of the savants were young men, recent graduates of l'École polytechnique or l'École des mines, les ponts, et chaussées. Some had not yet completed their studies and were still working for their degrees. Nearly all of them were in awe of Bonaparte and signed on for the expedition because of their faith in him even though they did not know where it was going. Two senior scholars, in their fifties, Gaspard Monge and Claude-Louis Bertholet, a geographer and a chemist respectively, played the major roles in recruiting these men and overseeing their activities in Egypt. Also looked to as a leader and highly regarded as a man of great learning was Jean Baptiste Joseph Fourier, still in his thirties, but soon to be the inventor of a system of mathematical analysis that would bear his name.

At the outset, the savants set up an Institut d'Égypt, modeled on the Institut de France. Here they held scholarly seminars, which were open to the public. Military men were welcome to attend. So were Egyptians, among whom one invited and impressed guest was the chronicler of the period, al-Jabarti. Al-Jabarti made note of all of the sophisticated scientific instruments that the scholars employed and marveled at the fact that the French had made a translation of the Quran and boasted a number of scholars who had a respectable mastery of Arabic.

One of the purposes of the Egyptian mission was to determine whether a waterway could be cut through the Isthmus of Suez to link the Mediterranean Sea with the Red Sea and the Indian Ocean. The engineer, Jacques-Marie Le Père, undertook the assignment. Harassed by Bedouins and forced to work at a breakneck pace, he came to the wrong conclusion. His report claimed that there was a 32.5-foot difference in elevation between the two bodies of water and therefore a canal would require an expensive set of locks.

If Le Père's work proved to be a failure, the French expeditions into Upper Egypt, ostensibly to bring the Mamluk forces based there under French rule, proved an unqualified scientific success. Although the French did not rout the Mamluks in Upper Egypt, the scholars whom they took with them compiled such an impressive amount of information on both ancient and modern Egypt that Kléber decided that their findings should be combined into a comprehensive and multivolume work, which would highlight all of the information that the French had discovered about Egypt. Thus was born the twenty-two-volume *Description de l'Égypte*, which appeared between 1809 and 1828. The work constituted the most detailed treatment of any country outside Europe and North America in 1800 at a time when Europe was beginning to spread its influence across the globe.

The twenty-two volumes contained ten volumes of plates, portraying ancient and modern Egypt, nine volumes of text, including memoirs and scholarly pieces describing ancient and modern Egypt, and three volumes of maps and atlases. Its influence on Europeans was stupendous. It sparked a fascination with ancient Egyptian civilization. It inspired cultured Europeans to collect Egyptian antiquities and to use Egyptian motifs in their household decorations and furniture. Although the savants were not trained archaeologists, the *Description* laid the foundations for studying the archaeology of Egypt. Bonaparte had brought savants to Egypt to facilitate French control over the country; yet these men were given such freedom to pursue their own intellectual interests that they succeeded in founding the field of Egyptology, which secured a privileged position in nineteenth-century European universities. (See figure 4 for an illustration from the *Description de l'Égypte* of the Sphinx as the French found it, covered entirely with sand up to its face.)

Critical to the new field of Egyptology was perhaps the most important discovery of the entire expedition. At the city of Rosetta, a French team came upon a stone tablet that contained a text in three languages—Greek, which, of course, scholars knew, demotic Egyptian, and hieroglyphs. It was clear from the outset that this find would be the key to deciphering hieroglyphs. Fortunately the French made engravings of the stone and shipped them back to France. When the French left Egypt, under the surrender terms, the British demanded that the French cede to the British everything that they had acquired in Egypt, including and especially the Rosetta Stone. A howl of protest that could be heard all the way to London and Paris ensued. The French savants, who had so painstakingly acquired artifacts and information about ancient and modern Egypt, refused to accept such terms and threatened to burn every item that they had collected. One of the scholars said that the loss to humankind would be on the order of the losses to world knowledge that had occurred when the library of Alexandria burned to the ground. The British

Figure 4. The Sphinx as seen by the French during their invasion of Egypt

relented and agreed to allow the French to take away items that were part of their possessions. This was not to include the Rosetta Stone, however, in spite of the claim by the French commanding general, Jacques Menou, that the Stone was as personal to him as his underwear and his embroidered saddles. The final terms compelled the French to turn the Rosetta Stone and much else over to the British, who eventually placed the Stone in the British Museum.

French and British competition over the Stone did not cease at this point. The scholarly world saw the Stone as the key to unlocking the mystery of hieroglyphs and opening the knowledge of the ancient Egyptians to the world. Two extraordinarily talented linguistic scholars, one a Briton, Thomas Young (1773–1829), and the other a Frenchman, Jean-François Champollion (1790–1832), set about feverishly to decipher the Stone. Champollion prevailed, although he acknowledged a debt to his competitor. So excited was he that he had found the key to unlocking hieroglyphs in 1822 that "he rushed to his brother's room at the Institut on the afternoon of the same day, cried 'I've done it' ('je tiens mon affaire'), and collapsed in a dead faint lasting five days."

The French invasion of Egypt set off a European wonderment with things Egyptian. But what difference, if any, did it mean to the Egyptians? Was the arrival of French forces another major turning point in the history of Egypt, comparable, let us say, to the appearance of Christianity and then Islam many centuries earlier? On the surface, it would seem not. The French forces, large as they were, remained in Egypt a scant thirty-seven months. For the most part they were confined to Cairo and made only occasional and mainly unsuccessful excursions beyond its confines. Certainly, the Cairenes felt the influence of the French, who occupied their best homes, exacted heavy taxes, and put down all signs of resistance with overwhelming and ruthless force. But unlike today, the population of Cairo was a mere 5 percent of Egypt's total.

This perspective, however, takes too cramped a view of these three years and especially their aftermath. By the time the Ottoman and British troops had arrived in Egypt, three armies totaling 150,000 troops were marching up and down the country, engaged in battles with one another and with elements of the Egyptian population, most particularly the Bedouin tribesmen. Moreover, the defeat of the vaunted Mamluk soldiers at the battle of the pyramids came as a shock to the Egyptian people and their Ottoman overlords. Not surprisingly, as we shall observe in the next section on Muhammad Ali, the lessons of modern warfare, and indeed much of the modernity that the French had brought to Egypt, were not lost on new leaders who emerged in a bitter struggle for power once the French had withdrawn.

MUHAMMAD ALI

The withdrawal of the French left Egypt in political turmoil. Three groups vied for power: the Mamluks, stung by their defeat at the hands of Napoleon's forces but eager to reestablish their supremacy; the Ottomans themselves, led by the sultan's primary agent, Khurshid Pasha; and an Albanian military man and adventurer, Muhammad Ali, who had come to Egypt with a contingent of Albanian troops on behalf of the sultan to force the French out and ostensibly then to restore Ottoman power. As it turned out, the group that would have seemed least likely to prevail—the Albanian forces of Muhammad Ali—seized power in 1805. Reluctantly, the Ottoman sultan recognized Muhammad Ali, often referred to as the Pasha, as the new ruler in Egypt, although Istanbul insisted that Egypt remain a province of the Ottoman Empire and continue to make annual tribute payments to Istanbul.

Muhammad Ali was born sometime in the late 1760s in the small Macedonian port city of Kavala. He lived until 1849, although he was compelled to step down as the ruler of Egypt in favor of his son Ibrahim in 1848. His father was an Ottoman soldier of Albanian or Kurdish roots as well as a tobacco merchant of some importance. Muhammad Ali worked in his father's tobacco business but also was schooled in warfare. In 1801, he was appointed deputy commander of an Albania military unit sent to Egypt for the purpose of expelling the French invaders. This unit, over which he was only second in command, was a small one, only 300 strong, but it joined other Ottoman forces that landed in Egypt in 1801.

The Ottoman forces in Egypt quickly divided into two camps—the Albanian troops and those that came from Anatolia itself and were entirely loyal to the Ottoman sultan. When the French withdrew, this division became intensified, and the shrewd Albanian leader, though illiterate, saw the virtue in appealing to important elements of Egyptian society. Muhammad Ali, who no doubt observed the way in which the French had curried the favor of Egyptian notables and scholars (the ulama), used the same strategy, making it appear to leading figures in Egyptian society that he, not his Ottoman adversary, Khurshid Pasha, was the man who had their true interests at heart. By 1805, he had vanquished the Ottoman forces and compelled those Mamluks still standing after their devastating encounters with the French to retreat to Upper Egypt. There they licked their wounds and awaited the opportunity to reacquire power as they had done so frequently in the past. Just why they accepted Muhammad Ali's invitation to meet with him in Cairo is somewhat hard to understand. But they did. What they got for their desire to wring a peaceful agreement from the Pasha was nothing short of a complete slaughter of their numbers following a banquet, ostensibly held in their honor at the Citadel of Cairo, but used by the Egyptian ruler to remove the last elements of opposition to his authority in Egypt. The defeat of the Mamluks left Muhammad Ali in the dominant position in Egypt. His control of the country was unchallenged, unlike that of his chief external opponent, the Ottoman sultan, who sought nothing less than to reacquire full sovereignty over the empire's most valuable province. Yet unlike Muhammad Ali, the sultan had internal groups, notably his Janissary corps, that were wedded to tradition and opposed the kinds of modernizing reforms that made Muhammad Ali such a strong ruler and potent adversary in Egypt.

Muhammad Ali realized that he was little more than a usurper of power, who would always have to deal with the political claims of Istanbul on Egypt. Hence, he immediately set about to upgrade his army. Indeed, the history of Egypt during the long reign of Muhammad Ali revolves around the gains and the losses of the Egyptian army. Nearly everything that the ruler did was dictated by his desire to strengthen his army and to make it the dominant force in the eastern Mediterranean. Although Muhammad Ali had been in Egypt only briefly while the French were there, he had learned enough of the French military successes in Egypt and in Europe to realize that Napoleon's armies were the best in the world. He wanted the skills and discipline that had so awed al-Jabarti when the Egyptian chronicler had seen the French army in action. What better way to acquire these qualities than to import French military advisers into Egypt. Not surprisingly, then, one of Muhammad Ali's first actions was to welcome a former Legion of Honor captain of Napoleon's armies, Joseph Anthelme Sève, to bring French military techniques to Egypt. Apparently, the approach was mutually beneficial, for Seve settled comfortably into Egypt, married an Egyptian woman, converted to Islam, took an Egyptian name and title, Sulayman Pasha, and helped to make the Egyptian military the most powerful force in the region.

Establishing a formidable military force in Egypt proved to be no easy task, however. At first Muhammad Ali sought to dragoon Sudanese recruits into his army. Many were taken as slaves in military raids as that country was brought under Egyptian control. But they balked, and also died in large numbers when they were transported to Egypt. Left with little alternative, he turned to the Egyptian peasantry, who, often kicking and screaming, provided the manpower of an Egyptian army that gradually expanded to 130,000 men and served in numerous campaigns outside Egypt itself. In addition to establishing an army, the Pasha, once again with the assistance of French advisers, created a navy and a naval arsenal at Alexandria.

At first Muhammad Ali used his army in the service of the Ottoman sultan. Fundamentalist Wahhabi religious and tribal groups had disrupted the political stability of the Arabian Peninsula. They had even sacked the holy cities of Mecca and Medina, where their advocates claimed that various practices that were anathema to good Muslims were taking place. The Ottoman sultan asked Muhammad Ali to send his new fighting force to the Arabian Peninsula and to bring order to the holy cities and to open the area to regular pilgrimages that the Wahhabis had prevented. The Egyptian army was dispatched to the Hijaz in 1812 and comported itself well, driving the Wahhabis out of the holy cities and restoring the annual pilgrimages. Next, the sultan asked the Egyptians to help put down the Greek nationalists who were seeking to establish an independent Greek state. The Pasha sent soldiers and his fleet, but this time his efforts did not meet with success. The Greeks had won the support of numerous European powers, which sent their fleets to the Mediterranean, where they sank the Egyptian flotilla at the battle of Navarino in 1827. The European states also provided additional diplomatic and military support for the Greek struggle. In 1829, the Greeks won their independence from the Ottoman Empire.

MUHAMMAD ALI'S MODERNIZATION PROGRAM

How do nations catch up when they find themselves lagging behind other, more powerful countries, as the Egyptian leaders discovered when they encountered Bonaparte's troops? One of the most determined, though ultimately failed, efforts was that carried out by Muhammad Ali. He did many of the things that countries seeking to transform themselves do, and he did them with a singularity of purpose that set him off from his regional competitors and that made him in the final analysis a threat to his more powerful and watchful European neighbors.

As we have seen, Muhammad Ali's pride and joy and his primary institution of change was his army. Yet he was smart enough to understand that a modern army had to be supported by a modernizing society. Moreover, he had seen the awesome power of the French and knew about France's economic and political exploits. He set about as soon as he had consolidated power to gain greater access to these sources of power. Not only did he bring European advisers to Egypt to impart their knowledge of European ways to his home country, but he also sent educational missions to Europe to imbibe the secrets of European strength. Egypt's first mission to Italy occurred in 1809, even before he had dealt with his chief adversaries in Egypt, the Mamluks. That he sent his next mission to Italy in 1813 suggests that he thought Italy had much to contribute to reformist projects at home. Thereafter, however, the Pasha was quite open-minded in his choice of European destinations. Educational missions went to Austria and France, with perhaps the largest numbers making their way to Paris.

Most of the students whom the Egyptian ruler sent on these missions were young men who had been schooled in Egypt's traditional religious schools. There was little choice at this stage when it came to selecting recruits since before he and his advisers had had a chance to set up Westernized schools (and these came along quickly), the raw material for the European training teams had to come out of the traditional Egyptian schools. Not only were the students expected to absorb their lessons in Europe and then to take on new occupations when they returned to Egypt, but they were also required to translate their textbooks, lectures notes, and other reading assignments into Turkish and Arabic. It was even said of the Pasha that he would lock returned students in rooms in the Citadel and require them to make full translations of pertinent European books before he freed them to enter the government bureaucracy.

The translation efforts were carried out with stunning energy. Having created Egypt's first press, in the Bulaq section of Cairo, the Pasha purchased 600 books in French and equipped each one of his new Westernized schools with a library of modern works in European languages as well as Arabic and Turkish translations of books that pertained to the materials being taught in the schools. Because so many of the translations at first were flawed and hard to read, the Pasha accepted the advice of one of his most brilliant students, Rafii al-Tahtawi, to set up a School of Translations for the express purpose of training individuals in European languages and making the school the center for translation efforts. Al-Tahtawi had accompanied one of the educational missions to Paris as the religious counselor of that mission and had studied widely while he was in Paris. He stayed on as the head of the School of Translation for sixteen years, during which period he facilitated numerous translations of important European works, and not just those in the fields close to the military predilections of his ruler. His translators also made available to the Egyptian reading public some of the works of the leading French enlightenment thinkers, including Rousseau and Voltaire.

Al-Tahtawi was an ideal mediator between Europe and Egypt. While in Paris, he studied Greek philosophy, history, mythology, the biography of Napoleon, travel books, European treatises on the Ottoman state, mathematics, engineering, geography, logic, and general philosophy. Later he wrote an influential treatise on his experiences in France, laying out as well what he thought Egypt needed to do in the way of assimilating European knowledge while protecting its own heritage. He also introduced the new field of Egyptology, at that time dominated by European scholarship, to the educated Egyptian public, writing a history of ancient Egypt and urging young Egyptians to obtain training in a field so vital to their country's national identity. The group of Egyptians who made significant contributions to the early history of Egypt, including the Egyptologist Ahmad Kamala and Marcus Samaria, the founder of the Coptic Museum in Cairo in 1908, owed a considerable debt to this remarkable thinker.

In his efforts to transform Egypt overnight into a state built on European foundations, Muhammad Ali also set up a number of schools of higher learning. Naturally he fostered a school for infantry, cavalry, and artillery, which promoted the organization of the Egyptian army on French lines, even to the point of playing French military music to inspire the soldiers. But he also created a school of law and a school of medicine. The school of medicine, the first of its kind in the Middle East, came into being in 1835 and was headed by a French military doctor, A. B. Clot. Not everything went smoothly for Clot. During an autopsy at the school, an offended Egyptian student attacked Clot, claiming that dissecting the human body violated Islamic norms. Clot gradually accustomed his students to human dissection by using dog cadavers, then waxen images of human beings before requiring them to work on human cadavers.

A large and modernizing army cannot exist in an impoverished society. The Egyptian Pasha recognized this reality and sought to stimulate all sectors of the Egyptian economy. Since Egypt was and had been from its origins an agricultural country, he turned first of all to the rural sector. Here he championed the introduction of new crops, the most important of which was long-staple cotton. For centuries, Egyptian peasants had cultivated cheap, short- and medium-staple cotton, which had little appeal to the outside world. Long-staple cotton was entirely different, however, for its fibers were strong and resilient and were especially attractive to English textile owners for the manufacture of fine cotton cloths. During the Muhammad Ali era a long-staple cotton, called Jumel, after the French scientist who introduced it, became Egypt's most lucrative export, accounting for nearly £1 million of Egypt's foreign trade in the late 1830s.

Cotton is a summer crop, grown during the low Nile season. It requires regular quantities of water. If Egypt wanted to become a major world exporter of this commodity, and Muhammad Ali devoutly wanted to enhance the state coffers through taxing the cultivation and export of cotton, it would need to make irrigation waters available to the countryside during the low Nile season. This project required the improvement of existing canals, the digging of new canals, and the construction of dams and weirs along the Nile, all for the purpose of raising the levels of water in the Nile and its canals so that farmers could take water from the canals and irrigate summer crops. Among the most important of hydraulic projects undertaken in this period was the cutting of a canal from the Nile to Alexandria. Known as the Mahmudiyya canal, it provided Alexandria with an ample water supply that in turn allowed its population to grow rapidly throughout the nineteenth century. Even more ambitious was the construction of a barrage across the Nile immediately north of Cairo at a location where the Nile divides into its two branches. Although this barrage did not become fully functioning until the British occupation, it provided additional irrigation waters so that farmers could grow cotton in the Nile delta.

The hydraulic works carried out during the reign of Muhammad Ali were a turning point in the agricultural history of Egypt. They began the transformation of Egyptian cultivation from the basin system, which depended on annual floods and had existed from ancient times, to a year-round form of irrigation, called perennial irrigation, by which the land was irrigated when and as the crops required water. Where perennial irrigation was introduced, two, even three, crops could be grown per year, not the single crop that had been traditional for millennia. Of course, under Muhammad Ali only the first steps in the changeover from basin to perennial irrigation took place. Most of Egypt continued to receive floodwaters and to employ basin irrigation, but a radical change had begun. It was only a matter of time and several large-scale irrigation projects, mainly based at Aswan, before flooding became a thing of the past and the Nile was tamed so that its waters were available the year round.

Agricultural modernization was not enough, however. The Egyptian ruler needed to promote economic development so as to be able to raise increasing amounts of government taxation revenue. Here, he drew on a late-eighteenth-century Mamluk practice. First he abolished the old tax-farming system that the Ottomans had employed, substituting state control over most of Egypt's agricultural land. Next he established a system of state monopolies for almost all of the agricultural commodities traded domestically and internationally. Establishing monopolies to buy agricultural outputs like wheat, barley, cotton, and sugar at low prices and selling these commodities at high prices either to local Egyptian consumers or, in the case of cotton, to foreign textile owners swelled the state coffers. The result was a large increase in government revenues, which, then, supported the enlarged army, the educational missions, the hydraulic improvements, and much else.

But this was not all. The Pasha introduced a program of industrialization, starting with textile factories in the 1810s and moving on to munitions, sugar refineries, indigo factories, rice milling, and tanning. The machinery and the industrial experts to run the factories were brought from Europe. The workforce numbered no fewer than 40,000 at its high point in the 1830s. Power to run the engines was a problem. Most of it was supplied by the workers themselves or by animals, for Egypt made use of only a few steam engines, largely because the ruler could not bring enough technicians to Egypt. Although the industrialization effort was a limited one, with substantial problems, such as a lack of purchasing power in a still-poor country and deficiencies in the power to run the industrial engines, Egypt's cotton textile factories were now using about one-fifth of the local cotton production.

MILITARY TRIUMPHS AND DIPLOMATIC DEFEATS

It was inevitable that Egypt and the Ottomans would clash. The sultan wanted to reestablish his control over Egypt, and Muhammad Ali had expansionist aspirations in the region. The clashes came in the 1830s when the Egyptian Pasha, eager to acquire access to the raw materials of Syria and to secure strategic military passageways from Egypt, sent his army into Syria. Two long campaigns occurred, in both of which Egyptian troops prevailed over the inadequately modernized Ottoman forces. The first took place between 1831 and 1833 and the second between 1839 and 1841. In the second the Egyptian army crossed the Taurus Mountains and advanced to within 100 miles of Istanbul, which lay within the grasp of the Egyptian forces. Yet on both occasions, the European powers, led by Lord Palmerston, Britain's foreign secretary, intervened and forced the Pasha to disgorge much of his territorial acquisitions.

The decisive Egyptian-Ottoman confrontation occurred during the second campaign. The European powers feared the dissolution of the Ottoman Empire and the emergence of Egypt as a formidable power in the eastern Mediterranean. Their intercession forced Muhammad Ali to withdraw his forces from Anatolia. What he got in return was recognition of his rule and that of his family over Egypt, which, however, remained formally a province of the Ottoman state. In addition, Muhammad Ali acquired lifetime control of the province of Acre in Syria. Much more significantly, the negotiations involving the Great Powers, the Ottoman Sultan, and the Egyptian government in 1840 and 1841 limited the size of the Egyptian army and compelled the Pasha to end his internal monopolistic buying practices. Henceforth, Europe's merchants were able to buy and sell freely in all internal Egyptian markets.

These were substantial blows to Egypt's modernizing effort. The Egyptian army was Muhammad Ali's pride and joy. State control of buying and selling in Egypt swelled government revenues. Some scholars have argued that European intervention prevented Egypt from becoming an economic, political, and military giant in the eastern Mediterranean, a worthy rival to its European neighbors. This argument, however, flies in the face of many facts. The Pasha's industrialization program had many deficiencies. His ambitions had begun to outstrip his resources. By the 1830s, the Pasha was already forced to dole out state lands to private, powerful individuals, creating the beginnings of Egypt's wealthy private landowning class. These land distributions were short-run financial successes since the Pasha now looked to private individuals to administer Egypt's land and to be responsible for tax collection, but in the long run, they reduced the state's revenues. No doubt the European powers stymied Muhammad Ali's ambitions to build a great eastern empire, using Egypt as his base. What he would have done had his troops marched into Istanbul and taken substantial territory from the Ottomans is a historical question worth posing, but difficult to answer. There is no doubt, however, that the exacting terms of the Treaty of London, especially those that reduced the size of the Egyptian army, deflated the Egyptian Pasha and led to an overall decline in modernizing energies during the 1840s.

Modernizing changes in Egypt came with a heavy price—a price exacted from the Egyptian peasantry. They were the recruits that served in Muhammad Ali's army and they also cultivated two, sometimes three crops a year. Military service was detested, and many peasants fled their villages or maimed themselves to keep from being forced into the army. In the early decades of the Pasha's rule the peasants gained additional income from their new labors. But later on, as taxes were increased, they suffered grievously.

The Pasha was hardly more than another of Egypt's many foreign rulers, a neo-Mamluk and a latter-day Ottoman in significant ways. Yet he was forced to draw the rank and file of the Egyptian population into state activities in ways that earlier Mamluks and Ottomans had not. He needed military recruits, even officers, when the supply of Albanians and Turks did not suffice. He expanded the bureaucracy, and the doors of his Westernized schools were open to native-born Egyptians. An Egyptian intelligentsia came into being, holding all of the aspirations of educated elites around the world at this time. They yearned for power and were attracted to European-style institutions, especially the parliamentary form of government. Muhammad Ali in his later years also doled out lands to private landholders, many of whom, but not all, were part of his Turco-Circassian clique. Important native-born Egyptian families also received lands from the Pasha, became wealthy over time, and began to constitute another powerful element dedicated to promoting their interests. Without willing or even wanting these changes, Muhammad Ali contributed greatly to dissolving the lines that separated the rulers from the ruled. A sense of a modern Egyptian national identity began to take shape. It would only increase as the century progressed.

KHEDIVE ISMAIL (1863–1879)

Khedive Ismail, son of Ibrahim Pasha and grandson of Muhammad Ali, ascended the throne in Egypt in 1863. He had a number of advantages as he came to power with ambitions to resume Muhammad Ali's modernizing energies. His two-year educational stint in Paris (1846–48) gave him a better understanding of the European world than his illustrious predecessor had had and also fueled his desires to make Egypt over in the image of Europe. In addition, he came to power at a time when Egypt's cotton crop was fetching high prices in international markets because the world's largest supplier of high-priced and extremely valuable long-staple cotton, the United States of America, was in the midst of a civil war. Lined up against him, however, were several massive obstacles, inheritances from the reign of his predecessor, Said, who ruled from 1854 to 1863. Said could not resist the temptation to borrow from European financial houses, and he left his successor a not inconsequential debt. Said also signed an agreement with his friend, the French entrepreneur Ferdinand de Lesseps, to build a canal that would link the Mediterranean and the Red Sea. Unfortunately, these concessions saddled Ismail with many financial burdens.

The Egyptian cotton export boom encouraged Ismail to continue borrowing from European financial houses, until his debt by the late 1870s had reached the staggering sum of £100 million, more than ten times the amount that Egypt collected annually in revenues. During the heady days of the cotton boom, Ismail had used the infusion of funds to beautify his major cities, to repair and extend the country's irrigation canal networks, to expand schools, and to enlarge the size of his army so that it could carry out military campaigns in Sudan and Ethiopia. But the high prices for cotton did not last, and by the 1870s the khedive now looked to Europe for funds to service the state debt rather than increase the country's economic productivity. When these funds only plunged the country into further debt, he employed short-run financial expedients, such as selling off state lands to private individuals and even pledging the taxation revenues of wealthy provinces to European debt service. His most desperate financial move was his decision to sell the government's holdings in the Suez Canal Company (a robust 44 percent of the company's equity) to the British government in 1875. At that point, the company had not yet started to pay the substantial dividends that it would later on, so Egypt received a mere £4 million for its huge land, labor, and financial contributions to the digging of the Suez Canal. In fact, it did not receive another penny from the Suez Canal Company until 1936, when the company, responding to nationalist attacks on the way it made money off the backs of the Egyptians, agreed to provide an annual contribution to the Egyptian government.

An inevitable but unintended consequence of the Ismail's modernizing efforts was the emergence of native-born educated Egyptians who now sought power for themselves. These individuals knew Europe and were eager to extend Egypt's transformation beyond the limits that Ismail imposed. European parliamentary democracies enthralled them. They saw no reason that Egypt, in emulating Europe, should not also have representative institutions so that they checked the powers of the khedive.

Among the intellectuals who emerged in the latter years of the reign of Ismail was the pan-Islamic leader Jamal al-Din al-Afghani. During his sojourn in Egypt, al-Afghani galvanized many of the young, Westernized, and educated Egyptians with his claim that Islam was under attack from Europe and that Islamic nations should unite to protect themselves from European ambitions. His most devoted disciple, a young Azhari shaykh, Muhammad Abduh, was destined to have an important religious and theological career in Egypt. Abduh joined with al-Afghani in trying to rally the educated Egyptian population to oppose growing European influence. Exiled by the British after their invasion of Egypt, the two men went to Paris, where they issued a journal, *al-Urwa al-Wuthqa*, which promoted pan-Islamic ideals and warned that Islam was itself threatened, perhaps even with extinction, by the superior military, political, and economic might of Europe and a European cultural onslaught. Later, Abduh returned to Egypt, made his peace with the British, served as the chief *qadi* (judge) in Egypt, and wrote essays on the ways that Islam could adjust to the challenge of the West without losing its identity.

Another important intellectual of this era, though more secular and more identified with the government, was Ali Mubarak. Educated in Egypt and France, he became a minister during Ismail's reign, serving as the minister of public works and the minister of schools. As a government official, he updated the Egyptian school system. His most enduring achievement was the modernization of parts of Cairo. Ismail placed a high value on making Cairo a capital city that could hold its own with the modern cities of Europe. He regarded Paris as the most beautiful and most modern of the European cities and wanted his urban planners to do for Cairo what Baron Haussmann had done for Paris during the reign of Napoleon III. Cairo was to have the same boulevards, plazas, and gardens that Haussmann had brought to Paris. That Ismail wanted to impress European visitors is attested by the fact that he had his urban engineers build structures around particularly ugly and run-down areas of the city so that outsiders would not have to behold unpleasant sights. His primary agent for urban modernization was Ali Mubarak.

Even today, much of downtown Cairo dates from the days of Ismail and owes its charm to the visions of these two men. Rather than tearing down parts of the old city, as the French urban planners did in Paris, Ismail, Ali Mubarak, and their planners used newly reclaimed lands west of the old city leading to the banks of the Nile River as the location of their new structures. The khedive enticed Barillet-Deschamps, the designer of the Bois de Boulogne and the Champs de Mars in Paris, to lend his creative efforts to the project and also brought the French horticulturalist Delchevalerie to fashion an elaborate set of gardens at Azbakiya. Replete with European and oriental tearooms and restaurants, pedal boats and bridges over a small lake, a Chinese pagoda, fencing school, and theaters, the gardens became a favored location for residents and visitors to relax. The center of the new Cairo was the plaza that is known today as Talaat Harb Square and from which impressive boulevards were constructed outwards in all directions like the spokes of a wheel. The buildings in the city center had flowery stone fronts and gratings, gargoyles, and roofs that were as fine as the best urban buildings in Europe's capitals. Nearby Talaat Harb plaza city planners built the grand opera house and the national theater, all underlining the reality that Cairo had indeed become "Paris along the Nile."

The high bureaucratic position held by Ali Mubarak revealed another significant development of Ismail's years—the rise of native-born Egyptians into positions of power once monopolized by Turkish elites. This new Egyptian element challenged the privileges that the Turkish-Circassian favorites of Muhammad Ali had enjoyed at all levels of government. Tensions were even felt within the army, where a group of native-born junior offices, led by Ahmad Urabi Pasha, vied for power and eventually provoked a rebellion that brought British military and political power into the country.

CONSTRUCTING THE SUEZ CANAL

Ferdinand de Lesseps had bullied the weak and vacillating Egyptian ruler Said into granting him the right to build a canal across the Isthmus of Suez. The first concession, in 1854, permitted de Lesseps "to form a financial company to pierce the isthmus" and operate a canal for ninety-nine years from its opening, while the second concession, granted in 1856, obligated the Egyptian government to provide four-fifths of the labor for the canal's construction. De Lesseps's company came into being in 1858, with the Egyptian government owning 44 percent of its shares and French investors, mostly members of the middle class and small holders, holding 52 percent. The average French holding was a mere nine shares; the largest group were landowners, of whom many were undoubtedly peasants, who had begun to acquire the habit of investing in business firms in the nineteenth century. The reason that the Egyptian government had to come to the financial rescue of the company was the determined opposition of the British government to the project and the unwillingness of British and other non-French investors to buy shares in a project that many were afraid would fail.

Lord Palmerston, British prime minister in the middle of the century, opposed the canal on political, not economic, grounds. He saw it as undermining the integrity of the Ottoman state, one of Britain's bulwarks to political stability in the eastern Mediterranean, and possibly leading to a collision between Britain and France. In 1851 he made Britain's position crystal clear. "It shall not be made, it cannot be made, it will not be made; if it were made, there would be a war between France and England for the possession of Egypt." His words proved prophetic.

But they did not keep de Lesseps from succeeding. Although the canal took longer to construct than he had predicted (fourteen years rather than six), and its cost of nearly £20 million was considerably more than projected, it opened for shipping on November 17, 1869. No one could dispute the critical role that de Lesseps played in making this dream of many French notables, including Napoleon and the scientific utopianists, the Saint Simonians, a reality. Nor could one discount the vital financial support that French peasants gave the project by buying shares in the company. But the canal would never have become a reality without Egypt's decisive support. Not only did the Egyptian government take up 177,642 shares, many of which de Lesseps had set aside for foreign, mainly British, investors, but the government provided corvee labor for digging the canal and the canal that brought fresh water from the Nile to the new city of Ismailia at the midpoint of the canal. When Khedive Ismail sought to terminate Egypt's obligation to provide corvee laborers because he needed the labor force to cultivate cotton during the boom years of the American Civil War, Egypt was compelled to pay compensation of more than £3 million to the Canal Company to rid itself of this obligation. This money helped to pay for the elaborate dredging equipment that the company brought to Egypt and without which the canal would surely never have been completed.

Is it any wonder that the Canal Company became an object of Egyptian nationalist resentment and a symbol of rapacious European capitalism? Nor should anyone have been surprised at the joy that the Egyptian population expressed when Nasser nationalized the Suez Canal Company in July 1956.

The Egyptian government marked the opening of the canal in 1869 with elaborate ceremonies, designed to demonstrate that Egypt had indeed become a legitimate and vital part of the European world. The government invited numerous European dignitaries, among whom the most famous were the emperor of Austria, the empress Eugenie of France, Émile Zola, and Henrik Ibsen. Khedive Ismail had tried to persuade Europe's leading composer, Giuseppe Verdi, to write an opera for the occasion. It was only later that Verdi took up the challenge and wrote *Aida* to celebrate ancient Egyptian civilization. *Aida* had its premier in 1871 in the newly built Egyptian opera house in Cairo. Verdi did participate in the ceremonies arranged for the opening of the canal. He agreed to allow the Egyptian government to perform the opera *Rigoletto,* and he also wrote several new cantatas and smaller pieces to celebrate the joining of the two seas.

Although Lord Palmerston had bitterly opposed the canal, British shippers and British tonnage dominated the canal's traffic right from the opening. Between 1871 and 1895 British tonnage passing through the canal was never less than 70 percent and remained above 50 percent until after World War II. As the builders understood, the canal dramatically shortened the vital sea route from Western Europe to India and East Asia. Previously European shipping to and from Asia circled the Cape of Good Hope in South Africa, but with steamships making their appearance on the oceans, the time and distance between Europe and Asia was severely reduced. A voyage from Bombay to London, which had required four months, now took only one month. Naturally, as Lord Palmerston had feared, Egypt loomed larger in British and French political aspirations. The French regarded the canal as their achievement; the British realized that the canal was a vital lifeline to their empire in India and to their vast trading networks in Asia.

THE URABI REVOLT AND THE BRITISH OCCUPATION

Ismail's mania for things European also propelled him into imperial escapades. Seeking even to outstrip his grandfather, Muhammad Ali, as conqueror of new territories, the khedive engaged in no fewer than ten military campaigns. He wanted nothing less than a massive Egyptian empire centered in Sudan and the Horn of Africa. Although he had a 90,000-man army and prominent European and American military advisers, his campaigns in Ethiopia in 1875–76 were so disastrous that they stirred resentment against him. Ultimately they led to a military rebellion, demands for parliamentary government, and the British occupation of the country.

By the 1870s Ismail's legitimacy was beginning to unravel. The country's massive indebtedness had forced the khedive to sell off precious assets and then to allow British and French advisers to assume control over the vital Ministries of Finance and Public Works. Perhaps he hoped that military adventures against the Ethiopian emperor for control over the Red Sea coast and large chunks of territory in the Horn of Africa would divert attention from the problems at home. But a badly disciplined and officered Egyptian army suffered humiliating defeats at the battles of Gundet and Gura in 1875 and 1876. The losses at Gura were entirely one-sided. While the Ethiopians lost only 900 men, 4,500 Egyptian soldiers were killed, wounded, or taken captive.

The shameful military defeats in Ethiopia exposed problems that had plagued the army ever since it began to expand under Ismail. The most severe of these concerns was tension between native-born Egyptian officers and the Turkish-Circassian elite who had monopolized the top positions in the army ever since the era of Muhammad Ali. Ahmad Urabi was the individual around whom much of the Egyptian discontent crystallized.

Ismail, however, saw the unhappiness in the army and the growing resentment of European influence as a way to reassert his power. In 1879 Egyptian indebtedness, European control, and army discontent crystallized over the proposal to reduce the size of the army from 93,000 to 37,000. Although the Ethiopian campaign had ended Ismail's ambitions for a vast African empire, it was the foreign powers that pressured the state for the reduction, citing cost savings as the grounds for their demand. Because most of the reductions would come at the expense of the native-born officer corps, these men, already resentful of the privileged position of the Turkish-Circassians, looked to Urabi to present their grievances. The officers submitted a petition of complaints to the khedive in February 1879, and Ismail in response dismissed his Council of Ministers, including the British and French ministers of finance and public works, and installed a new set of ministers loyal to him. European powers refused to accept this assertion of Egyptian national independence. They reacted by having the Ottoman sultan depose Ismail and replace him with Ismail's son, Tawfiq, who was to rule until 1892.

For a few years, Egypt settled back into the old arrangements. Britain and France continued to exercise substantial control over internal political decisions. But the resentment of European influence continued to grow. Not only was it felt strongly among the Egyptian officers, but it was shared by intellectuals like Jamal al-Din al-Afghani and Muhammad Abduh and landowners and merchants, who sought a larger place for themselves in the government and who championed enhanced powers for an Egyptian Chamber of Delegates that Ismail had created in 1866. Tensions came to a head when Urabi seized power and established his own Council of Ministers, threatening to limit the authority that Europe exercised over the country. Khedive Tawfiq fled to Alexandria and sought foreign intervention.

That it was the British who intervened, rather than the French, was perhaps not surprising. Although French investors held more of the Egyptian debt than did the British, the British regarded the Suez Canal as a chokepoint of their empire. Fearful that the French might steal a march on them, the liberal government of William Ewart Gladstone dispatched a large army to Egypt and routed the Egyptian army at the battle of Tel el-Kebir in September 1882. There was considerable irony in Gladstone's decision to send troops. While out of power, he had written an article in *Nineteenth Century* warning against an invasion of Egypt and predicting that a military intervention there would set off a scramble for imperial possessions throughout the African continent. His words proved prophetic. Britain's invasion of Egypt did, indeed, become a precipitating factor in the pell-mell European partition of the African landmass.

To calm the French and the other European powers and to assuage the opposition of the little Englanders at home, Gladstone's government promised a short-lived occupation. The ministers talked about a one- to three-year window of opportunity during which the British would restore the khedive to authority, reform the Egyptian administration, punish the Urabi rebels, and establish fiscal stability. In reality, the last British soldiers did not leave Egypt until 1956, no less than three-quarters of a century later than promised. What caused them to stay on were their own realization that reforms would take longer than anticipated and a growing sense that Egypt represented an extraordinary strategic, political, and economic asset to the British Empire.

What would have happened had the British not intervened is a historical conundrum almost impossible to answer. Urabi was not an effective leader; yet there were others who had administrative and financial talents. Moreover, the revolt produced an outpouring of nationalist sentiment that existed in few other African territories at the time and that might have been a foundation on which to establish a viable nation-state. Still, the age of imperialism had seized the minds and imaginations of Europeans. A prize like Egypt could not withstand these imperial ambitions.

CHAPTER TEN
The British Period, 1882–1952

Lord Cromer, Britain's consul general in Egypt from 1883 until 1907, was the virtual ruler of the country for the quarter of a century that he held that office. Although he was but one among many other foreign diplomats, he was backed up by a large British army of occupation. He expected to be obeyed, and he was. His power was no whit less than that of the khedives who had preceded him. Most Egyptians, especially the educated elite, who were his most vocal critics on many policy matters, conceded that he had brought political stability to the country and restored its finances to a healthy state. Yet when he left the country, with huzzahs cascading from the foreign community living in Egypt, the foreign press there and overseas, and the acclaim of the British public, he had not won the adulation of the Egyptian people. Egyptians are famously hospitable and generous to foreigners. They understand the importance of ceremony and tradition. Yet they bade Cromer farewell in near silence. All but three Egyptian politicians boycotted Cromer's farewell speech at the Cairo Opera House on May 4, 1907. On the day that he left Cairo, he rode through the streets that had been emptied of traffic and lined with troops to avoid any untoward incidents. The Egyptians were true to their historical traditions. As they had with the hated Hyksos and Persians, they showed their displeasure for foreign rulers who remained aloof from the people and who spurned Egyptian ways.

CROMER'S EGYPT, 1883–1907

Anticipating the wrath of the French, who had regarded Egypt as a special sphere of their influence ever since Bonaparte's invasion of the country, the British promised a speedy evacuation of the country after their invasion to protect access to the Suez Canal. This promise was hardly sufficient to assuage the feelings of the French, who believed that they had been outsmarted. Nor did the French trust the British to leave. Right up until 1904, when Britain and France resolved most of their international differences, France made difficulties for Britain in Egypt, reminding the British of their duty to evacuate and raising questions about Britain's handling of Egypt's finances.

The British chose Evelyn Baring (elevated to the peerage as the Earl of Cromer in 1892 and referred to hereafter as Cromer) as their consul general in Egypt. Cromer was a formidable figure. Although he had not attended one of the elite British universities, as had so many other high-ranking British colonial officials, he was a skilled administrator, first-rate in financial matters, an essential in the virtually bankrupt Egypt. He was learned in classical languages and history, mostly self-taught.

Cromer was a Gladstonian liberal in political and economic matters and thus the logical choice of the Gladstone government that had promised a quick reform of the Egyptian government and a speedy evacuation of British troops from the country. Cromer knew Egypt well. He had served in the country during the latter years of Khedive Ismail's reign. His experience as the financial adviser to Lord Ripon, the viceroy of India, also recommended him to the home government. It did not take long, however, for Cromer to alter his attitudes on Britain's mission in Egypt. A growing awareness of the severity of Egypt's financial jumble, a keener appreciation of the strategic importance of Egypt and the Suez Canal to an expanding British Empire at a time when the whole of Africa was being partitioned, and a conviction that he and British advisers alone could enact desperately needed reforms in Egypt led him to believe that the

British presence in Egypt must go on for some time. That Cromer's views were eventually accepted by the British ruling classes at home can be seen from the fact that Cromer served as Britain's consul general of Egypt from 1883 to 1907.

Yet Cromer's belief that Britain must remain in Egypt ran into many obstacles. More important even than the repeated British promises of a speedy evacuation was the French pressure for the British to leave a country in which France had such long-standing cultural and financial interests. French pressure came to a head right away when Cromer faced a challenge to resume full payments on the Egyptian debt by the end of 1887 or have the entire question of Britain's role in Egypt reopened for international discussions. Indeed, Cromer's first great political and fiscal triumph occurred when he won what he called "the race against Egyptian bankruptcy" in 1888 and thereby forestalled increased international controls over Egypt. The price that he had to pay, however, was a steep one. Aware that Egypt had an overextended empire in Sudan, he attempted to withdraw Egyptian forces from that country. Not only did the Egyptian political elite object to this loss of precious territory, but the mechanism for evacuating the Egyptian soldiers proved a disaster. Cromer's chosen agent for the evacuation could not have been worse. General Charles Gordon was not a man who understood the word *retreat*. Rather than leading the Egyptian troops out of Sudan, Gordon holed up in the capital city, Khartoum. He awaited an attack from Sudanese rebels under the leadership of Muhammad Ahmad, a self-proclaimed Mahdi and bitter foe of Egyptian influence in his territory. Foolishly, he expected the British to rush troops to his defense. In this strategy he made a grievous error, which cost him his life and ended the Egyptian administrative and military presence in Sudan, as Cromer had wanted all along.

Cromer was an official trained in the post–Indian-mutiny era of British colonial rule. He did not believe that "oriental and African races" could ever fully adopt British ways or achieve the levels of civilization that the British and other Europeans enjoyed. What Britain could do for Egyptians, whom he regarded as weighed down by "religious prejudice" and "antique and semi-barbarous customs," was look after the material interests of the common people, the Egyptian fellahin, and interfere as little as possible in religious and social affairs. Because the Egyptians were Muslims and the British Christians, British rule could not continue indefinitely, though Cromer believed that the era of British tutelage would last for many years, perhaps even centuries. Holding to this view, Cromer stressed lowering taxation rates, improving the irrigation system, and promoting law and order. Much further down the ladder of his concerns, much to the dismay of the Egyptian elite, was educational and social reform. In his view, a Westernized form of education had the prospect of producing half-educated graduates who were ill-suited for a colonial economy and polity and who would turn to nationalist demagoguery, stirring up discontent against the British, as had happened among the educated of India.

Another factor made Cromer's task difficult. Egypt was not a full-fledged British colonial possession. Because the British occupation was supposed to be a temporary one, Egypt remained formally a part of the Ottoman Empire. Nor did Cromer become a colonial governor, as did officials in British-controlled territories in Africa. Cromer's title was simply that of the British consul general in Egypt. Most of the British officials sent out to Egypt to operate the government were not appointed as ministers in the Egyptian government. Rather, they were advisers, who functioned behind the formal Egyptian ministers. Of course, their advice was expected to be heeded, but tensions repeatedly flared up into ugly disputes between the two groups. As one British official (Lord Alfred Milner) wrote, the British form of governing Egypt was a "veiled protectorate." The British did insist, however, that their representatives would be in full control of what they considered the two most important Egyptian Ministries, Finance and Public Works. And it was in these two arenas that the British had the most decisive influence over Egypt during the Cromer years.

Cromer's nearly twenty-five-year tenure of power in Egypt was full of many accomplishments and a number of failures. Although he was only a consul general, few Egyptians ever sought to defy his orders. A British army of occupation, ordinarily 5,000 men strong, backed up the proconsul's demands. The bulk of the troops occupied a central location in the city of Cairo and showed its strength in parades on high ceremonial occasions and marches through the delta. Today, the Nile Hilton hotel graces the area that held these British troops. Cromer also had the support of an Egyptian army, which had a British-appointed commanding general and other British officers, seconded from the British military. For most of the colonial era the British army of occupation in Egypt, which was raised to 10,000 strong during the interwar years, was the only contingent of British soldiers garrisoned throughout whole of the African continent.

As expected from a ruler who believed that the only way Britain could deal with Egypt was through improvements in the population's material standards of life, Cromer's achievements were in the realms of finance and public works. Having won the race against bankruptcy by 1888, Cromer continued to increase the country's revenues and to reduce the percentage of government revenues earmarked for the service of the debt. By the time he left the country in 1907, he had dramatically reduced the percentage of the state budget that went into debt service.

Critical to enhanced revenues were improvements in Egypt's irrigation networks. From the outset, the British imported hydraulic engineers who had gained crucial knowledge and experience on the great rivers of India. Using their Indian training in dam building and irrigation, they set about refashioning Egypt's control over the Nile waters. Beginning on a small scale, they improved the dams and weirs that had fallen into disrepair in the latter years of Khedive Ismail's rule. The most important undertaking in these years was a refurbishment of the barrage just north of Cairo that controlled irrigation waters for the southern provinces of the Nile delta. Here a notable expansion in cotton cultivation took place. Much later, as the finances of the country improved, the British undertook the construction of a large-scale dam at Aswan. This work took place between 1898 and 1902 and was heightened on two separate occasions in the twentieth century. For many years the largest dam in the world, the Aswan dam provided additional irrigation waters for both Upper and Lower Egypt.

Hydraulic reforms transformed the countryside and altered radically the routines of the Egyptian peasantry that had changed little over the millennia. In many parts of Egypt, particularly the delta, the annual Nile flood no longer occurred. Instead, for some cultivators water became available as and when it was needed. This change meant that farmers could grow two, sometimes even three, crops per year, the most important of which for the Egyptian economy was cotton, a summer, low-Nile crop that required regular watering throughout the growing season. These changes did what Cromer intended, at least in the early years of his rule. They put additional financial resources in the pockets of the ordinary peasant farmer. But as the amount of land held in large private estates grew apace, as it had done under Muhammad Ali and Ismail, much of the enhanced agricultural revenue flowed into the hands of large landowners. The peasants now found themselves forced to work the year round, with little enhancement in their standard of life and with an increase in their exposure to the water-borne and debilitating disease bilharzia.

A final achievement brought far more to the British than to the Egyptians. The reconquest of Sudan rounded out the massive British Empire in East Africa. In 1896, Cromer readied plans for retaking Sudan, which had fallen on difficult times once the Mahdi died in 1885 and was replaced by Abdallahi ibn Muhammad. The Egyptian army, under the command of British officers and headed by Herbert Kitchener, carried out the conquest, after which Sudan came under the dual control of Egypt and Britain. Unfortunately for the Egyptians, this unusual Anglo-Egyptian condominium was heavily weighted in favor of Britain. The British retained the top administrative positions in Sudan, leaving the Egyptian exchequer to make up the considerable financial deficits of the Sudanese government. These were a burden on the Egyptian budget until the outbreak of World War I. After the war, because of Egyptian attacks against British military officers in Sudan, the British went further in limiting Egypt's influence over a country that the Egyptians had occupied in the nineteenth century and that most Egyptians regarded as an integral part of their country.

The weaknesses of the Cromer years were as apparent as their strengths. In many ways, they were the opposite side of the coin of strengths. First, Cromer was a thoroughgoing autocrat. He brooked no dissent, neither from subordinate British officials nor from Egyptians. In his early days, before he became Lord Cromer, subordinates often referred to him as "over-Baring." He dominated the thinking at the British Consulate, the nerve center of power, insisting, in the words of one critic, that officers there "think to the right and think to the left." These authoritarian tendencies rubbed many the wrong way, especially Egyptian officials, who, as they listened to the British promises of a speedy evacuation, tried to chisel out some autonomous power for themselves. Such challenges to Cromer's authority were invariably dealt with severely. Any Egyptian official who showed too much independence found himself out of power. Cromer finally found his ideal Egyptian prime minister in Mustafa Fahmi, who held the office from 1895 until 1908 and who was the consummate collaborator.

A second problem of the Cromer years, and one that left him at loggerheads with educated Egyptians, was education. Cromer was highly suspicious of so-called educated "natives," regarding them as potential critics of British rule. Having imbibed the lessons of the Indian mutiny and Indian opposition to the Raj, he was reluctant to spend money on educational improvements.

While public works received state revenues in generous amounts, the education ministry was starved for funds. In a report published in 1903 Cromer revealed that the state had expended less than 1 percent of its revenues on education. Even as late as 1913, the Ministry of Public Instruction received a mere 3 percent of the Egyptian budget, compared to 16 percent to the Ministry of Public Works and 26 percent for tribute to the Ottoman Empire and debt repayment. Moreover, Cromer appointed a dour Scotsman, Douglas Dunlop, as adviser to the department of education. Dunlop was contemptuous of Egyptians, especially educated Egyptians, whom he regarded as bad-tempered upstarts. His collisions with Egyptian officials over educational policies were legendary.

When a group of leading Egyptian intellectuals approached Cromer in 1906 with plans for the establishment of an Egyptian university, they received a cold shoulder. In Cromer's estimation, Egypt was far from ready for university training. The most he was willing to concede was some additional funds for primary and secondary schooling. Unmoved by Cromer's logic, these individuals forged ahead with their plans and opened a private Westernized university in Cairo in 1908. In time this institution became Cairo University, one of the leading establishments of higher education in the Middle East.

A final area of weakness, at least in the minds of many Egyptians, was Cromer's unwillingness to promote elections and parliamentary government. While Cromer regarded Britain's parliamentary system as one of the supreme achievements of the British people and an essential element in its political and economic success, he held to the view that Egypt was not yet at a stage where parliamentary governance would work. Indeed, it is fair to wonder whether Cromer thought that Egyptians would ever master the intricacies of democracy. He regarded Islam as antithetical to science and reason and believed that efforts to reform Islam were doomed to fail. At best, the Egyptian people would have to go through an extended period of political training before they would be able to create a viable democracy. Meantime, the British would rule the country in a thoroughly autocratic fashion.

NATIONALIST DISCONTENT

The Urabi revolt had crystallized strong nationalist sentiment among educated and well-to-do Egyptians. For many the slogan that galvanized their hopes for the future was "Egypt for the Egyptians." Alas, the British army of occupation and the exiling of some of the leading figures in the Urabi movement dashed these hopes. A decade of relative political quiescence ensued, broken in the early 1890s when a young, tempestuous khedive, Abbas II, acceded to the throne in Egypt. Abbas chafed under Cromer's authoritarian ways.

When the khedive brought in a new prime minister without consulting Cromer, the consul general rebuked the young upstart and insisted on installing his own chief minister. Two years later, when the khedive criticized the deportment and training of the Egyptian army and its commanding general, Herbert Kitchener, he received another open reproach from British officialdom. Of course, Abbas learned the folly of challenging British preeminence in open ways, but he became for many of the elite a symbol of opposition to increasing British dominance over their country. Before long, the khedive sponsored a political party and a newspaper that regularly critiqued British policies.

Although the khedive was a thorn in the flesh of British rule, the mantle of its sternest critic fell to a young, educated law school graduate, Mustafa Kamil. Trained in the Egyptian School of Law, which was, in fact, the distant successor to al-Tahtawi's School of Translations, Kamil created a political party, the National Party, and founded a newspaper, *al-Liwa*, which espoused the policy of complete independence for Egypt. Seeking to win the favor of international groups, he looked to both France and to the Ottoman Empire to support his demands. Many French intellectuals were only too happy to find in Mustafa Kamil an instrument for reasserting France's longtime interests in Egypt, and the Ottoman sultan was pleased to see in Kamil an advocate of his pan-Islamist propaganda.

To Kamil, there was no question that Egypt deserved to be an independent country. He boasted of the country's long history of nationalist manifestations, dating from the Egyptian opposition to the French invasion of the country in 1798 and culminating in the Urabi revolt. Steeped in the history of the country and reveling in its ancient glories, he stressed the depth of Egypt's national identity, one that could be traced back to the earliest pharaohs. In truth, he held to a view of Egypt radically different from that of Cromer and other British officials. To him, Egypt was virtually unique among African and Middle Eastern states in that it had a racially, linguistically, and religiously homogeneous population. It had all the requisites that the Europeans claimed to be essential to nation-state existence. In one speech, he proclaimed that Egypt "was a dynamic and civilized nation, wishing and being able to govern itself." He also condemned the British for bringing into the country officials who did not know, or even care to learn about, the language and traditions of the country. "Foreigners," he asserted, "belong to free and prosperous countries. We have our miserable Egypt."

Cromer's views could not have differed more. In his widely read 1908 treatise, *Modern Egypt*, published just after he left the country, he depicted the country as a place of no fixed identity. For him, the country was composed of a conglomerate of racial, religious, and linguistic groups. It contained within its borders Jews, Coptic Christians, Greeks, Italians, French, Britons, Syrians, and Armenians, who, left to their own devices and lacking the overarching direction of British officials, would produce disabling internal divisions. The official population figures supported Kamil's claims, for in the censuses of 1917 and 1927 foreign minorities were only slightly more than 200,000 persons, less than 2 percent of the total. If Copts and Jews were added in, the total came to less than 10 percent. To Cromer, however, since the overwhelming majority of the Egyptians were relatively poor, uneducated, and illiterate peasants, authority could not be passed into Egyptian hands. The real ability to rule lay with a thin veneer of individuals who were of such different backgrounds that political unity could not be achieved through them.

The overt opposition to British rule came to a head in the last years of Cromer's tenure in Egypt. By the turn of the century, the nationalist press was unrelenting in its attack on British policies. *Al-Liwa* catalogued the rising number of British officials who were involved in virtually all aspects of the country's governance. It complained that the reconquest of Sudan had produced obstacles to the unity of these two territories. Even moderate nationalists, who had frequently praised the British for restoring order to the country and bringing fiscal discipline, now concentrated their attacks on Cromer's educational policies, claiming that the British sought to keep Egypt uneducated and illiterate in order to prolong their rule.

In 1906, this growing discontent crystallized. A clash occurred in the Egyptian delta between a small group of British soldiers out on a hunting expedition and peasants from the village of Dinshawai, who were enraged when one of the soldiers shot and killed their domesticated pigeons. A dispute took place, in the midst of which a British soldier died. A number of leading British officials were horrified, believing that nationalist messages had penetrated the countryside and were producing political instability and overt opposition to their authority. Important elements within the British decision-making elite in the British Consulate decided that they must demonstrate to the local people that challenges to British authority were unacceptable. At a hasty trial, the so-called ringleaders of the incident were found guilty of inciting violence and committing a murder. The punishment of those deemed guilty was barbaric beyond anyone's expectations. Six men were hanged and another six were flogged in front of the entire village, whose members were forced to assemble and to watch the sentences carried out. The repercussions were the very opposite of what the authorities had wanted. In Britain, the Parliament, the press, and the citizenry were appalled that a country that justified its existence in Egypt on the grounds of bringing a superior civilization to the downtrodden could behave in such an irresponsible and high-handed fashion. In Egypt, the nationalists took up the cause of the villagers and excoriated the British for what they considered criminal behavior.

In response to the rising crescendo of nationalist protest, Cromer tried to make concessions to his Egyptian critics as well as to show the iron fist of British authority. He brought the young moderate nationalist Saad Zaghlul (1857–1927) into the Council of Ministers as the minister of public instruction. The Egyptians hoped that the energetic and well-respected Zaghlul would give education a stronger voice in ministerial discussions. Cromer also revived the Egyptian National Assembly, fallen into disuse since the Urabi revolt. Although the Assembly was to have only advisory powers and the franchise was limited, Egyptians had reason to believe that these changes were the beginning steps in creating a parliamentary system and power sharing with the British. But Cromer's heart was not in these reforms. His time in Egypt was drawing to a close. He would surely have left with or without the Dinshawai incident, for he had grown tired and sick during his last years in the country. He left under a cloud, however. As he departed through the streets of Cairo, many turned out, but troops lined the entire road to prevent any disturbance. Silence reigned in ways that were eerily unfamiliar to the hustle and bustle of Cairo and reflected the general condemnation that the population now had for the consul general.

Although the British Parliament passed a resolution of gratitude for Cromer's lengthy service to the British Empire and made him the virtually unheard of grant of £50,000 as a manifestation of their respect for his work, in fact the debate in the House of Commons was strident. The rising voice of anti-imperialism, already stunned by the violence of the Boer War in South Africa (1899–1902), used this occasion to reflect on how far short of its imperial goals the empire was falling.

WORLD WAR I AND THE 1919 REVOLUTION

The tribulations inflicted upon Egyptians during World War I spread the resentment against the British from the educated elites to the rank and file of the population. War pressures hit the peasantry hard; they led directly to an uprising of major proportions in 1919 that caught the British unprepared.

At the time the war broke out Khedive Abbas II was visiting Istanbul. The British, fearing Abbas's opposition to their rule, deposed him summarily and replaced him with Husayn Kamil. They also introduced military rule and a state of emergency. The British officer in charge of the military in Egypt at the time, General John Maxwell, had few worries about the Egyptians accepting these dramatic changes. By November 1914 he had an 82,000-man army in Egypt. "I have got such a smashing force here now that it would be worse than folly for a few discontents to attempt any foolish act." Just before proclaiming martial law, he marched units of his army through the streets of Cairo, proclaiming the exercise "a great success—very impressive." In the same way, after announcing that Husayn Kamil would be the new sultan of Egypt, Maxwell ordered another show of force. This time he "marched 8,000 cavalry through the Cairo streets. I think the natives thought they would never stop. They took two and a half hours to pass the saluting point. Cairo's quite a sight, full of soldiers and great huge fellows they are." Such was the British technique for showing their power. Egypt remained quiescent during the war. They stored up all of their resentments until afterwards.

The war pitted the British, French, and Russians against the Germans, the Austro-Hungarians, and the Ottomans. Fearing that the Egyptian population might rally behind the Ottomans, who were employing pan-Islamic sentiments to win allies, the British severed Egypt's formal ties with the Ottoman Empire and then established a British protectorate over the country. To mollify Egyptian resentment, they announced that they alone would bear all of the burdens of the war, a promise that was violated almost from the outset when the British ordered the Egyptian army to the Suez Canal to counter an Ottoman invasion across Sinai.

By 1916 Egypt was fully engaged in the war. The British had no fewer than three armies based in the country, a total of 400,000 men, whose interactions with the Egyptian population produced many violent incidents and whose consumption of local products produced soaring price inflation that hurt the poorer Egyptian classes while enriching a few merchants. Even more distressful to the local population, especially those living in the countryside, was the recruitment of Egyptian workers and the use of Egyptian camels in the labor and camel corps, needed as support for the British forces under the command of General Edmund Allenby in a campaign to drive the Ottomans out of Palestine and Syria. The demands on the peasantry were large and onerous and carried out with a heavy hand of coercion. In *Modern Egypt*, his classic study of the British occupation, Cromer had boasted of having rid Egypt of the evils of the corvee, the courbash (the hippopotamus-hide whip), and corruption. These returned with a vengeance in 1916, 1917, and 1918. Local officials, required to recruit personnel and animals for the labor and camel units, resorted to the old tactics.

And these demands fell inequitably on the people. As one British military observer noted, "no fellah joined it [the labor corps] from a desire to save the country from invasion, and no educated Egyptian ever served in its ranks." The casualties among the labor corps were not great since its units served behind the military lines, although they suffered losses from disease, but the same could not be said of the camel corps. It saw action at the front and suffered considerable deaths and casualties in warfare.

By war's end the country seethed with resentment. Virtually every segment of Egyptian society held deep grievances against the British. Price inflation afflicted the city dwellers. Large landowners grumbled about the restrictions against cultivating cotton given the high prices that cotton fetched during and just after the war. The peasantry hated the labor exactions of the later war years. For the educated element in Egypt—the group that had mounted the most visible opposition to British rule in the period leading up to the war—the single most important development was American intervention in the war in 1917 and Woodrow Wilson's proclamation of his Fourteen Points. The message that resonated with the educated Egyptians was Wilson's proclamation of the doctrine of self-determination and the virtues of democratic government in a world free of the specter of war. Although Wilson had directed his ideas at the Central powers (Germany, Austro-Hungary, and the Ottoman Empire) in hopes of undermining the legitimacy of their monarchical forms of government and spurring their linguistic and ethnic minorities to challenge their rulers, the ideals spread with alacrity well beyond their European context. They found a ready audience in Egypt, where the leaders of the political parties that had sprung into existence in the decade and a half leading up to the outbreak of the war seized on the doctrine of self-determination and were sure that it should be applied to Egypt. After all, they reasoned, were Egyptians not as well prepared to rule themselves as Czechs, Poles, Serbs, and others?

Prepared to carry their nationalist aspirations to Europe in 1918 were two influential groups. First, the Egyptian ministers in power, Adli Yakin and Husayn Rushdi, insisted that they should lead a delegation to London to conduct political negotiations with the British cabinet. Espousing a more expansive view, Saad Zaghlul believed that an Egyptian delegation (a Wafd), representing a broader spectrum of Egyptian society and headed by himself, should go straight to the Paris Peace Conference and lay its demands at the feet of the assembled leaders there. Zaghlul was especially eager to meet with Woodrow Wilson, the new shining light of international politics and the enunciator of the new ideologies of self-determination and democracy.

Almost overnight, Zaghlul became the darling of the educated and politically informed. He had not always been the face of Egyptian nationalism. The son of a local notable, he had studied at al-Azhar, where he became a disciple of Muhammad Abduh in the period leading up to the British occupation. In the 1900s, he worked with the moderate Ummah Party, led by one of Egypt's most respected and moderate intellectuals, Ahmad Lutfi al-Sayyid. This party was not averse to cooperating with the British and viewed them as preparing Egypt for its ultimate political independence. For Ummah Party members, the Watani Party of Mustafa Kamil and Muhammad Farid was too radical, and the coterie of supporters gathered around Khedive Abbas II was too confrontational with the British. It was hardly surprising, then, that Zaghlul agreed to serve as minister of public instruction in Cromer's cabinet reshuffle of 1906 or that he served in the Egyptian Legislative Assembly in the years leading up to World War I.

The British rejected the Egyptian demands, arguing that their own ministers were fully engaged with the peace negotiations in Paris. They suggested that these matters could be dealt with after the Versailles conference had finished its work. When the Egyptian ministry resigned and the population flared up in violence, the British arrested Zaghlul and a few of his closest supporters and exiled them to Malta. This action led to widespread violence throughout the country. In the cities, students and government officials marched in protest. In the countryside, the peasants, egged on by local officials, tore up rail lines and attempted to isolate themselves entirely from Cairo and the powers of the central government. First, in Minya province and then in other provinces, local officials announced the formation of independent, provincially based republics. Even the release of Zaghlul from Malta and permission for him and his Egyptian delegation, the Wafd, to take their case to Paris did not quell the violence. When the allies, gathered at Versailles, refused to meet with the Egyptian delegates and President Wilson recognized the British protectorate over Egypt, the violence continued unabated in Egypt. The country had spun out of control. The British found themselves with only a modicum of authority in the big cities and nearly no authority over the countryside. It was only after Lord Allenby, sent to Egypt as a special envoy to restore order to the country, unilaterally proclaimed Egypt's political independence from Britain and the end of protectorate rule that the British felt confident that political stability could be sustained. In the new political arrangements, the ruler of Egypt, called the khedive before World War I and the sultan during and just after the war, now became the king. Of course, Allenby's proclamation of independence was carefully circumscribed. The British claimed four limitations on Egyptian independence: protection of foreigners and control over the operations of the Suez Canal, over Sudan, and over Egyptian foreign policy. In order to oversee these obligations, the British retained a military presence in the country, even larger, in fact, than the 5,000-man army that had occupied the country before World War I.

As part of his formula for restoring order to the country, Allenby asked the Egyptian political leaders to draw up a new constitution for governing the country. Although the Wafd boycotted the discussions that resulted in a new constitution in 1923, they agreed to participate in the elections that took place in 1924. As might have been anticipated, the Wafd won the elections, and Zaghlul was installed as Egypt's prime minister. His tenure of power proved short-lived, however, for the assassination of Lee Stack, the commanding general of the Egyptian army, who was inspecting troops in Sudan in 1924, caused the British to dismiss Zaghlul from office and to deny him the prospect of ever returning to power.

Thus, the 1919 revolution produced significant political changes, including a new constitution, a proclamation of Egypt's independence, and a newly elected government. It also resulted in a number of significant economic and social changes, in many ways far more radical than those that took place in the political sphere. As early as the Urabi revolt, Egyptians had realized that political independence without economic strength counted for little. Among the nationalist demands in the lead-up to World War I were industrialization, an economy less dependent on the export of a single commodity, no matter how high its world price, and a purely Egyptian bank, run by Egyptian directors and with Egyptian shareholders, that would undercut the monopoly enjoyed by the numerous foreign banks that operated in Egypt. But the critical moment for Egypt's economic transformation came during World War I when a leading group of Egyptian businessmen, some of them native-born Egyptians and some of them foreigners with long years of residence in the country, met as a commission to study Egypt's commerce and industry. Its report, published in 1918, laid out the new directions that the economy would take in the interwar years and beyond.

The members of the commission formed a veritable Who's Who of Egypt's business classes. Among the group were Talaat Harb, Egypt's most impressive entrepreneur in the interwar period; Ismail Sidqi, who would be a leading minister and sometimes prime minister in this era; Henri Naus, head of the Egyptian Sugar Company, the leading industrial organization at the time; and Yussuf Aslan Qattawi, a Jewish businessman with contacts throughout the world of commerce, finance, and business. The report had one overriding message: Egypt's great agricultural expansion and prosperity were destined to come to an end. The amount of new land that could be brought under cultivation through dam construction and irrigation improvements was limited. Meanwhile, the Egyptian population was growing at a fast clip. Already a landless element had begun to appear. If Egypt were to develop economically, an essential ingredient of its political future, it would need to promote local industries and stimulate a more diversified economy, less dependent on the export of a single crop. According to the authors of the report, the Egyptian

Sugar Company was already showing the way. It employed 17,000 laborers and produced no fewer than 100,000 tons of refined sugar per year. Similar industries could be established in food processing, cigarettes, wine and spirits, cement, and textiles, for which a local market already existed.

A single individual led the way after the war. Talaat Harb, whose statue graces one of the main squares in Cairo today, had been planning economic changes for many years. Now his opportunity to effect change arrived. Born in 1867, the son of a minor railway employee, Harb was educated at the Egyptian School of Law. For many years he worked in various government ministries, always demonstrating a skill in financial matters and thereby coming to the attention of Egypt's wealthy landlords. The landlord who became his champion was Umar Sultan, whose finances Harb straightened out and who then put the young business phenom in touch with other large landowners. As Harb surveyed the Egyptian economy, he came to the conclusion that almost all of the investment in Egypt and the business firms that operated in the country were foreign. He also believed that the most powerful economic institutions were Egypt's many foreign banks. They controlled the crucial funds that were lent to the landowning class at the beginning of the cotton-growing season or were made available for the purchase of new landholdings. Harb's trip to Europe before the war revealed to him that banks with large amounts of capital at their disposal, like the German great banks, had used their financial clout to stimulate Germany's late-nineteenth-century industrialization. Such a bank in Egypt, if owned and run by Egyptians, could play a similar dynamic role in diversifying and industrializing the Egyptian economy, Harb believed.

In 1920 Harb realized his dream of a purely Egyptian bank. He persuaded 124 wealthy individuals, many of them large landowners who admired Harb's financial acumen, to contribute £E80,000 to start the new bank. Its charter was avowedly nationalist, as befit this revolutionary era. All shareholders and directors were to be Egyptians. No foreign element was to be involved. Moreover, the bank, called Bank Misr (or the Bank of Egypt), was to play a role in creating other Egyptian companies, with a view to diversifying the economy. A number of important Misr companies followed in short order. Using capital from Bank Misr and from wealthy Egyptians and drawing heavily, though no longer exclusively, on Egyptian directors, Harb established a group of important textile factories, an airline, a navigation company, an insurance firm, and many other businesses. Between 1920, when the bank came into existence, and the outbreak of World War II in 1939 Bank Misr founded eighteen companies, with a paid-up capital in 1939 of slightly over £E2,000,000. Talaat Harb had, in fact, achieved his ambition to promote industrialization and economic diversification. Other wealthy Egyptians followed his lead, so that by the outbreak of World War II, slightly more than half of the capital invested in large-scale firms operating in Egypt was Egyptian, compared to 14 percent before 1914. Moreover, Harb had established his reputation as Egypt's most dynamic entrepreneur.

Alas, the story of Talaat Harb's economic exploits did not end well. In 1939, at the outbreak of the war, the bank found itself overextended at the very time when many depositors sought to withdraw their funds. Rebuffed in his efforts to receive funds from the National Bank, Egypt's equivalent of a central bank at this time, Harb looked to the government, which offered to bail out Bank Misr only if Harb resigned from the board and withdrew from the world of business. Citing ill health, he complied. Many at the time and later on believed that the British and influential Egyptian business figures and government officials had engineered the bank's crisis. The reality was otherwise. Over the years, often for political reasons, the bank had made large loans to influential landowners, many of which during the depression years had become nonperforming. Even more risky was the bank's aggressive financial sponsorship of the Misr companies, which left it constantly short of funds and thus unable to meet the run that depositors made on its funds. Its losses in 1939 totaled £E3 million, wiping out its entire operating capital of £E1 million, its reserve of £E800,000, and between £E1 million and £E2 million of the £E17 million of depositors' money. The sad lesson that Talaat Harb learned in 1939 was that a normal commercial bank, with a multitude of depositors, who could demand their funds at any moment, could not be a development bank that lent large sums on long-term investments.

Two other pressure groups also emerged during the 1919 revolution. One was dominated by Egyptian landlords, and the other by foreign businessmen who had made Egypt their home. The first, the General Egyptian Agricultural Syndicate, which was established as a pressure group by the large landowning and cotton-exporting elite, came into being in 1921. Its goal was to secure greater Egyptian control over the economy and to allow Egyptian cultivators to obtain more of the profits of cotton exports for themselves. Naturally, its members were thrilled by the establishment of Bank Misr because they regarded foreign banking and exporting establishments as the institutions that gained the most from Egypt's export- and import-oriented economy.

A year later, the Egyptian Federation of Industries was established. Although the founders, mostly European businesspersons resident in Egypt, sought and, to some extent, gained significant Egyptian representation within the association, Europeans dominated this organization from the outset. The federation represented the industrial wing of the Egyptian bourgeoisie and promoted those policies, such as protective tariffs, tax breaks for infant industries, and favorable labor legislation that would enhance efforts to create new industries. The guiding force of the organization, which issued a journal in French, English, and Arabic and which also published a scholarly publication dedicated to social, political, and economic issues, *l'Égypte contemporaine*, was an Egyptian Jew, I. G. Levi, whose role in promoting local industrialization was immense.

Radical social transformation also accompanied the political and economic changes of the interwar years. The most obvious transformation was the growth of Egypt's two major cities, Cairo and Alexandria. Cairo, which in 1800 had a population around one-quarter of a million (or approximately 6 percent of the total population) had burgeoned to more than one million, according to the census of 1927. Although it still constituted only 7 percent of the total Egyptian population, its growth was continuing at ever increasing, even alarming, rates. The exodus from the countryside also affected the city of Alexandria, which had a population of a half a million according to the 1927 census, far above the mere 6,000 who were residing in what was little more than a modest-sized fishing village in 1800 at the time of the French occupation. Although the vast majority of the Alexandrine inhabitants were Egyptians, they hardly made any impression on the powerful European residential elite. These wealthy, mainly commercial families lived in resplendent residential quarters, commuting into the center of the city by means of a comfortable tram line. Egypt's well-connected foreign residents have been immortalized in Lawrence Durrell's *Alexandria Quartet* (1957–60), which describes the cafés, restaurants, luxury hotels, and exquisite private manors of the European elite, without even so much as a hint that most Alexandrines were native-born, rather poor Egyptians. Later on, when the Egyptian intellectual Muhammad Husayn Haikal complained that Egyptians lived like foreigners in their own country, he could have easily pointed to Alexandria as the consummate example of this statement.

Let us once again return to a journey in from the Cairo International Airport to the center of the city. Our taxi goes through one of Egypt's most unusual residential areas, Heliopolis, which reflects many of the currents of the European-dominated first half of the twentieth century in Egypt. Heliopolis was the brainstorm of a wealthy Belgian financial tycoon, Baron Édouard Empain, who had fallen in love with Egypt and made it his principal residence. Realizing that Cairo's population was expanding at rapid rates, he bought up land to the northeast of the main city and then developed a housing estate there. He sold properties to the wealthy, foreigners and Egyptians alike, built estates and apartment buildings, created utility companies, including a tram line, which continues to run today and serves commuters as their main form of transportation from the suburb to their workplaces in the center of the city. Empain did everything in an outsized way. His architecture is oriental baroque, and the most stunning (or, should we say, outlandish) of the structures that he built was his own residence, now unoccupied, but a landmark for anyone traveling from the airport to the center of the city. Designed to resemble a Hindu temple, it contained a revolving tower that allowed the viewer to follow the path of the sun.

A question that haunted many Egyptians for years was whether Empain and other wealthy foreigners who settled in Egypt and invested their wealth and energy in the country brought real benefits to its people. Or did all of this foreign enterprise relegate Egyptians to a distant second-class status? The young officers who seized power in 1952 had no doubts: the foreign populations, especially the foreign wealthy classes, were parasites. They had to go, and they were sent packing. Yet there is irony here. One of Empain's most spectacular constructions, the Heliopolis Palace Hotel, was the finest hotel in Africa when it was first opened; now it is the residence of the Egyptian president, Husni Mubarak.

Women were less caught up in the social changes galvanizing the country during the first three decades of the twentieth century. Their education and literacy lagged significantly behind those of men, and their visibility in the professions and politics was much less. Yet during this period what some called the woman question roiled Egyptian politics and thought. In the first place, the small minority that formed the educated and upper crust of Egyptian female society came out in large numbers to support Zaghlul during the 1919 disturbances. The most admired woman of the period, and in many respects a pacesetter for new roles for Egyptian women, was the wife of Saad Zaghlul, Safiya Zaghlul, known to many as the mother of the Egyptian nation. She was never as radical as the most visible feminist of the period, Huda Sharawi, who stopped wearing the veil, founded the Egyptian Feminist Union, and worked for women's rights. Rather, Safiya sought to be a moderating influence, regarding her chief role as supporting her husband and then after his death preserving his memory.

The question of the place of women in Egypt society did not surface unannounced during the women's demonstrations in 1919, however. It had emerged as a controversial matter in the period before World War I. A progressive, Western-oriented, and relatively secular branch of the Egyptian intelligentsia believed that one of the forces accounting for Egypt's lagging behind Europe and its political subordination to the British was its treatment of women. In this regard, the leading spokesman for women's reform, Qasim Amin, found himself in complete agreement with Lord Cromer, who, in charting the major differences between the Orient and the Occident, argued that Europeans accorded freedom to women, while Muslims held them in a subordinate place. Qasim Amin wrote several treatises (*The Emancipation of Woman*, 1899, and *The New Woman*, 1900) demanding reform of the education of women and calling for an end to veiling. Ironically, his chief critic was none other than Egypt's most innovative entrepreneur, Talaat Harb, who published a rejoinder to Amin's two books on women's rights, in which he insisted that women should continue to be veiled as an assertion of one of the fundamental differences between the Muslim East and the Christian West.

The practice of veiling was known at the time by its Arabic word, *al-hijab* (which has a different meaning in contemporary Egypt, where it stands for the head scarf that covers the hair), while unveiling was called *al-sufur*. The most highly publicized moment of unveiling occurred in 1923 when the feminist and wife of a leading notable, Huda Sharawi, having returned from a women's conference in Rome, served notice that she would no longer wear a veil. Historians have seen this moment as the time when unveiling became a prominent concern among elite women. The reality was that by 1923 perhaps only 15 percent of the female population wore the *burqa*, the veil that covered the face from beneath the eyes. Ordinary peasant women had never worn veils, since that would have encumbered them as they worked in the fields. The most popular of the veils worn by upper-crust women in the prewar period was a thin white veil and was known as the *yismak*, but its popularity was already in decline by the end of the war.

THE INTERWAR YEARS

The primary political theme of the interwar years was a three-cornered struggle between the palace, the British Embassy, and the Wafd for political power. Even though Zaghlul died in 1927, his successor, Mustafa al-Nahhas. though lacking Zaghlul's charisma, inherited the mantle of the party as the champion of Egyptian independence. In relatively free elections, of which there were few, the Wafd was the sure winner. But the Wafd's periods of power were limited. The party had to deal with the antagonism of the British and King Fuad and his successor, King Farouk. The British retained a large army of occupation in the country, with which they could intimidate Egyptian politicians. The kings had the power to remove governments that they did not like. As a consequence, in spite of the fact that the Wafd was Egypt's primary political party, others formed, largely around well-known political leaders like Ismail Sidqi, and awaited the call of the king to form a government. Sidqi led the Egyptian government during the early years of the world depression (1930–33), when he endeavored to alter the Egyptian constitution in ways that would hamstring the Wafd. He was largely unsuccessful.

One important political event marked the interwar years, however. In 1936, with war clouds forming in Europe and Egypt's politicians fearful that the country would be drawn into a European maelstrom as it had been during World War I, the newly elected Wafd government finally signed a peace treaty with the British. This accord confirmed the 1922 British grant of political independence to Egypt, but continued to reserve certain powers to the British. These powers, as before, were protection of foreigners, the Suez Canal, Sudan, and foreign affairs, but Egypt obtained three concessions that were absent from the imposed peace agreement of 1922. The treaty was to run for only twenty years; the British force was to be limited to 10,000 men and was to be housed away from the major population centers of Egypt in the Suez Canal zone once a suitable base had been constructed; and Egypt was to obtain membership in the League of Nations. Nonetheless, these concessions hardly provided Egypt with the full-fledged independence that so many of the nationalists demanded. The Wafd lost a considerable degree of its legitimacy when it acceded to these arrangements.

In reality, there was much that was happening outside the realm of parliamentary politics and threatening to parliamentary forms of government that worried the Wafd as much as the British and the king did. In 1928, a young firebrand orator, reared in the delta but posted as a teacher to the Suez Canal region, where foreign privilege and wealth were palpable, established a new organization destined to shape political thinking throughout the entire Muslim world. Hasan al-Banna created the Muslim Brotherhood, asserting that a return to the authentic form of Islam as practiced in the early centuries of the faith would provide a full and sufficient answer to modern-day problems. He also argued that parliamentary governance was a sham imposed by the wealthy and powerful on the poor to keep them in their place. The Brotherhood spread its message far and wide within Egypt and beyond and over time created secret cells, which employed violence against its opponents. The Brotherhood was not the only organization opposed to parliaments and prepared to use violence to destabilize the state. A group known as Young Egypt, drawing its inspiration from Italian fascism, emerged and used street violence to challenge the establishment. As a consequence, the Wafd and other political parties responded by establishing their own youth groups, who used their paramilitary bodies to promote their causes as thuggishly as did the Muslim Brothers and Young Egypt. Egypt during the decade of the 1930s, when the depression was working its way through the country, was rife with calls for violent action, political assassinations, and electoral intimidation.

Secular nationalism and reformed Islam seemed to be on the rise at the turn of the century. Muhammad Abduh, Egypt's most respected Muslim scholar, made strong efforts to find compatibilities between Western learning and values and traditional Islamic teachings. The leading journals, like *al-Muqtataf*, and newspapers, such as *al-Ahram*, were beacons of scientific inquiry and champions of the virtues of Westernization efforts. Yet they had their opponents, whose strength was on the ascendant in the interwar years, in part because parliamentary governance did not realize its promises and the economy faltered. There were many controversies between the Westernizers and their opponents, but none as spectacular as those that involved two of Egypt's most outspoken westernizing intellectuals, Ali Abd al-Raziq and Taha Husayn. At the time that Mustafa Kemal Ataturk abolished the caliphate in Turkey, Ali Abd al-Raziq, at that point in his life an obscure judge in the Islamic legal system, issued a treatise, *Islam and the Bases of Rule* (1925), which contended that the caliphate had no basis in the scriptures or law of Islam. He added that the institution had been imposed by force on the people and that it was "a plague for Islam and Muslims, a source of evils and corruption." In Abd al-Raziq's view, Muslims did not need to be bound by the political traditions handed down for centuries. They could innovate, even establish polities that bore a close resemblance to those in the West.

A year later, the brilliant young scholar Taha Husayn, whose autobiographical work, *al-Ayyam*, won acclaim throughout the Arabic-speaking world as a portrait of a youngster growing up in a traditional environment but coming to grips with the modern world, wrote a book on the pre-Islamic period and early Islam in the Arabian Peninsula. In this work he applied historical criticism to the emergence of Islam and suggested that some of the stories concerning the early days of the faith were myths.

Taha Husayn and Abd al-Raziq were solidly in the tradition of higher Western criticism of religious texts. Both were pious Muslims, who had been inspired by the schools of higher criticism in the Western world's understanding of early Christianity and sought to employ the same methods in the study of Islam. The response that they generated, however, caught them and other advocates for a more relativist and historicist approach to religion and early religious institutions by surprise. Both writings were subject to intense discussion and criticism, especially from conservative quarters. Abd al-Raziq lost his standing among the corps of Egyptian scholars, and Taha Husayn had to withdraw the original text and republish an altered and more conservative version. The lessons were not lost on other liberal, secular, and modernist intellectuals, who now became wary of writing anything that openly challenged the deeply held religious beliefs of conservative Muslim scholars in Egypt. Moreover, after Muhammad Abduh's death, although his liberal, reformist agenda for Islam continued to influence intellectuals, his main disciple in Egypt, Rashid Rida, used the journal *al-Manar* to espouse a far more conservative and even anti-Western program than Abduh had favored.

THE WAR YEARS AND THEIR AFTERMATH

The leaders of the Wafd had signed the 1936 treaty with the British in order to spare Egypt the sufferings that the British had inflicted on the country during World War I. They were to be deeply disappointed when World War II broke out. The war came to the doorstep of the country when Rommel's German army crossed the Libyan-Egyptian border in 1942 and made straight for Egyptian population centers. Once again, Egypt found itself the center of large allied troop concentrations, and though the Egyptian army was not called on to hold the Germans off, several young officers put themselves secretly in touch with the German high command in hopes of ridding the country of the dreaded British military presence. So great was the tension in the country in early 1942 and so fearful were the British that the existing government might try to negotiate with the Germans behind their backs that they surrounded King Farouk's palace in Cairo with tanks and compelled him to install a pro-British Wafdist government. The ministry of Mustafa al-Nahhas did, in fact, back the British, whose forces stopped the German military advance at al-Alamein, but the once-ultranationalist Wafd received nothing but condemnation from many segments of Egyptian society for its collaboration with the British. No group was more offended by this abdication of authority to the British than the young officer corps of the Egyptian army, who held a grudge against the king for succumbing to British demands and against the Wafd for allowing themselves to be used by their occupiers. The stage was being set for the military coup d'état of 1952.

Much had to happen before the coup occurred. Political assassinations abounded. One of those to lose his life was none other than the founder of the Muslim Brotherhood, Hasan al-Banna. Parliament continued to falter, failing to address a host of social and economic problems. By then, everyone was aware that the distribution of wealth, especially land, was badly skewed. A few landowning families held vast amounts of land, while the mass of the population eked out a living on small estates or as landless laborers. The largest landholders by far were members of the royal family, reputed to own no fewer than 180,000 acres. An effort to pass land reform legislation failed to muster enough votes in a parliament dominated by the large landed classes. Ridding the country of the British military presence was another issue that remained unresolved. During the war, the British had built a mammoth military base in the Suez Canal zone, and instead of keeping not more than 10,000 troops in that base, as stipulated by the 1936 treaty, except in times of war, the British had as many as 100,000 men stationed there as their contribution to the American-led Cold War effort against Soviet ambitions in the Middle East. This huge military presence infuriated the Egyptians, who used guerrilla warfare tactics to make life intolerable for the British soldiers stationed there.

Many collisions took place between British forces and Egyptian nationalists in the early 1950s, one of which, in January 1952, saw the British launch an attack against a unit of the Egyptian police in the canal city of Ismailia. The reports that Egyptian police officials had died in the confrontation with British soldiers was greeted in Cairo with mob rioting against foreign establishments, especially those owned by Britons. The Egyptian army had to be called in to quell the disorder that left ten British subjects dead and much foreign property burned to the ground. Among the establishments destroyed were the famous Shepheard's Hotel, Barclays Bank, and the British Overseas Airways Corporation offices. That a massive British army of 100,000 men sat on their weapons while British subjects and British and foreign properties were being destroyed sent a message to all who observed these events. One of the grounds for stationing troops in Egypt, according to the treaties of 1922 and 1936, was the protection of foreign populations and their interests. Obviously the fact that British troops allowed foreign citizens to be killed and foreign property to be destroyed revealed to many that the days of the British Empire in the Middle East were numbered.

Egypt for the Egyptians, 1952–1981

Nasser and Sadat

In the stifling heat of the evening of July 22, 1952, a group of young Egyptian military officers, who had been plotting and planning the future of Egypt, seized the reins of authority. They struck late at night, taking control of the radio networks and the main military bases. They moved hastily, even slightly before they felt entirely confident of their success, conscious that King Farouk and his followers were gathering information about them and preparing to move to stymie their plans. Over Radio Cairo, Anwar al-Sadat, one of the Free Officers, announced the coup and asserted that the military was seizing power in order to transform Egyptian society. No longer would the country be ruled by corrupt politicians, headed by an immoral and reprehensible king, all of whom did the bidding of the British. The young men who captured the levers of power vowed that they would rule for the people, not in the interests of the privileged few.

The officers wasted little time in making good on their promises. Within days of taking power, they waved goodbye to King Farouk, who sailed away from Alexandria on his yacht, bound for his favorite playgrounds in Europe. Although the officers appointed his young son as heir to the throne, that fiction lasted only a little longer. By year's end the military men had done away with the monarchy, bringing an end to an institution that dated back to the radical modernizing figure Muhammad Ali. Nor did they stop there. By August, they had passed a land reform law, limiting individual landholdings to 200 acres, and a family's holdings to 300 acres. The shock was immense. Egypt for more than a century had been ruled by a few hyperwealthy landowners, who lived in splendor, vacationing in the high spots on the European continent during Egypt's searing summer season, and lording it over the rank and file of the population, who lived in abject poverty. As the military men went around the countryside, handing out the new certificates of ownership to peasant families, they were greeted with applause and enthusiasm. An outpouring of pride spread throughout the country. Finally Egypt was in the hands of authentic Egyptians who had risen from the ranks. And the officers promised even more. They said that education would be opened to all and that social mobility and economic improvement would follow.

Who were these men who had seemingly emerged from obscurity to lead the Egyptian nation at a time of incredible strain? They were young, many of them in their early thirties, holding the ranks of major and lieutenant colonel. The vast majority were native-born Egyptians, not the descendants of the old Turkish military class. Most had attended the Egyptian military school in the late 1930s when it had begun to take a larger number of better-educated young men, less connected to wealthy and aristocratic families. These men formed special bonds through their education and through their differences from older and more senior military officers. They conversed about Egypt's problems, not least of which was the continued British military presence in the country. A few had made contact with the Axis powers during the early stages of World War II when Rommel's desert army was advancing on Egypt. One of the most radical of the group, Anwar al-Sadat, thought that the German invasion of Egypt provided the ideal moment to effect a revolution against the British. He was found out and imprisoned. The young officers were acutely aware of Egypt's weaknesses and soon formed a secret organization, called the Free Officers Group, most probably in 1949, with a view to diagnosing Egypt's weaknesses and seeking solutions to its manifold problems. On the eve of the 1952 coup, the organization had anywhere from 280 to 340 members. (See figure 5 for a picture of some of the important Free Officers.)

Because these young officers were politically sensitive, they formed ties with outside groups, also concerned about Egypt's political future. Some gravitated toward the Muslim Brotherhood; others were

Figure 5. Nasser, Sadat, and Neguib and other Free Officers

influenced by Communist and socialist thought and organization. What they detested most, however, were the established politicians, notably the Wafd, who had allowed themselves to be coerced into ruling Egypt during the troubled year of 1942 and who in their return to power in the election of 1950 had been unable to rid the country of British troops.

For many of the young officers, a turning point was the failed 1948 Egyptian military campaign that the Arab states, led by the Egyptian army, launched against Israel at the time of its creation. The Arab armies showed poorly on the battlefields, unable to prevent the establishment of a separate Jewish state in Palestine as the British prepared to bring an end to their colonial rule in that territory. The Egyptian public and its politicians had displayed only minimal interest in the early years of the dispute over Palestine. They took hardly any notice of the declaration of Lord Balfour, the British foreign secretary, promulgated in 1917 at the height of World War I, that his government would work to create a homeland for the Jews in Palestine. But as Arab-Jewish tensions mounted, the Egyptian community was drawn in. The 1930s witnessed bloody confrontations between Jewish and Arab groups. By the end of World War II, Egyptian nationalist and pan-Arab elements had become so deeply involved in the future of Palestine that the anniversary of the Balfour Declaration served as a day on which to protest growing Zionist influence in Palestine. On occasions, the protests became violent; much of the hostility was directed against the property and commercial establishments of wealthy Jewish businesspersons.

Egyptian officers were deeply embarrassed by their military defeats in the 1948 Arab-Israeli war and blamed the politicians for sending them into battle with faulty weapons, grossly unprepared. One of the young officers who harbored ill will against the old order and who was wounded during battles in the Negev was Gamal Abdel Nasser. He was destined to emerge as the leader of the Free Officers. In his opinion, the Israeli adversaries fought with the qualities of zeal and ruthless determination that were lacking on the Egyptian side. Nasser and the others held the politicians in Cairo, and especially the corrupt king, responsible for their losses. They looked forward to the day when new rulers, perhaps they themselves, would clean the Augean stables of the old order.

Nasser and the other Free Officers had imbibed enough of the criticisms of democratic rule in the 1930s to be reluctant to trust the fate of Egypt to elections. Soon after seizing power, they abolished the old parties, allowing only the Muslim Brotherhood to remain in existence. When the Brotherhood did not cooperate with the military men, it, too, was outlawed. Although Nasser was the guiding figure from the outset, he stayed well behind the scenes at first. Believing that the populace was likely to be skeptical of being ruled by such young and inexperienced men, they encouraged a senior officer, General Muhammad Neguib, who had been sympathetic to their ideas, to become the figurehead leader. This arrangement, however, did not last. Neguib let his growing popularity go to his head and began to aspire to real authority. In a showdown over power in 1954, Nasser prevailed and became the supreme leader of the military government. Although the officers continued to meet as a body, called the Revolutionary Command Council, in reality, from 1954 onwards until his death in 1970, Nasser was the unquestioned leader.

GAMAL ABDEL NASSER

Nasser was an inspiring figure, the right man at the time for the task. He was in his mid-thirties, battle-tested, highly respected within the officer corps. Although he brooked no opposition, he shunned the trappings of power and lived a modest personal life. He dressed in ordinary civilian suits although he had a passion for striped ties, of which he owned 250, had no ambitions to ostentatious ways, chain-smoked three packs of American cigarettes a day, and resided in a modest house with his wife and much-sheltered children. At first he was only a tolerable public speaker, but with the passing of time he became a brilliant orator, far more at home in colloquial Egyptian that the ordinary listeners preferred than in modern standard Arabic, with its classical overtones. Once he got started in a speech, he could carry on for hours, repeating over and over his litany of political themes—that Egypt had suffered grievously at the hands of the British for nearly a century, that Western capitalism robbed Egypt of its wealth and dignity, and that the pathway toward power in the Middle East and toward a solution of the vexing Arab-Israeli problem was through an Egyptian-led pan-Arab unity. The last theme put him at loggerheads with many of the more conservative and royalist politicians and political potentates in the Arab world. Employing Radio Cairo, which broadcast his message of Egyptian leadership throughout the entire Arab world, he created many enemies, but won the hearts and minds of the young, well-educated Arab progressives.

The Anglo-Egyptian treaty of 1936 had proved the undoing of the Wafd and gave the military its chance to seize power. If the Free Officers accomplished nothing else, they had a solemn duty to rid the country of the hated British military occupation. Negotiations were long and arduous. The British were determined to hold on to their magnificent and huge base in the Suez Canal zone, which they regarded as an essential element in deterring Soviet expansionism into the Middle East. Here they enjoyed American support. But no Egyptian could tolerate the presence of large British forces in their country, however well-meaning the cause. Finally, in 1954, the two sides reached an accord. All British uniformed troops would depart by early 1956. The British would retain a small staff of nonuniformed officers to oversee the maintenance of the base, which the British could reoccupy in the event of an attack in the area.

The military put the best face on the agreement, celebrating the fact that British troops would finally be gone in 1956 after a stay of seventy-four years. But the critics thought otherwise, observing that British military observers would remain behind along with a plethora of British international firms, whose task it was to keep the base up to its previously high state of readiness. So angered was a segment of the population that a Muslim Brother attempted to assassinate President Nasser as he was giving an open-air speech in Alexandria in early 1954. Nasser was unharmed and used the moment to rouse his audience with the words that assassins might kill him, but other Nassers would arise to carry forward his mission. At the same time, he ended his already deteriorating relationship with the Muslim Brotherhood, imprisoning many of its leaders.

Of the many weaknesses of the young military officers the most obvious was a lack of mastery of economic matters. The officers recognized their economic deficiency and installed a traditional, mainline economist as their first minister of finance. They made only one intervention in the minister's first budget proposals, vetoing a proposal for an increased tax on cigarettes on the grounds that smoking was one of the few pleasures that the common man could afford.

Yet their lack of expertise in economic matters did not mean that they had no general economic agenda. Quite the contrary; these men were brought up in a generation that admired the rapid economic progress of the Soviet Union, with its five-year plans, its heavy and rapid industrialization, and its military defeat of Nazi

Germany. They believed that a combination of central planning and creative entrepreneurial energies could transform the Egyptian economy overnight. They also held to the view that one of the major factors impeding Egypt's economic progress was British colonial rule and the role that foreign capital played in keeping Egypt an agricultural producer and exporter and an industrial midget. Hence, they wanted their government to be active in the economic arena, to set high, but attainable economic growth rate targets, to limit the power of foreign capital, and to be energetic in redistributing wealth from the superrich to those most in need. Of course, they believed that their land reform program had set the tone for such wealth redistribution and new directions. Not only would the poor smallholder peasants, and even some of the landless, receive that most valuable of Egyptian assets, land, but people with resources would now see the value of investing in other forms of wealth, such as industrialization.

The military men went through a series of finance ministers until they found the man who best suited their aspirations. This was Dr. Aziz Sidqi, a Harvard-trained economist who believed wholeheartedly in planned economic development and was confident that Egypt could become the industrial giant of the Middle East. The scheme that Sidqi and Nasser agreed would be the foundation block of Egypt's new diversified economy was a new, immense dam just south of the old, twice-heightened Aswan dam. Known as the High Dam from the outset, this project entailed financing, constructing, and the holding back of waters on a scale not yet seen in hydraulic works around the world. Its advantages to Egypt were obvious. In the first place, and of vital importance to the Egyptian planners, the whole project would be accomplished within Egypt's borders. Unlike other plans for maximizing the irrigation waters of the Nile, many of which the British hydraulic engineers had put forward, this scheme would not involve a series of dams along the Nile stretching from Central Africa and Ethiopia through Egypt. The defect of the British plans, in the minds of the Egyptian planners, was that, however environmentally sound they were and however much they contributed to the overall economic development of the entire Nile basin, they placed Egypt's agricultural and industrial well-being in the hands of non-Egyptians. There were other obvious advantages to a High Dam at Aswan. A large set of turbines could generate significant amounts of cheap electricity that would power Egypt's new industries. Additionally, the floodwaters being held back in a massive lake behind the dam, subsequently named Lake Nasser, would ensure a regular distribution of Nile waters season after season. All parts of Egypt could be converted to perennial irrigation, and new, previously nonarable parts of Upper and Lower Egypt could be made cultivatable. Finally, the old specter of high and low Niles wreaking havoc with Egypt's agricultural production would be removed.

But significant disadvantages existed, not the least of which, for Egyptians and foreigners alike, was the huge cost. Egypt would not be able to finance the dam construction on its own. It would need significant foreign assistance. The big lake that would come into being behind the dam would require the resettlement of a large number of Nubian villagers living in the region, and would also submerge many of the region's outstanding antiquities, the most famous being the massive statues of Ramses at Abu Simbel. In addition, hydraulic engineers feared that silt deposits at the base of the dam would build up and compromise its integrity. As for the disadvantages that would occur downstream in Egypt, the most obvious was that no part of the country would any longer receive the renewing supply of silt that the Nile in flood brought from the Ethiopian highlands. Egyptian farmers would require large infusions of expensive fertilizers if the soil were to retain its high levels of productivity. Already bilharzia was a scourge of the peasant population. Now with waters remaining in the canals the year-round and with peasants working in these canals all the time, bilharzia was certain to become widespread and endemic. Finally, the Nile waters would no longer sweep through the delta. The result would be that the Mediterranean Sea would steadily push into the interior of Egypt and render the lands in the lower delta less fertile.

Nonetheless, the hydraulic experts in weighing costs and benefits concluded that given Egypt's exploding population its main economic hope for the future was such a dam. This being the case, the government's primary task was to secure outside funding and technical assistance.

The Egyptians turned first of all to the West. The British had been the chief hydraulic engineers throughout the twentieth century and had the greatest technical knowledge of the Nile River basin. The Americans, with their controlling influence in the World Bank, were the essential financial resource, in addition to having considerable experience with large-scale hydraulic projects, like the Tennessee Valley Authority.

Here, however, the plans hit many snags that ultimately plunged Egypt and the great powers into an international crisis. At first the Western powers were sympathetic. The Americans worried that the project might put too great a strain on the Egyptian economy and dispatched Eugene Black, the head of the World Bank, to place budgetary restrictions on the Egyptians so that Egypt would not put itself in financial jeopardy and risk defaulting on its repayments to the bank by attempting to undertake other costly projects. Black admitted that the High Dam was "the largest single project which the Bank has ever been asked to consider," adding that "it ranks among the major development projects in the world." Black may have thought his meeting with Nasser went well. Nasser had a different view. Like so many Egyptians, he was steeped in the history of his country and acutely sensitive to those moments when the Western powers had lorded it over Egyptians. As he talked with Black, he could not help but recall numerous moments in the nineteenth century when the British and the French imposed humiliating economic terms on his country. Nasser later remarked that the face of Black seemed to transform itself into that of Ferdinand de Lesseps, who in the middle of the nineteenth century had saddled the overmatched ruler, Said, with one-sided concessions for the construction of the Suez Canal. Although Nasser did not rule out an accommodation with the Americans and the World Bank, he did not want a repeat of Egypt's nineteenth-century experience. He feared that the bank would impose neocolonial restrictions at the very moment that Egypt had finally achieved its full independence.

The Egyptian–World Bank negotiations are a tangled story that a few highly detailed diplomatic histories have unraveled. The outlines tell a simple and painful tale, however. The Americans, the British, and the World Bank constantly dithered, although, over time, they put together an impressive team of foreign hydraulic and electrical companies interested in building the High Dam and installing its electrical fixtures. Matters changed drastically in September 1955 when the Egyptian government purchased arms from Czechoslovakia, a Soviet bloc country. It is not hard to understand the Egyptian decision to turn to the Soviets. Their efforts to acquire weapons from the West availed them little. At the same time a confrontation between units of the Egyptian and Israeli armies on the Gaza border left a number of Egyptian soldiers dead and filled the high command with an acute sense of Egypt's military inferiority to the Israelis. At the time Egypt had only six serviceable planes and tank ammunition that would last only through a one-hour battle. Nasser and the other Free Officers were acutely aware that nothing could undermine their legitimacy more swiftly than growing discontent in the army over military preparedness.

Nonetheless, this purchase stunned the Western powers, which had always been Egypt's source of weaponry. Was the door opening for further Soviet intrusions into Egypt and the rest of the Middle East? After long debates and considerable indecision, the American secretary of state, John Foster Dulles, a cold warrior of the first order, who believed that countries were either with the United States in the Cold War or enemies and who regarded Nasser's efforts to follow a stance of positive neutrality a contradiction and an anathema, decided that the Egyptians should be taught a lesson in Cold War diplomacy. In mid-1956, under constant prodding from the Egyptians for a definitive decision on the High Dam project, the Americans, the British, and the World Bank withdrew their support for the scheme. Dulles's reasoning did not articulate the true reasons for his decision. Instead, he asserted that the West was worried that the project was beyond the financial capacities of the Egyptian government, certainly a legitimate concern. But in truth,

Dulles wanted to let Nasser and others who would be watching know the high price that they would pay for a flirtation with the Soviet Union.

What followed was a set of events so stunning that they caught many of the primary actors surprised and unprepared. In the late afternoon of July 26, 1956, as Nasser was giving a speech to an assembled crowd in Alexandria, Egyptian technicians and military men moved into the Suez Canal zone and took over control of the Suez Canal Company. The signal for action was when Nasser referred to the old canal nemesis, de Lesseps, in his speech, at which point officials of the state were to assume control of the operations of the Canal Company. After mentioning de Lesseps, Nasser went on to proclaim that the West would not stymie Egypt's effort to modernize the country through the withdrawal of financial and technical assistance for the High Dam. In retaliation, Nasser announced to a jubilant audience that Egypt would nationalize the Suez Canal Company, paying off its shareholders at the share price on the day of nationalization, and would use its assets to finance the High Dam.

Egypt's actions should not have jolted the West. The American State Department and the British Foreign Office had long worried that Egypt might nationalize the Canal Company, whose concession, in any case, had only another thirteen years to run. In 1969 the company was scheduled to revert to Egyptian hands. Moreover, as the Law Officers of the British Foreign Office acknowledged in an unpublished but widely read internal report, the Egyptian government had a legal right to nationalize what according to the company's charter was a full-fledged Egyptian company. Arguments about the international status of the canal and the Suez Canal Company to the contrary, the consensus among the international legal experts was that the various international treaties governing the company and traffic through the canal did not impinge on Egypt's sovereignty over the canal zone.

These arguments made nary a dent on the political leaders in Britain, France, and Israel. From the moment of nationalization, they plotted against the Egyptians, notably against Nasser, who, for many of these leaders, conjured up images of fascist dictators in the 1930s challenging the international order. Each power had its own reasons for wanting to take Nasser down. The French were incensed at Radio Cairo for supporting the Algerian nationalists, who were seeking to end French rule. The Israelis feared Nasser's opening to the Soviet Union and his acquisition of Soviet weaponry. And the right wing of the British Conservative Party, then in power, wanted to roll back the concessions that previous governments had made to colonial nationalists and to slow down the dissolution of the British Empire. The British prime minister, Anthony Eden, forever eager to get out from under the shadow of his predecessor, Winston Churchill, played the most decisive role in portraying Nasser as Britain's implacable foe. In the opinion of Anthony Nutting, one of his close advisers, turned critic, "Eden began to behave like an enraged elephant charging senselessly at invisible and imaginary enemies in the international jungle." Eden told Nutting that he wanted Nasser destroyed, not isolated or neutralized. When Nutting warned Eden that this outcome was likely to cause political chaos in Egypt, the prime minister replied: "And I don't give a damn if there's anarchy and chaos in Egypt." Finally at a secret meeting in Sèvres, France, between October 21 and 24, the main French and Israeli leaders agreed to cooperate in an invasion of Egypt. They also dispatched the French foreign minister, Christian Pineau, to secure the participation of the British.

Nasser had a completely different mind-set from his adversaries'. In the first place he believed that the nationalization decree was quite legal. He also realized the outrage that would sweep through the West, but he was certain that with the passage of time sensible politicians in the West would come to see the force of Egypt's case. In this regard, the interview he had with prime minister Robert Menzies of Australia was telling. Menzies argued that the great powers in the world could not leave Egypt in charge of a waterway that was of such vital importance to so many countries. Some kind of international control needed to be established. Nasser did not dispute the force of Menzies' argument. He merely countered by saying that as soon as the British internationalized the port of London, which was even more critical to international shipping, he would do the same with the Suez Canal.

Nasser believed that time was on his side. He estimated, quite rightly, it turned out, that it would take the British and the French at least three months to mobilize a full-scale naval invasion of Egypt. By then he believed that cooler heads would prevail. He also believed, quite wrongly in this case, that the British would never conspire with the Israelis, since such an alliance would rebound against British interests and undermine Britain's reputation throughout the Middle East. Where he truly misjudged his opponents was in the determination of a small cabal of Conservative political leaders, headed by prime minister Anthony Eden, to sweep all of these problems aside and go forward with their secret plans for an invasion of Egypt.

On October 29, perhaps as many as 45,000 Israeli soldiers poured across Sinai in an attack against Egypt. France and Britain said, quite disingenuously, that they had to intervene in order to separate the warring antagonists. In fact, the French and the British had worked out these arrangements months in advance. They began landing roughly 80,000 troops at Port Said and along the canal zone on November 5; yet almost from the outset, the military and political plans of the British, French, and Israelis went awry. No one was taken in by the deception that the invasions had not been agreed upon in advance. Although a few Egyptian cabinet members counseled immediate surrender, Nasser and the rest decided that they must fight on no matter how outmanned they were. The Egyptians were, in fact, badly outnumbered. Counting raw conscripts, the Egyptian army was fewer than 90,000 men and did not have the advanced weaponry that their adversaries employed. Yet the invaders did not anticipate the reaction of world opinion or the outrage of the American political elite. Rather than backing their British, French, and Israeli allies, the American president, Dwight D. Eisenhower, called for an immediate cease-fire and the withdrawal of all enemy troops from Egyptian soil. The Soviets also chimed in, saying that if the European powers did not withdraw, the Soviets would rain down bombs on Paris and London. When the Americans withdrew financial support for the British pound, the outcome was no longer in doubt. Britain could not stand a run on sterling and had to stop its invasion and withdraw its forces even before it had achieved the minimum goal: securing control over the Suez Canal zone. Whether the British, French, and Israelis could have imposed a new, more compliant government on Egypt remained a moot point. France and Israel followed the British in evacuating their forces in short order. Nasser had seized an immense international political victory from the jaws of military defeat. He had nationalized the Suez Canal Company and fended off a large-scale invasion. His reputation among the Arab peoples soared.

Other consequences, less spectacular, but no less significant, followed. The Egyptian leadership, many of whom feared for their lives, took out their revenge on the British, French, and Jewish businesses and foreign communities living in Egypt. Many of these individuals, especially the Egyptian Jews, who numbered no fewer than 80,000 at the conclusion of World War II, had deep roots in Egypt. These counted for little. British, French, and Jewish firms were nationalized and placed in Egypt's expanding public sector. British and French nationals were expelled from the country. One individual whose family's ties to the Arab world went back to the eighteenth century and who sat on the boards of many of the country's most important private sector business firms, had his passport stamped at the time of leaving, "never to return to Egypt." Jews who could not prove their Egyptian nationality status, and many could not, had to leave as well. By and large, wealthy Jews, who had important foreign connections, left for Western Europe or the United States. The poorer Jews made their way to Israel. The Jewish exodus from Egypt was spread over a number of years, but by the 1970s only several hundred Jews remained in Egypt.

In many respects, the populations who held foreign nationality or who had thrown in their lot with non-Egyptian groups had brought on their own expulsion. They lived in enclaves cut off from the rank and file of the Egyptian population. Rarely did they speak the local language. They congregated in their privileged sporting clubs, which began to admit a trickle of well-to-do and well-connected

Egyptians only after World War II. They were deeply resented, particularly by young educated Egyptians, like the military officers, who believed that these foreign groups kept Egyptians from holding the main levers of power in their country. But the Egyptian elite overestimated their own abilities at this stage of political and economic independence and underestimated their need for foreign technical and business acumen. While it was true that Egyptians ran the Suez Canal with exemplary efficiency, proving the naysayers in the Western world completely wrong, they were hardly as successful absorbing into the public sector and running efficiently the large number of British, French, and Jewish industrial, commercial, and financial firms that were taken over after the 1956 invasion.

One of the reasons that the Egyptians ran the Suez Canal so effectively is that the difficulties of running ships through the canal had been grossly exaggerated by the old Suez Canal Company as a justification for the company's massive profits. In fact, the canal had no locks, like the Panama Canal, and had several large interior lakes where ships going in one direction could be held while ships traveling in the other direction passed. Moreover, the Egyptians were determined to prove to the world that they could run the canal as effectively as the largely French-administered company had done. Alas, this was not true for most of the other foreign firms that entered into Egyptian hands after 1956. Here, the government was not so careful in selecting its public sector managers. Many inexperienced and frankly incompetent military officers occupied important seats on the boards of these firms. In addition, Nasser's expansion of the educational system came with a lethal promise. He guaranteed a position in one of the many governmental bureaucracies to all graduates of Egypt's universities. The civil bureaucracy was already overblown. The government now took to placing the many university graduates in public sector business firms, whether or not their services were required. Egypt's industries, commercial establishments, and financial institutions became bloated with employees far beyond their needs. As a result the companies produced commodities and rendered services that were either too expensive for the ordinary Egyptian to purchase or were sold at prices below cost because the government made up for the losses. These became a drag on the Egyptian economy by the late 1960s.

Nasser and his advisers did not foresee these results as they continued to enlarge the public sector at the expense of private investment. By the early 1960s, the state had taken over virtually every large-scale business firm, and the entrepreneurial elite that had promoted development through the private sector during the interwar period found itself idled and even held accountable for the failures of the Egyptian economy. Nasser and his colleagues embraced the Soviet model of economic expansion, drafting ambitious five-year plans and opening a host of new government-run industries that were expected to be the engine of economic progress. During the publication of the first five-year plan, Nasser in a burst of optimism stated that the country would double its standard of living within ten years and would reach the British standard of living within two decades.

He was wrong. The country made little economic progress. Committed to internal economic change and cutting off most of its economic ties with the Western world, the Egyptian government ran huge budgetary deficits and found itself unable to provide the essentials of life for most of the inhabitants. Although the state subsidized bread and fuel, there were still massive shortages. When the state purchased products in high demand from overseas, such as cheese, toilet paper, and the like, and made them available at government-run stores, the lines of customers ran for blocks.

The one unquestioned economic achievement of the Nasser years was the building of the High Dam at Aswan. Nasser had ostensibly nationalized the Suez Canal Company to gain the revenue to finance the construction of the dam. In reality the Soviets stepped in and provided most of the financing and technical assistance. Say what the critics might, the Soviets did a splendid job with the dam. By the time that it was up and functioning at full capacity in the 1970s its twelve massive generators produced about 50 percent of Egypt's electricity output. It also permitted new lands to be brought into cultivation. In spite of the many negative environmental impacts of the High Dam, it is inconceivable that Egypt could have found the resources for its rapidly expanding population without it.

The otherwise dismal performance of the economy was not Nasser's most critical failing, however. It was in the foreign policy arena, where he had started out so spectacularly with the resolution of the Suez crisis. The Egyptians had followed the Suez triumph with what were impressive gains in pan-Arab politics. Syria and Egypt joined together to form the United Arab Republic in 1958. Egypt endeavored to extend its influence into the Arabian Peninsula, dispatching a large contingent of troops in support of antiroyalist forces in Yemen. Both of these ventures failed, however, and proved to be harbingers of future foreign policy setbacks. The United Arab Republic dissolved in 1961, with the Syrians claiming that the Egyptians treated them as second-class citizens. The Egyptian military forces were unable to score a decisive victory in Yemen and became bogged down in long, drawn-out warfare. But these were minor losses compared with the renewal of the Arab-Israeli conflict in 1967. Nasser's decision making here was deeply flawed and brought about radical changes in the geopolitical environment of the Middle East.

After the Suez invasion, Israel withdrew its troops to their original boundaries with Egypt, and Egypt permitted United Nations observers to station themselves along the hot border spots between Egypt and Israel, always, however, on the Egyptian side. In mid-1967 tensions erupted along the Syrian-Israeli border. Rumors abounded that the Israelis were mobilizing forces in that area. Nasser's Arab world critics taunted the Egyptian president that he was hiding behind United Nations observers at a time when the Egyptian army was needed to rein in the Israelis. Nasser then made a fateful decision. After meeting with the commander of the Egyptian forces, Abdel Hakim Amr, and gaining Amr's assurance that the Egyptian army was now in a position to hold its own against Israeli forces and even to defeat them, Nasser demanded that the UN withdraw its observers from Egyptian territory. Three weeks later, the Israelis, fearing that Egypt and Syria might launch an attack, sent planes against the Egyptian air force and troops into Sinai. The air strike was stunningly successful, destroying 300 of the 430 Egyptian combat airplanes and providing Israel with command of the air space. Lacking air cover, the Egyptian forces stationed in Sinai were easy targets for advancing units of the Israeli army and air force. Egypt lost an estimated 20,000 soldiers, most of them in a desperate retreat across Sinai. When Syria and Jordan joined the battle against Israel, the Israelis took large chunks of Jordanian and Syrian territory. By the time that a cease-fire was imposed, only six days after the first shots had been fired, Israel had taken the Old City of Jerusalem and the West Bank of the Jordan River from Jordan. It had also overrun the Golan Heights from Syria, and its forces had control over Sinai. It was preparing to build a military defense on the east bank of the Suez Canal, subsequently called the Bar Lev line, which Israel hoped would prevent the Egyptians from crossing the canal and attacking Israeli forces stationed on the east bank of the canal.

For the frontline Arab states the war was a disaster. For the Israelis the military triumphs secured their military and political predominance in the region. But pride often goes before a fall, and here it did. The Israeli military became complacent and arrogant, believing that their Bar Lev line rendered them invulnerable to their most serious military challenger, the Egyptians. Some Israelis held the view that they would trade the occupied Arab lands, except for Jerusalem, which no Israeli politician was prepared to give up, for a peace treaty and Arab recognition of the Israeli state. But another segment of Israeli society had a different view of these lands. They saw the occupied territories as lands that could be filled with Israeli settlers and provide the country with more secure boundaries while fulfilling a perceived religious imperative to reclaim all of the land that the Israelites held in ancient times.

In Egypt, the state could not hide its military and political defeat. Israeli forces occupied the Sinai Peninsula, from which Israeli oil companies quickly began to pump oil from wells that the Egyptians had built and exploited. The Egyptian military had blamed politicians for the 1948 military debacle. Now they had only themselves to blame. Nasser offered his resignation, accepting full responsibility for the failure. But the country was unwilling to see its fabled leader step down. With encouragement from paid supporters, the people of Cairo and other major Egyptian cities turned out en masse to demand that Nasser stay on as president of the republic. Bending to their wishes, he withdrew his resignation. Yet by then he was dispirited and disillusioned, in ill health. Just over three years after the Six Day War of June 1967, Nasser died of heart failure.

Nasser's death marked the end of a dramatic two decades of transformations. The masses turned out in record numbers to pay tribute to a man who had restored Egypt's lost dignity, defied the great powers, promoted massive redistributions of wealth through land reform and the expansion of public education, and to many symbolized the very essence of Egyptianness.

ANWAR AL-SADAT

Anwar al-Sadat was Egypt's vice president at the time of Nasser's death. Although he was one of the early Free Officers and involved in the 1952 military takeover, few expected him to succeed to Nasser's mantle of power. He lacked the gravitas of his predecessor. Many thought that Nasser had installed Sadat in the vice presidency because he represented no threat to the president's power. But here his critics were badly mistaken. After a short tussle for power, Sadat emerged the victor and proved a worthy, though quite different, successor to Nasser.

Nasser and Sadat were men cut from different cloths. Nasser was a quiet, reserved family man. He shunned the limelight in the early stages of the revolution and never seemed comfortable with his world prominence or in his dealing with the great statesmen of the Western world. He wore simple suits, eschewed signs of opulence, was fastidious and austere in his daily routines. About him there was not the slightest hint of corruption. Sadat was a mirror opposite. He loved the world stage, delighted in talking with the great statesmen of the West and being interviewed by leading journalists and television personalities. He was flamboyant in nearly everything that he did. He wore his religion on his sleeve just as he wore the most exquisitely tailored Western suits and most elegantly produced

Figure 6. Anwar al-Sadat and his wife, Jihan

Western shoes. His wife, Jihan al-Sadat, was as modern a woman as Nasser's wife appeared to be a traditional Muslim wife. She was an outspoken feminist whom he married as his second wife when she was only sixteen years of age. Like her husband, she came to enjoy public attention. She sought to use her political influence to better the lot of Egyptian women. (See figure 6 for a picture of Sadat and his wife, Jihan.)

Not only did Sadat and Nasser have radically different political styles and personalities, they also pursued radically different domestic and international policies, although in the last years of his life Nasser embarked on some of the same policies that Sadat championed. As a young man, Sadat had burned with a nationalist passion. He claimed that by the time he left secondary school "a certain feeling had struck root in me—a hatred for all aggressors and a love and admiration for anyone trying to liberate the land." These drives had put him in touch with the Germans during World War II and had made him the Free Officers' liaison with the Muslim Brotherhood. Yet once he had seized power in 1970, he put aside many of these radical ambitions to pursue more pragmatic initiatives. Sadat's new directions had a domestic and an international component, but were based on a single fundamental precept. He believed that the Soviet Union had failed Egypt, primarily because it had no compelling interest in helping Egypt resolve its long-standing conflict with Israel. The situation of no war and no peace with Israel, which prevailed in Egyptian-Israeli relations after the 1967 war, served the Soviets well, but kept the Egyptian population saddled with the constant, draining requirement to prepare to take on an adversary whose military superiority had been proven in all of the confrontations with Egypt. In contrast, the Americans wanted peace in the region and had the political and military clout to bring about durable peace arrangements between the Arab states and Israel. Hence Sadat's first step was to curtail Egypt's long-standing dependence on the Soviet Union, which he did in 1972, when he required Soviet advisers, political as well as military, to leave the country.

Sadat followed this demand with an even more dramatic, daring, and completely unexpected move. In October 1973 (during the month of Ramadan in the Muslim world) he launched an attack across the Suez Canal against the Israeli forces seemingly safely ensconced behind their impregnable Bar Lev fortifications. To the surprise of nearly everyone, even the Egyptian military planners, the attack succeeded beyond their wildest expectations. The Egyptians broke through the Israeli defenses in many places, routed the Israeli army, which withdrew in disarray, fleeing across Sinai, leaving vast quantities of armor behind. Numerous Egyptian generals urged Sadat to press on with the attack, advancing into Israeli territory. But Sadat feared provoking an international crisis and bringing the Americans into the war on the side of the Israelis if the Egyptian army actually threatened the security of Israel. Instead, he held his forces back, during which period the Americans hurriedly sped replacement military equipment to Israel.

The Israeli counterattack was rapid and ferocious. Its replenished army drove the Egyptians back across Sinai. Units of the Israeli army surrounded a large segment of the Egyptian army on the west bank of the Suez Canal. Here, Sadat's faith in an American intervention paid off. The Americans, with Soviet backing, prevailed on the Israelis to accept a truce and to allow the defeated Egyptian army to withdraw with no further loss of life. The grounds were thus prepared for an Egyptian rapprochement with the United States and for changes in Egyptian relations with Israel.

A series of rapid and transforming events followed the ending of the 1973 war. American advisers and technicians began to move into Egypt as rapidly as Soviet personnel departed. In 1977 Sadat went much further, stating that he would be willing to go to Israel and speak in the Israeli Knesset in an effort to resolve differences between Egypt, the Arabs, and the Israelis. The Israelis welcomed the overture, and Sadat flew to Jerusalem on November 19, 1977, where in a speech in the Knesset he offered to broker a peace settlement between his country and Israel and to resolve the host of problems that separated Israel and the displaced Palestinian peoples living in refugee camps in the Israeli-occupied West Bank and Gaza territories, in Jordan, and in Lebanon. The American president, Jimmy Carter, seized upon this initiative, and at hard bargaining sessions at Camp David, outside Washington, D.C., Sadat, Menachem Begin, the Israeli prime minister, and President Carter hammered out the terms of a peace accord between Egypt and Israel. In return for signing a peace treaty and recognizing Israel, Egypt would receive back the whole of the Sinai Peninsula. Other terms of the agreement included promises on both sides to work to solve the underlying problems that separated Israel and the Palestinian peoples and to work to bring a Palestinian state into being.

The agreement between Egypt and Israel ended a thirty-one-year period of hostility between the two countries, punctuated by four major conflicts, in 1948, 1956, 1967, and 1973, and numerous skirmishes and violent incidents. Thus, Egypt became the first Arab state to reach an accommodation with Israel. To Sadat and many Egyptians the peace agreement was essential, a prerequisite to creating a more stable and prosperous future for the Egyptian people. Before the peace agreement, the prospect of going to war loomed over the entire population, none more so than young Egyptian men, who were forced into compulsory military service and had to put on hold marriage and career plans.

The Egyptian-Israeli peace agreement was not greeted with enthusiasm among the Arab states, however, all of whom condemned Sadat for deserting a hallowed pan-Arab commitment to the Palestinian Arabs and who expelled Egypt from the Arab League. To punish the Egyptians the government of Saudi Arabia cut off all of its financial support, a figure that was running at nearly $5 billion annually. Sadat counted on the Americans to fill the financial gap. Nor did the agreement, while ending the limbo status of no war, no peace, meet with resounding approval at home. Many critics felt that Egypt had abandoned a sacred commitment to the Palestinians by initialing a unilateral treaty with their great foe. The general Egyptian population also felt the sting of being viewed as a pariah state within an Arab world, where Egyptians had always assumed that their country was the cultural, intellectual, and political leader.

Peace with Israel and rapprochement with the Americans were the international dimensions of Sadat's vision for a transformed Egypt. Another element was a radically altered economic program. Sadat's economic program entailed curtailing government-dominated economic planning in favor of restoring the private sector and encouraging private foreign investment capital. On the surface, Sadat's economic vision seemed made to order for Egypt and the rest of the

Middle East. Called the *infitah*, or the opening, the intention was to open the Egyptian economy to foreign investment, most notably investment funds coming from the now spectacularly oil-rich countries of the Gulf. The Egyptian premise was that these states would see in Egypt all of the ingredients required for an industrial transformation, led by a private sector, and would provide needed capital. Unfortunately, implementation proved more difficult than expected. In the first place, the Egyptian public sector fought back, using the red tape of the government's bureaucracy to impede the movement of foreign investment into the country. Food riots in 1977 compelled the government to terminate most of its efforts to reduce subsidies on essential food products and other commodities. An even more decisive impediment, however, was Egypt's rapprochement with the Israelis. This departure was anathema to the Saudis, the richest of the Arab countries, and not that much more palatable to the smaller oil kingdoms of the Arabian Peninsula. Foreign investment did not flow into the country as Sadat had hoped, and state-initiated economic planning remained a still important ingredient of the country's economic program.

Sadat never had a chance to see his economic vision gain momentum. On October 6, 1981, while reviewing a military parade to celebrate the anniversary of the 1973 war, a small group of armed Islamic militants poured out of a military vehicle at the rear of the parade, firing at the parade grandstand where the president sat with other dignitaries. The chief assassin, Lieutenant Khaled Islambouli, approached the grandstand and fired point blank at Sadat. Sadat was rushed to the military hospital, but was pronounced dead on arrival. At his trial, Islambouli boasted, "I have killed Pharaoh."

Sadat's funeral was an entirely different affair from that of his predecessor. Attended by dignitaries from all over the Western world, including three American presidents (Jimmy Carter, Gerald Ford, and Richard Nixon), but boycotted by the entire Arab world except for President Gaafar Nimeiry of Sudan, the funeral procession passed through an almost silent capital. The ordinary people of Egypt used the occasion to express their displeasure with a man who had ruled over them but not won them to his side as Nasser had.

The assassins revealed one element of the opposition to the Egyptian president. The government had always dealt with the Muslim Brothers in contradictory and quixotic ways. When it suited its purposes, the state put them in jail, and when it thought they would support the government, it let them out. When Sadat came to power, many Muslim Brothers were in prison. In an effort to win their support for initiatives that were departures from Nasser's, Sadat opened up the prisons and courted the support of the Muslim Brothers. They gained in strength during the decade of the 1970s, but just one month before his assassination, realizing that radical elements among the Islamists were plotting against him, he ordered a massive roundup of dissidents. Most of the radical Islamists returned to jail, except for at least for one Brotherhood cell, the one headed by Islambouli of the Islamic Jihad Group that had avoided detection and arrest. Just how this group was able to join the parade with their weapons and ammunition was a cause for many conspiracy theories. No unit was supposed to carry live ammunition during the parade, so there were many who believed that well-placed leaders in the military establishment had a hand in Sadat's death. Yet to this day no charges have been brought beyond the group who actually carried out the killing.

The Sadat assassination also reminded long-time Egyptian observers that extremely radical and militant branches of the Muslim Brotherhood now existed in Egypt as well as in many other Muslim countries. Much of the inspiration for this group came from the martyred Egyptian Sayyid Qutb, who took up the intellectual leadership of the Muslim Brotherhood after the 1948 death of Hasan al-Banna, the group's founder. A trip to the United States after World War II traumatized the youthful Sayyid Qutb. There he found such loose morals and such a close mixing of the sexes to cause him to see Western civilization as a poisonous plant to be avoided at all cost in the Muslim world. His treatises became increasingly anti-Western and pro-Muslim, but a turning point in his life came when the Nasser government imprisoned him and tortured him. Qutb was in jail from 1954 to 1964, when he was briefly released, then reimprisoned. He was executed in 1966. During these grim prison years, he wrote passionately about the need to take action against the spread of Western influence, using violence if necessary, and he espoused the fullness and correctness of Islam as practiced in the earliest days by Muhammad and the early devouts.

Qutb's most important work, *Milestones*, was composed while he was in prison, briefly banned, but circulated widely, though secretly. An expert on Qutb's writings said of *Milestones* that it was "the seal of Qutb's life's work, the culmination of an enormous literary production, much of which has nothing to do with Islamic preaching." Its message was that the ideologies of capitalism, collectivism, and colonialism were bankrupt and godless and that "the turn of the Muslim community has come to fulfill for mankind [that] which God has enjoined upon it." But the triumph of Islam would require a vanguard of believers, willing to combat the elements that ruled the world and kept it in a state of darkness. Contemporary Muslims needed to look back to the time of the Prophet and the early believers to rediscover the pure Islamic doctrines, the message that was based entirely on the original principles sent by God to this generation of faithful, not yet adulterated by knowledge derived from Greek, Roman, and Persian sources.

CHAPTER TWELVE
Mubarak's Egypt

Eight AM is the height of the rush hour at the Maadi metro station. Although Maadi is one of Cairo's wealthiest residential areas, a place where foreigners intermingle with well-off Egyptians, it has undergone an enormous expansion over the last several decades. The platform is packed with commuters anxious to arrive on time at their workplaces in center city. Anyone familiar with the old Helwan to Bab al-Luq train line on which the present tram runs would hold out little hope of getting on board. But there are obvious and promising differences in the new system. No long line of pushing and shoving passengers forcing their way to the head of the queue to purchase tickets exists. Riders buy as many metallic-coded coupons as they will require for the next few weeks and use them to enter and leave through turnstiles located at station entrances. In this and other ways Cairo's new tram system, opened in 1989, resembles the Paris underground, whose engineers installed the Cairo network. A sleek nine-car train arrives almost exactly two and a half minutes after the previous one left. Two middle cars are reserved for women. Any man entering is shooed away, even if it means that he must wait for the next train. Originally, the first two cars of the train had been set aside for female passengers, but a tragic collision of the train at the end of the line involving the deaths of many women riding in the first car persuaded the transit authorities to move the women's cars to a safer location in the middle of the train.

The cars are jammed with people, even the last ones, which tend to attract younger riders since passengers have to walk longer distances to get to them. But are the crowded conditions any different from those occurring daily in Paris, London, Tokyo, and New York during the rush hours? Perhaps a little. but then Cairenes are accustomed to living in cramped spaces. In comparison with travel in the pre-metro days, the ride is comfortable and civilized. Previously, riders shoved and poked one another. Brave folks hung out the doors, risking their lives if the train hit a car at one of its many level crossings. Accidents occurred more frequently than anyone liked to admit. Women suffered grievously from unwanted groping. Commuters delight in the changes. They take pride in this advance into first-world status.

The old line from Helwan to Bab al-Luq ran entirely above ground. The new metro system descends underground just beyond the Old Cairo station, allowing the train to call at stations in the center of the city whose names salute Egypt's modern heroes: Urabi, Nasser, Sadat, Zaghlul, and Mubarak. It comes to the surface in the northeast and ends its journey at el-Marg, thirty miles from its starting point. Three miles of the route are underground. A second, shorter line intersects underground with the main Helwan-el Marg line in the center of Cairo. Traveling east and west, it descends beneath the Nile and connects the working-class residential area of Shubra with Cairo University. Cairo's metro is nothing less than a modern-day miracle. It operates with an efficiency that existed in no part of the city twenty years ago. Rarely are trains late; yet they carry over two million passengers daily.

The metro has had another, perhaps, unanticipated consequence. It has addressed one of the main causes of urban rioting, namely Cairo's overused and once completely inadequate transportation system. Riots have been a periodic feature of modern-day Cairo. The quickest trigger for urban violence has been abrupt increases in food and gasoline prices. But second in the list are transportation woes.

By accident I happened to be swept up in an urban demonstration and experienced its doleful consequences. On January 1, 1975, I had an appointment across the city. I took the old train line from Maadi to Bab al-Luq and called in at the huge government building, the Mugamma, just off the main square at Midan al-Tahrir, before making my journey across the city. Disturbances seemed to be taking place in the central plaza, but the official with whom I talked at the Mugamma assured me that all was safe. I set out on my walk, which ordinarily would take fifteen minutes, and climbed the pedestrian walkway that encircled the main plaza, Midan al-Tahrir, in those days. To my astonishment, below me on the main streets several taxis and buses were burning. Protesters had gathered. Had the government official whose advice I had sought known what was going on outside? I quickly discovered that he had not. Looking down Cairo's busy thoroughfare, Sharia Qasr al-Aini, which runs from the Midan al-Tahrir to the Qasr al-Aini hospital, I witnessed an alarming spectacle. There, running in place no more than one hundred yards away, with clear visors over their faces, batons in one hand, and wooden shields in another, was a large and formidable contingent of riot police. I fled, just in time. As I was making my way to the nearby Corniche, the riot police descended on the protesters in the Midan, beating and arresting those who were not quick enough to escape.

The protesters had gathered for one reason. They were workers at the Helwan iron and steel factory. Each day they had to reach their work destination through the old train line. If they were late, as they often were because of delays in the train schedule, employers docked their pay. The new line has transformed Cairo's transportation network. It moves workers to their work destinations on time. It relieves the above-ground transportation—the buses, cooperative taxis, and private taxis—so that now people can make plans to be at certain places at agreed-upon times. Cairo has changed in many exciting and unusual ways.

President Sadat initiated many of the changes that are now visible in Cairo, Alexandria, Egypt's other major cities, and even the countryside. But most of the innovations came to fruition during the long presidency of Husni Mubarak, who succeeded to office at the time of Sadat's assassination. Mubarak has had a longer tenure of power than any contemporary Egyptian ruler except for the founder of the Egyptian monarchy, Muhammad Ali, who ruled for forty-three years, from 1805 to 1848.

HUSNI MUBARAK

The vice president at the time of Sadat's assassination was Husni Mubarak. Many believed that he, like his predecessor, had been selected for the position because of his mediocrity, which posed no threat to the president. He was little known outside inner official circles, but generally he was thought to be a well-meaning if not particularly adept bureaucrat. The impression that he was not an astute politician continued for some time, even in the face of mounting counterevidence. A common joke among the Cairenes, who enjoy nothing more than poking fun at their leaders, is that Mubarak's facial appearance and his actions resembled those of the smiling cow on the most popular packaged cheese in Egypt. In fact, Mubarak set about to prove critics wrong. Before long, through shrewd, mainly behind-the-scenes action, he demonstrated that he was, indeed, a resourceful political leader, able to outsmart rivals and retain a stranglehold on power. To date, he has been in office nearly thirty years and has won five presidential plebiscites.

Mubarak was not one of the Free Officers. Only twenty-three years at the time of the coup, he became a respected member of the military, a bomber pilot, who in time established an exemplary record in the Egyptian air force. He rose quickly in the ranks, becoming commandant of the Air Force Academy in 1967 and air force chief of staff in 1969. Through distinguished action in the 1973 war, he was elevated to air marshal. Thus, he quieted the fears of the powerful military establishment that Sadat's successor would not be one of their own. Moreover, in much less flamboyant and aggressive ways, he went about the task of strengthening Sadat's new departures while appeasing those who had been uncomfortable with his predecessor's radical visions. He strengthened Egypt's relationship with the United States, which after the peace agreement with Israel in 1979 became the major supporter of the Egyptian economy and the military with massive infusions of assistance. As a new and seemingly more chastened leader, Mubarak also repaired Egypt's relations with the other Arab states and regained his country's membership in the Arab League. Obviously, it did not damage the Egyptian position that several other Arab countries, including Jordan and Syria and eventually the Palestinians, engaged in diplomatic negotiations with the Israelis. By 2008, however, only Jordan had signed a peace agreement with Israel.

In the last years of his tenure, President Sadat had begun to open up the polity, allowing several new parties to compete in parliamentary elections. He also permitted a greater degree of press freedom than had existed previously. His assassination temporarily put a stop to these liberalization measures. Upon assuming the presidency, Mubarak proclaimed a state of emergency (which has remained in effect ever since), arrested Muslim Brothers who had eluded the police network under Sadat, banned the Muslim Brotherhood outright, and increased control of the press. Yet the Egyptian president also lightened the government's grip on power, largely under pressure from the educated and increasingly prosperous middle class. New political parties came into being, many of them avowed critics of the government. Elections to the People's Assembly, although carefully controlled, resulted in the triumph of many opposition candidates, though never enough to threaten the solid majority of the government party, the National Democratic Party. The most powerful opposition group remained the Muslim Brotherhood, despite the continuing ban against the organization. In the elections to the People's Assembly of 2005 the government returned a convincing majority, but eighty-four Muslim Brothers were elected out of a total 444 Assembly seats, although, of course, these individuals could not openly declare themselves to be members of a banned organization.

Mubarak is not the showman that his two predecessors were. He is much less comfortable with crowds. No doubt, being on the parade grandstand when Sadat was gunned down and he was wounded has made him far more conscious of threats to life than his predecessors had been. According to some accounts, he has survived no fewer than six assassination attempts. Not surprisingly, then, when he ventures out, he does not travel in an open car, welcoming the admiration of the populace as was the custom of Nasser and Sadat. He moves about with overwhelming security. It is easy to know when

Mubarak or an important foreign diplomat is traveling through the city. The streets over which his or the foreign diplomat's vehicle will travel are lined with security police, who actually stand with their backs to the streets scanning the crowds and the buildings overlooking the streets so that no unwanted event can occur. Constantly surrounded by bodyguards, he resides in a presidential palace in Heliopolis under heavy protection.

Mubarak has maintained the essentials of Sadat's foreign policy. The Egyptian relationship with Israel remains solid and peaceful though seemingly in jeopardy on tense occasions. It has suffered whenever the Israelis repressed Palestinian dissidents in Gaza and the West Bank. The Egyptian leaders were deeply embarrassed when Israel invaded Lebanon in 1982 and even more so when Israeli troops remained in occupation of the southern part of Lebanon for nearly two decades. But the peace accord has held even in spite of vocal protests by the Egyptian populace.

In much the same way the Egyptian government has been America's major Arab ally. The Egyptians sent an estimated 35,000 troops in support of President George H. W. Bush's international force to repel the Iraqi invasion of Kuwait in 1991. They gave only limited support, however, to the 2003 invasion of Iraq under President George W. Bush. Although the Egyptian government allowed American troops to transit through Egypt on their way to Iraq, Mubarak made his opposition to the war clear, warning that "instead of one bin Laden we will have one hundred bin Ladens" if the Americans continued their aggressive policies in the Middle East.

An important reason that the Egyptians have maintained their rapprochement with the Americans has been the substantial American financial, technical, and military assistance to Egypt. By 2004 the Americans had invested $25.5 billion in the Egyptian economy. This support has begun to decline and at a rapid rate recently, however. In 1979, the year in which the Egyptians and Israelis signed their peace accord, the Americans provided Egypt with $1.1 billion in economic aid and nearly twice that figure in military aid. By an agreement reached in 2000, America stated that it would reduce its economic assistance to Egypt by $40 million per year until the aid package leveled off at just a little more than $400 million in 2009. Just how significant this decline is can be seen by considering the following statement. Had the Americans continued their economic contributions to the Egyptian economy at the $1.1 billion figure of 1979, the funds turned over to the Egyptian government would have totaled $4.5 billion in 2004 dollars.

Sadat had signed a peace treaty with the Israelis and initiated his *infitah* (opening) economic policies with the hope that they would jolt the economy into action and lead to sustained and impressive economic progress. Mubarak continued these policies, but the goal of rapid economic development continued to elude Egypt. The country's gross domestic product per person in 2006 was $5,000, and its income per capita was $1,260. By World Bank measurements Egypt is among the low-income countries in the world. Its income per capita is better than Pakistan's and Bangladesh's and on a par with that of the former Soviet satellite countries in East and Central Europe and some of the richer African countries. Sadly, it is next to last among the Arab countries, providing a higher standard of living only than in Sudan. The place of agriculture in the country's gross domestic product, once at the top, has shrunk to 14 percent. Manufacturing is 19 percent of GDP, and if mining (including oil) is factored in, that number increases to 38 percent. Increasingly, Egypt has turned itself into a service-oriented economy, which sector now accounts for nearly half of GDP.

A fair-minded analysis of the performance of the Egyptian economy during the Mubarak years would give the country passing grades but not stellar ones. The 1980s was a decade of disappointingly slow and erratic economic growth. New policies are often difficult to implement, and this was certainly true of the new economic arrangements that aroused the opposition of public sector bureaucrats and did not win immediate support from foreign investors. In addition, the oil-rich Arab states, big financial backers of the Egyptian economy before the Egyptian-Israeli peace accord, withdrew their financial support during the first half of that decade. Only American financial assistance filled the gap.

In time, however, the new economic policies took hold. Instead of raising the price of bread, the most essential of all Egyptian food-stuffs, which the government had attempted to do in 1977, only to provoke the most massive riots the country had seen since the military came into power, the government kept it the same but reduced the size of the standard loaf on sale. Similar gradual adjustments were made in the prices of other subsidized commodities, especially petroleum products, with the result that by the turn of the century the government's outlay on subsidies was no longer consuming a large part of the state budget. Finally, in 2003, the government floated the Egyptian pound, bringing it into alignment with the free-market price and undercutting the once robust black market.

The annual economic growth rate between 1990 and 2005 was an impressive 4.2 percent. In the following two fiscal years (2006 and 2007), the rate rose to 6 percent, providing some indication that the policies for so long recommended by the International Monetary Fund, encapsulated by the IMF phrase "getting the prices right," were finally working. Alas, the global economic meltdown of 2008 poses a whole new set of economic dilemmas.

The open-door, liberalizing economic policies did not deal with one of Egypt's most pressing issues. They did not eradicate or, for that matter, greatly reduce poverty. In 2005, as was the case in 1980 and 1990, nearly 20 percent of the Egyptian population lived below the poverty line, unable to meet all of their basic needs for food, health care, housing, and education. In spite of improvements in the gross domestic product, the growth rate of employment between 1990 and 2005 was a disappointing 2.6 percent per year, hardly sufficient to absorb the graduates of high schools and universities entering the job market each year.

Sadat and Mubarak promised a liberalization of the polity and freedom of expression to go along with a liberalization of the economy. The changes that have come about thus far have not been as much as hoped for, but represent significant improvements over the Nasser days. While Nasser was in power, people feared to say anything against the government, even in the privacy of their homes. They worried that their conversations might be reported to the secret police or overheard in police cars patrolling residential areas and equipped with electronic bugging equipment. Mubarak tried to curry the favor of large segments of the Egyptian populace when he first became president. He freed imprisoned Muslim Brothers and entertained many of them at a gala official reception. He permitted Muslim Brother candidates to run for seats in the People's Assembly, though, of course, they had to declare themselves as independents. He gave official recognition to the secular, oppositional political parties.

Mubarak's relations with the Muslim Brotherhood began to cool in the 1990s. The Brothers refused to endorse his fourth run for the presidency in 1995 and proved unwilling to condemn the growing number of violent attacks on foreigners perpetrated by militant Islamic groups.

Under Sadat and Mubarak the press has enjoyed more freedom than it had under Nasser. The opposition political parties, including the Muslim Brotherhood, publish newspapers and journals that attack the government. But the resources of these groups pale in comparison with the funds that the state pours into government-controlled newspapers, radio, and television. In any contest to reach the population with political and cultural messages, the government overwhelms the efforts of opposition groups.

The educated middle class prospered under a more open and private-sector-oriented economy. Tourism flourished, notwithstanding efforts of radical Islamists to frighten foreigners from coming to Egypt. Some attacks were grimly spectacular, notably in 1997 when militant opponents of the regime killed sixty tourists at the site of Queen Hatshepsut's temple in Upper Egypt and again in 2005 in the resort city of Sharm el-Sheikh on the Red Sea when militants destroyed a hotel frequented by tourists. Egyptian industrialization surged under government support, and Egypt became a center for the production of fine textiles, pharmaceuticals, and processed food, all of them industries that had earlier successes in Egypt. Although the major cities, led by Cairo and Alexandria, grew beyond anyone's expectations, the government endeavored to keep pace with the increased number of urban dwellers by building flyover highways, a tunnel leading cars into the center of Cairo from one of the northeastern suburbs, and a superb metro system.

Egypt's wealthy had little to complain about through the Mubarak years, except for a clampdown on freedom of expression and assembly. The wealthy quarters and suburbs of Cairo and Alexandria have access to local and imported products in abundance. Good restaurants abound, and city dwellers are now able to place takeout orders for prepared foods of high quality. The hotels in Cairo and Alexandria reach first-world standards, and the resorts along the Red Sea as well as the tourist attractions in Upper Egypt delight local residents as well as foreign visitors.

But the poor have not shared in the improved standards of living. Egypt, which experienced a significant redistribution of wealth during the Nasser years, now finds itself with a highly maldistributed pattern of wealth. In the 1990s the World Bank was so concerned about the income distribution in Egypt that it singled it out as having such a skewed division of wealth as to jeopardize the country's political stability. The poor living in cities like Cairo eke out their existence in slum areas, having little access to health care and education. In the countryside, where more than 40 percent of the population still resides, the life chances are even bleaker. Here schools are in short supply and access to health care is not satisfactory. The country finds itself divided into a large and increasing group of haves but also a substantial group of have-nots, who turn to opposition groups, such as the Muslim Brotherhood, to voice their discontent in hopes that these organizations will improve their conditions.

In spite of the turbulence of the twentieth century (or perhaps because of it), the struggles with the British, the wars with the Israelis, the triumphs and failures of foreign policy, and the tribulations of remaining a relatively poor country with aspirations to be a rich and modern state, Egypt has retained its cultural ascendancy throughout the Arab world. Its films and television serials, mostly soap operas, have a wide pan-Arab audience. Its writers, poets, essayists, and intellectuals set the tone for much of the cultural life of the Arab world. Egypt produced the first novel written in Arabic. Its two most famous and beloved writers of fiction during the interwar years were Taha Husayn and Tawfiq al-Hakim, whose widely read novels, *al-Ayyam* (Childhood Days), Taha Husayn's autobiographical account of growing up in an Egyptian village, and *Awdah al-Ruh* (The Return of the Spirit), al-Hakim's portrait of the Egyptian revolution of 1919, now form core reading materials in any class wishing to understand modern Egypt and learn modern Arabic.

Of the many inheritors of the literary mantle of Taha Husayn and Tawfiq al-Hakim, none stands out more prominently than Naguib Mahfouz, winner of the 1988 Nobel Prize in Literature. Mahfouz was influenced by Tawfiq al-Hakim, for he, too, bristled at the brutality that the British troops displayed to Egyptian protestors in 1919 and tried to carry forward many of the themes that had animated al-Hakim's work. A more prolific writer one could not find. Author of more than thirty novels, 350 short stories, countless plays and film scripts, Mahfouz is best known for his *Cairo Trilogy*, written in the 1950s, a portrait of the severe social changes but enduring family ties that exist in some of the poor neighborhoods of Cairo. Although Mahfouz began his literary career with an ambition to depict the whole of Egypt's marvelous and tangled history through historical novels, he abandoned this enterprise to explore the daily lives of ordinary Egyptians.

His fame brought him a fair share of critics, some of them openly hostile. His defense of Sadat's peace initiative with the Israelis caused his books to be banned for a time in many Arab countries. His criticism of Nasserism and of militant Islam put him on the death list of radical groups, one of whose members attacked him in 1994, causing him severe nerve damage. In spite of these and other setbacks, he retained his deep sense of humanity and his accessibility to all segments of Egyptian society. One of his customs was to gather one night a week at a fashionable Cairo café to discuss political and literary affairs with friends and anyone who wished to be part of the conversation.

When cataloguing change and continuity over long periods of time, sometimes cold statistical figures are not as revealing as personal observations. I have been in and out of Egypt, especially Cairo, numerous times since my first six-month stay there in 1960. Actually, I did not return to Egypt for fifteen years after my first visit. In 1973–74, I lived in Maadi for twelve months, which were devoted to research. One change was staggeringly obvious: the Egyptian people were bigger, healthier, more robust, and less afflicted with bodily injuries and defects than they had been a decade and a half earlier. In 1960 I saw an elite combat unit of the Egyptian army. These young men looked like supermen in size and strength compared with the rest of the population. By 1973, most Egyptians looked the way the soldiers of 1960 had. Some of the credit goes to Nasser and his wealth redistribution and educational expansion plans. But the lion's share of the glory belongs to the Americans, ironically enough, because these years were tendentious ones in American-Egyptian political and military relations. In spite of rejecting Nasser's efforts to follow a neutralist stance in foreign affairs, the Americans supplied Egypt with vast quantities of grain under a government ordinance, known as PL-480.

Not only did the American government ship grain to Egypt, but it also allowed the Egyptians to repay in blocked Egyptian pounds. For a time, it seemed as if the Egyptians would never extinguish the debt. During this period, American researchers enjoyed a bonanza. American libraries were able to buy up virtually every book that was published in Egypt (and many were) and American researchers were able to flock to Egypt to study all aspects of Egyptian history, polity, economy, and culture. Their fellowships, like the Arabic books that American libraries put on their shelves, were paid for out of these blocked funds. I benefited personally, receiving two American Research Center in Egypt fellowships in the 1970s and having at my fingertips the massive and renowned Arabic collection of Princeton University's Firestone Library. Alas, those funds dried up. Today Egypt pays for its food imports in hard currency, and American researchers and libraries also have to find hard currency for their purchases and fellowships.

It was a delight to see the Egyptian people looking so healthy in the 1970s. On the other hand, it was dismaying to find the economy in such a state of stagnation. Even rich foreigners found living conditions stressful. Few imported products were available. The streets were empty. Families did not own cars, a relief to pedestrians, to be sure, since they could jaywalk across main streets. I used to frequent the library of *l'Égypte contemporaine* on Ramses street in downtown Cairo, at present a main boulevard, choked with traffic. In the early 1970s I strolled across the street anywhere in the road and at any time of the day.

The *infitah*, the effects of which could be seen by 2000, have since changed the face of Cairo. Streets are full of traffic. Pedestrians move about gingerly, forced to walk in the streets, dodging speeding cars. The sidewalks serve as emergency parking areas during day and night. The wealthy display their riches ostentatiously. An alarmingly high proportion of Mercedes Benzes, an automobile that costs a local resident upwards of $50,000 if purchased legally, clutter the streets, more so than one would see in almost any other city in the world. In the 1970s the Nile Hilton Hotel, built in the 1960s, and the Mena House, located at the pyramids, were the city's only five-star hotels. One could not find a first-class restaurant anywhere in Cairo. My wife and I used to treat our two little children to an ice cream sundae at the Swiss Restaurant in downtown Cairo because the executive chef had ice cream flown in from Switzerland.

At the high end, then, the Cairo of the new millennium is a new creation. It has five-star hotels and restaurants, fast food houses, Internet cafés, health spas, and boutique specialty shops, featuring the latest imports from Europe and America. Its merchants cater to the well-to-do. Yet in the face of great wealth, poverty remains all too evident, and the poor continue to suffer. But they are now less visible, especially for dwellers in the posh districts of Zamalek, Maadi, Garden City, and Muhandeseen, whose residents can more easily avert their eyes from the poor than they could thirty or forty years ago. And the well-to-do rarely venture into poorer areas, like Shubra and Imbaba. These districts are out of bounds to the state authorities, run by their own communities, overtly hostile to the state and resentful of the extreme differentials of wealth that are so visible today.

THE FUTURE UNDER MUBARAK AND AFTER MUBARAK

Modern Egypt has seemed perennially at a crossroads. It was so when Napoleon's forces invaded the country and yet again when Muhammad Ali and his successors endeavored to bring the country into the modern world without succumbing to European imperial ambitions. The leaders of the 1952 military coup promised to lead the country to modernity. While they realized a number of their goals, they failed on many others, leaving the present government to face a whole series of dilemmas: What role does Islam have in Egypt's future? Can Egypt's large population ever hope to attain economic well-being? Does democracy have a chance, and what will happen in the country after Mubarak leaves office? Questions abound; answers are difficult to find.

Is Islam the Solution?

Islam is a powerful force in contemporary Egypt. Its message is that Islam is the solution to Egypt's many problems, a message that has captivated many believers and well-wishers. Egyptian Muslims and non-Muslims alike resonate to its critique of secular modernity. Like the Islamists, many contemporary Egyptians repudiate the capitalist message of the West—too materialist, individualistic, and exploitative of the poor. They also reject communist formulas—godless, mechanistic, politically oppressive, and now a proven failure. Where the Islamists falter in their appeals for broad support is the nature of the society that an Egypt under Islamic authority would have. Among the Muslim groups a tenuous consensus exists that an Islamic Egypt would look to the Prophet Muhammad and the early converts for inspiration, that the legal system would draw upon the sharia, and that the country would seek alliances with other Muslim nations rather than the United States. But the implementation and specifics splinter Muslim groups and alarm secularists.

Much of the fragmentation within Egypt's resurgent Islam has stemmed from the widespread opposition to the heinous and violent acts of the militants, many of whom, wishing to cripple the Mubarak regime, attacked and killed hundreds of policemen, soldiers, civilians, and tourists during the 1990s. Perhaps no event was more responsible for creating revulsion and arousing opposition to the agenda of the militants than the killing of scores of tourists visiting Queen Hatshepsut's mortuary temple in Upper Egypt in 1997. The organization responsible for the Upper Egypt massacres as well as many others was an umbrella body bearing the name al-Gamaa al-Islamiyya, which inherited the banner of militant Islam from the Muslim Brotherhood after this body repudiated the use of violence in the 1970s. Its most visible advocate was Shaykh Omer Abd al-Rahman, the blind cleric, a disciple of the fourteenth-century Islamic purist Ibn Taymiyya and the Egyptian militant Sayyid Qutb. After being expelled from Egypt and spending time in Afghanistan in contact with al-Qaeda leaders, Shaykh Omer entered the United States. American authorities believed that he was involved in planning the World Trade Center bombing in 1993 and subsequently convicted and sentenced him to life imprisonment for conspiring to blow up New York City landmarks. In Egypt, Mubarak, the target of many militants, responded vigorously to the challenges posed by Islamic militants, imprisoning many of the members of al-Gamaa al-Islamiyya, which has since renounced the use of violence and seen the government release many of its adherents from prison.

Were free and fair elections held today, most observers believe that they would result in a victory for the Muslim Brotherhood. The popularity of the Brotherhood exists because of its fervid opposition to the government and its provision of social services to those in need. This has been especially evident during moments of crisis, as, for instance, during an earthquake, which caused severe damage to various quarters of Cairo in 1992, leaving 520 dead and 4,000 injured. At the time of the earthquake Muslim Brothers were on the scene with rescue workers and medical attendants more rapidly than government officials. Moreover, Muslim Brothers have formed large and powerful blocs among university students and in most of the professional organizations. Many of their preachers have been outspoken critics of the regime, accusing it of corruption and irre-ligion. The tapes of the best known of these clerics circulate widely. None seem to be in greater demand than those of the blind Azhari imam Abdul Hamid Kishk, whose popularity is so widespread that the government has left him alone in spite of his inflammatory comments against the regime.

A striking manifestation of the strength of Islam can be seen in the revival of religious piety, often of a very public nature. Men riding the metro chant verses of the Quran. Attendance at Friday prayers has increased. Devout Muslim men take pride in the black spot that forms on their foreheads (called *zabib* in Arabic, mean-ing "raisin") from repeated prostrating of themselves in prayer. As for women, an increasingly proportion of them now wear the head scarf, the hijab.

The widespread use of the head scarf represents a surprising shift in feminine dress, and perhaps much more. In the 1920s and 1930s educated and well-to-do women began to discard the veil and em-braced the vision of a new Egyptian woman, perhaps not completely Westernized, but certainly wearing European-style clothing and moving out of the home into public spaces with a freedom that had not existed previously. But beginning in the 1960s and 1970s, this same segment of female society began to adopt the head scarf and, in some cases, to stress their religiosity and their distinctive-ness from Western women. In part the changes stemmed from a desire to reestablish a separate Egyptian identity; in part from disil-lusionment with the promises of a better way of life that the West held out but no longer appeared capable of providing. But Egyptian women did not surrender their independence or bow to the wishes of men in their adoption of the hijab. They used scarves and other items of clothing to display their individuality, spurning the tradi-tional black that women in earlier times had worn and rivaling one another in the variety of colors that their headdresses featured. In addition, many women took to wearing head scarves to demonstrate their separate identity from men and their disappointment with the failed egalitarian promises of modernity and their own stressed and burdensome lives. Often they blamed their husbands and fathers for their difficult situations. (See plate 25 for a picture of Egyptian school girls wearing head scarves.)

The rise of these different Islamic groups, radical and moderate, has had another dramatic historical effect. It has undercut the influence of the Sufi brotherhoods, which since the twelfth and thirteenth centuries formed the major institutional setting for popular belief and practice (see chapters 7 and 8). These traditional brotherhoods were a source of social and religious activity and communal solidarity, but the Muslim Brotherhood supplanted the Sufi lodges as the primary meeting place and the social network for the great mass of the Egyptian population. In addition, the established ulama, who had long viewed Sufi organizations with much skepticism, used the declining influence of Sufism to strengthen their attack on these organizations.

Yet contemporary Islam's hard edge alienates Egyptian secularists and many moderate Muslims. The radical militants who took up Sayyid Qutb's call to engage in violence, attacking moderate Egyptians and foreigners, have only succeeded in driving a deep wedge within the Islamic movement. Representing a small fraction of the Islamists, they divert international attention away from the moderates and serve as a convenient pretext for government suppression of the Brotherhood.

The intolerance of the right wing of the Islamists has produced ugly disputes with moderates and secularists. The most notorious of the showdowns involved Nasr Hamid Abu Zaid, a professor of Islamic Studies at Cairo University, whom conservative Islamists accused of having maligned Islam, the Quran, and the Prophet Muhammad. Conservative Islamists attacked his major publications, pointing out that he argued for approaching the Quran as a work of literature, possessing mythical elements. The dispute found its way into the Egyptian courts, which held against Abu Zaid, declaring that he was an apostate and therefore outside the Muslim community. The court went even further, ruling that because he was an apostate, his marriage was no longer valid in Islamic law, but was null and void. Both he and his wife fled the country and settled in the Netherlands.

Egypt has experienced other incidents of intimidation and censorship at the hands of ultraconservative Islamists. Religious fanatics killed the liberal Egyptian intellectual Faraq Fuda and harmed the Nobel Prize–winning writer Naguib Mahfouz. At the present time, professors in academic institutions are burdened with worries about whether their reading assignments will antagonize conservative Muslims and create problems with deans and other administrators. Two telling incidents occurred at the American University in Cairo. The first originated when a conservative Muslim intellectual demanded in an article published in Egypt's leading daily newspaper, *al-Ahram*, that the state ban the circulation and reading of the French Arabist Maxime Rodinson's biography of Muhammad, a work originally published in 1971, widely read in the Muslim world, and generally considered to be sympathetic to the Prophet. The critic, Salah Muntasir, asserted that the biography denigrated Islam and the Prophet's life. At the time, the book was required reading in a course at the university. Under heavy public pressure, the university administration had the book withdrawn from circulation at the university's library. Not much later, a tenured faculty member and professor of Arabic literature at the American University in Cairo encountered similar objections when she assigned an autobiographical work by a young Moroccan writer. Several parents wrote letters of protest to the university's administration. They asserted that the work was pornographic, hardly suitable for young minds. When the professor refused a request from the administration that she alter her reading list, the case exploded into the headlines of Egypt's leading newspapers.

Such is the chilling effect that conservative Islamists have had on scholars and literary figures, who must think a second time before publishing anything that might raise the hackles of the religious authorities. One well-known author and publisher opined: "I reread any story I write several times. Given the number of possibilities and my inability to determine them I have resorted to a legal adviser, a young lawyer, who is my neighbor. He reads every story that I write and every book I publish, especially by a naïve writer. My agony begins as soon as the book enters the print shop."

Egyptian-Christian relations have also suffered under a rising Muslim intolerance of the presence of the Coptic community. During the interwar years and under the presidencies of Nasser, Sadat, and Mubarak it was customary, even essential, to have at least one Coptic minister, usually put in charge of an important office. Influential Coptic ministers included Makram Ubayd, who was a strong supporter of the Wafd under Zaghlul before he fell out of favor with the Wafd and created his own political party. In the post–World War II era, Butrus Butrus Ghali, a scion of one of the most influential and wealthy Coptic families, held high political office, serving for a time as Egyptian minister of foreign affairs before becoming Secretary General of the United Nations. Yet these bows to the legitimacy of the Copts have not kept fundamentalist Islamists from venting their anger against them. In parts of Upper Egypt, where a large segment of the Coptic population resides, Muslim groups have made attacks on the Copts and have inhibited efforts of this community to refurbish their churches and celebrate their holy days.

Can the Nile Become Even More Bountiful?

Egyptians have counted on the Nile to create wealth. They do so again today. With a present population close to 80 million, estimated to rise to 100 million by 2030 and not to stabilize before 2065 at 115 million, the need for new land and resources is pressing. Of the numerous programs being put forward to expand the country's living and arable space, none is more breathtaking than the Toshka project. Conceived of in 1992, the plan calls for the channeling of the waters held in Lake Nasser behind the Aswan High Dam onto the vast tracts of land in Egypt's western desert. At present this area is part of the New Valley governate, which comprises 38 percent of Egypt's total area but is the least populated governate in the country.

The most optimistic projections for Toshka are little short of miraculous. Said to be able to create a second Nile River basin, the scheme is scheduled for completion in 2020 at a cost of $70 billion. Its goal is nothing less than to double the arable land in Egypt, create two million new jobs, and attract over 1.6 million people into an area that was once one of the world's most arid and inhospitable locations. In 2005, the main pumping station came into being at a cost of $5.5 billion, appropriately named for President Mubarak, who has staked much of his reputation on this endeavor. The pumping station will eventually drive water into a main irrigation canal, called the Sheikh Zayid Canal, which will run thirty miles westward and feed four side branch canals.

Responsibility for preparing this area for agricultural uses and urban development falls to a newly created government entity, the Southern Regional Development Authority. It plans to dole out large segments of the arable land to private development companies, who in turn will divide up the estates into large holdings for big agrobusinesses and smaller holdings for individual families.

But will this dream come to fruition? Many critics think not. They have dubbed it Mubarak's pyramid (yet another reminder of how the past intrudes on the present), reminding listeners that similar claims were made but never fulfilled for the expansion of agricultural lands after the construction of the high Aswan dam. They also assert that even if the project achieves some successes, profits will be siphoned off into the coffers of foreign investors, who have been written in for most of the scheme's financing.

Even more troubling, however, are the demands that are certain to be made in the near future for a redivision of the Nile waters. Egypt is unlikely to be able to count on obtaining an increase in the allocation set aside for it in the last Nile waters agreement of 1959, negotiated between Egypt and Sudan. At the time Egypt received 56 milliards of the estimated 84 milliards of Nile waters that passed through Aswan each year. Sudan's total was 18 milliards, with 10 milliards expected to be the amount of water held in the Lake Nasser reservoir. These 10 milliards are precisely the amount of water that the Egyptian hydraulic engineers propose to channel off into the western desert. But can Egypt expect to retain such a large share of the Nile waters now that all of the riverine states, especially Ethiopia and Uganda as well as Sudan, have their own increasing needs for the Nile's waters? Without doubt the Egyptians face a troubled future in their control over the Nile, for the Middle East and North Africa in general have 6 percent of the world's population but only 2 percent of renewable water supplies. The planners have said that Egypt can respond to increased demands on Nile waters from riverine states by reducing the usage of irrigation waters in the delta and conserving and even increasing water supplies along the whole of the Nile River basin. But are these likely to be realizable goals? Yet the consensus among experts, much as it was when Egypt moved ahead with its high Aswan dam, is that Egypt has no viable alternatives to Toshka given the parlous state of its expanding population and its desperate need for new land and new resources.

Where Will They Live?

Nearly one-third of all Egyptians live in Cairo (population 18.5 million in 2008) and Alexandria (population 4 million in 2008). Cairo is one of the world's quintessential primal cities, holding no less than 25 percent of Egypt's total population. Its explosive growth has defeated the shrewdest of the city's urban planners. Sewerage projects, new electricity grids, telephone networks, increased water filtration plants and supply systems, new bridges over the Nile, and bigger and speedier highways have proven to be inadequate and out of date almost from the moment that they were completed. Well-to-do Cairenes today refuse to use the public water supply even though objective reports confirm that it is safer than all of the bottled water on sale in local stores. No doubt the public water is safe as long as it reaches residences without being compromised because of ancient and rusted piping systems. Most residents refuse to take that chance.

In 1969, at the end of the Nasser period, urban planners launched the Greater Cairo Region Master Scheme. Its major goal was to open up new cities as a way to relieve pressure on Cairo. The first plan called for the establishment of four satellite cities in the deserts surrounding Cairo. Sadat supported the new initiative, demanding even bolder visions, nothing short of "a new population map for Egypt." Under his guidance the greater Cairo master plan was expanded to include fourteen new urban centers. The revised plan envisioned three different types of cities: satellite cities that would be close to Cairo and would serve as commuter locations; freestanding cities, further afield, supporting a more diversified economy and becoming self-sufficient; and, finally, new settlements, located near Cairo and other urban areas but destined to enjoy economic and political independence from nearby cities. The plan contemplated that the new cities would start out with target population figures of half a million, hopefully to grow to and even beyond the million mark. A final and decisive part of the plan was the construction of a ring road around Cairo that would not only ease traffic congestion in and out of the city but also serve as a barrier to urban sprawl.

The first of these cities came into being in the 1970s. Two of them (the Tenth of Ramadan and the Sixth of October) have been reasonably successful, a third (Sadat City) has thus far failed, while a fourth one (New Cairo), not originally part of the master scheme and a recently developed urban location, is likely to outstrip all of the others in population and performance.

The Tenth of Ramadan is located along the Cairo-Ismailiya desert road about thirty miles outside Cairo. It has succeeded in attracting middle-sized industries and managerial and professional individuals who run the new factories. Thus far, however, the city lacks a residential labor force. The factory workers prefer to live among their friends in Cairo and to commute to and from work. The urban planners lament this development since they envisioned the Tenth of Ramadan as a self-contained city. But it does not seem to disturb the city's residents, who have created a largely upper-middle-class urban paradise for themselves, replete with golf courses, swimming pools, and irrigated lawns, gardens, and trees.

Much the same has occurred in the Sixth of October, less than twenty miles from Cairo. Its residents, mainly middle- to upper-middle-class professionals, have established Egypt's most attractive gated community. The Sixth of October serves several important economic functions. Like several of the new desert cities the Sixth of October has become a major wholesale marketing city, taking over many of the functions once handled by the Rod al-Farag agricultural market in Cairo, previously Egypt's only wholesale agricultural market. Before the new desert cities appeared, all agricultural produce came into the central Rod al-Farag market in Shubra district before being distributed to the rest of the country and the other parts of Cairo. The Sixth of October has also become important because it has seven private universities, including two private medical schools.

The words of Mustafa Kishk, an expatriate Egyptian who had been living in Los Angeles but was determined to return to his country, are worth hearing. Kishk settled in Cairo, which nearly destroyed his dream of living in Egypt once again. He found its crowdedness, noise, pollution and disorderliness, even for an Angelino, intolerable. The move to the Sixth of October City brought him precisely what he had aspired to: "I felt like I was in a brand new country. I love the higher altitude and the clean cool air it brings. People are flocking to these new cities because they are sick and tired of Cairo. I really can't think of one bad thing to say about them." Kishk is right. The Sixth of October has more land than Zamalek and fewer buyers. The housing prices are well below the rates in Cairo and Alexandria. The names that the inhabitants give to their residential quarters, such as Beverly Hills in the Sixth of October, bespeak the modern, Western world that the people believe they are creating in the desert.

Sadat City, bearing the name of the country's most energetic apostle of new urban development, was supposed to be the path-breaking urban city. Instead it has been its most palpable failure. Located along the desert road from Cairo to Alexandria, it has turned out to be too far from Cairo (fifty-five miles northwest of the city) and much too far from Alexandria. The residents of the desert cities still wish to frequent the capital or to go to the Mediterranean. They find life at such a distance from these centers of political and cultural life unattractive. Despite pouring resources into Sadat City, the government has been unable to attract a large and stable population.

New Cairo, on the other hand, has simply taken off as a place to reside, despite its distance from the center of the city. It is expected to have a population of 4.5 million by 2020, attracted mainly by the extraordinary university development taking place there and also by its reasonable proximity to Cairo. The anchor of the city is the new, expensive, and luxurious campus of the American University in Cairo.

Can Education Be an Instrument of Social Mobility Once Again?

Over the last two hundred years, education has been a powerful force for social mobility. Muhammad Ali and his successors sent native-born Egyptians, not members of their Albanian-Turkish ruling class, for schooling in the West and enrolled them in Egypt's Westernized schools. By the time Khedive Ismail came to the throne in 1863 an educated, native-born Egyptian elite was in a position to challenge the authority of the Turko-Circassians. A second era of rapid social mobility occurred during the Nasser years. The funds available for public schools increased, and university education enjoyed a remarkable expansion. At the same time, the private schools that had thrived under the British were no longer favored. Talented Egyptians, often from poor rural families, were able to use the new educational opportunities to move into the professions, government, and the business world.

Under Sadat and Mubarak education has become an instrument of the status quo. It solidifies the position of the wealthy and powerful and erects barriers to the aspiring among the poor. Private schools are now the rage, forcing public schooling into the shadows. Everywhere in the educational system money is the key factor. The wealthy send their children to the proliferating private, mostly foreign-run elementary and secondary schools. The German school, the French lycée, a British school, and the most expensive of them all, exceedingly well endowed, Cairo American College (the

American private elementary and secondary school), have become the training arenas for government service and the private sector. The German school has such a respected reputation for the rigor of its training and its excellence in language instruction, including, of course, the essential language of Egyptian governmental and business life, English, that parents line up years in advance to gain admittance for their offspring even though there is no use for the German language in Egyptian life. The Cairo American College is like an expensive private school in the United States. Its class sizes are small; its facilities, educational and extracurricular, are unmatched. It has an Olympic-size swimming pool, first-rate track resources, and numerous playing fields. Alas, its fees are so high that it has few Egyptian students. The majority of the students are sons and daughters of American diplomats and businesspersons. The school also educates a large number of the children of well-off Middle Eastern families.

During the Nasser years, particularly after the 1956 British-French-Israeli invasion of Egypt, the government sequestered many of the private British and French private schools. It also undercut the legitimacy of the American University in Cairo, refusing to recognize its diplomas for entrance into government service. The result was that these schools attracted only those young people who wanted to acquire a fluency in English and who intended to pursue careers in the shrinking private sector, especially in tourism, where knowledge of English was mandatory.

Under Mubarak the social and economic situation changed radically. Tourism accounts for 10 percent of gross domestic product, and an even larger proportion in Cairo, where the educated want to live. And tourism demands command of foreign languages, the knowledge of which is more fully acquired in the private, foreign-run schools. The American University in Cairo, once a pariah institution, a school of last resort for members of the elite who could not get their children into one of the prestigious faculties of Cairo University (notably medicine, engineering, and law), has experienced a stunning revival. Its graduates are to be seen in the higher echelons of government. Mubarak's wife, Suzanne, and his son, Gamal, are both AUC graduates, and many sons and daughters of leading members of the government attend AUC or are recent graduates.

In September 2008, the American University in Cairo opened its new campus in New Cairo. It had little alternative to relocating outside the center of Cairo. The government wanted it to vacate some of the most valuable property in the city, and the university needed more room than it could find in central Cairo for its expansion. Hence it moved out of its famous central campus site, with its elegant administration building, originally known as the Gianaclis building, after the Greek business entrepreneur, located just off Midan al-Tahrir, along with its other two campuses, and relocated in a spacious area though distant from the center of the city. The old campus will be put to good use. The Gianaclis building will be restored to its original form and will serve as a general cultural center while the old campus will house a café, a bookstore, and a reading area, becoming an oasis for the public from the hustle and bustle of the city.

Meanwhile, the new campus projects the rosy future that the AUC trustees and administration see for the university. The new site will feature three campuses and splendid architectural designs. The lower campus will be the face of the university to the outside world. It will feature a park sporting desert plants and an amphitheater for important public lectures. The middle campus will be the core of the university's academic life. It will contain all of the different degree-granting schools, the administration buildings, and the library. Students and faculty will enter the middle campus through a domed and arched gateway designed along the lines of the great mosque of Cordoba. The upper campus will contain the classrooms as well as the socializing facilities for students and faculties, dominated by a multipurpose campus center building.

While the American University in Cairo is the principal and most highly regarded of the private, foreign-run universities, it is not the only one. British, French, German, and Canadian groups have shown interest in entering the higher-education scene. A group of wealthy Canadian businesspersons with Egyptian roots opened the Canadian International College in 2004. This school emphasized science and technology and affiliated itself with the Cape Breton University of Nova Scotia. In addition to believing that their institution could fill a gap in Egypt's higher science education, the founders also wanted to make money. The school became a for-profit institution, whose originators expected to benefit financially from the unfulfilled demand among Egyptians for an English-based education. The founders obviously had done market research, for the enrollment figures for the first year greatly exceeded anyone's projections. Rather than turn away fee-paying students in the face of the school's newness the Canadian trustees instructed the local administration to take all of those who qualified for enrollment. This action was taken with a heavy heart by the dean, but the school opened to a spectacular enrollment and much acclaim.

The flourishing of the private institutions at all levels is a severe indictment of public sector education, which had been one of Nasser's cherished revolutionary goals. Public sector education continues to play a major role in Egypt. It educates far more students than do the private schools, but even here money talks. At whatever level of schooling, success in the classroom depends on obtaining extra coaching and reading materials, all of which cost money. Parents pay for tutors, seek to get special handouts from teachers for their children, and tape lectures or ask for (and pay for) the lecture notes of university professors, who often teach large classes, not all of whose attendees can find a seat for themselves in inadequate lecture halls.

What Happens after Mubarak?

Although President Mubarak is in no danger of breaking the longevity record of Ramses II, who ruled for sixty-six years, his stay in power has been a lengthy one. He is now in his eighties. On everyone's mind is who or what will succeed him. Unlike his predecessors, he has not designated a vice president. Much evidence exists that he would like to hand the mantle of power to his son Gamal, who has steadily ascended the power hierarchy of the National Democratic Party. In 2006 Gamal Mubarak became the assistant secretary general of the party. Although his succession has aroused opposition in many quarters, he has shown himself to be an astute and in certain ways a progressive leader. He was responsible for bringing younger, more technically proficient, liberal economists into the government cabinet in 2005.

Although the military is likely to have the final say on who will succeed Mubarak, the populist opposition movement, known as Kifaya, that surfaced during the 2005 elections suggests that the will of the people cannot be brushed aside as easily as it has in the past. Kifaya crystallized when a group of prominent intellectuals, alarmed that President Mubarak would seek a fifth term as president and that he was preparing for his son to succeed him, called a conference on September 22, 2004. Attended by 500 intellectuals and non-NDP political leaders, the conference leaders created what they called a movement of opposition, rather than a political party. Its formal name was the Egyptian Movement for Change, but it quickly became known by its nickname, *kifaya*, which in Arabic means "enough." Kifaya brought together a host of disparate elements—Islamists, New Wafd members, labor supporters, Nasserists, the Ghad or Tomorrow Party, led by the charismatic businessman, Ayman Nour, and the Socialist (or Tagammu) Party. Its unifying principle was a singular and popular one—opposition to Mubarak and his continuing control of the Egyptian polity.

Although Kifaya failed to win at the polls, it did achieve some striking victories. First, it forced President Mubarak to alter the procedures for selecting and then electing the president. Previously, the task of selecting the president fell to the People's Assembly, which always nominated President Mubarak, since the Assembly was dominated by NDP members. Under popular pressure, Mubarak allowed other candidates to enter the hustings and to run against him. His principal opponent was Ayman Nour of the Ghad Party, and though Nour won only 8 percent of the vote, he so alarmed Mubarak and the NDP that they brought charges against him of having falsified names on his petition to run for the presidency. Following the election, Nour was found guilty of these charges and sentenced to a term in prison.

The election showed how formidable were the powers of the state. The National Democratic Party controlled the radio and television networks and had the most widely circulated newspapers in its camp. Yet the Kifaya movement demonstrated the depth of opposition to the government. Its supporters took advantage of the new electronic instruments gaining widespread use in Egypt to blunt some of the NDP's advantage with the traditional media. Using cell phones, email, and Internet access, Kifaya whipped up the populace against the government, using a simple set of slogans and words to solidify its message. Bloggers informed readers of when the next mass demonstration would occur and circulated Kifaya posters against the NDP. Naturally, the state countered with its usual doses of intimidation. Some of the demonstrations were large. Others were so poorly attended that the riot police outnumbered the protestors. Every time Kifaya assembled its followers, a massive police presence appeared.

The fact that Mubarak and the NDP won the 2005 elections suggests that the Egyptian population is still far from being able to seize power. In any case, fractures began to appear within the Kifaya organization, particularly between the Islamists and the secularists. A dividing issue was the head scarf, which some of the secularists wished to condemn and which the Islamists defended. Democracy is far from ready to break out in a country with a long history of authoritarian one-man rule. But the opposition to the status quo and Mubarak's increasing police state grows by the day.

Numerous problems face future Egyptian leaders. Population growth is in many ways the knottiest of them all. One Egyptian economist given to irony and humor stated that he had a solution to Egypt's population dilemmas. Egypt should introduce mandatory birth control and make it retroactive to 1910. The new cities, the Toshka irrigation project, the expansion of private schooling, industrialization, and new and more productive crops and seeds are some of the answers that have been put forward to cope. But many of these proposals are fraught with serious defects.

Egypt through the Millennia

History abounds in Egypt. Everywhere one turns are reminders of the past. In the countryside, although annual floods no longer occur, the ancient *shaduf* and the buffalo-driven water wheel are ever present. Peasant women help their husbands and their fathers till the fields as they have for millennia. Not far off are pharaonic and Islamic antiquities that astonish Egypt's countless visitors but are no more than a taken-for-granted feature to the Egyptian population. At a greater distance from the settled parts of Egypt are monasteries and ancient churches, reminders of a distant Christian era. Greek and Roman remains fill the cities, which also reflect the drive to modernity of the last two centuries. Exclusive sporting clubs create oases of repose and pleasure, once enjoyed only by wealthy foreigners, now open to the affluent of Egypt. Yet they exist only short distances from some of the most impoverished quarters, grim locations where the poor attempt to eke out a desperate existence. A modern metro system, built on the model of the Paris metro, snakes its way from Helwan, an industrial suburb in the south, to Abbasiya and Heliopolis in the north.

Visitors flock to Egypt. They arrive to step back into history, lured by the immensity of the pyramids, the massive and egotistical monuments of Ramses II that are reminders of outsized imperialist ambitions, and antiquities that bespeak the great Alexander, Cleopatra, and Roman legions. They travel to the Monastery of Saint Catherine in Sinai and ascend Mount Sinai there where many believe that God gave the Ten Commandments to Moses. They visit other monasteries in the deserts to relive the experiences of the early desert fathers. Cairo is a veritable treasure trove of medieval Muslim life, full of stately mosques, caravanserais, majestic walls, and heavy gates that separated the royal city from its outlying quarters.

In the face of such historical abundance contemporary Egypt gets short shrift. The elegance of downtown Cairo and the beauty of Alexandria's cornice are too often overlooked. Modern Egypt seems entirely distant from the ancient and the medieval periods. Radical changes have transformed modern Egypt's history. In a country where the inhabitable area has expanded only a little and where, even in the best of times, no more than 6 million people resided, now 80 million compete for space. Although the urban dwelling area where Cairo now exists has been Egypt's political center since pharaonic times, its present-day daily population of 18.5 million would have been unimaginable to anyone even as late as 1950. Although Egyptians have long had a sense of their national integrity, the country is a land of immigrants. Libyans, Nubians, Syrians, Persians, Greeks, Romans, Arabs, Berbers, Kurds, Turks, Britons, and Frenchmen and women have settled in the Nile River basin, intermarried, and stayed on, eventually becoming Egyptians themselves. The country's religious past is as diverse as its population. Pharaonic cosmologies gave way to Greek and Roman gods, which were supplanted by the Christian God and then by the Islamic Deity. For a time Jesus Christ was worshipped as the Son of God, but his followers became a minority after the country was absorbed into powerful Islamic empires. With Islam came Arabic. Ancient Egyptian, Greek, Latin, and Coptic died out, as did much of Egypt's connection with its distant past.

Not only have different religious beliefs prevailed at different moments and diverse populations entered the country, but the country's present economic life bears little relationship to what it was up to the beginning of the nineteenth century. No longer do annual Nile floods wash over Egypt's farming lands and order the daily routines of peasant life. Hydraulic constructions, even more spectacular than those of the architects of Egypt's massive antiquities, enable a year-round control of the Nile's high and low waters. High dams, intermediate barrages, and small weirs have eliminated annual flooding, evened out the flow of water to the lands between the summer and winter months, and allowed cultivators to grow three crops per year. Egypt, once the granary of the eastern Mediterranean and Southwest Asia, became the world's leading exporter of high-staple cotton at the end of the nineteenth century. Though its cotton exports continue to be important, they have lost some of their economic significance to industrial products and specialized fruits, vegetables, and flowers, all of which make their way to high-income countries in Europe and the Americas.

Yet despite the immensity of change, a considerable persistence marks Egypt over many millennia. These persistences are the theme of the final chapter.

GEOGRAPHY IS DESTINY

Geography has determined the history of few countries as profoundly as it has that of Egypt. What nature first gave to Egypt—isolation from outside influences and an opportunity to build a deep and abiding sense of Egyptian identity—human ingenuity then removed. Surrounded by deserts on the west and east, cataracts in the south, and the Mediterranean in the north, the Egyptian people launched their history in an isolated location, ensconced along the banks of the Nile and dependent on its annual floods but entirely protected from foreign peoples. The pharaohs of the ancient kingdom stamped their power and ideology on the people. They, the civil and military officials, and the priestly class forged an enduring Egyptian character and suffused it through the dwellers in the Nile basin. But technological breakthroughs brought Egypt into closer contact with the outside world and forced the Egyptians to defend their uniqueness against other peoples. Some they conquered; others conquered them. The domestication of the horse and the camel enabled warriors and merchants to traverse long distances and even to pierce the deserts. Hyksos horses and chariots came out of Southwest Asia in the seventeenth century BCE to bring the Middle Kingdom to an end. The Hyksos tribesmen became Egypt's first conquerors. In turn, Egyptian pharaohs mastered horse and chariot technology and extended Egypt's sway eastward into Syria, Palestine, and beyond and south into Nubia. Next, when Greeks and Romans learned the mysteries of ocean currents and improved their sailing technologies, Egypt also confronted powerful seaborne peoples. By this time, Egypt's strategic geopolitical importance had become obvious. It lay astride three continents—Asia, Africa, and Europe. Aspiring world conquerors, and there were as many in these early centuries as there have been in later centuries, including Persian satraps, Greek warlords, and Roman legionnaires, recognized the geopolitical centrality of Egypt. Arab Muslim warriors followed in the footsteps of these early empire builders and incorporated Egypt into their far-flung territorial possessions. In the Fatimid era Egypt itself sought world dominion. Later, in the thirteenth century, Egyptian Mamluk soldiers brought a halt to a Mongol project of world conquest. The Ottoman Turks, having finally driven Christians from the city of Constantinople in 1453, a decisive moment in world history, turned their attention away from eastern and central Europe and looked southward. They incorporated Egypt into their empire. It became their most important Arabic-speaking possession.

In modern times powerful European states competed for preeminence in Egypt. Europe's first expansionists, Spain and Portugal, turned away from the Middle East, honoring the strength of the Ottoman Empire. They focused their attention on the New World. By the nineteenth century, however, Britain and France, aspiring to a world domination that had eluded the Spanish and Portuguese, eyed Egypt as a prize in their global struggles. Napoleon Bonaparte's invasion of 1798 was an abortive first salvo, while de Lesseps's construction of the Suez Canal heightened the country's strategic importance, especially to the British, whose shipping dominated traffic through the canal and who needed it to move troops to the east if colonial possessions gave trouble. A British invasion and occupation were well-nigh inevitable. In 1882 it occurred. Britain's control over Egyptian affairs lasted until after World War II.

Yet in spite of these invasions and the repeated incorporation of Egypt into someone else's empire, the sense of Egypt's unique identity, first implanted in the pharaonic era, endured. Conquerors came and went. Egyptians stayed on and defended the integrity of their ways of life. Indeed, large numbers of the foreign populations that moved into Egypt blended into the local population. They were eager to reside in a land endowed with cloudless days, friendly people, and prosperous living standards. Those rulers that remained aloof from the local people and refused to assimilate to Egyptian ways, notably the Hyksos in ancient times and the British in modern times, ultimately incurred the wrath of the people. They and their collaborators were driven away.

RULERSHIP

The fundamental characteristics of the Egyptian identity are elusive, but several stand out. From 3000 BCE to the present, absolutist rulers have exercised sway. In ancient times, poets and artisans celebrated the exploits of Thutmose, Akhenaten, Hatshepsut, and Ramses II in verse and stelae. Alexander and Cleopatra graced Egypt's Graeco-Roman eras, and Fatimid caliphs created the magnificence of Cairo. Napoleon Bonaparte left his mark on Egypt, and Lord Cromer held the reins of power in Cairo when the British Empire was at its height. Although Nasser, Sadat, and Mubarak claimed to restore authority to the people, they ruled as autocratically as their predecessors.

Just why "big men," and, occasionally, "big women," have dominated Egypt's historical record is a historical conundrum. The unification of southern and northern Egypt—the delta and the long sliver of land in the south—required extreme military might, as the Narmer palette, showing an athletic warrior beheading his opponent, demonstrates. Religious and cosmological ideas underscored the legitimacy of the monarch. Priests and civil servants proclaimed the divinity of the ruler, asserting that he alone ensured the regular and smooth functioning of the Nile River and maintained social order, *maat*. Even when social disorder prevailed, during the intermediate periods between the Old, Middle, and New Kingdoms, important local notables came to the fore and became responsible for providing some semblance of social order.

Ancient Egypt was a male-dominated culture. The eldest male was the dominant figure in the household, responsible for the orderliness of his extended family. So just as the oldest, or in most cases, the most respected male in an extended family held unchallenged power, so the pharaoh, as head of the family of Egyptian people, held supreme authority and enjoyed unquestioned legitimacy.

Although control over the Nile waters was at first a local affair and did not involve day-to-day regulation by a central government, as the Egyptians gained greater knowledge and control over its high and low waters, the central government became a major actor. Its officials measured the rising waters during the flood stages, assessed the tax according to their knowledge of whether the year would be favorable or unfavorable to cultivators, and stored grain seeds for the next harvests. Egypt never was the most highly regulated of the world's centralized hydraulic societies, given the general predictability of floods; nonetheless the role of the government in hydraulic affairs was vital. It became even more critical in the modern era when vast hydraulic projects, like the immense dams at Aswan, brought Nile flooding under control and allowed a system of perennial irrigation to replace the traditional basin system. In this period—the last two hundred years—Egypt's most influential bureaucrats have been its hydraulic engineers, not its political rulers.

Islam, especially the Sunni version, blended well with the autocratic traditions of the pharaohs. Muhammad, the Prophet, exercised political as well as religious authority. His successors, first, the four "rightly-guided" caliphs, then the Umayyad rulers, and, after them, the Abbasid caliphs, carried forth the expansion of Islam. Although they did not possess clerical authority, since that function was reserved to Muslim scholars, the ulama, caliphs demanded that peoples living under their authority be obedient. Of course, Muslim rulers were obligated to rule according to Muslim law, and if and when they diverged from this path, their subjects had the right to revolt.

The centralizing and absolutist tendency within the Islamic world became even more pronounced as caliphs began to import Turkish slave-warriors into their military organizations and to make them the military prop of their authority. This practice reached a high point in Egypt during the Mamluk era from the thirteenth century to the beginning of the sixteenth century and was retained, with adjustments, under Ottoman rule. When the French invaders were expelled from Egypt in 1801, a neo-Mamluk ruler, Muhammad Ali, solidified his control over the country. He ruled as autocratically as had his predecessors, the Mamluks and the Ottomans, except for the fact that he sought to come to terms with Western powers and brought the country into contact with Western culture. One of the unintended consequences of his opening to the West was the rise of a native-born, Western-educated Egyptian intelligentsia. This group would ultimately see Egypt as a prototypical nation-state, no different from France or Britain, and therefore deserving of rule by native-born Egyptians rather than by foreign agents, be they the Turko-Circassians of Muhammad Ali's and Ismail's reigns or the British of the British occupation.

Under British rule, Lord Cromer, though technically merely consul general, exercised as much authority over the country as had his predecessors, Muhammad Ali and Ismail. Although Cromer believed in Britain's parliamentary regime as the pinnacle of good government, he did not cultivate representative government in Egypt. He asserted that Egypt was not yet ready for such an advanced political system. Cromer believed that British advisers and officials should rule Egypt autocratically for an extended period of political tutelage. It was only during the interwar years, when Egypt attained a modicum of independence from the British, that Egyptians gained any experience in democratic governance. Yet while Egypt had the trappings of democratic rule, in the form of regular elections, political parties, and parliamentary governance, the powers of the British and the Egyptian monarchy, still in the hands of the family of Muhammad Ali, made it nearly impossible for the will of the people to make itself felt through elections.

In 1952, a group of young military officers overthrew the parliamentary regime and expelled the monarch, King Farouk. Like so many military regimes in Africa, Asia, and Latin America, these young officers were skeptical that democracy could achieve the goals that they had set for themselves and for Egypt. They wanted nothing short of full political independence from the British and from all binding external alliances, rapid economic development, income redistribution, and social justice. As a consequence, for more than a half century, three military men have determined the destiny of the country. The first two—Nasser and Sadat—were Free Officers themselves while the third—Mubarak—was a decorated military man of a generation later than the Free Officers. Each, in his own distinctive way, maintained the power of the Egyptian presidency and has kept parliamentary and democratic governance in check.

RELIGIOSITY

The Egyptians have been and continue to be a deeply religious people. Religion has surfaced as a bulwark of the social order or a force of transforming change in every period of the country's history. It is a core feature of Egyptian life and has affected all of the communities with whom the Egyptians have come into contact.

The ancient religious beliefs of the pharaohs suffered a bad name, given them by the advocates of Judaism and Christianity. The Hebrew prophets and the authors of the New Testament set their religions off against that of the Egyptians, extolling their monotheism and ridiculing the Egyptians for their zoomorphic and multitudinous gods. Yet these two Abrahamic religions and Islam, which saw itself as successor to Judaism and Christianity, owed much to the cosmology of the ancient Egyptians. Within its polytheistic religious universe, ancient Egyptian religion tended toward monotheism. The inhabitants of different locales believed that their areas were protected by a single, powerful deity. During the Middle and New Kingdoms, priestly classes elevated the sun gods, Ra and Amun-Ra, to the status of a high god. The "heretic king," Akhenaten, claimed that Aten, the sun disk god, was the only divine being. In addition, Christianity and Islam both embraced the belief in an afterlife, fundamental to the ancient Egyptians, and the Christian belief in God as a trinity (Father, Son, and Holy Ghost) had parallels in the Egyptian narrative of Isis, the godly mother figure, Osiris, the father,

318

and Horus, the avenging son. Moreover, Egyptian religion depicted a battle between a good deity, often seen as Osiris, and an evil force, Seth, Osiris's brother. In one of the most widely disseminated tales, which has parallels to Christian theology, Seth killed his brother, Osiris, and dismembered his body, only to have Horus, the son of Isis and Osiris, defeat Seth and resurrect Osiris. Horus became the god of the sky and protector of the reigning pharaoh. Isis became the goddess of life and civilization, whose cult continued into the Greek and Roman periods, and Osiris the god of death, resurrection, and fertility.

Yet religion has not always promoted the powers of the state and served as a force for the status quo. In ancient times, priests amassed great power and wealth and challenged the authority of the pharaohs. One of the reasons for Akhenaten's religious innovation and his move of the political capital from Thebes to the city of Akhetaten was to rid himself of priestly privilege and to rule on his own. In the era of the Roman Empire, Christianity arose as a religion of opposition to the political power and religious beliefs of the emperors. Egypt was a bastion of the new religion, a center of high theological thought at the Catechetical School in Alexandria, and the original fount of eremetic and cenobitic monastic life.

Islam, erupting out of the Arabian Peninsula, became the force that overthrew the Persian Empire and drove the Christian Byzantine Empire into retreat. Gradually Islam became the majority religion within its own boundaries, replacing Christianity and Zoroastrianism. In 1453, Ottoman soldiers brought an end to the Byzantine state when they overran the city of Constantinople. As a religious system Islam provided strong support for state power. The ulama rallied around Muslim caliphs and sultans, and the people's Islam, Sufism, tended not to challenge political authority. Nonetheless, Islam had within its fold oppositional elements. In the Mamluk era, Muslim scholars, like Ibn Taymiyya, called for a return to the pure Islam of the early days of the faith and made no brief for the rulers of Egypt. Shiism was always a force of opposition, especially where Shiite communities formed a vocal and discontented minority, as they did in many regions of the Ottoman Empire.

CONCLUSION

In the late twentieth century radical Islam became the most powerful opposition movement within the Muslim world and a challenge to the hegemony of the United States and its allies. As anyone with knowledge of the intellectual prominence of Egypt might have expected, Egyptian Muslims assumed leadership in this Islamist movement. The intellectual guide to radical and militant Islam was Sayyid Qutb, an Egyptian, who was put to death by the Nasser government. His writings, many of which were composed and circulated while he was imprisoned, called for Muslims to return to the solid foundations of their original faith and to use whatever means they could to restore their territories and the larger world to the unimpeachable teachings of the Prophet Muhammad. Egypt's experience with violent Islam has repelled many of the country's citizens, but it has not diminished the attraction of religion. Religiosity, so vital to the civilization of the ancient Egyptians, remains a fundamental force in Egyptian society today.

At the beginning of the twenty-first century, two of Egypt's most fundamental qualities—its one-man rule and its religiosity—are at war with each other. A revived, pragmatic, and flexible form of Islam has achieved deep roots in the Egyptian population. Its proponents want the ruling regime to deliver on its earlier promise to empower Egyptians and foster democratic rule. But the present government, heir to the long tradition of autocratic and highly personalized authority, is loathe to cede power to other groups. Egypt's destiny is not clear, but, as in the past, it will be hotly contested.

NOTES

CHAPTER ONE
The Land and People

Page 2 Kepel, *Muslim Extremism in Egypt*, p. 213.
Pages 5 and 6 Godolphin, *The Greek Historians,* pp. 92 and 105–6.
Page 6 Godolphin, *The Greek Historians*, p. 94.
Page 7 Maisels, *Early Civilization*, p. 31.
Page 10 Godolphin, *The Greek Historians*, p. 97.
Page 10 Mayer and Prideaux, *Never to Die*, pp. 94 and 96.
Page 13 Hurst, *The Nile*, p. 40.
Page 15 Diop, *African Origins of Civilization*, p. xiv.

CHAPTER TWO
Egypt during the Old Kingdom

Pages 26 and 27 Baedeker, *Egypt and the Sudan*, pp. 137–38.
Page 27 Romer, *The Great* Pyramid, p. 19.
Page 28 Assmann, *The Mind*, p. 22.
Page 31 Breasted, *History*, p. 106.
Page 39 Romer, *The Great Pyramid*, p. 75.
Page 44 Breasted, *The Dawn*, p. 65.
Pages 46 and 47 Mayer and Prideaux, *Never to Die*, pp. 120–24.
Page 48 Mayer and Prideaux, *Never to Die*, p. 49.
Page 49 Bell, "Dark Ages," pp. 9–12.
Page 49 Bell, "Dark Ages," p. 23.

CHAPTER THREE
The Middle and New Kingdoms

Page 52 Breasted, *History*, p. 356.

Page 56 Breasted, *History*, p. 116.

Page 57 Parkinson, *The Tale*, pp. 30, 31, and 40.

Pages 60–61 Mayer and Prideaux, *Never to Die*, p. 116.

Page 61 Breasted, *History*, p. 376.

Page 65 Hornung, *Akhenaten*, p. 7.

Pages 67–68 J. Wilson, *Culture of Ancient Egypt*, p. 117.

Page 69 Reeves, *Egypt's False Prophet*, p. 146.

Page 69 Hornung, *Akhenaten*, p. 46.

Page 70 Hornung, *Akhenaten*, p. 44.

Page 73 Burckhardt, *Travels in Nubia*, pp. 90–91.

Page 77 Watterson, *Women*, p. 54.

Page 78 Robins, *Women*, p. 75.

CHAPTER FOUR
Nubians, Greeks, and Romans, circa 1200 BCE–632 CE

Page 81 Green, *Alexander of Macedon*, p. 274.

Page 83 J. Wilson, *Culture of Ancient Egypt*, p. 305.

Page 84 Welsby, *The Kingdom of Kush*, p. 5.

Page 84 Heeren, *Reflections*, p. 294.

Page 85 Grimal, *History of Ancient Egypt*, p. 339.

Page 90 Burkert, *Orientalizing Revolution*, p. 26.

Page 91 Green, *Alexander to Actium*, p. 84.

Page 92 Wiegand and Davis, *Encyclopedia of Library History*, p. 21.

Pages 95–96 Zabkar, *Hymns to Isis*, p. 15.

Page 97 Tyldesley, *Cleopatra*, p. 63.

CHAPTER FIVE
Christian Egypt

Page 110 Haas, *Alexandria in Late Antiquity*, pp. 138–39.

Page 111 Atiya, *History of Eastern Christianity*, p. 34.

Page 112 Brown, *The World*, p. 96.

Page 114 Krawiec, *Shenoute*, p. 13.

Page 118 Potter, *Roman Empire at Bay*, p. 419.

Pages 118–119 Watterson, *Coptic Egypt*, p. 45.

Page 120 Atiya, *History of Eastern Christianity*, p. 17.

CHAPTER SIX
Egypt within Islamic Empires, 639–969

Page 124 Peters, *Muhammad*, p. 23.
Page 125 Arberry, *The Koran Interpreted*, p. ix.
Page 128 Arberry, *The Koran Interpreted*, p. x.
Page 130 Butler, *Arab Conquest of Egypt*, p. 194.
Page 131 Raymond, *Cairo*, p. 16.
Page 131 Hitti, *The Arabs*, p. 69.
Page 132 Raymond, *Cairo*, p. 12.
Page 135 Hodges and Whitehouse, *Mohammed*, p. 126.
Page 136 Lewis, *Islam*, p. 70.
Pages 141–142 Colla, *Conflicted Antiquities*, pp. 79–81.
Page 142 El Daly, *Egyptology*, p. 48.

CHAPTER SEVEN
Fatimids, Ayyubids, and Mamluks, 969–1517

Page 153 Brett, *Rise of the Fatimids*, p. 219.
Page 155 Lev, *State*, p. 185.
Pages 160–161 Gibb, *Saladin*, pp. 167 and 111.
Pages 164–165 Lewis, *Islam*, vol. 1, p. 84.
Page 166 Ayalon, *Islam*, vol. 4, p. 32.
Page 170 Petry, *The Civilian Elite*, p. xxi.
Page 172 Dols, *Black Death*, pp. 156 and 67.
Page 172 Raymond, *Cairo*, p. 139.

CHAPTER EIGHT
Ottoman Egypt, 1517–1798

Page 175 Tietze, *Mustafa Ali's Description*, pp. 28, 29, and 30.
Page 176 Tietze, *Mustafa Ali's Description*, pp. 37 and 40.
Page 177 Salmon, *Ottoman Conquest*, pp. 45 and 111.
Page 184 Inalcik, *Ottoman Empire*, p. 10.

Page 189 al-Jabarti, *History of Egypt*, vol. 1, pp. 331–32.
Page 192 Winter, *Egyptian Society*, p. 225.
Page 193 al-Jabarti, *History of Egypt*, vol. 2, p. 9.

CHAPTER NINE
Napoleon Bonaparte, Muhammad Ali, and Ismail

Page 197 al-Jabarti, *Al-Jabarti's Chronicle*, p. 3.
Page 197 al-Jabarti, *Al-Jabarti's Chronicle*, p. 8.
Page 198 Burleigh, *Mirage*, pp. 41–42.
Page 199 al-Jabarti, *Al-Jabarti's Chronicle*, p. 26.
Page 199 al-Jabarti, *Al-Jabarti's Chronicle*, p. 32.
Page 199 al-Jabarti, *Al-Jabarti's Chronicle*, p. 31.
Page 200 al-Jabarti, *Al-Jabarti's Chronicle*, p. 37
Page 200 Herold, *Bonaparte in Egypt*, pp. 90–91.
Page 200 Herold, *Bonaparte in Egypt*, p. 100.
Page 202 al-Jabarti, *Al-Jabarti's Chronicle*, p. 84.
Page 202 al-Jabarti, *Al-Jabarti's Chronicle*, p. 90.
Page 202 al-Jabarti, *Al-Jabarti's Chronicle*, p. 93.
Page 207 Parkinson, *Breaking the Codes*, p. 35.
Page 222 Myntti, *Paris along the Nile*, title page.
Page 222 Farnie, *East and West*, p. 33.
Page 223 Farnie, *East and West*, p. 29.

CHAPTER TEN
The British Period, 1882–1952

Page 230 Owen, *Lord Cromer*, p. 215.
Page 230 Cromer, *Modern Egypt*, vol. 2, p. 130.
Page 231 Milner, *England in Egypt*, p. 24.
Page 234 Tignor, *Modernization*, p. 58
Page 237 Kamel, *Egyptiens et Anglais*, pp. 88 and 120.
Page 239 Tignor, "Maintaining the Empire," p. 182.
Page 240 Tignor, "Maintaining the Empire," p. 182.
Page 241 Elgood, *Egypt and the Army*, p. 241.
Page 253 Gershoni and Jankowski, *Egypt*, p. 61.

CHAPTER ELEVEN
Egypt for the Egyptians, 1952–1981

Page 264 Tignor, *Capitalism*, p. 106.
Page 267 Nutting, *No End*, p. 32.
Page 269 Tignor, *Capitalism*, p. 132.
Page 276 Sadat, *In Search*, p. 5.
Page 279 Kepel, *Muslim Extremism in Egypt*, p. 42.
Page 281 Kepel, *Muslim Extremism in Egypt*, p. 42.

CHAPTER TWELVE
Mubarak's Egypt

Pages 299–300 Mehrez, *Egypt's Culture Wars*, p. 20.
Page 303 Stewart, "Cities in the Desert," p. 462.
Page 304 *Egypt Today*, vol. 30 (January 2009).

BIBLIOGRAPHY

'Abd al-Rahman, 'Abd al-Rahim. *Al-Rif al-Misri fi-l-qarn al-Thamin Ashr*. Cairo, 1974.

Abd al-Rahman, Abd al-Rahim, and Wataru Miki. *The Village in Ottoman Egypt and Tokugawa Japan: A Comparative History*. Tokyo, 1977.

Abdel-Fadil, Mahmoud. *Development, Income Distribution, and Social Change in Rural Egypt (1952-1970): A Study in the Political Economy of Agrarian Transition*. Cambridge, 1975.

Abdel-Malek, Anouar. *Égypte: Société militaire*. Paris, 1962.

——. *Idéologie et renaissance nationale: L'Égypte moderne*. Paris, 1969.

Abdo, Genieve. *No God but God: Egypt and the Triumph of Islam*. Oxford, 2000.

Abduh, Muhammad. *Rissalat al-Tawhid*. Translated by Michel el Razik. Paris, 1925.

Abu-Lughod, Ibrahim. *Arab Rediscovery of Europe*. Princeton, 1963.

Aburish, Said K. *Nasser: The Last Arab*. New York, 2004.

Adams, Charles C. *Islam and Modernism in Egypt*. London, 1933.

Ades, Henry. *A Traveller's History of Egypt*. Northhampton, MA, 2007.

Aldred, Cyril. *Akhenaten: King of Egypt*. London, 1998.

Allen, James P. *The Ancient Egyptian Pyramid Texts*. Atlanta, 2005.

——. *Middle Egyptian: An Introduction to the Language and Culture of Hieroglyphs*. Cambridge, 1999.

Allouche, Adel. *Mamluk Economics: A Study and Translation of al-Maqrizi's Ighathah*. Salt Lake City, UT, 1994.

American University in Cairo. *AUC Today*. Cairo, 2008.

Anis, Muhammad. *'Arba'a Febrayar 1942 fi Ta'rikh Misr al-Siyasi*. Beirut, 1972.

——. *Dirasat fi Watha'iq Thawrah 1919*. Cairo, 1963.

——. *Thawra 23 Yulya 1952 wa Usuluha al-Ta'rikhiya*. Cairo, 1969.

'Aqqad, Abbas Mahmud al-. *Sa'd Zaghlul: Sirah wa Tahiyah*. Cairo, n.d.

Arberry, A. J. *The Koran Interpreted*. Oxford, 1980.

BIBLIOGRAPHY

Armbrust, Walter. *Mass Culture and Modernism in Egypt*. Cambridge, 1996.

Arnold, Dieter. *Building in Egypt: Pharaonic Stone Masonry*. Oxford, 1991.

Assmann, Jan. *Egyptian Solar Religion in the New Kingdom: Re, Amun and the Crisis of Polytheism*. Translated by Anthony Alcock. London, 1995.

———. *The Mind of Egypt: History and Meaning in the Time of the Pharaohs*. Translated by Andrew Jenkins. New York, 2002.

———. *Of God and Gods: Egypt, Israel, and the Rise of Monotheism*. Madison, WI, 2008.

Atiya, Aziz S. *A History of Eastern Christianity*. London, 1968.

Awadi, Hesham al-. *In Pursuit of Legitimacy: The Muslim Brothers and Mubarak, 1982–2000*. London, 2004.

Ayalon, David. *L'esclavage du Mamelouk*. Jerusalem, 1951.

———. *Gunpowder and Firearms in the Mamluk Kingdom*. London, 1956.

———. *Islam and the Abode of War: Military Slaves and Islamic Adversaries*. Aldershot, England, 1994.

Ayubi, Nazih N. M. *Bureaucracy and Politics in Contemporary Egypt*. London, 1980.

———. *The State and Public Policies in Egypt since Sadat*. Reading, England, 1991.

Badran, Margot. *Feminists, Islam and the Nation: Gender and the Making of Modern Egypt*. Princeton, 1995.

Baedeker, Karl. *Egypt and the Sudan: Handbook for Travellers*. Leipzig, 1929.

Baer, Gabriel. *Studies in the Social History of Modern Egypt*. Chicago, 1969.

Bagnall, Roger S. *Egypt in Late Antiquity*. Princeton, 1993.

———, editor. *Egypt in the Byzantine World, 300–700*. Cambridge, 2007.

———. *Later Roman Egypt: Society, Religion, Economy, and Administration*. Aldershot, England, 2003.

Bagnall, Roger S., and Bruce W. Frier. *The Demography of Roman Egypt*. Cambridge, 1990.

Baines, John, and Jaromir Malek. *Atlas of Ancient Egypt*. New York, 1980.

Baker, Raymond William. *Egypt's Uncertain Revolution under Nasser and Sadat*. Cambridge, 1978.

———. *Islam without Fear: Egypt and the New Islamists*. Cambridge, 2003.

———. *Sadat and After: Struggles for Egypt's Political Soul*. Cambridge, 1990.

Bakker, Egbert J., Irene J. F. deJong, and Hans van Wies, editors. *Brill's Companion to Herodotus*. London, 2002.

Baraka, Magda. *The Egyptian Upper Class between Revolutions, 1919–1952*. Reading, England, 1998.

Barakat, 'Ali Muhammad Muhammad. *Tatawwur al-Milkiya al-Zira'iya fi Misr wa-Atharuhu 'Ali al-Haraka al-Siyasiya, 1846–1914*. Cairo, 1973.

Barnes, Timothy D. *Athanasius and Constantius: Theology and Politics in the Constantinian Empire.* Cambridge, 1993.

Baron, Beth. *Egypt as a Woman: Nationalism, Gender, and Politics.* Berkeley, 2005.

———. *The Women Awakening in Egypt: Culture, Society, and the Press.* New Haven, 1994.

Battles, Matthew. *Library: An Unquiet History.* New York, 2003.

Beattie, Kirk J. *Egypt during the Nasser Years: Ideology, Politics, and Civil Society.* Boulder, CO, 1994.

Beckwith, Christopher I. *Empires of the Silk Road: A History of Central Eurasia from the Bronze Age to the Present.* Princeton, 2009.

Behrens-Abouseif, Doris. *Cairo of the Mamluks: A History of the Architecture and Its Culture.* London, 2007.

———. *Egypt's Adjustment to Ottoman Rule: Institutions, Waqfs, and Architecture in Cairo. 16th and 17th Centuries.* Leiden, 1994.

Beinen, Joel. *Was the Red Flag Flying There? Marxist Politics and the Arab-Israeli Conflict in Egypt and Israel, 1948-1965.* Berkeley, 1990.

Beinin, Joel, and Zachary Lockman. *Workers on the Nile: Nationalism, Communism, Islam, and the Egyptian Working Class, 1882-1954.* Princeton, 1987.

Bell, Barbara. "The Dark Ages in Ancient History, I, The First Dark Age in Egypt." *American Journal of Archaeology,* vol. 75, no. 1 (1971), pp. 1-26.

Berkey, Jonathan P. *The Formation of Islam: Religion and Society in the Near East, 600-1800.* Cambridge, 2003.

Bernal, Martin. *Black Athena: The Afroasiatic Roots of Classical Civilization.* Volume 1, *The Fabrication of Ancient Greece, 1785-1985.* London, 1987.

Berque, Jacques. *L'Égypte: Impérialisme et révolution.* Paris, 1967.

Bingen, Jean. *Hellenistic Egypt: Monarchy, Society, Economy, Culture.* Edinburgh, 2007.

al-Bishri, Tariq. *Al Dumuqratiya wa Nizam 23 Julya, 1952-70.* Beirut, 1970.

———. *Al-Haraka al-Siyasiya fi Misr, 1945-1952.* Cairo, 1972.

Borsch, Stuart J. *The Black Death in Egypt and England: A Comparative Study.* Austin, TX, 2005.

Bowman, Alan K. *Egypt after the Pharaohs: 332 BC-AD 642: From Alexander to the Arab Conquest.* London, 1986.

Bowman, Alan K., and Greg Woolf, editors. *Literacy and Power in the Ancient World.* Cambridge, 1994.

Bowman, Alan K., and Eugene Rogan, editors. *Agriculture in Egypt: From Pharaonic to Modern Times.* Oxford, 1999.

Brakke, David. *Athanasius and the Politics of Asceticism.* Oxford, 1995.

BIBLIOGRAPHY

Breasted, James Henry, editor and translator. *Ancient Records of Egypt: Historical Documents from the Earliest Times to the Persian Conquest.* Chicago, 1906.

———. *The Dawn of Conscience: The Sources of Our Moral Heritage in the Ancient World.* New York, 1933.

———. *A History of Egypt from the Earliest Times to the Persian Conquest.* New York, 1950.

Brett, Michael. *The Rise of the Fatimids: The World of the Mediterranean and the Middle East in the Fourth Century of the Hijra, Tenth Century CE.* Leiden, 2001.

Brewer, Douglas J., Donald B. Redford, and Susan Redford. *Domestic Plants and Animals: The Egyptian Origins.* Warminster, England, 1994.

Brown, Nathan J. *Peasant Politics in Modern Egypt: The Struggle against the State.* New Haven, 1990.

Brown, Peter. *The Making of Late Antiquity.* Cambridge, 1978.

———. *The Rise of Western Christendom: Triumph and Diversity, AD 200-1000.* Oxford, 2003.

———. *The World of Late Antiquity: From Marcus Aurelius to Muhammad.* London, 1971.

Bulliett, Richard W. *The Camel and the Wheel.* Cambridge, 1975.

———. *Conversion to Islam in the Medieval Period: An Essay in Quantitative History.* Cambridge, 1979.

Bunson, Margaret. *A Dictionary of Ancient Egypt.* New York, 1991.

Burckhardt, John Lewis. *Travels in Nubia.* London, 1819.

Burkert, Walter. *The Orientalizing Revolution: Near Eastern Influence on Greek Culture in the Early Archaic Age.* Translated by Margaret E. Pinder and Walter Burkert. Cambridge, 1992.

Burleigh, Nina. *Mirage: Napoleon's Scientists and the Unveiling of Egypt.* New York, 2007.

Burns, William J. *Economic Aid and American Policy Toward Egypt, 1955-1981.* Albany, NY, 1985.

Butler, Alfred J. *The Arab Conquest of Egypt and the Last Thirty Years of the Roman Dominion.* Oxford, 1978.

Butzer, Karl W. *Early Hydraulic Civilization in Egypt: A Study in Cultural Ecology.* Chicago, 1976.

Cabrol, Agnes. *Amenhotep III: Le magnifique.* Paris, 2000.

Cameron, Averil. *The Mediterranean World in Late Antiquity, AD 395-600.* London, 1993.

Capponi, Livia. *Augustan Egypt: The Creation of a Roman Province.* New York, 2005.

Cartledge, Paul. *Alexander the Great: The Hunt for a New Past.* Woodstock, NY, 2004.

Chuvin, Pierre. *A Chronicle of the Last Pagans*. Translated by B. S. Archer. Cambridge, MA, 1990.

Clive, Eric H., and David O'Connor, editors. *Thutmose III: A New Biography*. Ann Arbor, 2006.

Clot Bey, A. B. *Aperçu général sur l'Égypte*. Paris, 1840.

Cole, Juan. *Colonialism and Revolution in the Middle East: Social and Cultural Origins of Egypt under Urabi's Movement*. Princeton, 1992.

——. *Napoleon's Egypt: Invading the Middle East*. New York, 2007.

Colla, Elliott. *Conflicted Antiquities: Egyptology, Egyptomania, Egyptian Modernity*. Durham, NC, 2002.

Collins, Robert O. *The Nile*. New Haven, 2002.

Colombe, Marcel. *L'évolution de l'Égypte, 1924-50*. Paris, 1951.

Cook, Michael. *Early Muslim Dogma: A Source-Critical Study*. Cambridge, 1981.

——. *The Koran: A Very Short Introduction*. Oxford, 2000.

——. *Muhammad*. Oxford, 1983.

——. "Pharaonic History in Medieval Egypt." *Studia Islamica*, no. 57 (1983), pp. 67-103.

Cortese, Deha, and Simonetta Calderini. *Women and the Fatimids in the World of Islam*. Edinburgh, 2006.

Crecelius, Daniel. *The Roots of Modern Egypt: A Study of the Regimes of Ali Bey al-Kabir and Muhammad Bey Abu al-Dahab, 1760-1775*. Chicago, 1981.

Creswell, K. A. *A Short Account of Early Muslim Architecture*. Harmondsworth, England, 1958.

Cromer, Evelyn Baring, Earl of. *Abbas II*. London, 1915.

——. *Ancient and Modern Imperialism*. New York, 1910.

——. *Modern Egypt*. New York, 1908. 2 volumes.

Crone, Patricia. *God's Rule: Government and Islam*. New York, 2004.

Crone, Patricia, and Michael Cook. *Hagarism: The Making of the Islamic World*. Cambridge, 1977.

Crone, Patricia, and Martin Hinds. *God's Caliph: Religious Authority in the First Centuries of Islam*. Cambridge, 1986.

Crouchley, A. E. *The Economic Development of Modern Egypt*. New York, 1938.

——. *The Investment of Foreign Capital in Egyptian Companies and Public Debt*. New York, 1977.

Cuno, Kenneth. *The Pasha's Peasants: Land, Society, and Economy in Lower Egypt, 1740-1855*. Cambridge, 1992.

Daftary, Farhad. *The Ismailis: Their History and Doctrines*. Cambridge, 1990.

BIBLIOGRAPHY

——. *A Short History of the Ismailis: Traditions of a Muslim Community.* Princeton, 1998.

Daly, M. W., editor. *The Cambridge History of Egypt.* Volume 2, *Modern Egypt from 1517 to the End of the Twentieth Century.* Cambridge, 1998.

Daly, Okasha El. *Egyptology: The Missing Millennium: Ancient Egypt in the Medieval Arabic Writings.* London, 2005.

Al-Damadurdashi's Chronicle of Egypt, 1688-1755. Translated and annotated by Daniel Crecelius and Abd al-Wahhab Bakr. Leiden, 1991.

Darnell, John Coleman, F. W. Dobbs-Allsopp, Marilyn J. Lundberg, P. Kyle McCarter, and Bruce Zuckerman, with the assistance of Colleen Manassa. "Two Early Alphabetic Inscriptions from Wadi el-Hol: New Evidence for the Origins of the Alphabet from the Western Desert of Egypt." *Annual of the American Schools of Oriental Research,* vol. 59 (2005), pp. 63, 65, 67-71, 73-111, 113.

David, Rosalie. *Ancient Egyptians: Beliefs and Practices.* Brighton, England, 1998.

Davis, Eric. *Challenging Colonialism: Bank Misr and Egyptian Industrialization, 1920-1941.* Princeton, 1983.

Deeb, Marius. *Party Politics in Egypt: The Wafd and Its Rivals, 1919-1939.* London, 1979.

Dennett, Daniel. *Conversion and the Poll Tax in Early Islam.* Cambridge, 1950.

Derda, Tomasz. *Administration of the Fayum under Roman Rule.* Warsaw, 2006.

Derda, Tomasz, Tomasz Markiewicz, and Ewa Wipszycka. *Alexandria: Auditoria of Kom el-Dikka and Late Antique Education.* Warsaw, 2007.

Di-Capua, Yoav. *Gatekeepers of the Arab Past: Historians and History Writing in Twentieth-Century Egypt.* Los Angeles, 2009.

Diop, Cheikh Anta. *The African Origin of Civilization: Myth or Reality.* Edited and translated by Mercer Cook. New York, 1974.

Disuqi, 'Asim Ahmad. *Kibar Milak al-'Aradi al-Zara'iya.* Cairo, 1975.

Dodwell, Henry. *The Founder of Modern Egypt.* Cambridge, 1931.

Dols, Michael. *The Black Death in the Middle East.* Princeton, 1977.

Donaldson, Dwight M. *The Shiite Religion.* London, 1933.

Donner, Fred McGraw. *The Early Islamic Conquests.* Princeton, 1981.

Doxiadis, Euphrosyne. *The Mysterious Fayum Portraits: Faces from Ancient Egypt.* London, 1995.

Dunand, Françoise, and Christiane Zivie-Coche. *Gods and Men in Egypt, 3000 BCE to 395 CE.* Translated by David Lorton. Ithaca, NY, 2002.

Dunn, John P. *Khedive Ismail's Army.* London, 2005.

Economist Intelligence Unit. *Country Report* and *Country Profile.* London, 2008.

Efendi, Huseyn. *Ottoman Egypt in the Age of the French Revolution*. Translated by Stanford J. Shaw. Cambridge, 1964.

Egberts, A., B. P. Muhs, and J. Van Der Vliet, editors. *Perspectives on Panopolis: An Egyptian Town from Alexander the Great to the Arab Conquest*. Leiden, 2002.

Ehrenberg, Margaret. *Women in Prehistory*. London, 1989.

El Shakry, Omnia. *The Great Social Laboratory: Subjects of Knowledge in Colonial and Postcolonial Egypt*. Stanford, 2007.

Elgood, P. G. *Egypt and the Army*. Oxford, 1924.

Erlich, Haggai. *Students and University in Twentieth-Century Egyptian Politics*. London, 1989.

Fahmy, Khaled. *All the Pasha's Men: Mehmed Ali, His Army, and the Making of Modern Egypt*. Cambridge, 1997.

———. *Mehmed Ali: From Ottoman Governor to Ruler of Egypt*. Oxford, 2009.

Farnie, D. A. *East and West of Suez: The Suez Canal in History, 1854–1956*. Oxford, 1969.

Finkel, Caroline. *Osman's Dream: The History of the Ottoman Empire*. New York, 2005.

Fluck, Cecilia, and Gisella Helmeche, editors. *Textile Messages: Inscribed Fabrics from Roman to Abbasid Egypt*. Leiden, 2006.

Frankfort, Henri. *Ancient Egyptian Religion: An Interpretation*. New York, 1948.

Frankfurter, David. *Religion in Roman Egypt: Assimilation and Resistance*. Princeton, 1998.

Freed, Rita E., editor. *Ramses II: The Great Pharaoh and His Time*. Denver, 1987.

Freed, Rita E., Yvonne J. Markowitz, and Sue H. D'Auria. *Pharaohs of the Sun: Akhenaten, Nefertiti, Tutankhamen*. Boston, 1999.

Gaffney, Patrick D. *The Prophet's Pulpit: Islamic Preaching in Contemporary Egypt*. Berkeley, 1994.

Gardiner, Alan. *Egypt of the Pharaohs: An Introduction*. London, 1961.

Gershoni, Israel, and James P. Jankowski. *Egypt, Islam, and the Arabs: The Search for Egyptian Nationhood, 1900–1930*. New York, 1986.

———. *Redefining the Egyptian Nation, 1930–1945*. Cambridge, 1995.

Gibb, Hamilton A. R. *Saladin: Studies in Islamic History*. Edited by Yusuf Ibish. Beirut, 1974.

Gillispie, Charles Coulston, and Michel Dewachter, editors. *Monuments of Egypt: The Napoleonic Edition*. Princeton, 1987.

Gilsenan, Michael. *Saint and Sufi in Modern Egypt: An Essay in the Sociology of Religion*. Oxford, 1973.

Godolphin, Francis R. B., editor. *The Greek Historians: The Complete and Unabridged Works of Herodotus*. Translated by George Rawlinson. New York, 1942.

Goedicke, Hans, editor. *Perspectives on the Battle of Kadesh*. Baltimore, 1985.

Goehring, James E. *Ascetics, Society, and the Desert: Studies in Early Egyptian Monasticism*. Harrisburg, PA, 1999.

Goitein, S. D. *Letters of Medieval Jewish Traders*. Translated by S. D. Goitein. Princeton, 1973.

——. *A Mediterranean Society: An Abridgement in One Volume*. Revised and edited by Jacob Lassner. Berkeley, 1999.

Goldberg, Ellis. *Tinker, Tailor, and Textile Worker: Class and Politics in Egypt, 1930-1952*. Los Angeles, 1986.

——. *Trade, Reputation, and Child Labor in Twentieth-Century Egypt*. New York, 2004.

Goldschmidt, Arthur, Jr. *A Brief History of Egypt*. New York, 2007.

Goldschmidt, Arthur, Jr., Amy J. Johnson, and Barak A. Salmoni, editors. *Re-envisioning Egypt, 1919-1952*. Cairo, 2005.

Goodman, Martin, with the assistance of Jane Sherwood. *The Roman World: 44 BC-AD 180*. London, 1997.

Gordon, Joel. *Nasser's Blessed Movement: Egypt's Free Officers and the July Revolution*. New York, 1992.

——. *Revolutionary Melodrama: Popular Film and Civic Identity in Nasser's Egypt*. Chicago, 2002.

Grajetzki, Wolfram. *The Middle Kingdom of Ancient Egypt*. London, 2006.

Gran, Peter. *Islamic Roots of Capitalism, 1760-1840*. Austin, TX, 1979.

Green, Peter. *Alexander of Macedon, 356-323 BC: A Historical Biography*. Harmondsworth, England, 1974.

——. *Alexander to Actium: The Hellenistic Age*. London, 1990.

Griggs, C. Wilfred. *Early Egyptian Christianity: From Its Origins to 451 CE*. Leiden, 1993.

Grimal, Nicolas. *A History of Ancient Egypt*. Translated by Ian Shaw. Oxford, 1994.

Gritly, A.A.I. El-. "The Structure of Modern Industry in Egypt." *L'Égypte contemporaine*, nos. 241-42. Cairo, 1947.

Haas, Christopher. *Alexandria in Late Antiquity: Topography and Social Conflict*. Baltimore, 1997.

Hahn, Peter L. *The United States, Great Britain, and Egypt, 1945-1956: Strategy and Diplomacy in the Early Cold War*. Chapel Hill, NC, 1991.

Hansen, Bent. *The Political Economy of Poverty, Equity, and Growth: Egypt and Turkey*. Oxford, 1991.

Halm, Heinz. *The Empire of the Mahdi: The Rise of the Fatimids*. Translated by Michael Bonner. Leiden, 1996.

——. *The Fatimids and Their Traditions of Learning*. London, 1997.

Hamdan, Gamal. *Collected Works*. Part 1, *Studies on Egypt*. Edited by Saleh Hamdan. Guizeh, Egypt, 2000.

Hanna, Nelly. *Construction Work in Ottoman Cairo*. Cairo, 1984.

——. *In Praise of Books: A Cultural History of Cairo's Middle Class, Sixteenth to the Eighteenth Century*. Syracuse, NY, 2003.

——. *Making Big Money in 1600: The Life and Times of Ismail Abu Taqiyya, Egyptian Merchant*. Syracuse, NY, 1998.

Hanna, Nelly, and Raouf Abbas, editors. *Society and Economy in Egypt and the Eastern Mediterranean, 1600-1900: Essays in Honor of André Raymond*. Cairo, 2005.

Harik, Iliya F. *Economic Policy Reform in Egypt*. Gainesville, FL, 1997.

Harris, J. R. editor. *The Legacy of Egypt*. Oxford, 1971.

Hartog, François. *The Mirror of Herodotus: The Representation of the Other in the Writing of History*. Berkeley, 1988.

Hathaway, Jane. *The Politics of Households in Ottoman Egypt*. Cambridge, 1997.

——. *A Tale of Two Factions: Myth, Memory, and Identity in Ottoman Egypt and Yemen*. Albany, NY, 2003.

Hathaway, Jane, and Karl K. Barbir. *The Arab Lands under Ottoman Rule, 1516-1800*. London, 2008.

Hawtung, G. R. *The First Dynasty of Islam: The Umayyad Caliphate, AD 661-750*. London, 2000.

Healey, John F. *Reading the Past: The Early Alphabet*. London, 1990.

Heeren, A.H.L. *Reflections on the Politics, Intercourse, and Trade of the Ancient Nations of Africa*. Translated by David A. Talboys. Oxford, 1832.

Heikal, Mohammed. *Autumn of Fury: The Assassination of Sadat*. New York, 1983.

Herold, J. Christopher. *Bonaparte in Egypt*. London, 1963.

Heyworth-Dunne, James. *An Introduction to the History of Education in Modern Egypt*. London, 1968.

Hinnebusch, Raymond A., Jr. *Egyptian Politics under Sadat: The Post-populist Development of an Authoritarian-Modernizing State*. London, 1988.

Hitti, Philip. *The Arabs: A Short History*. Chicago, 1985.

Hodges, Richard, and David Whitehouse. *Mohammed, Charlemagne, and the Origins of Europe*. Ithaca, NY, 1983.

Hodgson, Marshall G. S. *The Order of the Assassins*. The Hague, 1955.

——. *The Venture of Islam: Conscience and History in a World Civilization*. Chicago, 1974. 3 volumes.

Hoebl, Gunther. *A History of the Ptolemaic Empire*. Translated by Tina Saavedra. London, 2001.

Hoffman, Michael A. *Egypt before the Pharaohs: The Prehistoric Foundations of Egyptian Civilization*. Austin, TX, 1991.

Holt, P. M. *The Age of the Crusades: The Near East from the Eleventh Century to 1517*. London, 1984.

——. *Egypt and the Fertile Crescent, 1516–1922*. London, 1966.

Hopkins, Keith. *A World Full of Gods: The Strange Triumph of Christianity*. New York, 2000.

Hornung, Erik. *Akhenaten and the Religion of Light*. Translated by David Lorton. Ithaca, NY, 1995.

——. *Conceptions of God in Ancient Egypt: The One and the Many*. Translated by John Baines. Leiden, 1982.

Hourani, Albert. *Arabic Thought in the Liberal Age, 1798–1939*. New York, 1962.

——. *A History of the Arab Peoples*. New York, 1991.

Hunter, Archie. *Power and Passion in Egypt: A Life of Sir Eldon Gorst, 1861–1911*. London, 2007.

Hunter, F. Robert. *Egypt under the Khedives: From Household Government to Modern Bureaucracy*. Pittsburgh, 1984.

Hurst, H. E. *The Nile: A General Account of the River and the Utilization of Its Waters*. London, 1952.

Ikram, Khalid. *The Egyptian Economy, 1952–2000: Performance, Policies, and Issues*. London, 2006.

Inalcık, Halil. *The Ottoman Empire: The Classical Age, 1300–1600*. Translated by Norman Itzkowitz and Colin Imber. New York, 1973.

Irwin, Robert. *The Middle East in the Middle Ages: The Early Mamluk Sultanate, 1250–1382*. London, 1986.

Issawi, Charles. *Egypt at Mid-Century*. New York, 1954.

——. *Egypt in Revolution*. New York, 1963.

Ivanow, W. *A Brief Survey of the Evolution of Ismailism*. London, 1952.

——. *The Rise of the Fatimids*. London, 1942.

Jabarti, Abd al Rahman al-. *Al-Jabarti's Chronicle of the First Seven Months of the French Occupation of Egypt (Tarikh Muddat al-Faransis bi Misr)*. Translated and edited by S. Moreh. Leiden, 1975.

——. *History of Egypt*. Edited by Thomas Philipp and Moshe Perlman. Stuttgart, 1994. 5 volumes.

Jankowski, James. *Egypt: A Short History*. Oxford, 2000.

Jiritli, 'Ali al-. *Khamsa wa Ashrun Amman: Dirasu Tahliliya lil-Siyasat al-Iqtisadiya fi Misr, 1952–1977*. Cairo, 1977.

Jong, Frederick de. *Sufi Orders in Ottoman and Post-Ottoman Egypt and the Middle East*. Istanbul, 2000.

——. *Turuq and Turuq-Linked Institutions in Nineteenth Century Egypt: A Historical Study in Organizational Dimensions of Islamic Mysticism.* Leiden, 1978.

Jong, Frederick de, and Bernd Radtke, editors. *Islamic Mysticism Contested: Thirteen Centuries of Controversies and Polemics.* Leiden, 1999.

Joseph, George Cheverghese. *The Crest of the Peacock: Non-European Roots of Mathematics.* London, 1991.

Kamel, Mustafa. *Égyptiens et Anglais.* Paris, 1906.

Karabell, Zachary *Parting the Desert: The Creation of the Suez Canal.* New York, 2003.

Keddie, Nikki R. *Scholars, Saints, and Sufis: Muslim Religious Institutions in the Middle East since 1500.* Berkeley, 1972.

Kedourie, Elie. *The Chatham House Version and Other Middle Eastern Studies.* London, 1970.

Kemp, Barry J. *Ancient Egypt: Anatomy of a Civilization.* London, 1989.

Kennedy, Hugh. *The Armies of the Caliphs: Military and Society in the Early Islamic State.* London, 2001.

——. *The Prophet and the Age of the Caliphates: The Islamic Near East from the Sixth to the Eleventh Century.* London, 2004.

Kepel, Gilles. *Muslim Extremism in Egypt: The Prophet and Pharaoh.* Berkeley, 1984.

Kerr, Malcolm H. *The Arab Cold War: Gamal abdal-Nasr and His Rivals, 1958-1970.* London, 1971.

Kienle, Eberhard. *A Grand Delusion: Democracy and Economic Reform in Egypt.* London, 2001.

Killearn, Miles Lampson, Baron. *Politics and Diplomacy in Egypt: The Diaries of Sir Miles Lampson, 1935-1937.* Edited by M. E. Yapp. Oxford, 1997.

King, Joan Wucher. *Historical Dictionary of Egypt.* London, 1984.

Kitchen, K. A. *Pharaoh Triumphant: The Life and Times of Ramses II.* Cairo, 1990.

Korayem, Karima. "Toshka Potential for Employment and Income Generation." Cairo, 2003. Unpublished paper kindly lent by the author.

Krawiec, Rebecca. *Shenoute and the Women of the White Monastery: Egyptian Monasticism in Late Antiquity.* Oxford, 2002.

Kuhrt, Amélie. *The Ancient Near East, c. 3000-330 BC.* New York, 1995.

Kunz, Diane B. *The Economy Diplomacy of the Suez Crisis.* Chapel Hill, NC, 1991.

Kyle, Keith. *Suez.* London, 1991.

Lacouture, Jean, and Simone Lacouture. *Egypt in Transition.* New York, 1958.

Laissus, Yves. *L'Égypte: Une aventure savante, 1798-1801.* Paris, 1998.

337

BIBLIOGRAPHY

Landau, Jacob M. *Parliaments and Parties in Egypt*. Tel Aviv, 1953.

Lane, Edward W. *The Manners and Customs of the Modern Egyptians*. London, 1842.

Lapidus, Ira M. *A History of Islamic Societies*. Cambridge, 2002.

——, editor. *Middle Eastern Cities: A Symposium on Ancient, Islamic, and Contemporary Urbanism*. Berkeley, 1969.

Lashin, Abd al-Khaliq Muhammad. *Sa'd Zaghlul*. Cairo, 1970.

Laurens, Henry. *L'expédition d'Égypte, 1798-1801*. Paris, 1989.

Lefkowitz, Mary R., and Gary MacLean Rogers, editors. *Black Athena Revisited*. Chapel Hill, NC, 1996.

Lehner, Mark. *The Complete Pyramids*. Cairo, 1997.

Lellouch, Benjamin. *Les Ottomans en Égypte: Historiens et conquérants au XVIe Siècle*. Paris, 2006.

Lerner, Gerda. *The Creation of Patriarchy*. New York, 1986.

Lev, Yaacov. *Saladin in Egypt*. Leiden, 1999.

——. *State and Society in Fatimid Egypt*. Leiden, 1991.

Levanoni, Amalia. *A Turning Point in Mamluk History: The Reign of al-Nasir Muhammad Ibn Qalawun, 1310-1341*. Leiden, 1995.

Lewis, Bernard, compiler. *Islam from the Prophet Muhammad to the Capture of Constantinople*. New York, 1974. 2 volumes.

——. *The Middle East: Two Thousand Years of History from the Rise of Christianity to the Present Day*. London, 1995.

——. *The Origins of Ismailism*. Cambridge, 1940.

Lewis, Naphtali. *Life in Egypt under Roman Rule*. Oxford, 1983.

Lloyd, Alan B. *Herodotus: Book II, Introduction*. Leiden, 1975.

Lloyd, George Ambrose. *Egypt since Cromer*. London, 1933. 2 volumes.

Lloyd, Selwyn. *Suez 1956: A Personal Account*. London, 1978.

Loprieno, Antonio. *Ancient Egyptian: A Linguistic Introduction*. Cambridge, 1995.

Lowry, Heath W. *The Nature of the Early Ottoman State*. Albany, NY, 2003.

Lowry, Joseph E. *Early Islamic Legal Theory: The Risala of Muhammad ibn Idris al-Shafi'i*. Leiden, 2007.

Lyons, Malcolm Cameron, and D.E.P. Jackson. *Saladin: The Politics of the Holy War*. Cambridge, 1982.

Mabro, Robert, and Samir Radwan. *The Industrialization of Egypt, 1939-1973: Policy and Performance*. Oxford, 1976.

MacCoull, Leslie S. B. *Dioscorus of Aphrodito: His Work and his World*. Berkeley, 1988.

Macleod, Arlene Elowe. *Accommodating Protest: Working Women, the New Veiling, and Change in Cairo*. New York, 1991.

Madelung, Wilfred. *The Succession to Muhammad: A Study of the Early Caliphate*. Cambridge, 1997.

Maisels, Charles Keith. *Early Civilization of the Old World: The Formative Histories of Egypt, the Levant, Mesopotamia, India, and China.* London, 1999.

Manning, Joseph G. *Land and Power in Ptolemaic Egypt: The Structure of Land Tenure.* Cambridge, 2003.

Manning, Joseph G., and Ian Morris, editors. *The Ancient Economy: Evidence and Models.* Stanford, 2005.

Mayer, Josephine, and Tom Prideaux. *Never to Die: The Egyptians in Their Own Words.* New York, 1938.

McCarthy, Justin. *The Ottoman Turks: An Introductory History to 1923.* New York, 1997.

Mehrez, Samia. *Egypt's Culture Wars: Politics and Practice.* New York, 2008.

Melchert, Christopher. *The Formation of the Sunni Schools of Law: Ninth and Tenth Centuries, CE.* London, 1997.

Meskell, Lynn. *Archaeologies of Social Life: Age, Sex, Class, et cetera in Ancient Egypt.* Oxford, 1999.

———. *Private Life in New Kingdom Egypt.* Princeton, 2002.

Milner, Alfred, Viscount. *England in Egypt.* London, 1892.

Mitchell, Richard P. *The Society of the Muslim Brothers.* London, 1969.

Mitchell, Timothy. *Colonising Egypt.* Cambridge, 1988.

Montserrat, Dominic. *Sex and Society in Graeco-Roman Egypt.* London, 1996.

Morimoto, Kosei. *The Fiscal Administration of Egypt in the Early Islamic Period.* Dohosha, Japan, 1981.

Mostyn, Trevor. *Egypt's Belle Epoque: Cairo, 1869-1952.* London, 1989.

Myntti, Cynthia. *Paris along the Nile: Architecture from the Belle Epoque.* Cairo, 1999.

The Nag Hammadi Library in English. Translated by members of the Coptic Library Project of the Institute for Antiquity and Christianity. New York, 1977.

Nasser, Gamal Abdel. *Egypt's Liberation.* Washington, DC, 1955.

Nasir, Jamal Abd al-. *Mudakirat 'Abd al-Nasir an Harb Falastin.* Cairo, 1978.

Newby, P. H. *Saladin in His Time.* London, 1983.

Northrup, Linda. *From Slave to Sultan: The Career of al-Mansur Qalawun and the Consolidation of Mamluk Rule in Egypt and Syria (678–689 A.H./1279-1290 A.D.)* Stuttgart, 1998.

Nutting, Anthony. *No End of a Lesson: The Story of Suez.* London, 1967.

O'Connor, David, and Eric H. Cline, editors. *Amenhotep III: Perspectives on His Reign.* Ann Arbor, 2001.

———, editors. *Thutmose III: A New Biography.* Ann Arbor, 2006.

BIBLIOGRAPHY

Oren, Michael B. *Six Days of War: June 1967 and the Making of the Modern Middle East*. Oxford, 2002.

Oweidat, Nadia, Cheryl Bernard, Dale Stahl, Walid Kildani, Edward O'Connell, and Audrak Grant. *The Kefaya Movement: A Case Study of a Grassroots Reform Initiative*. Santa Monica, CA, 2008.

Owen, Roger. *Cotton and the Egyptian Economy, 1820-1914*. Oxford, 1969.

———. *Lord Cromer: Victorian Imperialist, Edwardian Proconsul*. Oxford, 2004.

———. *The Middle East in the World Economy, 1800-1914*. London, 1981.

Pagels, Elaine. *Blind Faith: The Secret Gospel of Thomas*. New York, 2003.

———. *The Gnostic Gospels*. New York, 1979.

Parkinson, R. B. *Breaking the Codes: The Rosetta Stone and Decipherment*. London, 1999.

———. *The Tale of Sinuhe and Other Ancient Egyptian Poems, 1940-1640 BC*. Oxford, 1997.

———. *Voices from Ancient Egypt: An Anthology of Middle Kingdom Writings*. London, 1991.

Pearson, Birger A. *Gnosticism and Christianity in Roman Coptic Egypt*. New York, 2004.

Peters, Francis E. *The Harvest of Hellenism: A History of the Near East from Alexander the Great to the Triumph of Christianity*. London, 1972.

———. *Muhammad and the Origins of Islam*. Albany, NY, 1994.

Petry, Carl F., editor. *The Cambridge History of Egypt, 640-1517*. Cambridge, 1998.

———. *The Civilian Elite of Cairo in the Late Middle Ages*. Princeton, 1981.

———. *Protectors or Praetorians? The Last Mamluk Sultans and Egypt's Waning as a Great Power*. Albany, NY, 1994.

———. *Twilight of Majesty: The Rise of the Mamluk Sultans al-Ashraf Qatbay and Qansuh al-Ghawri in Egypt*. Seattle, 1993.

Philipp, Thomas, and Ulrich Haarmann, editors. *The Mamluks in Egyptian Politics and Society*. Cambridge, 1998.

Piquet, Caroline. *La compagnie du canal de Suez: Une concession française en Égypte. 1888-1956*. Paris, 2008.

Poliak, A. N. *Feudalism in Egypt, Syria, Palestine, and Lebanon*. London, 1939.

Pollard, Lisa. *Nurturing the Nation: The Family Politics of Modernizing, Colonizing, and Liberating Egypt, 1805-1923*. Berkeley, 2005.

Pomeroy, Sarah B. *Women in Hellenistic Egypt: From Alexander to Cleopatra*. Detroit, 1990.

Popper, William. *Egypt and Syria under the Circassian Sultans, 1382-1468, Systematic Notes to Ibn Taghri Birdi's Chronicles of Egypt*. Berkeley, 1955-57. 2 volumes.

Potter, David S. *The Roman Empire at Bay, AD 180–395*. London, 2001.

Powell, Eve M. Troutt. *A Different Shade of Colonialism: Egypt, Great Britain, and the Mastery of the Sudan*. London, 2003.

Pritchard, James B., editor. *The Ancient Near East: Anthology of Texts and Pictures*. Princeton, 1973. 2 volumes.

Quirke, Stephen. *The Cult of Ra: Sun Worship in Ancient Egypt*. London, 2001.

Qutb, Sayyid. *Milestones*. New Delhi, 2005.

Raafat, Samir W. *Cairo, the Glory Years: Who Built What, When, and for Whom . . . .* Alexandria, 2003.

Rachida, Besrour. *Études en histoire social Égyptienne sous les Mamelouks*. Tunis, 2006.

Ramadan, Abd al-Azim. *al-Sara al-Ijtimai wa-l Siyasi fi Misr*. Cairo, 1975.

Rathbone, Dominic. *Economic Rationalism and Rural Society in Third Century AD Egypt: The Heroninos Archive and Appianus Estate*. Cambridge, 1991.

Raymond, André. *Artisans et commerçants au Caire au XVIIIe siècle*. Damascus, 1973–74. 2 volumes.

——. *Caire des janissaires: L'apogée de la ville Ottoman sous Abd al-Rahman Katkhuda*. Paris, 1995.

——. *Cairo*. Translated by Willard Wood. Cambridge, 2000.

Redford, Donald B. *Akhenaten: The Heretic King*. Princeton, 1984.

——. *Egypt, Canaan, and Israel in Ancient Times*. Princeton, 1992.

——. *The Oxford Encyclopedia of Ancient Egypt*. Oxford, 2005.

Reid, Donald M. *Whose Pharaohs? Archaeology, Museums, and Egyptian National Identity from Napoleon to World War I*. Berkeley, 2002.

Reeves, Nicholas. *Egypt's False Prophet: Akhenaten*. London, 2001.

Rice, Michael. *Egypt's Legacy: The Archetypes of Western Civilization, 3000–300 BC*. London, 1997.

——. *Egypt's Making: The Origins of Ancient Egypt, 5000–2000 BC*. London, 1990.

Richmond, J.C.B. *Egypt, 1798–1952*. New York, 1977.

Rifaat, Mohammed. *The Awakening of Modern Egypt*. New York, 1947.

Rivlin, Helen Anne B. *The Agricultural Policy of Muhammad Ali in Egypt*. Cambridge, 1961.

Robins, Gay. *The Art of Ancient Egypt*. Cambridge, 1997.

——. *Women in Ancient Egypt*. London, 1993.

Robinson, Francis, editor. *The Cambridge Illustrated History of the Islamic World*. Cambridge, 1996.

Robinson, Ronald, and John Gallagher. *Africa and the Victorians: The Climax of Imperialism*. Garden City, NY, 1961.

Robinson, Warren C., and Fatmah H. El-Zanaty. *The Demographic Revolution in Modern Egypt*. Lanham, MD, 2006.

Roehrig, Catherine H., editor. *Hatshepsut: From Queen to Pharaoh*. New York, 2005.

Romer, John. *Ancient Lives: The Story of the Pharaoh's Tombmakers*. London, 1984.

———. *The Great Pyramid: Ancient Egypt Revisited*. Cambridge, 2008.

———. *People of the Nile: Everyday Life in Ancient Egypt*. New York, 1982.

Rousseau, Philip. *Ascetics, Authority, and the Church in the Age of Jerome and Cassian*. Oxford, 1978.

———. *Pachomius: The Making of a Community in Fourth-Century Egypt*. Berkeley, 1985.

Rowlandson, Jane. *Landowners and Tenants in Roman Egypt: The Social Relations of Agriculture in the Oxyrhynchite Nome*. Oxford, 1990.

Sadat, Anwar al-. *In Search of Identity: An Autobiography*. New York, 1978.

———. *Revolt on the Nile*. London, 1957.

———. *Waraqa Uktubir*. Cairo, 1974.

Sagiv, David. *Fundamentalism and Intellectuals in Egypt, 1973-1993*. London, 1995.

Said, Rushdi. *The River Nile: Geology, Hydrology, and Utilization*. Oxford, 1993.

Salmon, W. H. *An Account of the Ottoman Conquest of Egypt in the Year A.H. 932 (A.D. 1516)*, translated from the third volume of the Arabic Chronicle of Muhammad Ahmed Ibn Ayas, an Eyewitness to the Scenes he Describes. London, 1921.

Sanders, Paula. *Creating Medieval Cairo: Empire, Religion, and Architectural Preservation in Nineteenth-Century Cairo*. Cairo, 2008.

Sasson, Jack M., editor-in-chief. *Civilizations of the Ancient Near East*. Volume 2. New York, 1995.

Saunders, J. J. *A History of Medieval Islam*. London, 1965.

Sayyid-Marsot, Afaf Lutfi. *Egypt and Cromer: A Study in Anglo-Egyptian Relations*. New York, 1966.

———. *Egypt in the Reign of Muhammad Ali*. Cambridge, 1984.

———. *Egypt's Liberal Experiment, 1922-1936*. Berkeley, 1977.

———. *A History of Egypt from the Arab Conquest to the Present*. Cambridge, 2008.

———. *Short History of Modern Egypt*. Cambridge, 1985.

———. *Women and Men in Late Eighteenth-Century Egypt*. Austin, TX, 1995.

Schacht, Joseph. *An Introduction to Islamic Law*. Oxford, 1964.

———. *The Origins of Mohammedan Jurisprudence*. Oxford, 1960.

Scholch, Alexander. *Egypt for the Egyptians! The Socio-Political Crisis in Egypt, 1878-82*. London, 1981.

Schroeder, Caroline T. *Monastic Bodies: Discipline and Salvation in Shenoute of Atripe*. Philadelphia, 2007.

Schroeder, Eric. *Muhammad's People: A Tale by Anthology*. Portland, ME, 1965.

Sharkey, Heather J. *American Evangelicals in Egypt: Missionary Encounters in an Age of Empire*. Princeton, 2008.

Shaw, Ian. *Ancient Egypt: A Very Short Introduction*. Oxford, 2004.

———, editor. *The Oxford History of Ancient Egypt*. Oxford, 2000.

Shaw, Ian, and Paul Nicholson. *The British Museum Dictionary of Ancient Egypt*. London, 2002.

Shaw, Stanford. *The Budget of Ottoman Egypt, 1005–1006/1596–1597*. The Hague, 1968.

———. *The Financial and Administrative Organization and Development of Ottoman Egypt, 1517–1798*. Princeton, 1962.

———. *Ottoman Egypt in the Eighteenth Century*. Cambridge, 1962.

Shayyal, Jamal al-Din al-. *Ta'rikh al-Tarjamah w-al-Harakah Thaqafiyah fi 'Asr Muhammad Ali*. Cairo, 1951.

Sijpesteijn, Petra M., and Lennart Sundelin, editors. *Papyrology and the History of Early Islamic Egypt*. Leiden, 2004.

Simpson, William Kelly, editor. *The Literature of Ancient Egypt: An Anthology of Stories, Instructions, Stelae, Autobiographies, and Poetry*. New Haven, 2003.

Springborg, Robert. *Mubarak's Egypt, Fragmentation of the Political Order*. Boulder, CO, 1989.

Stewart, Dona J. "Cities in the Desert: The Egyptian New Town Program." *Annals of the Association of American Geographers*, vol. 86, no. 3 (1996), pp. 459–80.

Strassler, Robert B., editor. *The Landmark Herodotus: The Histories*. New York, 2007.

Sublet, Jacqueline. *Les trois vies du Sultan Baibars*. Paris, 1992.

Sullivan, Earl L. *Women in Egyptian Public Life*. Syracuse, NY, 1986.

Takacs, Sarolta A. *Isis and Sarapis in the Roman World*. Leiden, 1995.

Talhami, Ghada Hashem. *The Mobilization of Muslim Women in Egypt*. Gainesville, FL, 1996.

Thompson, Dorothy J. *Memphis under the Ptolemies*. Princeton, 1988.

Thompson, Jason. *A History of Egypt From Earliest Times to the Present*. Cairo, 2008.

Thoreau, Peter. *The Lion of Egypt: Sultan Baybars I and the Near East in the Thirteenth Century*. Translated by P. M. Holt. London, 1992.

Tietze, Andreas. *Mustafa Ali's Description of Cairo of 1599*. Vienna, 1975.

Tignor, Robert L. *Capitalism and Nationalism at the End of Empire: State and Business in Decolonizing Egypt, Nigeria, and Kenya, 1945-1963*. Princeton, 1998.

——. *Egyptian Textiles and British Capital, 1930-1956*. Cairo, 1989.

——. "Maintaining the Empire: General Sir John Maxwell and Egypt during World War I." *Princeton University Library Chronicle*, vol. 53, no. 2 (1992), pp. 173-99.

——. *Modernization and British Colonial Rule in Egypt, 1882-1914*. Princeton, 1966.

——. *State, Private Enterprise, and Economic Change in Egypt, 1918-1952*. Princeton, 1984.

Tignor, Robert L., and Gouda Abdel Khalek, editors. *The Political Economy of Income Distribution in Egypt*. New York, 1982.

Toledano, Ehud R. *State and Society in Mid-Nineteenth Century Egypt*. Cambridge, 1990.

Torok, Laszlo. *Transfigurations of Hellenism: Aspects of Late Antique Art in Egypt, AD 250-700*. Leiden, 2005.

Trigger, Bruce G. *Early Civilizations: Ancient Egypt in Context*. Cairo, 1993.

Trigger, Bruce G., B. J. Kemp, D. O. Connor, and A. B. Lloyd. *Ancient Egypt: A Social History*. Cambridge, 1983.

Tucker, Judith E. *Women in Nineteenth-Century Egypt*. Cambridge, 1985.

Tyldesley, Joyce. *Cleopatra: Last Queen of Egypt*. London, 2008.

Vandier, Jacques. *La famine dans l'Égypte ancienne*. Cairo, 1936.

Vasunia, Phiroze. *The Gift of the Nile: Hellenizing Egypt from Aeschylus to Alexander*. Berkeley, 2001.

Vitalis, Robert. *When Capitalists Collide: Business Conflict and the End of Empire in Egypt*. Berkeley, 1995.

Vatikiotis, P. J. *The Egyptian Army in Politics*. Bloomington, IN, 1961.

——. *The Fatimid Theory of State*. London, 1957.

——. *The History of Egypt*. Baltimore, 1980.

——. *The History of Egypt from Muhammad Ali to Mubarak*. Baltimore, 1991.

——. *Nasser and His Generation*. London, 1978.

Volney, M. C. *Travels through Syria and Egypt in the Years 1783, 1784, and 1785*. London, 1805.

Ward, Ann. *Herodotus and the Philosophy of Empire*. Waco, TX, 2008.

Waterbury, John. *The Egypt of Nasser and Sadat: The Political Economy of Two Regimes*. Princeton, 1983.

Watt, W. Montgomery. *Muhammad at Mecca*. Oxford, 1953.

——. *Muhammad at Medina*. Oxford, 1956.

Watterson, Barbara. *Coptic Egypt*. Edinburgh, 1988.

——. *The Gods of Ancient Egypt*. New York, 1984.

——. *Women in Ancient Egypt*. New York, 1991.

Watts, Edward J. *City and School in Late Antique Athens and Alexandria*. Berkeley, 2006.

Weaver, Mary Anne. *A Portrait of Egypt: A Journey through the World of Militant Islam*. New York, 1999.

Weeks, Kent R. *The Lost Tomb: The Greatest Discovery in the Valley of the Kings since Tutankhamun*. Cairo, 1998.

Weigall, Arthur. *The Life and Times of Akhnaton, Pharaoh of Egypt*. New York, 1923.

Welsby, Derek A. *The Kingdom of Kush: The Napatan and Meroitic Empires*. London, 1996.

Wengrow, David. *The Archaeology of Early Egypt: Social Transformations in North-East Africa, 10,000 to 2650 BC*. Cambridge, 2006.

Wenke, Robert L. *The Ancient Egyptian State: The Origins of Egyptian Culture (c. 8000–2000 BC)*. Cambridge, 2009.

Wiegand, Wayne A., and Donald G. Davis Jr., editors. *Encyclopedia of Library History*. New York, 1994.

Wilkinson, Richard H., editor. *Egyptology Today*. Cambridge, 2008.

Wilkinson, Toby A. H. *Early Dynastic Egypt*. London, 1999.

——, editor. *The Egyptian World*. London, 2007.

Williams, Caroline. *Islamic Monuments in Cairo: The Practical Guide*. Cairo, 2002.

Williams, Rowan. *Arius: Heresy and Tradition*. Cambridge, 2002.

Wilson, Arnold. *The Suez Canal*. New York, 1939.

Wilson, John A. *The Culture of Ancient Egypt*. Chicago, 1951.

Winter, Michael. *Egyptian Society under Ottoman Rule, 1517–1798*. London, 1992.

——. *Society and Religion in Early Ottoman Egypt*. New Brunswick, NJ, 1982.

Winter, Michael, and Amalia Levanoni. *The Mamluks in Egyptian and Syrian Society and Politics*. Leiden, 2004.

Wittek, Paul. *The Rise of the Ottoman Empire*. London, 1938.

Woolf, Gregg, editor. *The Cambridge Illustrated History of the Roman World*. Cambridge, 2003.

Wright, Lawrence. *The Looming Tower: Al-Qaeda and the Road to 9/11*. New York, 2006.

Yeomans, Richard. *The Art and Architecture of Islamic Cairo*. Reading, England, 2006.

Yubil Bank Misr. Cairo, 1970.

Zabkar, Louis V. *Hymns to Isis in Her Temple at Philae*. London, 1988.

INDEX